BRANDING AS A CULTURAL FORCE

ROBIN LANDA

BRANDING
AS A
CULTURAL
FORCE

Columbia University Press
Publishers Since 1893
New York   Chichester, West Sussex
cup.columbia.edu

Library of Congress Cataloging-in-Publication Data
Names: Landa, Robin, author.
Title: Branding as a cultural force : purpose, responsibility,
    and resonance / Robin Landa.
Description: New York : Columbia University Press, [2025] |
    Includes bibliographical references and index.
Identifiers: LCCN 2025020019 | ISBN 9780231217057 (hardback) |
    ISBN 9780231561518 (ebook)
Subjects: LCSH: Branding (Marketing)—Social aspects. | Branding (Marketing)—
    Environmental aspects. | Artificial intelligence.
Classification: LCC HF5415.1255 .L358 2025 | DDC 658.8/27—dc23/eng/20250821
LC record available at https://lccn.loc.gov/2025020019

Printed in the United States of America

Cover design: Amaya Grullon Hernandez and Deborah Ceballos

GPSR Authorized Representative: Easy Access System Europe, Mustamäe tee 50,
10621 Tallinn, Estonia, gpsr.requests@easproject.com

Dedicated to the brands, organizations, and creative partners who lead with integrity—those who protect the planet, champion justice, and uplift the communities they serve. Your work reminds us that branding, at its best, is a cultural force for good. ∼

CONTENTS

FOREWORD

LELAND MASCHMEYER, COFOUNDER/CEO OF COLLINS

I n *The Hucksters*, a movie from 1947, there's a scene that perfectly captures the crude beginnings of industrial-scale brand building. Sydney Greenstreet's Mr. Evans, a grandiose soap tycoon with the subtlety of a foghorn, delivers what was then considered the height of marketing wisdom: "Beauty Soap! Beauty Soap! Beauty Soap!" he thunders, each iteration accompanied by the sort of desk-pounding one normally associates with Soviet diplomacy. His strategy, if one may dignify it with such a term, amounts to "repeat your brand name until consumers mumble it in their sleep."

How exotically antiquated this now seems. Today's brands operate on a plane that would leave Mr. Evans and his ilk as dazed as a sailor handed a smartphone in an age of sextants. Brands have transcended their humble origins as commercial identifiers to become cultural institutions. They hoist self-identity, shape public discourse, carry geopolitical narratives, and command a devotion that would make most cult leaders envious.

The modern brand must juggle the demands of profit with the exigencies of ethics and citizenship. Saluting Milton Friedman's bland mantra of shareholder primacy is no longer acceptable. Society demands more. Our soap must not only cleanse our dishes but also the grime from our world.

Robin Landa's book arrives as a sparkling guide for an era where a simple transaction of selling soap has evolved into a complex social contract. Filled with wit and wisdom, it dazzles the reader with an array of examples from those leaders building purpose-driven brands. Incisive commentary and vivid case studies chart a course for those ambitious enough to see the modern brand not as a cudgel for consumer manipulation but as a platform for societal improvement. True success, the book argues, demands more than selling; it requires listening, inspiring, and innovating in ways that ring far beyond the cash register.

Poor Mr. Evans, were he here today, would still be pounding his desk with the vigor of a man who mistakes volume for vision. But the era of brute-force branding has long passed. The horizon belongs to those who elevate their enterprises into agents of genuine progress. The brands that thrive will not be those that shout the loudest but those that matter the most. Landa's book shows us why—and, more importantly, how.

BRANDING AS A CULTURAL FORCE

INTRODUCTION

This is our clarion moment.

The decisions we make now will shape our future for decades. Corporations and their brands have the power to drive positive change while still achieving prosperity. Profit and working for the common good are not mutually exclusive.

Moving beyond mere transactions requires committing to well-funded, long-term initiatives that drive lasting systemic change. Companies can transcend profit-making by raising awareness and making a meaningful impact on environmental and social issues. By leveraging the strategic and creative expertise of their advertising agencies, branding firms, and design studios, corporations can support just causes, positively influence culture, and promote the well-being of individuals, communities, and the planet.

People recognize that their spending power can drive change. By supporting brands that prioritize sustainability, social justice, and social responsibility, they contribute to a broader movement for positive impact. This awareness adds significance and purpose to their purchasing decisions.

Environmental sustainability is a significant concern for Gen Z and Millennials, with about 60 percent expressing anxiety about climate change. They believe businesses should offer sustainable purchasing options. A recent survey of twenty-three thousand respondents from forty-four countries found that protecting the environment is viewed as the most urgent societal challenge where companies can make a significant impact. This perspective shapes their behavior and expectations of businesses.[1]

In addition to delivering on product or service promises, people increasingly expect brands to actively contribute to the common good. Consumers, especially Gen Z, prefer to patronize companies that address their immediate needs and contribute to a sustainable future.[2] To do so, companies must actively commit to making positive societal and environmental contributions beyond their core business activities by implementing ethical practices, supporting community initiatives, reducing environmental footprints, and promoting social and financial equity. Accountability requires transparently reporting on efforts and progress, taking responsibility for actions, and addressing shortcomings. This approach builds trust with consumers, employees, and other stakeholders, reinforcing the brand promise and fostering engagement.

Brands should prioritize building and nurturing communities by actively engaging with and supporting the groups they serve. This involves investing in local, national, and global communities through sponsorships, community service projects, and partnerships with leaders, organizations, creators, and influencers. By aligning with cultural values and audience interests, brands can stay relevant and resonate with their target markets. Engaging with culture—encompassing music, the visual and performing arts, sports, cuisine, language, technology, festivals, and more—feeds the creation of compelling narratives that reflect shared experiences and shape cultural norms and aspirations. By building communities and fueling cultural expression, brands can forge emotional connections, deepen their influence, and become integral to people's lives, ultimately driving advocacy.

Brands must recognize their varying levels of influence and the power imbalances they create within industries and communities. Taking responsibility for their impact—whether positive or negative—and committing to ethical practices, transparency, and accountability are vital components of corporate social responsibility. This commitment includes addressing the social, environmental, and ethical challenges associated with their influence, such as promoting diversity and inclusion, advancing sustainability, supporting fair labor practices, economic equity, gender equality, and social justice.

In addition to practicing corporate social responsibility today, companies can embrace "cathedral thinking"—a long-term vision inspired by the multi-generational construction of medieval cathedrals. This mindset emphasizes goals that benefit future generations, demonstrating a commitment to initiatives whose impact unfolds over time, such as environmental conservation and infrastructure development.

Successful branding as a cultural force requires understanding a brand's role within the broader cultural landscape and how it relates to prevailing issues, values, and public conversations. Not every strategy will succeed across all cultural contexts. Recognizing this enables brands to stay responsive—adjusting their approach without compromising core values and tailoring their messaging to resonate authentically within specific communities or moments.

This book deviates from conventional branding or brand identity design guides, focusing instead on how corporations and their creative partners use branding, design, and advertising to advance the common good through impactful initiatives and advocacy. I curated the featured campaigns for their significant contributions to cultural and social causes, *without any endorsements or sponsorships influencing my selection*. I aim to critically analyze these exemplary practices and inspire readers to adopt transformative strategies for positive social impact, ultimately motivating the creative industry to harness its influence as a force for good.

To provide a comprehensive view of how distinguished practitioners and thought leaders positively shape culture, I interviewed some of the world's most prominent figures. These conversations offer valuable insights into strategic creative thinking.

Gaëtan du Peloux, chief creative officer and co-chief executive officer of Marcel Paris, encapsulates the core message of this book when he asserts: "I believe companies have both rights and duties. It's an implicit understanding between people and businesses: we allow companies to make money, but in return, we expect them to contribute positively to society. This collective responsibility is crucial, and I emphasize this to all my clients."[3]

Audiences and Uses

This book is a roadmap for identifying and refining branding strategies and creative solutions that create a positive cultural impact, featuring insights from prominent voices worldwide. It is suitable for anyone interested in advertising, branding, design, marketing, and consumer culture, but is particularly valuable for the following audiences:

Faculty in Advertising, Branding, Design, and Marketing will find this book enhances curricula in ideation, strategy, and creative execution. Emphasizing purpose-driven solutions and a triple bottom line approach, it includes insights from esteemed global professionals, making it an indispensable resource for those prioritizing strategic creativity and social impact.

Undergraduate and graduate students will discover actionable content that provides long-term career value. Drawing from my experience teaching thousands of students who have gone on to build successful creative careers, this book offers guidance that helps students secure desirable positions, stay competitive, and advance swiftly in their fields.

Creative practitioners at all levels will benefit from the book's focus on strategic creativity, with an emphasis on advertising and branding for social good.

Through fresh perspectives and real-world examples, it helps professionals rejuvenate their approach and craft work that resonates and drives positive impact.

Marketers and business professionals seeking career advancement and a deeper understanding of the creative process will find invaluable insights in this book. It helps readers grasp key concepts, think strategically, build strong brand constructs, and connect with varied audiences, setting them apart in increasingly competitive fields.

Team leaders, managers, and project managers will find practical guidance on leading with impact, elevating team performance, and driving impactful brand engagement. This book delivers actionable insights into what makes brands succeed and how to align teams around shared goals through effective, purpose-driven leadership.

Ultimately, this book is for those who see branding not merely as commerce, but as a cultural force—a catalyst for meaningful change.

CHAPTER 1

MOVING AT THE SPEED OF CULTURE

"**F**ootball is like a religion here.

"But the Women's World Cup isn't even broadcast on TV? That alone highlights the issue," Gaëtan du Peloux, co-CEO and co-chief creative officer of Marcel Paris, told me.[1] The Marcel Agency's challenge was to show the world the greatness of women's soccer (referred to globally as *football*) in a way that would actually change minds.

For the Women's World Cup, Marcel partnered with Les Artisans du Film Paris and Prodigious Paris to create the short film *WoMen's Football* for the French telecom giant Orange (figure 1.1). The video opens as an exciting highlight reel featuring male star players from the French national team—Kylian Mbappé and Antoine Griezmann among them—showcasing their skills and spectacular goals. Midway through, the ad surprises viewers by revealing that the true athletes behind these incredible moments are actually players from the French women's team.

This execution required weeks of meticulous research in the French Football Federation's archives to identify specific technical moves by women players. The production team then matched these moves with identical ones by male players and used visual effects (VFX) techniques to seamlessly present the women's footage as men's highlights. The message was clear: when Orange supports *les Bleus* (the men's team), Orange also supports *les Bleues* (the women's team).

The film went viral worldwide, sparking global conversations about women's football and demonstrating how creative execution can elevate important social messages.

1.1 Frame from video: "WoMen's Football." Brand: Orange; Creative Agency: Marcel Agency; CCO & CEO: Gaëtan du Peloux & Youri Guerassimov; Creative Director: Xavier Le Boullenger; Copywriter: Antonin Jacquot; Art Director: Vincent Teffene; Publicis Conseil: CCO Publicis France: Marco Venturelli; Executive Creative Director: Fabrice Delacourt; Production—Prodigious; CEO: Christopher Thiery; Head of Production: Timothé Rosenberg

As the world's most popular sport, soccer offers a vast platform for promoting gender equality. Yet significant gender disparities persist: Men comprise 95 percent of coaches and 91 percent of referees, and it wasn't until 2022 that a woman officiated a World Cup match.[2]

Heather Reid, the former executive director of Women's Soccer Australia, told CNN Sports that while practical barriers to gender equality such as pay gaps, limited viewership, ad revenue, poorer facilities, and fewer opportunities are significant, "sexist attitudes" and "shifting attitudinal barriers" remain formidable challenges.[3]

Promoting equality and diversity is a fundamental commitment for Orange. "We observed that women's soccer is often underestimated, less followed, and even mocked, despite the impressive skills of the players and the emotional intensity of their matches, which rival those of men's games," an Orange spokesperson told CNN. "We wanted to correct these misconceptions and challenge these preconceived notions."[4]

Leading a Cultural Conversation

Have a purple M&M.

For the first time in a decade, M&M'S, part of Mars Inc., added Purple—a new "spokescandy" to its crew of characters.[5] Characterized by her self-expression, self-awareness, authenticity, and confidence, Purple is designed to symbolize acceptance and inclusivity. She brings a quirky nature to the legendary cast of M&M'S characters, who Mars recently refreshed with updated looks and more nuanced personalities.[6] To highlight her individuality, Purple made her musical debut by releasing a single and music video titled "I'm Just Gonna Be Me."

As part of the M&M'S "FUNd," a global initiative aimed at increasing a sense of belonging for ten million people, "I'm Just Gonna Be Me" is available on all major music streaming platforms to support inclusive arts and entertainment. For every stream, the brand will donate one dollar (up to $500,000) to Sing for Hope, a non-profit organization that harnesses the power of the arts to bring hope, connection, and purpose to millions of people worldwide through music.[7]

The M&M'S FUNd offers resources, mentorship, opportunities, and financial support in the arts and entertainment space to ensure broader access to experiences that foster belonging. FUNd's advisory council includes experts from Disability:IN and GLAAD, organizations that share these inclusive values. Mars's goal is to create a more inclusive world through authentic representation.[8]

Ingraining a brand into the fabric of popular culture has become essential for parent companies. When brands seamlessly integrate into societal conversations, they cultivate genuine enthusiasts who eagerly share what they value (or perhaps love) with their networks.

Moreover, forward-thinking brands go beyond cultural participation to cultural influence. They leverage their reach, creative resources, and visibility to drive substantive change. This approach creates business value: research shows that a brand's social purpose and values drive consumer purchase decisions more than traditional product attributes.[9]

With ever-growing opportunities for people to share their thoughts about culture beyond their immediate circles on platforms such as Instagram, TikTok, Twitter/X, and Reddit, brands have unprecedented chances to insert themselves in relevant and organic ways. These "shareworthy" opportunities influence purchasing decisions and drive positive cultural conversations. People are willing and often eager to share and engage with compelling advertising stories across media channels—content that creates powerful connections through storytelling.[10]

"A brand's social value and purpose are now more important than ever in activating a consumer's sense of value and meaning. Identifying which of the brand's values resonate and how they line up with a consumer's values has become more critical to the work of growing brands with greater consumer loyalty, stronger brand trust, and higher financial returns," reported Milos Bujisic, a clinical associate professor of marketing and statistics in NYU's School of Professional Studies and lead author of a recent Corporate Social Value Index study.[11]

FOCUS: EBM's "SCHOOLGIRL NEWSCASTERS" / IMPACT BBDO, MIDDLE EAST AND PAKISTAN

Pakistan is ranked 153 out of 156 in the 2021 Global Gender Gap Report.[12] UN Women reports that institutions deny 53.6 percent of women in Pakistan access to education, training, and employment, a stark contrast to the 7.4 percent of men facing similar deprivation.[13] Pakistan's education system is characterized by significant gender disparity, with parents often pulling girls out of school early. As a result, only 34.2 percent of girls reach high school, primarily due to the widespread belief that education is unnecessary for women.[14]

On World Human Rights Day, "to move the needle in its quest to correct imbalance in gender equality," as stated by Ali Rez, the regional chief creative officer for the Middle East, North Africa, and Pakistan regions at Impact BBDO, the creative agency orchestrated a news broadcast takeover on behalf of their client, the leading Pakistani food company EBM. The campaign, titled "Schoolgirl Newscasters," aimed to boost the enrollment of girls in schools across Pakistan.[15] Two schoolgirls, who were illiterate just three years prior, took over as newscasters for the evening, delivering news to millions on Pakistan's three leading news channels. The message: When empowered with literacy, girls' potential is unlimited.

Outdoor brand REI went beyond traditional product placement, commercials, and short films by co-producing full-length feature films in collaboration with other producers and studios. REI showcased these films at film festivals and distributed them through streaming services and theaters, significantly expanding their cultural influence beyond typical brand marketing. REI Co-op Studios, the in-house content arm for REI, released the feature films *Canary* and *Frybread Face and Me* to highlight narratives about climate change and the profound connections historically underrepresented groups have with nature, offering insightful perspectives.[16]

"The films we're bringing to audiences explore some of the most important and pressing topics at the forefront of outdoor culture and beyond: climate change and racial equity," said Paolo Mottola, REI Co-op's director of brand and content marketing.[17] *Frybread Face and Me* (overseen by executive producer Taika Waititi) follows a boy spending the summer with his grandmother on a

Navajo reservation. This tribute to cultural awakening earned selection for the 2023 Toronto International Film Festival's Global Indigenous Cinema program.

Making Meaningful Connections

Building strong connections with target audiences drives every successful brand strategy. Pop culture, politics, and pressing social issues offer abundant opportunities for brands to engage in dialogue and build relationships through shared experiences and pertinent conversations.

Before the advent of Instagram and TikTok, I wondered, "How do you make a brand social?" Social media platforms have since afforded marketers the tools to do just that. These platforms capture cultural moments that dominate conversations, emerging swiftly and fading just as fast. These opportunities are hard to ignore, even for brands not actively monitoring cultural trends. From massive shared events like the Super Bowl to niche interests such as true crime podcasts to album releases from music superstars Taylor Swift and Beyoncé, the right timing and execution can help brands tap into widespread cultural excitement.

Industry leaders from Steve Jobs, the co-founder of Apple, to Evan Horowitz, the co-founder and CEO of Movers+Shakers, have emphasized the importance of staying one step ahead by anticipating consumer needs and desires before they're even expressed. Deep insights and clear audience understanding can drive widespread engagement. By cultivating authentic relationships, brands can move beyond mere transactions and become integral to their consumers' lives.[18]

For instance, through its First Strides initiative, Diageo North America Inc.'s blended Scotch whisky brand Johnnie Walker has turned its "Keep Walking" tagline into a catalyst for supporting underrepresented groups in culture. The initiative includes a grant program with IFundWomen; a creator grant program with writer/producer Kenya Barris and Blacktag (a global platform for Black creatives) supporting five projects from Black creators; and a social media video series produced by comedian Lilly Singh. To date, the brand has provided over $1 million in funding to its partners.[19]

To engage effectively in current conversations, it's essential to identify trending topics that align with your audience and brand's mission. Monitoring social media, news, and pop culture offers insights into public sentiment and interests. Successfully leveraging real-time conversations to engage fans and broader audiences requires careful and consistent monitoring. While quick responses are crucial during major cultural events, maintaining a balance between timeliness and thoughtful action is key for sustained engagement.[20]

Consumers today want more from brands than just a transaction; they seek to be part of something larger. Many are eager to align with movements, contribute to real change, and feel at the forefront of innovation. They don't want to stand on the sidelines; they want to actively participate—think of it as marching in the parade or participating in the rally. When a brand reduces its messaging and interactions to mere economics, engagement dwindles and the magic is lost.

For a movement to truly thrive, it must nourish the collective spirit, feeding the shared values and sense of purpose that unite its participants. This communal energy sparks deeper emotional connections, fostering lasting interest and genuine excitement. One has only to think of brands such as Dove, Patagonia, or Ben & Jerry's to understand this phenomenon—these companies have built communities around shared beliefs and values, extending far beyond simple transactions.

At a time when our planet, societies, and individuals are facing numerous challenges, it's more important than ever for brands to take a stand and invest in positive change. However, some companies hesitate when they or others face backlash for supporting a community or cause. Understanding that "everyone" is never a brand's actual audience is crucial. By taking tangible action rather than focusing solely on messaging, brands can drive real change and reshape public perception. If a company is committed to making a difference, branding becomes a cultural force.

As creative consultant Luke Flynn told me, "The more we contribute to culture and respect it, the more we get out of it."[21]

Interview: Gaëtan du Peloux, Chief Creative Officer and Cochief Executive Officer, Marcel

Born and raised in Paris, Gaëtan is the eldest of seven children. He started his career as a copywriter at the international advertising agency CLM BBDO in 2004. He's now 44 years old and works at Marcel as chief creative officer and co-chief executive officer. Along with his creative partner, Youri Guerassimov, Gaëtan has produced outstanding and award-winning work for a large span of national and international brands.

Gaëtan is one of the most acclaimed French creatives of his generation: he has won more than 300 awards, including two Cannes Lions Grand Prix, three D&AD Black Pencils, a D&AD White Pencil, a One Show Green Pencil, a One show SDG pencil, two NY Festivals Best of Show, eleven Eurobest Grand Prix, two Grandy, and many Grand LIA and Grand Clio awards.

Gaëtan du Peloux

He has been honored to take part in the judging and chairing of many advertising festivals, including Eurobest, Cannes Lions X2, D&AD, One Show, London International Awards (LIA), New York Festivals, AD STARS [now rebranded to MAD STARS], Grand Prix Strategies, the French Art Directors Club Annual Awards, and the CPS Awards organized by the Collectif du Planning Stratégique (Strategic Planning Collective).

Gaëtan is a happy husband and a father of three. He tries to spend more time with them than with Youri. Yes, he tries . . .

What was the inspiration, strategy, and creative process behind the WoMen's Football campaign for the telecom giant Orange?

Orange, a French multinational telecom company, similar to Verizon in the United States or Deutsche Telekom AG in Germany, has a long-term partnership with French football. They sponsor the French National Federation, which covers all levels of football—from amateur to professional—across all age groups.

In the lead-up to the Women's World Cup, Orange faced a challenging context: no TV broadcaster had picked up the event three weeks before its start. Orange wanted to highlight their commitment to women's football and draw attention to the sport. They asked us to create a campaign to showcase their support and encourage people to watch women's football.

Our inspiration came from how football fans, including my 14-year-old son, constantly share highlight compilations on social media. Our goal was to address the faulty perception that women's football is less technical, less spectacular, and less entertaining than men's football. We aimed to show men what they were missing and let them judge for themselves, without asserting that women's football is better, or just as good.

To achieve this, we created a surprising moment by using VFX [special effects technology]. By matching camera angles from women's and men's football games, we replaced male players with female players in highlight reels. This technical feat took fourteen weeks and involved meticulous work by flame artists [professionals skilled in using Autodesk Flame, a high-end visual effects software suite]. We wanted to reveal the truth—that women's football is just as thrilling—without relying on AI [artificial intelligence], to maintain authenticity.

In creating the campaign, we were sensitive to challenging viewers' preconceptions. We needed to convey the message without alienating our audience, just as sensitive topics discussed in an ad campaign, like Gillette's "The Best a Man Can Be," can backfire if not handled carefully. Focusing on authenticity and showcasing real highlights allowed the audience to see the reality of women's football.

Our goal was simply to present the truth, so we avoided using AI. Instead, we relied on flame artists to create a genuine and impactful visual experience. We curated highlights from the French national women's team's matches and meticulously paired them with matching angles from men's games. The only truly gender-neutral aspect of football is the camera placement, which allowed us to blend the footage seamlessly.

During this painstaking process, flame artists transformed female players into male players, ensuring every detail was accurate. By blending footage of women's and men's football, we drew attention to the similarities in skill and excitement. The result was stunning, showing the same level of skill and excitement in women's football as in men's.

What made the campaign truly brilliant was its organic success. Despite meticulous planning, the human element—the emotional connection—ultimately drives a campaign's success. People shared the video widely, making it their own and contributing to its viral spread.

Our approach focused on finding solutions to a significant issue: men generally don't watch women's football. This problem is prevalent in countries outside the United States, where women's football is often perceived as less technical, less spectacular, and less entertaining. However, people form these opinions without actually watching the games. We aimed to showcase women's football in a way that allowed viewers to form their opinions. Inspired by the highlight compilations my kids and their friends share daily, we sought to create something widely appealing.

We didn't aim to prove that women's football is better or just as good as men's. Instead, we wanted to present it authentically and let the audience decide for themselves (see figure 1.1).

You uphold the philosophy, "They didn't know it was impossible, so they did it." Would you elaborate on this, please?

I love this sentence because advertising can be the worst job in the world if you just follow the same old recipe and only do what the client asks. You'll end up feeling uninspired and depressed after a couple of years. But if you approach it with a spirit of innovation and passion, you realize how lucky you are to do this job. We have the opportunity to create things that have never been done before or to make something truly brilliant.

This mindset makes all the difference. It excites you to come to the office and work with your team. I really live by this philosophy because I believe being a bit naïve is just another way of being passionate. We work incredibly hard in advertising; you need that extra passion to achieve something great.

This philosophy reflects our agency Marcel's approach to advertising. If we only follow client instructions without creativity or passion, the work becomes uninspiring. Embracing naiveté and passion allows us to achieve extraordinary results, making our job fulfilling and motivating.

The WoMen's Football campaign showcased the beauty of taking risks and trusting in human creativity and emotion, proving that even the most challenging topics can be successfully addressed with the right approach.

The unpredictability of human response is what makes advertising both challenging and beautiful.

The WoMen's Football campaign for Orange promoted a telecom company and championed professional women's sports. As the mind behind award-winning culture-creating work, you understand the intricate process of fostering brand engagement within cultural conversations. How can brands effectively initiate and shape these discussions, ultimately influencing the cultural landscape?

I believe companies have both rights and duties. It's an implicit understanding between people and businesses: we allow companies to make money, but in return, we expect them to contribute positively to society. This collective responsibility is crucial, and I emphasize this to all my clients.

A company's credibility is key. If a brand has a long history of supporting women's causes, it can rightfully speak about these issues, and people will listen. However, if a company without prior involvement suddenly tries to capitalize on a social trend, it can backfire. I find such opportunistic behavior off-putting and potentially damaging to the brand's reputation.

How do you make a brand matter, or make it more valuable to people?

I believe that agency teams, often composed of younger individuals, reflect the pulse of society. They are in tune with emerging trends and the evolving landscape. My goal is to create honest work for our clients, ensuring they stay relevant by connecting them with the current times. Timing is crucial—our WoMen's football campaign, for instance, might not have had the same impact if released three years earlier or later. Brands must resonate with the present, finding their legitimate space and relevant topics to engage with. This approach adds value to the brand.

Unfortunately, some brands are led by individuals who may not be as open-minded or in touch with younger audiences. Convincing CEOs, corporate executives, or marketing officers to embrace ideas that are truly in the zeitgeist often relies on building long-term relationships. The best work at our agency has come from partnerships spanning at least four years. Trust is essential. At the beginning, we need to demonstrate our honesty and commitment to the client's success, showing that we care about their company as much as they do. Over time, the passion and dedication we bring to our work help build this trust. Although we sometimes fail, our consistent effort to find true solutions to real problems often leads to success stories such as WoMen's Football.

Are there times when a client believes they have one problem to address, but you recognize that the real issue is something entirely different?

Absolutely, it happens often. For instance, in a previous campaign for a carpooling company, the client thought their main issue was perception, but we identified a larger problem: biodiversity in Europe. We urged them to leverage their influence to address this pressing issue, which not only aligned with their values but also had the potential to improve their public image. By taking positive actions instead of just conveying a message, they could enact real change and alter public perception. Eventually, they listened to our advice, leading to a campaign for French supermarket giant Carrefour called "The Black Supermarket," which won a Grand Prix for creative effectiveness. It's a prime example of addressing the underlying issue to achieve significant impact.

In the Black Supermarket campaign, Carrefour took a stand against a restrictive EU law that allowed access to only 3 percent of fruits and vegetables listed in the European Union's Official Catalog of Authorized Species, leaving the remaining 97 percent effectively illegal.

Across France, so-called Black Supermarkets unveiled herbaria [specialized in-store displays] showcasing 600 "illegal" fruits and vegetables. A web film supplemented the campaign, supported by print and outdoor advertising.

Visitors were urged to sign a Change.org petition advocating for legal reform, which garnered over 85,000 signatures. The brand, Carrefour, broke the law to advocate for its reform. However, it actually succeeded in changing the EU laws in the process.

What responsibilities do creatives hold when tapping into cultural moments? How do you ensure responsible, respectful, and authentic engagement with these moments?

Creatives are responsible for ensuring that their engagement with cultural moments aligns with the brand's core message and values. If leveraging a cultural moment adds depth or a new perspective to the brand's narrative, it can be highly effective. However, if the connection feels forced or insincere, it's best to approach with caution.

I believe in long-term consistency over short-term gains. While jumping on cultural moments can provide a temporary boost, it's essential to maintain a consistent brand story over time. This requires establishing a clear storytelling strategy, often embodied in the brand's tagline or creative platform.

In our agency, we work closely with strategic planners to develop a creative platform for each brand. This platform serves as a guiding principle for storytelling, ensuring that our creative executions are both inventive and consistent with the brand's identity. While the strategy provides a framework, creativity allows us to adapt the storytelling to different contexts and cultural moments while remaining relevant and authentic.

We always think long-term about the storytelling of our brand. My teams and I establish a guiding principle, or "North Star," for our storytelling. We work with strategic planning to create a creative platform for each brand, often reflected in the tagline. This platform allows us to adapt our storytelling in diverse and relevant ways while maintaining consistency. This flexibility makes being a creative so exciting—balancing innovation with relevance and consistency is key.

Does the tagline encapsulate the overarching strategy?

Absolutely, yes. The tagline plays a pivotal role in defining the overall strategy. It's often the first thing people see alongside the logo, making it a critical component of brand messaging. While the tagline should be concise and memorable, it should also reflect the brand's essence and values. From there, other creative elements such as claims or sub-baselines [text or graphic elements positioned below the main baseline of the primary text] can expand on the tagline, but it all starts with crafting a compelling and resonant tagline.

How much of the creative platform and the strategy comes from the client?

When it comes to developing the creative platform and strategy, it's often a collaborative process between the client and us. While we receive specific briefs outlining their goals and expectations, building the brand typically involves input from both sides. We start with the foundation the client provides, but we also bring our expertise and insights to the table to shape the overall direction. Ultimately, it's about balancing between honoring the client's vision and leveraging our creativity to produce impactful work.

Our approach involves gathering good data to provide the necessary elements for strategic thinking, which allows us to develop smart strategies with creative potential. From a business standpoint, this is crucial because ultimately, companies are focused on results. We're not just here to enjoy ourselves, but to convey our clients' messages effectively.

Sometimes, this means promoting a product or offering discounts. Other times, it involves challenging biases; for example, encouraging people to look at women's football objectively. Whatever the objective, our goal is to find the best way to deliver our clients' message and achieve tangible results.

Do you find that some clients are skittish about purpose-driven work? For example, there have been recent backfires to purpose-driven advertising in the United States.

In our agency, we're fortunate to have a diverse team with individuals who are passionate about feminism and other important topics. This diversity is crucial because it ensures we approach sensitive issues with care and empathy. We value everyone's input and actively listen to each other's advice and perspectives.

We build our team dynamic on collaboration and mutual respect. My creative partner, Youri Guerassimov, and I have been working together for twenty years, and we attribute our success to our ability to work as a team. We've realized that our openness to each other's ideas and perspectives has been a key factor in our achievements.

We believe that diversity enriches our work. By embracing different viewpoints and experiences, we can create more impactful campaigns. We constantly seek feedback and input from each other, recognizing that no single person has all the answers. This collaborative approach not only strengthens our work but also fosters a culture of inclusivity and respect within our agency.

CHAPTER 2

DIFFERENTIATION

No voice need ever be lost.

Released on the International Day of Persons with Disabilities, Apple's campaign "The Lost Voice" highlights its new accessibility feature, Personal Voice. This technology enables individuals at risk of losing their ability to speak, due to amyotrophic lateral sclerosis, multiple sclerosis, or dementia, to communicate using a digital recreation of their voice, instead of a generic text-to-speech reader.

In the campaign's hero film, directed by Taika Waititi, a young girl journeys through the woods searching for her "lost voice," guided by an imaginative, bunny-eared friend. The film features a real-life father using Personal Voice to read a bedtime story to his daughter, creating a deeply personal connection. The story is narrated with a track composed entirely of human voice samples, enhancing the emotional impact.

The campaign also included a hardback storybook and a free, accessible e-book on Apple Books, garnering global attention with 18 million views and acclaim from disability advocates, industry press, and the public.

"Thank you, Apple, for telling stories that speak disabled truths," said disability activist Maayan Ziv.[1]

Apple exemplifies brand differentiation through every aspect of its market presence. By integrating cutting-edge products, exceptional design, a cohesive ecosystem, distinctive customer experiences, effective marketing, and a commitment to high quality and user experience, Apple embodies the ethos of "think different" and aligns with its audience's desire to do the same.

What Makes a Brand

"What is a brand?" asked Leland Maschmeyer, cofounder of the renowned brand consultancy COLLINS and Sway the Future.

At a recent executive-level meeting with a company valued at over four billion dollars, Maschmeyer and the executives discussed the role of branding in the business's transformation. What Maschmeyer expected to be a straightforward agreement on the definition of a brand turned into a twenty-minute debate. Although five people responded, none captured the exact definition, Maschmeyer recounted to the audience at the 2024 Web Summit Rio.

Maschmeyer addressed a common misconception, explaining that many think of a brand as merely a color, tagline, or package design. "The reality is that brand is differentiation," Maschmeyer said. That's the simplest, best, and most accurate definition. He explained that without a brand, a product lacks differentiation and fails to stand out from the competition, thereby becoming a mere commodity. The core function of a brand is to provide consumers with a reason to choose your product or service over others.[2]

And there you have it.

Differentiation transforms brands from options into preferences. While distinctiveness ensures people notice and remember a brand, differentiation makes them choose it. This advantage can emerge from various sources—a breakthrough creative platform, unique benefits, emotional resonance, ethical commitments, or a singular voice—but it always establishes a meaningful edge over competitors. Whether through innovation, superior quality, or deeply held values, differentiated brands don't just compete for attention; they command choice. Consumers gravitate to differentiated brands.[3]

Salience

When you do market orientation, things that you didn't think were important become very important. Salience: your biggest job as a marketer is salience; it's making your brand come to mind in buying situations. You don't see that if you're not market-oriented.

—Mark Ritson, marketing and branding strategist,
former professor of marketing, Melbourne Business School

Salience is how easily a brand comes to mind in relevant moments—whether a consumer faces a pain point or scans a store shelf. High salience means that the brand is top of mind: the first one consumers think of in a category without prompting. This mental availability directly drives purchasing decisions.[4]

To achieve salience, consider the following core elements necessary for a brand's success:

Heart: At the heart of a brand lies a core purpose—its raison d'être—and that should radiate through every message and action. This foundation remains constant in principle while staying flexible in practice, adapting to change without losing identity.

Meaning: Understanding a brand's significance in people's lives builds relationships. Brands deepen connections by making individuals feel valued and understood. The critical question becomes: How does the brand enhance lives or enable people to accomplish things they couldn't before?

Strategic associations: Effective branding establishes one or two key connections you want people to make with the brand. These strong associations enhance brand salience by "owning" a specific attribute or value that distinguishes them from competitors, as detailed in chapter 3. For instance, Volvo owns safety, while BMW owns performance.

A creative platform supports these strategic associations by providing a tactical foundation for all campaign elements. It encompasses the central idea, messaging framework, visual identity, and emotional tone that express the brand's essence. This platform ensures that all creative work stays consistent with the brand's core values and target audience, guiding compelling narratives, designs, and experiences that reinforce key associations. At its best, a creative platform delivers four essential qualities:

Singular: A distinctive and differentiated brand captures attention, increases awareness, and creates mental availability, which sparks stronger consumer desire and builds preference over competitors.[5]

Remarkable: A brand captures attention when it is exceptional. As Nick Law notes, it embodies "something unique that others can't easily replicate." Recent research using Lippincott's Brand Aperture® performance measurement tools reveals that consumers perceive only 5 percent of brands as truly unique.[6]

Anticipatory: The most powerful brands anticipate needs and desires before people explicitly express them. As Steve Jobs, cofounder of Apple, often emphasized, people frequently don't know what they want until you show it to them. This means addressing unspoken requirements and leading audiences toward new possibilities through innovation and foresight.

Immersive: Engaging brand experiences create lasting impressions and influence behavior. Whether entertaining, informative, or both, these experiences enable brands to build connections with audiences while staying true to their core identity.

Beyond strategy, a strong creative platform shapes how we experience a brand visually and emotionally. Originally from film and theater, *mise-en-scène*—the deliberate arrangement of visual elements to create meaning—provides a powerful framework for this visual orchestration.

In branding, this approach transforms how brands create atmosphere, distinction, and narrative cohesion. Rather than random visual choices, mise-en-scène demands intentional composition that serves a strategic purpose. This framework operates across four key dimensions:

> **Visual identity**: Deliberate arrangement of color, typography, imagery, and layout creates a distinctive brand presence. Each element works in harmony to establish recognition and differentiation in saturated markets.
>
> **Atmospheric design**: Like film directors setting the mood through visual choices, curated environments establish emotional tone. This atmosphere becomes integral to the brand experience, not merely decorative.
>
> **Visual communication**: Visual elements align with brand values to tell cohesive stories. Every design choice reinforces the brand's core message, fostering organic audience connections.
>
> **Cross-platform consistency**: Applied across packaging, advertising, retail spaces, and digital touchpoints, mise-en-scène creates a unified visual language that strengthens recognition and recall.

Meaningful Differentiation

Differentiation drives brand preference, while distinctiveness ensures brand visibility. Recent analysis quantified the value of differentiation, showing that brands described as "Meaningfully Different to More People" achieve up to five times greater market penetration than those with minimal meaningful difference, according to Kantar's Meaningful, Different, and Salient (MDS) framework.[7]

"For the first time, we've integrated a decade of attitudinal brand research with actual shopper behavior to comprehensively understand the tangible impact of marketing on growth," explains Jane Ostler, Kantar's EVP of thought leadership.

"One key finding is the importance of emotional connections in advertising. When optimized, these connections foster differentiation and predispose consumers toward a brand, thereby boosting sales and loyalty."[8]

One powerful method for differentiating a brand is creating richer emotional connections by honoring people's heritages, communities, and passions. Research shows that divergent thinking and creativity enable brands to develop assets with emotional impact.[9] When brands celebrate cultural identity with

FOCUS: APPLE'S SUERTE / TBWA\MEDIA ARTS LAB LATAM

Apple's fantastical short film *Suerte*, shot entirely on an iPhone, pays tribute to Mexican culture. It follows Iván Cornejo, an emerging Música Mexicana artist, as he overcomes a creative block by exploring his cultural roots. Characters from the traditional game of Lotería—a fish, the devil, and a mermaid—guide him on a surreal journey that inspires new music.

Directed by the Mexican American duo Cliqua (Pasqual Gutiérrez and Raúl "RJ" Sanchez) and created by TBWA\Media Arts Lab LATAM, the 13-minute film features unconventional shots that merge the worlds of Música Mexicana, a Latin music subgenre, and Lotería, the classic Mexican bingo game. Alongside Cornejo, the film features other Música Mexicana musicians, including Edén Muñoz, María Zardoya, and producer Camilo Lara.

Cliqua, known for their innovative music videos for artists including Bad Bunny, Rosalía, J Balvin, and The Weeknd, used iPhone 15 Pro features such as 5x optical zoom, action mode, and cinematic mode to create the piece. Following Apple's epic *lucha libre* film, *Huracán Ramírez vs. La Piñata Enchilada*, this work continues Apple's music-driven ethos while enriching its connection to Mexican heritage.

respect and nuanced understanding, they distinguish themselves beyond product features.

Apple's short film *Suerte*, for instance, celebrates Latinx heritage through storytelling that is culturally authentic and distinctly Apple in its cinematic approach.

Brands that embed societal, cultural, and environmental responsibility into their core promise stand out from competitors. This commitment can influence consumer choices significantly, often swaying preferences toward brands that genuinely support societal causes. While supporting social issues may sometimes invite backlash, authentic advocacy within a space where the brand has earned credibility typically strengthens its reputation for contributing to the greater good. Research indicates that a robust brand reputation fosters a stronger emotional attachment, which drives greater brand advocacy.[10]

Interview: Nick Law, Creative Chairperson, Accenture Song

Nick Law is Accenture Song's creative chairperson and leads its Creative Strategic Priority initiative. He
is one of the world's most innovative
and versatile creative leaders. He
believes all technology needs creativity to make it human, and all creativity needs technology to make it real.

Before coming to Accenture, Nick held many positions at major global companies: he was vice president for Marcom Integration at Apple, where he was
one of three leading the global design and marketing group; he was the chief
creative officer of Publicis Groupe and president of Publicis Communications,
helping to drive a unified creative vision across the Groupe's Brands; and he
was the vice chairman and global chief creative officer at R/GA—where, during
his 17-year tenure, he led it to be one of the most awarded agencies in the world.
Nick's career in design, advertising and digital media has spanned thirty years
and four continents, and he has worked with the brightest and best across multiple creative disciplines. He is a two-time honoree of the Creativity 50 list of
the world's most influential creative people. A native of Sydney, Australia, he
now lives in Brooklyn.

Please share and tell us about Accenture Song's Eight Principles for the Future of
Creativity.

The essence of a successful creative company lies in its differentiation. You
want to offer something unique that others can't easily replicate. To achieve
this, it's crucial for a company to have unwavering principles. This has been
true for companies such as R/GA, Apple, and Nike.

When your principles are consistent, even as the practices and tasks you
engage in are constantly changing, you have a clear framework guiding your
approach. This paradoxically allows for greater speed and differentiation. With
solid principles in place, you don't waste time figuring out how to approach
new challenges, enabling you to act quickly and maintain your unique edge.

For instance, in our company, we have identified eight key principles and four
core adversaries. These principles guide our actions and decisions, ensuring that
we stay true to our unique identity while adapting to changing circumstances.

1. *To make new things, first remake yourself.* Acknowledge that the first creative
   act of any company is to design itself: structuring the organization and fostering a culture that will lead to the desired work. When embarking on new

projects, you need to reverse engineer everything based on the goal. Often, this necessitates changes in organizational structure, personnel, and processes.

Many companies falter when they attempt to produce something new without adjusting their existing frameworks. This has been particularly detrimental for agencies struggling with new media and digital innovations. Therefore, the first principle is clear: to make new things, first remake yourself.

2. *Foster a singular vision within a collaborative culture.* For creative companies, collaboration is essential because creativity thrives on the combination of diverse ideas and perspectives. The best way to achieve this is by having individuals with different skill sets work together to create something they couldn't achieve alone.

   In advertising, a prime example is the revolutionary pairing of copywriters and art directors, which transformed the industry during the Bernbach era. At R/GA, we embraced a similar approach with our "stories and systems" methodology, where campaign creatives collaborated with digital designers to produce innovative work that stood out.

   Collaboration is the engine of modern creativity, but it needs a clear, singular vision to be effective. Projects require a well-defined vision to guide the collaborative process. Without this, teams can waste time and resources due to misaligned goals. Conversely, companies with a strong vision but poor collaboration struggle to execute effectively because they can't agree on what they're trying to achieve and can't bring the right elements together.

   Therefore, the second principle emphasizes the importance of a clear vision to guide collaborative efforts, ensuring that all team members are aligned and working towards a common goal.

3. *Be loose with ideas, tight with executions.* In any creative exercise—whether it's design, storytelling, or general innovation—there are two distinct modes of operation.

   The first mode is the dreaming phase, characterized by looseness and freedom. This is when you brainstorm, combine disparate ideas, and entertain audacious thoughts. It's a chaotic and open-ended process where you generate a multitude of ideas, knowing that not all will be feasible or successful. This phase thrives on creativity and exploration, encouraging a broad and unrestricted flow of ideas.

   The second mode is the execution phase, where discipline and craft become paramount. Here, you take the best ideas from the dreaming phase and refine them into polished, executable plans. This phase demands precision, attention to detail, and a commitment to quality. Execution is a vertical exercise, focusing on excellence and thoroughness.

   Balancing these two modes creates a T-shaped organization: the horizontal axis represents the breadth of creative ideation, while the vertical axis signifies the depth of executional expertise. Some companies excel in idea generation but falter in execution, while others rush to execution without adequate ideation. Recognizing and managing these two modes is essential for successful creative endeavors.

4. *Solve before you sell.* This is a fundamental principle, especially in service industries, where there's often pressure to prioritize sales. However, selling before solving can be counterproductive in the long run. Instead, the focus should be on truly solving the problem at hand, as this leads to greater success in the long term.

   The incentive to sell should be balanced with the understanding that providing genuine solutions leads to stronger client relationships and better outcomes. When something new emerges, there's often a gap that needs to be filled, much like at the dawn of the Internet. By prioritizing solving over selling, you position yourself to seize these opportunities and remain ahead of the curve. This approach ensures that you're not just selling products or services but actively shaping the future of your industry.

5. *Be best in class and create next in class.* By being the best in class at what you do and consistently innovating, you not only address current needs but also anticipate and meet future ones.

   For instance, during my time at R/GA, there was a surge in demand for websites as every company recognized the need for an online presence. This created a booming industry of website development, with companies scrambling to get online. What set R/GA apart from its competitors was our commitment to craftsmanship, excellence, and deep expertise. While it was initially challenging to distinguish ourselves in a crowded market, our dedication to quality and innovation paid off as the internet matured. As the internet evolved, our lead only grew stronger. While many small web shops faded away, we thrived because we were not just best in class but also ahead of the curve. This experience taught us the importance of staying ahead of emerging trends and technologies.

   Now, with Generative AI, we find ourselves in a similar position. Our clients recognize the importance of staying ahead in this rapidly evolving landscape. It's not just about meeting their immediate needs but doing so with excellence and foresight. By consistently delivering outstanding results, we ensure that we remain the go-to partner for our clients, even as the technology landscape continues to evolve.

6. *Creativity needs technology, technology needs creativity.* Creativity and technology are inherently intertwined. You can't truly be creative without a medium, and that medium requires creativity to be effectively utilized. Whether it's a pencil or cutting-edge digital tools, technology and creativity must be symbiotic.

7. *Go deep, then simplify.* This principle recognizes the pivotal role of designers and creatives in distilling complex systems into something accessible and

understandable. Whether it's in interface design or advertising, the task is to take intricate technology or messaging and make it digestible for the average person.

In interface design, for instance, the challenge is to simplify the workings of a complex machine into an intuitive and user-friendly experience. Similarly, in advertising, the goal is to distill the essence of a product into a message that resonates with consumers.

This principle echoes Blaise Pascal's sentiment. In his *Lettres provinciales*, the French philosopher and mathematician Pascal famously wrote: "I would have written a shorter letter, but I did not have the time."

It emphasizes the importance of investing time and effort to gain a deep understanding of the complexities before simplifying them into a form that is easily comprehensible. By going deep into the intricacies of a system or message, designers and creatives can then simplify it in a way that is both concise and has strong impact.

8. *Make it matter by starting in the middle.* This is a crucial concept in advertising today. In an era where everyone has access to vast amounts of information at their fingertips, the traditional marketing funnel is obsolete. The idea that consumers start with broad awareness and then narrow their choices down linearly no longer holds true.

Instead, think of the consumer journey as an onion. Consumers have a limited awareness of options due to the difficulty of creating widespread awareness in today's fragmented media landscape. From this limited awareness, they conduct their own research using YouTube, Reddit, and other platforms, expanding their consideration set. They then narrow it down again based on their findings.

However, the industry is structured like an hourglass, with brand marketers (the top) and performance marketers (the bottom) working in silos. The top focuses on creating beautiful, broad-reach campaigns that few people see, while the bottom produces data-driven, often unattractive ads that everyone sees. This disconnect is problematic because it fails to address the consumer's need for understanding.

The middle is where understanding happens—where consumers look for information that bridges their initial awareness and final decision. Both brand and performance marketing need to incorporate more of this middle layer. Campaigns should focus on clarity and conveying the value of the product to make consumers both feel and act. Effective advertising clarifies the product's value and engages the audience meaningfully, rather than merely trying to capture attention through persistent but shallow tactics.

In summary, starting in the middle means creating campaigns that help consumers understand and appreciate the product, blending the best of brand and performance marketing. This approach ensures that the top creates compelling narratives that resonate and the bottom drives action through clear, value-focused messages.

Then we have four core adversaries, which represent what we need to avoid both as a company and as an industry. These enemies are personified to clarify the pitfalls we must steer clear of:

1. Stowaways: Either do the work or support those who do. This guards against a management culture that is detached from the actual work.
2. Zombies: Blank compliance kills quality. We prioritize quality over mere compliance.
3. Lemmings: Consensus does not equate to a good idea. A consensus-driven culture often stifles creativity, which thrives on bold, distinctive ideas.
4. Roosters: The loudest voice isn't always the most expert. Decision-making should be based on expertise, not authority or volume.

These enemies highlight the behaviors and attitudes that can undermine a creative culture. Avoiding these pitfalls ensures we stay true to our principles and foster an environment where creativity can flourish.

You have expertise in design, branding, and advertising. What are the common issues and elements that creatives must address?

Creativity thrives on the synergy between different disciplines and perspectives. Take, for example, the collaboration between designers and copywriters, each bringing unique skills and insights to the table. This dynamic interaction is where true innovation occurs.

In the realm of collaboration, it's crucial to distinguish between mere transfer connections and compound connections. Transfer connections involve the exchange of information but lack the depth of engagement needed for true creativity. On the other hand, compound connections occur when different disciplines work together to enhance each other's output. This requires a delicate balance of conversation and information exchange, neither too sparse nor overwhelming.

At the heart of creative collaboration lies the symbiotic connection. Whether in design, advertising, or any creative field, this model involves a close-knit team engaging in ongoing dialogue rather than a simple handoff of tasks. However, tribalism and structural barriers can impede this collaborative spirit. Overcoming these obstacles requires fostering a culture that values diversity and encourages interdisciplinary cooperation.

Furthermore, while technology such as Adobe Photoshop or Generative AI can automate certain tasks, true creativity flourishes when multiple human minds engage with the medium. Even as technology advances, human collaboration remains essential for pushing the boundaries of creativity.

Ultimately, successful collaboration hinges on establishing the right connections with individuals who bring diverse perspectives and expertise to the table. By embracing diversity and fostering meaningful dialogue, creative teams can unlock their full potential and drive innovation forward.

When you combine the expertise of someone who understands images with someone who understands copy, you get ads like Volkswagen's "Lemon" ad, where the synergy between the visual and textual elements is crucial. If you remove one element, the entire concept falls apart, showcasing the magic that happens at the intersection of these two ways of thinking. This process highlights the most important aspect: true collaboration.

There are many tasks we do daily that we call "collaboration," but they are not the type of collaboration that leads to creative breakthroughs. For example, receiving a company newsletter from Accenture, customized to the recipient, is a form of communication but not genuine collaboration. I call this a "transfer connection," where information is passed from one point to another without interaction.

The second type of connection is between disciplines, such as strategy, creative, and production. When one phase enhances the next, I call this a "compound connection." You can diagnose this connection by assessing whether the strategy is improving the creative output. If not, you have two levers to adjust: the amount of conversation and the amount of information shared. There is a "Goldilocks" amount of information—neither too little nor too much—that is ideal for a creative person to work effectively.

This balance is achieved through a more organic back-and-forth interaction. It's not just about handing over a brief and walking away, nor is it about micromanaging the creative process. Instead, it's about finding that perfect level of engagement.

The most crucial connection, where true creativity lives, is what I call a "symbiotic connection." This involves a small, close-knit group of people, typically two or three, working together in a conversation-based, organic interaction. This dynamic allows for the creation of something neither could achieve alone.

Two main obstacles prevent people from forming these connections: tribalism and structure. At R/GA, we had a designer culture and an advertising culture, each with a tendency to prefer working within their own group. Overcoming this instinct is essential for fostering creativity and innovation. You also need the right structural connections. It's not about having a weekly call but about creating the right environment for people to come together and figure things out. There is also a third obstacle: the instinct to rely solely on technology. While technology like generative AI can enhance creativity, it still benefits from human interaction and collaboration.

Effective collaboration requires overcoming tribal instincts, designing the right structural connections, and balancing technology with human creativity. This approach ensures that the creative process is enriched by diverse perspectives and expertise.

How can a brand have social impact?

I recently gave a presentation at the NYCxDesign event, focusing on social impact. I began by emphasizing that, as a designer, the most significant impact you can have is to excel at your job. How you apply your skills and what you apply them to are crucial decisions. Feeling strongly about a social issue is useless unless you can apply your expertise to address it.

Design is about manipulating your medium to create something meaningful. There have been three major revolutions offering designers opportunities to leverage their skills for impact:

1. The Industrial Revolution: This was about making everything, enabling mass production and generating enormous wealth, but also causing environmental degradation.
2. The Internet Revolution: This connected everything, providing access to information, people, and opportunities, but also leading to chaos and information overload.
3. The AI Revolution: This is about combining everything, enabling the creation of things we never imagined possible, but also fostering distrust due to a lack of transparency.

Each revolution has its trade-offs. The challenge for designers is to maximize the positive aspects and minimize the negative ones. For example, the Industrial Revolution lifted many out of poverty but also polluted the planet. The Internet has democratized access but also created chaotic information environments. AI offers unprecedented creative potential but also raises issues of trust.

As designers, our role is to navigate these trade-offs. We should strive to make mundane tasks frictionless and humane experiences textured. This means deciding when to simplify a process for ease of use and when to add complexity to enhance engagement and understanding.

Silicon Valley often advocates for a frictionless experience, but this can strip away human agency and richness. Most people desire the convenience of a frictionless world without losing their humanity. Therefore, designers need to judiciously remove friction when it benefits users and add texture when it enhances their experience.

Purpose in design comes from having a clear framework to make these decisions, understanding the trade-offs, and applying your expertise to create meaningful solutions. This approach has far more impact than merely expressing opinions on social media.

How do you make a brand matter or more valuable to people?

This is why I think the word "brand" is a suitcase word—it's vague, like saying something is "nice." What does that really mean? The simplest way I can explain it is that a brand represents what you expect from a company. Building a brand is crucial because if people don't know your company, they have no expectations.

You build a brand by doing useful and interesting things. Sometimes, something is just interesting; other times, it's interesting because it's useful. Either way, this interaction shapes the brand. When media becomes too abstract, focusing solely on reach rather than being useful or interesting, it degrades the brand. For instance, performance marketing that relentlessly chases transactions with banners can diminish the brand if it lacks usefulness or interest.

Creatives often mediate a company's marketing strategies and its relationship with its customers. Creatives possess empathy and can envision what people might find useful and interesting. This contrasts with purely data-driven approaches, which, while valuable, can't replicate the creative insight into customer needs.

I appreciate technology and the expertise of technicians—they can do things I can't. However, their skills complement mine. The value I bring lies in making things useful and interesting, which is essential for building a strong brand.

If you were addressing university students studying advertising or branding, what's the one thing that you would emphasize about storytelling?

To me, storytelling is a unique way of thinking. Unlike the systematic, architectural mindset prevalent in the tech world, where people see relationships and patterns spatially, great storytellers approach things temporally. They focus on one moment at a time rather than everything at once.

The power of storytelling lies in the revealed moment and the drama that unfolds. This can happen over a narrative arc or in a single instance. Even in mundane tasks, like creating a PowerPoint presentation, the drama from slide to slide is what keeps the audience engaged. A story is compelling because of these moments of revelation that offer new insights or emotional experiences.

A good story should make the audience feel like they've gained a deeper understanding of themselves or the world. Without these revelatory moments, a story falls flat. While anyone can tell a story, great storytellers excel in creating these dramatic, high-impact moments.

CHAPTER 3

NORTH STAR BRAND CONSTRUCT

No filter should tell you how to look.[1]
Yet, the most widespread use of augmented reality (AR) isn't in gaming; it's in face filters on social media.[2] Some 54 percent of girls prefer their appearance in edited photos, contributing to distorted perceptions of beauty and self-esteem.[3]

Social media platforms provide face-altering augmented reality filters, typically for harmless effects such as adding flower crowns or dog ears. However, using generative AI, TikTok introduced the Bold Glamour filter, which dramatically airbrushed users' faces to conform to a narrow beauty standard. Though it sparked controversy, with critics calling for a ban due to its potential harm to mental health, the filter quickly gained popularity among influencers and everyday users. As the creator of the No Digital Distortion movement and the Dove Self-Esteem Project, Dove felt compelled to respond.

Recognizing that influencers were driving Bold Glamour's popularity, Dove enlisted influencers to counteract the trend with the #TurnYourBack campaign. This simple, replicable action invited users to turn their backs on the filter, making participation as easy as a dance challenge or reaction prompt on TikTok.

Dove partnered with sixty-eight influencers to shift the conversation. Actor Gabrielle Union's video post, for example, showed her using the Bold Glamour filter, discussing its effects, and then turning her back. This format enabled both influencers and everyday users to participate and fuel the countertrend.

The #TurnYourBack campaign garnered 54 million video views and over 567,000 engagements, with a 94 percent positive sentiment rate in key markets. It also received 174 media placements, including features in *Women's Health*, *WWD*, *PopSugar*, and *Vanity Fair Italia*.[4]

In branding, the term "North Star" refers to a guiding principle or core strategy that drives all aspects of concepting, creative solutions, messaging, and executions. It represents the brand's ultimate purpose or mission, as a constant point of reference that aligns the brand's actions with its core values and long-term vision.

Identifying a North Star ensures consistency in messaging, copy, art direction, design, and brand experiences, keeping the brand focused on what matters most and helping it navigate market challenges or changes. Essentially, it's the brand's true north—a guiding direction that informs everything from product development to marketing efforts, helping ensure all initiatives align with the overarching mission.

Although #TurnYourBack is a more recent campaign, Dove's North Star has guided its efforts for over twenty years, shaping how the beauty industry and culture at large perceive and define "real" beauty. Dove has remained committed to this purpose, which gives it the credibility to speak in that space. Here is the Dove Real Beauty Pledge: "Dove is committed to making beauty a source of happiness for all women, not anxiety, today and for generations to come. We believe that every woman should be able to define beauty on their own terms: making it a source of joy and self-expression."[5]

Dove's North Star steers their branding, advertising, and design strategies. Not only did Dove change their narrative over twenty years ago, but they also changed the cultural narrative of beauty. Over the past two decades, major beauty brands have increasingly showcased a diverse range of "real women" (as opposed to professional models who adhere to hegemonic beauty standards) in their ads. Dove's narrative drove a shift that caught arch-competitors' attention and influenced their strategies.[6]

The campaign grew out of Dove's heritage, dating back to when David Ogilvy wrote its ad copy in the 1960s. Maureen Shirreff, who served as the group creative director under Ogilvy, notes that Dove has always favored using "real women" over conventional models in its ads. The campaign was also a reaction to TV shows of the time, such as Fox's *The Swan*, which promoted "extreme makeovers" for women.

The brief for the original campaign was to create a mission for Dove that transcended product advertising and aimed to "widen the definition of beauty," Shirreff explained. "This meant including women who had never been featured in beauty ads before."[7]

Over twenty years later, the success of Dove's approach is evident, with global sales reaching $6.5 billion—more than double the $3 billion it recorded before the campaign launched.[8]

Brand Building Strategy

Define your aspirational north star including why you exist, what makes you special, and how your brand comes to life in a compelling and actionable way.

—Wolff Olins

Wolff Olins's "About" page outlines its approach to purpose and brand strategy as: "We're here to help our clients defy convention, redefine expectations and ignite positive change."[9]

Strategically creative branding does more than highlight a product, service, or entity's utility—it transforms it into something more meaningful, setting new expectations and creating a positive impact for both the business and society. While this might sound grandiose, it's evident in the success of brands such as Dove, Instacart, Converse, and Apple. In a worldwide marketplace with endless options, strategically creative branding provides a compelling reason for consumers to choose one product over another by endowing a brand with distinctive and differentiated characteristics and imagery that make it stand out and remain salient.

A strong brand strategy defines the brand's promises and aligns with the audience's desires, anticipating future needs while reflecting the company's and the audience's core values. This alignment is crucial for success. About 84 percent of people surveyed globally agreed with the statement "I need to share values with a brand in order to buy it," according to the Edelman Trust Barometer Special Report: Brands and Politics (fifteen countries; fifteen thousand people; more than one thousand respondents per country). Moreover, for many brand categories, shared values matter even more to younger generations.[10]

The strategy shapes the brand's stance and drives purposeful, impactful action. Creative experts then refine and elevate this strategy, transforming it into something truly irresistible. Key factors to consider include:

- *Capabilities*: What the brand promises to deliver, encompassing its functional benefits.
- *Expressive case*: How a brand communicates its identity, values, and emotional appeal to connect with its audience meaningfully. Rather than focusing solely on functional benefits or logical arguments, an expressive case emphasizes the brand's personality, beliefs, and emotional benefits. It highlights the brand's story, mission, and values, aiming to forge a more personal bond with consumers by aligning with their values and emotions.
- *Emotional connection*: The primary emotions associated with the brand and the emotional benefit promised. (Best practice dictates identifying no more than two closely related associations.)

- *Need*: What the target audience wants or genuinely needs, often filling a gap or void.
- *Positioning*: What the brand delivers; what differentiates it; what makes it relevant, unique, and credible within the space.
- *Facilitation*: How the brand facilitates change, sparks transformation, and helps people reach their goals.
- *Integration*: How the brand fits into people's lives, delivering undeniable value and thus becoming irreplaceable; this encompasses what the brand means to individuals.
- *Values*: Articulation of the core principles that guide the brand's actions and decisions, clearly defining the values, beliefs, behaviors, and ethics that underpin the entity's mission and goals. Think of it this way: It's not what a brand says about its values but about what the values say about the brand.
- *Worldview*: The broader context for how the brand's values are expressed and understood in relation to environmental, societal, and global issues.
- *Value communication*: Clearly and effectively conveys a brand's core benefits and unique qualities to its target audience, articulating its core values, how it stands out from competitors, and why it is relevant and valuable to consumers, often highlighting its additional value.
- *Conscientiousness*: By moving beyond a limited understanding of corporate social responsibility, a company aligned with its values and perspective operates not merely as a profit-driven entity or in a performative way, but as an engaged and emotionally intelligent global citizen. It embraces a genuinely proactive and ethical approach to conducting business.
- *Responsiveness*: The brand can rethink, adapt, and pivot as needed. Circumstances that could prompt a brand to reevaluate its position include unforeseen cataclysmic events (e.g., pandemics or natural disasters), political changes, significant market shifts, technological advancements (think AI), major social issues, new forms of green energy, environmental impacts, and changes in consumer behavior or needs.
- *Key messages*: Address the needs, desires, and aspirations of the target audience; articulating shared values; expressing how the brand wants to be perceived.

Once they consider these factors, creative experts conceive, develop, and create externally facing visual and written communications for the brand. These communications must be well differentiated and have a tangible impact to be meaningful to the target audience, through the use of elements including but not limited to:

- *Brand narrative*: A dynamic and interconnected story framework that shapes the brand's portrayal and positioning, offering a cohesive narrative that demonstrates how the brand's capabilities align with the audience's needs and aspirations, driven by the brand's core values. Creatives conceive and craft the stories that shape a brand's narrative—stories designed to entertain, inform, educate, or inspire, fostering a sense of purpose and deepening the emotional connection with the audience.

- *Image attributes*: Communicating a consistent tone, personality, essence, credibility, and authenticity, while emphasizing the brand's uniquely differentiated characteristics.
- *Evocative visual and written expressions*: Outward representations of the brand's identity that make the abstract components unmistakable, memorable, and unique.
- *Totality of brand experiences*: Ensuring the audience experiences the brand's promises and values through participatory, unforgettable experiences delivered across traditional, emerging, interactive, multi-sensory, or entertainment-driven channels.

When defining a brand's North Star, you clarify its purpose, highlight what differentiates it, and articulate how it comes to life in a compelling and actionable way. As global brand consultancy Wolff Olins explains, "By 'brand,' we mean an organization that doesn't just sell something but also means something to people."[11]

Brand Building: A North Star Brand Construct

Imagine sailing the open seas when you spot a pirate flag waving from a distant ship. What emotions would surge through you?

Over two decades ago at the One Show Festival, Brian Collins, an expert in design (and cofounder of renowned brand consultancy COLLINS), opened his presentation with this evocative scenario. His insights have since become a cornerstone that I frequently reflect on.

Collins used pirate flags as a vivid example to illustrate the enduring power of branding. He highlighted how, historically, the sight of a pirate flag with its skull and crossbones immediately conveyed a clear message: danger and impending doom. As ships drew closer, every action reinforced this brand promise, creating an immersive experience. Over time, pirates consistently delivered on their brand promise of death and plunder, establishing a reputation that instilled fear and often led to surrender without resistance. Collins argued that their success stemmed from effectively linking their brand promise to their actions and performance.

Any product, service, organization, company, or individual remains indistinguishable within its category until it establishes uniqueness through elements including a distinctive name, symbol, cohesive identity design, functional and emotional benefits, strategic associations, origin story, and a compelling narrative

FOCUS: CANADIAN DOWN SYNDROME SOCIETY'S "INPLOYABLE" / FCB CANADA

North America is experiencing an unprecedented labor shortage, with over 6.8 million job openings. Employers are urgently seeking dedicated and dependable workers. Yet, more than 50 percent of individuals with Down syndrome face significant barriers in securing meaningful, paid employment.

Inployable is the first employment network for individuals with Down syndrome on LinkedIn. By consolidating willing candidates into one accessible platform, Inployable simplifies the process through which employers can tap into a more diverse and inclusive talent pool. The program provides resources for employers on inclusive hiring practices, training processes, and interview modifications to help them successfully integrate individuals from the Down syndrome community into their workforce.[12]

Since its launch in 2022, Inployable has rapidly expanded, connecting with over eight hundred individuals on LinkedIn. Working with partners LinkedIn and Adecco, the Canadian Down Syndrome Society (CDSS) is enhancing Inployable to offer more job opportunities, a greater pool of talented job seekers, and increased support for career development, inclusive hiring, and employment professionals.[13]

At the end of this chapter, you can learn more about the Inployable initiative in the interview with Nancy Crimi-Lamanna, the chief creative officer of FCB Canada.

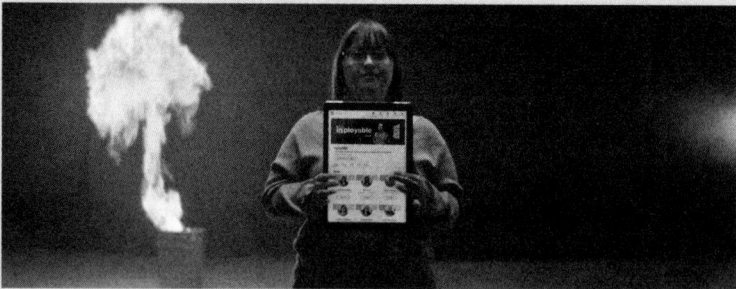

3.1 Campaign: "Inployable." Client: Canadian Down Syndrome Society (CDSS); Chair: Ed Casagrande; Executive Director: Laura LaChance; LinkedIn Canada Country Manager: Diana Luu; Head of Marketing: Jonathan Li; Creative Agency: FCB Canada; Chief Creative Officer: Nancy Crimi-Lamanna; Executive Creative Director: Andrew MacPhee; Associate Creative Director: Sara Radovanovich; Associate Creative Director: Sally Fung; Creative Director: Ryan Dzur; Creative Director: Sam Cote with supporting stories. Consistently delivering quality and fulfilling promises enhances differentiation and distinctiveness, shaping stakeholders' perceptions.

Conceiving A North Star Brand Construct

You must know your North Star and your why. You have to be authentic to that because if you're not, it won't last. It's not just about supporting women's sports; KPIs [Key Performance Indicators] are important . . . but doing good in the world is really important. Women's sports are part of that . . . Understanding your North Star is the first step . . . We've built relationships, not transactions.

—Kristyn Cook, EVP and chief agency, sales & marketing officer, State Farm[14]

A North Star brand construct is the foundational framework that captures and defines the essence and purpose of a brand. It serves as a guiding model, helping all stakeholders—audience, marketers, designers, and creatives—understand the brand's core identity, values, and strategic connections. This framework shapes the brand's narrative and visual identity, fostering clarity, sharper positioning, and strategic action. It's what keeps everything aligned, clear, and moving with purpose.

Reflecting on Apple CEO Tim Cook's advice to George Washington University graduates—"Your values matter. They are your North Star"—this principle holds universal relevance.[15]

A clearly defined brand construct helps an entity establish a distinctive position in the consumer's mind, creating strong associations with specific attributes or values. Leading brands such as Microsoft, Samsung, and Coca-Cola exemplify the power of a well-defined construct across all consumer touchpoints. This framework enables a brand to assert its unique qualities and stand out from competitors. For instance, Patagonia embodies environmental sustainability, Disney represents magical experiences, and LEGO symbolizes creative potential.

Six Factors Driving a Brand Construct

Six key factors drive the creation of a brand construct.

1. **Purpose**: A brand's reason for existing lies in its "why." It addresses both current needs and future potential, striving for salience—ensuring the brand remains top of mind when consumers seek solutions. Achieving this requires consistently delivering on its promises.

A significant majority of consumers (59 percent) believe that brands with a positive impact are worth paying more for because they've earned their trust (62 percent), even when the products are otherwise similar.[16]

2. **Impactful emotional connection**: A brand should evoke emotional resonance and foster a meaningful connection that elicits strong responses. Brands that align with consumers' values, identity, and beliefs build genuine affinity. Branding can strengthen this connection by prioritizing corporate citizenship and demonstrating a purpose beyond profit. For example, 55 percent of US adults believe businesses should publicly address climate change, while 52 percent think companies should advocate for mental health issues.[17]

    Providing practical value while addressing broader societal and ethical concerns helps brands foster deeper emotional connections and a shared sense of purpose. Sixty-three percent of Millennials and 59 percent of Gen Zers feel a connection with others who use the same brands.[18]

3. **Alignment**: Continuously adapting a brand's offerings and messaging to meet current and future needs ensures it aligns with and resonates with the values of its target audiences.

4. **Differentiation**: Setting a brand apart from its competitors prevents it from becoming a commodity, ensuring it stands out and offers consumers compelling reasons to choose it over others. A brand construct doesn't need to be entirely unique, but it must distinguish the brand from the competition.

5. **Distinction**: Emphasizing the unique benefits and attributes that set a brand apart in a crowded market requires design excellence, crafting an iconic visual identity across all touchpoints, integrating visual dynamism, and cultivating instant recognition and emotional resonance.

6. **Lifestyle or business integration**: Ensuring the brand integrates seamlessly into people's personal lives, work environments, or business operations enhances its practicality and relevance. Integration reinforces habitual use.

Essential Considerations for Crafting a Brand Construct

Apple Inc. often comes to mind when considering a tech giant renowned for design excellence and user-centric products. Apple consistently champions innovation, guided by leading experts in its creative initiatives. As Nick Law, Accenture Song's creative chairperson, notes, "The essence of a successful creative company lies in its differentiation. You want to offer something unique that others can't easily replicate. To achieve this, it's crucial for a company to have unwavering principles. This has been true for companies such as R/GA, Apple, and Nike."[19]

From the beginning, Apple has aimed to meet customer needs and to inspire them. This philosophy is the cornerstone of their marketing strategy, which centers on building a profound emotional connection with consumers.

> We believe that business, at its best, serves the public good, empowers people around the world, and binds us together as never before.
> —Apple's CEO Tim Cook

A well-defined North Star construct clarifies a brand's essence, purpose, and values, providing a foundation for cohesive stories across all touchpoints. This framework must be authentic, setting transformative goals for customers, reducing ambiguity about the brand's purpose, and consistently delivering on promises through actionable initiatives.

A brand construct should be "ownable"—not necessarily in a legal sense, unless protected by a patent, but in its consistent and passionate expression of the brand's identity. This sense of "ownership" builds a strong association between the construct and the brand, making it difficult for competitors to replicate. By focusing on one or two distinctive associations and communicating them consistently, a brand boosts its memorability and salience.

Within this guiding North Star framework, a brand defines its identity. However, public perception ultimately shapes it, influenced by factors such as human presence, atmospheric cues, semiotics (the meaning behind symbols), distinctive assets (e.g., music, sound effects, animations, color), social media interactions, conversations, and that ever-valuable buzz.

Consider the following distinctions:

- *Brand archetype* presents the brand as a persona, embodying its symbolism, values, behaviors, and messages. When applied thoughtfully and responsibly, an archetype enhances recognition and relatability by drawing on universal human experiences, helping people quickly connect with the brand's story and meaning. (For more on brand archetypes, refer to chapter 15 and the Tool: Scrutinizing Archetypes at the end of this book.)
- *Brand identity* represents how a business or any entity wants to be perceived by its audience, much like an individual's character. A brand's teams shape its identity by creating and managing cohesive visual, written, verbal, haptic, and sonic assets. For insights into how a brand is actually perceived, particularly if it's well established, refer to the concept of brand image.
- *Brand image* refers to people's perception or impression of a brand shaped by their experiences, interactions, and associations. Multiple factors shape and convey this image, including the brand's messaging, marketing efforts, ad campaigns, endorsements by influencers or celebrities, media mentions (such as in songs, TV shows, videos, or films), content creators, reviews,

company initiatives, product quality, customer service, and visual identity. It reflects what people think and feel when they encounter the brand.

- *Brand narrative* encompasses the overarching theme and individual stories told to articulate its identity to internal and external stakeholders. It offers context for past actions, explains current initiatives, and outlines future goals. For a deeper exploration, see chapter 12 on the power of stories.
- *Brand personality* refers to the set of human traits and characteristics attributed to a brand, shaping how the audience perceives it.
- *Brand tone* emerges in the style, manner, and attitude a brand uses to communicate with its audience. It reflects the brand's personality and identity conveyed through imagery, word choice, and interactions across all touchpoints. The tone shapes the emotional context of communication and influences how people perceive and connect with the brand. For example, Nike's tone is consistently motivational, while Wendy's is famously sassy.

KEY QUESTIONS TO DEFINE A BRAND IDENTITY

Differentiation is crucial for standing out in a crowded, competitive market.[20]

To clearly define a brand identity and guide its evolution, address these foundational questions. Each response should highlight what differentiates the brand and what makes it uniquely meaningful to people. This emphasis ensures that the brand becomes memorable, recognizable, and associated with a defining essence—and of course, salient.

- **Who are you?** Start with the brand's origin story and mission, then consider how every message, narrative, and visual or verbal element reflects that identity.
- **What do you want people to instantly think or feel when they hear the brand name?** Clarify the emotional and cognitive associations you want to trigger. These should align with the brand's purpose and promise.
- **What's the top association with your brand name or logo?** Associations reflect the primary impression or emotional connection consumers form and should align with the brand's core values.
- **What do you offer?** Consider both the functional advantages and emotional benefits the brand delivers.
- **How was the customer's life before using the brand?** Now, envision how the brand transforms their routine, mindset, or business and the meaning it adds.

- **How do you do it?** Highlight any proprietary methods, unique processes, or distinctive approaches that set your brand apart.
- **Why do you do it?** Pinpoint the underlying purpose driving the brand, its reason for being, as emphasized by Simon Sinek in *Start with Why*.[21]
- **When?** Always. Consistently delivering on brand promises builds credibility and earns trust.

Ideally, every entity or brand owner should have clear answers to these questions. However, many brands turn to specialized external partners, such as brand communications firms, design studios, and advertising agencies. These experts play a vital role in formulating, positioning, and executing the core concepts, design, and advertising that define a brand.

Navigating Brand Building: Internal Strategy vs. Agency Expertise

Building a brand requires distinct yet complementary contributions from the company or brand owner and its partner agencies, each bringing unique expertise to the process.

A thorough understanding of the brand's history, mission, business plan, long-term goals, and values is essential for the company or brand owner. This knowledge informs integration across functions, such as research, product development, sales, customer service, and so on, allowing internal teams to collaborate effectively. Together, they guide ongoing branding efforts, ensuring a cohesive identity that builds the customer base over time.

Creative agencies, on the other hand, bring an external perspective and specialized expertise. Their experience with diverse projects offers fresh insights and strategically creative ideas that can lead to compelling campaigns. With dedicated resources and a focus on creativity, agencies craft campaigns that captivate audiences and enhance brand engagement.

Company/Brand Owner Side

- **Deep brand knowledge**: Internal executives and teams possess a thorough understanding of the brand's origin, history, mission, values, benefits, and long-term goals. This insight provides a comprehensive perspective and supports consistent branding efforts across the organization.

- **Integration**: Branding initiatives should align with key business functions, such as research and development, product/service innovations, sales, and customer service, to promote cohesion and organizational unity.
- **Stewardship**: Unlike agencies focusing on project-based work, internal branding requires ongoing stewardship and responsiveness to market shifts. Dedicated brand stewards ensure continuous alignment with the brand's evolving objectives and strategies.
- **Internal resources**: Although company teams may lack the specialized creative expertise of external agencies, they leverage internal insights, data, and stakeholder knowledge to inform branding strategies.
- **Stakeholder involvement**: Branding decisions often require input from multiple internal stakeholders, including executives, product managers, sales teams, and others. While this collaborative approach brings diverse perspectives, it can slow decision-making and dilute ideas due to differing viewpoints and the need for consensus.
- **Long-term focus**: Internal branding emphasizes developing and maintaining a long-term brand identity and reputation, aiming to build sustained salience and cultivate enduring customer relationships.

Creative Agency Side

- **Emphasis on strategic creativity**: Award-winning agencies prioritize creativity and innovative solutions, often pushing boundaries to develop standout campaigns that capture attention. The level and quality of creative output vary across agencies.
- **Diverse creative expertise**: Agencies offer a broad range of specialized skills, including branding, design, strategy, advertising, AR/VR/XR, AI-generated content, experiential design, motion/animation, social media campaigns, and influencer or content creator marketing. This breadth of expertise enables them to deliver comprehensive creative solutions.
- **Outside viewpoint**: Agencies bring an external and objective perspective, providing fresh insights and ideas that internal teams might overlook. This outside lens often reveals new opportunities and unlocks fresh approaches.
- **Client diversity**: By working with various industries and clients, agencies gain extensive experience and best practices. This exposure deepens their understanding of multiple sectors, including competitors' businesses, and sharpens their strategic thinking.
- **Project focus**: Agencies typically operate on a project basis, executing specific campaigns or brand initiatives with defined objectives and timelines. Unless designated as the agency of record (AOR), their involvement is often short-term. Some creatives find that longer partnerships are more effective for building trust. (For more about establishing trust, please refer to

the interview in chapter 1 with Gaëtan du Peloux, chief creative officer and co-chief executive officer, Marcel.)

- **Resources**: Agencies have extensive strategic planning and creative development resources, supported by specialized partners in areas such as social media and experiential design. Their broader client base and larger project budgets enable them to employ dedicated market research professionals and other resources.

Interview: Nancy Crimi-Lamanna, Chief Creative Officer, FCB Canada

Named by *Adweek* as one of Toronto's Brand Stars shaping the city into the creative hub it is today and a Campaign US 40 Over 40, Nancy has played a key role in FCB's creative resurgence, helping elevate the agency to Creative Network of the Year at the 2021 Cannes Lions, the most awarded agency at the 2020 One Show, and *Adweek*'s 2020 Global Agency of the Year. Her work has been presented to the United Nations twice, and she also has the distinction of bringing home Canada's first Integrated, Commerce, Strategy and Creative Data Cannes Lions. In 2023, FCB Canada was named the #2 North American Agency of the Year at the Cannes Lions, and the Agency of the Year at both the Effies and WARC where it brought home several Best of Show honors and the Cannes Grand Prix in Direct for adidas Runner 321. This year, her long-standing partnership with the Canadian Down Syndrome Society was recognized with a coveted One Show Penta Pencil, which awards agency/client partnerships that deliver creative excellence—another Canadian first.

Since joining FCB Canada eight years ago, the agency's creative work has been among the most celebrated and innovative in the industry, including its work for BMO/BMO Harris, adidas, Ontario Lottery and Gaming, and the Canadian Down Syndrome Society. This thinking has helped FCB Canada achieve the honor of being named the Media Innovation Agency of the Year for two years in a row, the Digital Agency of the Year for seven years, and the most-awarded Canadian agency at Cannes for four years.

Beyond creating iconic campaigns, Nancy is an industry thought leader. She has served on several international juries, including as jury president at the Cannes Lions, Clios, and D&AD. She also volunteers her time for industry panels, sits on the ADCC advisory board, and serves on school advisory boards for advertising students in Canada.

How do you go about conceiving, executing, and thinking about a brand campaign from a strategic perspective, platform perspective, and business solution perspective?

At FCB, strategy and creative are so intimately connected that they are basically two sides of the same coin. We like to say everything is strategy and everything is creative, and the moment you start to pull those things apart is the moment you get yourself into trouble. We have a robust set of strategic tools that we use to get us to really smart work, but they're really account management, data, and creative strategy tools because we use them together, and we tackle the business problems of our clients as a team—from a strategic point of view, from a creative point of view, we do it all together.

From a platform perspective, we like to build brand platforms that can evolve with a brand and its consumers over time—long-standing platforms from which we can create provocative and behavior-changing work for years to come. For example, our work for the Canadian Down Syndrome Society (CDSS) is based on an enduring platform that addresses different moments in the journey of families and people living with Down syndrome.

Please tell us about your work for the Canadian Down Syndrome Society.

The Canadian Down Syndrome Society is a small Canadian charity. Our work has been focused on driving change by addressing specific moments in the journey of a person with Down syndrome. Its aim has been to drive real change, but the byproduct has also been to shift perceptions of what a person with Down syndrome is capable of by taking them out of the role of victim and placing them into new roles as experts, teachers, and activists. In Canada, despite a growing movement toward diversity and inclusion, bias continues to be pervasive against people living with disabilities; there is still a very long way to go, but progress happens in small systemic steps that address specific barriers.

Our work over the eight years has aimed to push through these boundaries: boundaries that limit the potential of people with Down syndrome and boundaries that limit how we think about advertising itself.

This is demonstrated in our work that has far exceeded the scope of what we think of as traditional advertising initiatives, solving problems not usually tackled by marketing agencies—such as partnering with Google, the world's largest technology company, to make their voice algorithms more inclusive, and orchestrating a globally unprecedented research study that proved the oversized impact that exercise has on cognition for people with Down syndrome.

Our relationship has been built on trust and respect, with a shared ambition to push the boundaries of typical disability advocacy work. We have never lost sight of the fact that the true experts are those living with Down syndrome themselves and have always made them the champions of each initiative.

Together, we've done much more than simply raise awareness of issues faced by the community; we've taken concrete actions to improve the representation of and inclusiveness in the lives of those with Down syndrome.

Over the course of our partnership, CDSS has become the global leader in advocacy and change for the Down syndrome community. CDSS has twice been asked to speak at the United Nations about our work together. The collaboration between FCB and CDSS is empowering a community and building lasting change.

Our creative platform demonstrated what people with Down syndrome can do, and a humanizing approach employed throughout this journey empowered them to advocate and make change for themselves.

Year 1: They became the true experts in answering expectant parents' questions. *Down Syndrome Answers*: a series of searchable videos where people with Down syndrome answered the forty most frequently Googled questions about Down syndrome by expectant parents.

Year 2: They became agents of change through the campaign "Anything but Sorry." Our Down syndrome experts once again explained that any profanity-laden reaction is better than the worst word of all: "Sorry" (figure 3.2). With our work being presented at the UN, they were effecting global change.

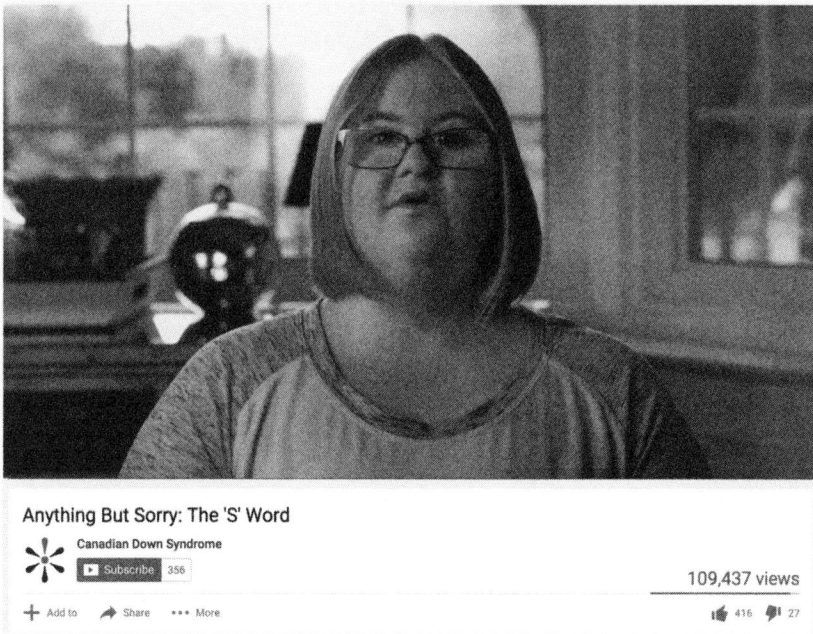

Anything But Sorry: The 'S' Word
Canadian Down Syndrome
Subscribe 356
109,437 views
Add to   Share   ••• More   416   27

3.2 Campaign: "Anything But Sorry." Client: CDSS; Chair, Board of Directors: Laura LaChance; Vice-Chair, Board of Directors: Ed Casagrande; Creative Agency: FCB Canada; Chief Creative Officers: Nancy Crimi-Lamanna, Jeff Hilts; Sr. Copywriter: Marty Hoefkes; Sr. Art Director: Michael Morelli; Art Director: Cody Sabatine, Gira Moin; Copywriter: Joseph Vernuccio

Year 3: They became teachers making voice technology inclusive. To improve Google's voice technology, we turned individuals with Down syndrome into Google's teachers. We worked with Google—a technology that usually teaches *us*—and empowered people with Down syndrome to be the ones teaching *it*.

Year 4: They became researchers leading a global research study. Despite being one of the most common genetic disorders, Down syndrome is among the least studied, so doctors often give poor advice to their patients. So, our Down syndrome experts provided hundreds of hours of scientific data in a globally unprecedented study to prove the link between exercise and cognition for the Down syndrome community (figure 3.3).

Year 5: They became valued employees by partnering with LinkedIn to connect the community to employers. North America is facing a historic labor shortage, yet over 50 percent of people with Down syndrome still struggle to

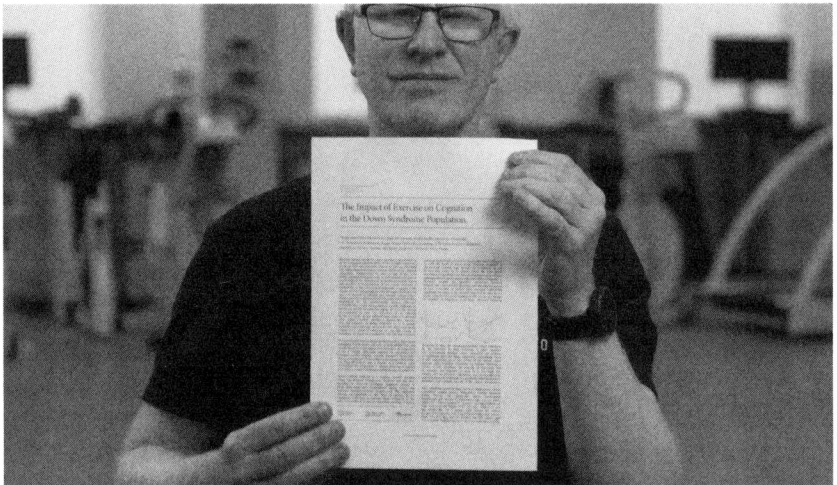

3.3 CDSS, "The Mindsets Paper with Dr. Dan Gordon." Client: CDSS; Chair: Ed Casagrande; Interim Executive Director: Laura LaChance; Marketing & Communications Manager: Kristen Halpen; Board Member: Ben Tarr; Partners: Anglia Ruskin University, Posit Science /BrainHQ, Creative Agency: FCB Canada; Chief Creative Officer: Nancy Crimi-Lamanna; Chief Creative Officer: Jeff Hilts; Executive Creative Director: Andrew MacPhee; Associate Creative Director: Michael Morelli; Associate Creative Director: Marty Hoefkes; Copywriter: Jon Dawe; Art Director: Jerry Yang

The CDSS collaborated with Dr. Dan Gordon and his research team at Anglia Ruskin University, as well as Dr. Michael Merzenich and his team at BrainHQ, to conduct a research study and awareness campaign aimed at exploring the possible connection between physical and mental fitness in individuals with Down syndrome.

find paid, meaningful work. Introducing **Inployable**: The world's first employment network for people with Down syndrome on LinkedIn (see figure 3.1). [*https://inployable.com/*]

You are an inaugural member of the Times Up Advertising movement addressing gender inequality and you've committed FCB Canada to #FreeTheWork, an effort to champion diversity in the workplace. Why are these initiatives important?

We are finally starting to recognize the contributions of women in advertising and other industries. By being an advocate for change, we are making advertising a safer and stronger space for women and other underrepresented communities. I have been a panelist for See It Be It, a Cannes initiative that is addressing the gender imbalance that continues to persist in the creative sector, several times.

#FreeTheWork focuses on the production space globally and we are proud to be one of the inaugural agencies in Canada to join. I also helped champion BIPOC production houses in Canada by providing them with exposure to Canada's top advertising executives and a series of feature articles in *Strategy Magazine*, one of Canada's leading industry publications.

These initiatives are important, not only from an equality perspective but from a business perspective. There has been a seismic demographic shift in North America. The myriad racial and ethnic groups that shape the foundation of our society today require us to champion diversity not only in our work—to be more relevant to multicultural subgroups within the population at large—but also within the workplaces where that culturally relevant work is created.

Consumers are demanding that brands recognize and celebrate their unique culture and heritage. They require a deeper level of intimacy for brands to truly understand and accurately connect to the fluidity of their cultural differences and nuances. As an agency, we must continuously evolve to meet them where they are going.

Your creative solutions push boundaries and innovate. Very simply, how do you manage to do that year after year?

My motto is "Leap and a net will appear." Doing what's been done only limits us and allows us to achieve what's already been achieved. New challenges require new ways of disrupting. I like to push the boundaries of what's possible and inspire my teams to do the same. We disrupt channel conventions, mess with best practices, and break a few rules, but all in the journey to do the most effective work. We harness data and technology to unlock new opportunities. We invent new ways of working and blow up old models. Our superpower is reimagining what a marketing solution can be.

Creating groundbreaking work, whether it's for adidas, CDSS, BMO [Bank of Montreal], or any other client, only requires the space to take risks and be more afraid of not trying than failing. In order to do that, we embed innovation into the creative department by including a creative innovation lead and a production innovation lead in our creative teams.

You've been a jury president at Cannes and served on several international juries, including the Cannes Lions, D&AD, Clios, and One Show. What are your criteria for creating and judging work that fosters cultural conversations and impact?

Great work always involves risk. It is always brave, even audacious. Let's change Google's voice algorithm, make lottery tickets wearable, and turn driveways into showrooms. Great work drives sales, builds brands, and becomes part of the cultural conversation. These are just a few of the things I look for, but my criteria are quite broad and often calibrated with the category I'm judging. Some of the general things I look for when evaluating work:

- Provocative. Does the idea make you stop and think? If a brand's work is only being noticed, how much value does it really have? You can spend your way into simply being noticed, but it's an expensive proposition. If the idea doesn't stick with people, it hasn't created enough value.
- Behavior change: Does the idea invite people to participate? It should be work that not only makes people think differently but also makes them behave differently, work that moves your audience from passive to active.
- Longevity: Is this idea so big that it scales across platforms and time? It should be an idea that when people see it, they see the future; they know there is more to come. This idea can build long-term brand equity or can sustain a brand for years to come at every moment of the journey.
- Relevance: The work should be addressing current and relevant cultural issues by providing insights and driving engagement for positive change.
- Authenticity: The best work is authentic work. It involves sincerity, genuine expression, and a true connection, whether it's with the customer or the brand itself. Is the idea itself true to the brand?
- Inclusivity: This is work that aims to be inclusive, that embraces and engages with diverse perspectives to create a more comprehensive dialogue where appropriate.
- Craft: An important criterion, in my judgment, is the level of care and attention involved in bringing an idea to life, and this truly elevates the work. My focus will shift depending on the category, but high production values, including cinematography, editing, sound design, and overall technical quality, are essential. Award-winning work is always well-produced and demonstrates a high level of craftsmanship in execution.

CHAPTER 4

BRAND-BUILDING IDEAS

"Find your place with us."[1]

Millions of refugees from Ukraine have crossed the Polish border.[2] Using data to help Ukrainian refugees in Poland find the best cities to settle in based on personal factors, Mastercard launched its "Where to Settle" campaign. Recognized for advancing the UN's Sustainable Development Goals at the Cannes Lions Festival, this campaign highlighted the potential of data-driven solutions.

As Ukrainian refugees opened 10 percent of new businesses in Poland, competition increased. In response, Mastercard introduced "Room for Everyone," showcasing how Polish and Ukrainian businesses can thrive together. The campaign promotes "Where to Start," a tool that matches businesses based on complementary data, fostering symbiotic relationships (for example, bakeries near barber shops or bookstores near jewelry stores).

By encouraging Polish entrepreneurs to collaborate with Ukrainian businesses, the campaign shifted the narrative from competition to cooperation. As a result, up to 40 percent of new businesses used the tool, and positive sentiment toward Ukrainians rose by 10 percent.[3]

While these campaigns have significantly improved the lives of millions, they have also revolutionized Mastercard's business, resulting in a 67 percent revenue increase and a 56 percent growth in brand value since 2018.[4]

When Mastercard and its creative agency McCann introduced the "Priceless" campaign in 1997, it resonated deeply with audiences through its relatable idea that in a society focused on materialism, the truly valuable experiences are those that "money can't buy." For instance, the 2005 "Cardboard Box" TV spot, directed by Steven Soderbergh, beautifully illustrates this concept: it showcases the joy of a toddler playing with a simple cardboard box rather than a store-bought toy, highlighting that such moments are indeed priceless.

In 2019, Mastercard and McCann recognized that to uphold the essence of "Priceless," the brand could not ignore the 1.4 billion people worldwide excluded from the financial system due to discrimination, exploitation, and other barriers. By making financial inclusion central to Mastercard's brand purpose, "Priceless" has evolved from a messaging campaign into a series of product innovations, tools, and platforms.

When I give presentations at universities across the United States, I show-case examples of branding, advertising, and design rooted in worthwhile ideas. I track the ideas that resonate most with students. Among the most resonant is Mastercard's "True Name" card, part of the Inclusive by Design campaign, which allows transgender individuals to use their preferred names (as opposed to birth names) on their credit and debit cards, without requiring a legal name change.

Mastercard's core message is compelling: "connecting everyone to priceless possibilities." Mastercard describes its aim as linking individuals, businesses, and organizations across more than 210 countries and territories, to unlock opportunities for people worldwide, now and for future generations.[5] This commitment is reflected in all aspects of the brand's messaging, highlighting its dedication to supporting local initiatives and tackling global challenges.

Mastercard's Purpose Manifesto states:

> We see a connected world. Where humanity unites, prosperity is possible and opportunity is open to us all.
> Our responsibility is to let basic human decency serve as our guide,
> Innovate with purpose
> And unlock potential for people everywhere . . .
> We see beyond what technology can build, to what passion can do, transforming economic growth into inclusive, sustainable growth, rewriting the future as we go.
> Our connection with each other fuels us to connect the world. And when we believe and build together, it creates Priceless possibilities for everyone.[6]

What Makes a Brand Idea Resonate

For a brand idea to truly stand out, it must be more than clever; it must address a specific need, desire, or gap in the market. The essence of a compelling brand idea lies in differentiating itself from competitors and forging a relationship with its target audience. Offering clear and convincing reasons for consumers to prefer one brand over another is essential. Without a distinct differentiation, there is little motivation for consumer preference, and if uniqueness isn't recognized or valued, it's unlikely to drive sales. For a brand idea to resonate effectively, it must be relevant to its intended audience, align with their values, and deliver on its promises.

Key Elements of a Resonant Brand

A brand insight leads to an idea: A compelling brand idea begins with a deep understanding of the target audience. By gathering and analyzing data on consumer behavior, preferences, attitudes, perceptions, existing customers, competitors, and the broader market, you create a foundation that can lead to valuable insights. Identifying unique opportunities or gaps others might overlook can offer a strategic advantage. These insights should be grounded in a thorough examination of category dynamics, brand audits, competitive successes and failures, and customer behavior and feedback, revealing key strengths, weaknesses, and areas for improvement.

It is salient: Ensuring that a brand evokes key strategic associations helps to ensure that it stays top-of-mind for consumers whenever they consider a specific need or product category—for instance, Mastercard's association with "priceless," Volvo's with "safety," or Apple's with "think different." (No other brand in the Kantar BrandZ Global Top 100 scores higher for salience than Apple.)[7] The key association should align with the brand construct (see chapter 3) and be distinctive and differentiated, setting the brand apart in the consumer's mind.

It performs: A brand fulfills its promise by answering the needs and desires of its target audience while ensuring financial viability. By continuously adapting to changing consumer needs, the brand can drive growth and achieve long-term success.

It provides value: Resonance begins by delivering something valuable to the audience—utility, information, entertainment, an emotional benefit, or a sense of belonging. The brand must earn the audience's time and attention by embodying its values and positively impacting every community it serves.

It is in alignment: A brand's ethos should be grounded in responsibility and integrity, remaining true to its core principles, which involve a genuine commitment to sustainability, community engagement, uplifting people, and ethical practices. Transparent communication of the brand's mission and vision across all channels fosters trust by openly addressing achievements and challenges.

Take Gen Z (born between 1997 and 2012) as a prime example. This demographic, influential in today's socially conscious and online world, uses brands to express their values and beliefs. Their choices reflect a strong commitment to their principles, setting high expectations for brands. Brands that fail to meet these standards may face significant backlash. To build trust and maintain engagement with Gen Z, brands must communicate openly and demonstrate their values authentically through meaningful actions.[8]

It offers transparency: The link between brands and politics is becoming more evident across global demographics. Nearly 80 percent of consumers evaluate brands through a political lens. For Gen Z, specifically, a brand's silence on societal issues is often seen as a political stance. In fact, 58 percent of consumers believe that a brand's lack of communication suggests inactivity or an effort to withhold information, which highlights the fact that brands cannot avoid political scrutiny, whether through their actions or their silence, as noted in Edelman's *The Brands and Politics* special report.[9]

Consistently addressing these core questions will clarify strategic goals and objectives:

- **What are our strategic goals and objectives?** Define your aims and outline how you plan to achieve prominence and salience in the market.
- **What do we stand for?** Specify what the brand will and will not represent.
- **Who should represent us?** Decide who should and should not represent the brand, including influencers, creators, and talent.
- **Who is our target audience?** Identify who you will and will not target.

Crafting Impactful Ideas: The Three G's Framework

Generating truly impactful ideas requires more than conventional brainstorming. To elevate the ideation process, consider using The Three G's framework—Goal, Gap, and Gain—as introduced in my book *The New Art of Ideas: Unlock Your Creative Potential.*[10] This approach helps generate ideas that are strategic, original, and worthwhile.

1. Clarify the **Goal**: Define what you aim to achieve, whether it's boosting brand awareness, reaching new audiences, enhancing brand perception, addressing community concerns, or increasing customer engagement.
2. Identify and fill a **Gap**: Determine if your goal addresses an unmet need within the sector or industry. Assess whether it might serve an overlooked audience, fill a market void, or explore new opportunities. Gaps may include underserved communities, specific niches, geographic locations, or product, service, or process deficiencies.
3. Assess the **Gain**: Evaluate whether the idea offers tangible or emotional benefits for the environment, individuals, and business. An impactful idea

should positively contribute to the triple bottom line—planet, people, and prosperity—beyond mere profit or novelty.

Addressing short- and long-term gains related to diversity, disability, sustainability, urban development, land conservation, and marine life is crucial, as these considerations have significant and far-reaching implications.

The Flexibility of the Three G's Framework

The Three Gs—Goal, Gap, and Gain—framework offers flexible pathways for generating impactful ideas. You can start with any "G" depending on what resonates most. Whether you first identify a gap or pain point that leads to an exploration of associated goals and potential gains, or instead begin with a societal benefit and work backward to define relevant goals and gaps, this adaptable process encourages innovation.

To create truly impactful ideas, consider their broader societal implications. Ideas that improve lives, promote sustainability, and contribute positively are highly valued within this framework. Embracing the triple bottom line—planet, people, and prosperity—ensures that ideas balance financial success with social and environmental responsibility, driving meaningful change.

STRATEGICALLY ADDRESSING MARKET GAPS FOR DIFFERENTIATION

Identifying and addressing market gaps strategically differentiates and positions a company through the following approaches:

Identifying unique opportunities: Identifying gaps in areas such as product features, customer segments, geographic regions, sustainable practices, renewable energy sources, habitat protection, waste management, access to clean water, water scarcity, biodiversity enhancement, sustainable food production and demand, community support, or service levels allows businesses to innovate and stand out. This differentiation adds meaningful value.

Purpose space: Determining the scope within which a brand can authentically engage with its audience involves understanding relevant topics, experiences, communications, and innovations. A brand's purpose

(*continued on next page*)

(continued from previous page)

> space reflects the trust, "permission," and approval of stakeholders and customers, aligning brand activities with societal norms and expectations.
>
> *Tailoring solutions*: Addressing identified gaps enables businesses to develop products or services designed explicitly for overlooked or underserved segments. This tailored approach enhances consumer satisfaction and engagement.
>
> *Creating a competitive advantage*: Effectively filling a gap positions a company as a leader or specialist in that niche, setting it apart from competitors who may not have addressed the exact needs.
>
> *Building brand identity*: Addressing specific gaps enhances a company's brand identity by highlighting its uniqueness, responsiveness to market demands, and commitment to environmental and social responsibility, thereby solidifying its position in consumers' minds.

Interview: Ben Miles, Chief Design Officer, APAC, R/GA

Ben Miles

Ben Miles is a renowned global design leader who champions transformative work in brands and company culture and advocates for meaningful ideas rooted in understanding human behaviors. His strong sense of responsibility drives him to use creativity to make a positive impact.

Heading R/GA's creative team, Ben has built a diverse and innovative team of APAC's best brand designers, experience designers, strategists, and technologists. Together, they share a common belief that brands should not merely appear in culture but significantly contribute to it.

Ben received a "World Changing Ideas" accolade from *Fast Company* for the impactful G' AY MATE project supporting marriage equality. In 2023, his leadership earned two D&AD Yellow Pencils and a Cannes Lions for the Indigenous social enterprise We Are Warriors (WAW).

Please tell us about Australia's First Nations group, We Are Warriors.

We Are Warriors was cofounded with Nooky, an Indigenous Australian rapper, radio host, entrepreneur, and father (figure 4.1). The platform is designed to empower and unlock the potential of Indigenous Australian kids, who are statistically the most incarcerated youth in the world despite making up just 3 percent of Australia's overall population. It connects them to First Nations role models and offers consultation for major brands about how they can better represent this community.

Systemic racism takes Indigenous youth away from their families and pushes them into detention centers at an alarming rate—that's a hard reality to grow up in. So, where do young Indigenous kids go to be inspired?

Having confronted his own uncomfortable truths, Nooky saw the need to create a platform that inspires young Mob, unlocking their Warrior spirit and driving positive change. We developed a socially conscious, politically charged brand with the goal of empowering Indigenous youth to succeed by spotlighting Blak excellence.

In the past, other organizations have focused on improving outcomes for First Nations youth by attempting to change how nonindigenous Australians saw Indigenous people; challenging negative perceptions and behaviors. However, the positive impact on Indigenous youth had been limited. So, we flipped it. Rather than ask nonindigenous Australians to change the way they saw Indigenous youth, we needed to change how Indigenous Youth saw themselves.

The problem is—as the adage goes—you can't be what you can't see. Australia's mainstream media fails to provide positive Indigenous role models for youth. Instead, stereotypes are perpetuated, leaving many Indigenous young people with the impression that there are limited options ahead of them. To change the way Indigenous youth saw themselves, we needed to make Indigenous success stories more visible: "See it to be it."

Our Warrior stories—from music, fashion, sport, photography, performance, and beyond—are at the heart of everything we do, representing the bravery, strength, and resilience it takes to succeed against all odds. We celebrate their greatness by focusing on building positivity, rather than fighting negativity.

We Are Warriors has evolved into one of Australia's most attitudinal brands, expanding its impact across various channels, initiatives, and collaborations. Significant achievements include Blak Powerhouse, an event subverting the symbolism of Australia Day to diminish its power over Indigenous Australians, and taking over Sydney New Year's Eve fireworks, sharing a message of love, hope, and greatness with over 425 million people globally.

A huge part of the brand's success is because of its personality: bold, unapologetic, and fierce. It's just the beginning for We Are Warriors, as we continue to grow and encourage everyone to join the WAW and make a difference.

What strategies should creatives employ to prioritize Indigenous or Blak perspectives and cultivate meaningful connections with various communities?

A lot of initiatives I've worked on have been in response to societal issues in Australia. But they've always been created in collaboration with the

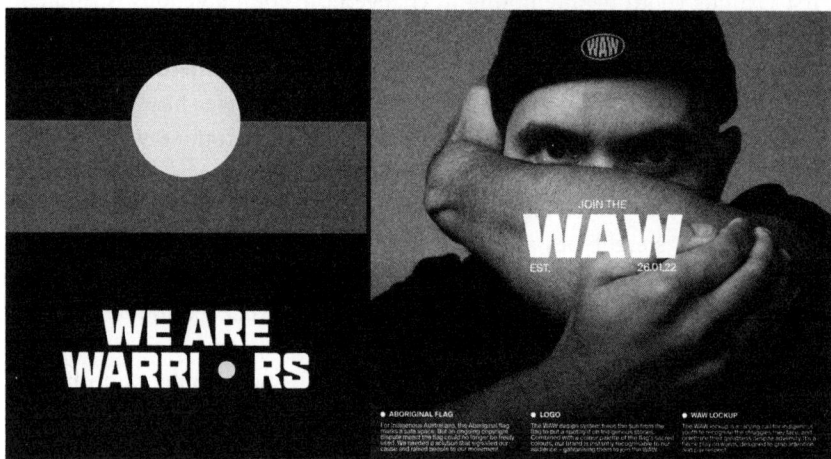

4.1 We Are Warriors

Non-Profit Client, "We Are Warriors," Sydney; Founder: Nooky AKA Corey Webster; Creative Agency: R/GA Australia; Global Chief Creative Officer: Tiffany Rolfe; VP, Executive Creative Director, Brand Design & Consulting: Ben Miles; VP, Chief Creative Officer APAC: Seamus Higgins; Design Director: Henry Cook; Photographer: Rob Hookey (seen here); Paven Gill, Sonder Films (next page)

communities they support. To do this with impact, creatives have to reach out and make authentic connections—and do it for the right reasons.

We Are Warriors started as an uncomfortable conversation—I initially reached out to Nooky in 2020 during the height of the Black Lives Matter movement. We met at The Gladstone Pub in Sydney for a raw and honest

4.1 (*continued*) Photographer: Paven Gill, Sonder Films

conversation that would become the genesis of an internationally acclaimed movement. Nooky told me if you're going to come talk to me, don't bullshit. Let's talk. I didn't come to Nooky with solutions for what was happening (or not happening) in Australia—I just listened.

Here are the strategies I'd give to creatives to prioritize different perspectives and to make long-term connections.

It starts with listening, learning, and committing.

Purposeful presence: Understand your "why"—your reason for being there, your potential value, and how you can help.

Start with humility: Avoid assuming you have all the answers. Listen before making grand promises. Play back what you've heard, welcome corrections, and embrace guidance. It's not always about being right.

Engage empathetically: Spend time with the community, listen with empathy, and foster two-way communication while building understanding.

And lastly, vulnerability and trust: Open up, show commitment through action, and aim to create a positive, safe space for open dialogue.

Why is it critical to decolonize branding and advertising?

Brands are increasingly using design to engage with different cultures and communities around the world; there's no room for cultural faux pas anymore. Decolonizing branding and advertising is crucial in today's consumer culture. However, brands need to make a lasting commitment to this process. And actions always speak louder than words.

Rather than giving you theoretical principles, let me give you an active example of how we decolonized a day and a colonial institution.

Australia is the only country in the Commonwealth to celebrate its national day on the day it was colonized. For many, Australia Day, held on January 26th, is known as Invasion Day—and celebrating it displays a shameful level of indifference toward First Nations lives.

We Are Warriors and R/GA approached the Powerhouse Museum, a major branch of the Museum of Applied Arts & Sciences (MAAS) in Sydney and owned by the Government of New South Wales, with an idea. For a government institution like this to take a stance and own a perspective on this controversial day was a huge achievement in itself.

To kickstart the WAW brand and change the narrative around Australia Day, we took over the Powerhouse Museum, subverting the symbolism of the day and diminishing its power over Indigenous people. The event name needed to match our provocative stance, yet still feel uplifting. Challenges came in the form of getting an institution of this stature to modify its name, and pushback from those who celebrate the day. But "Blak Powerhouse" brings together the community and the institution in a show of collective strength. The nod to the US civil rights movement also invokes a legacy of resistance, activism, and pride.

Adding "Blak" may be a simple change, but it is an enormously potent one. With its unique spelling, the name was a powerful expression of acceptance for Indigenous Australians. Seeing this immediately signaled that this was an event for them, by them, while the allusion to the political slogan of "black power" also signposted to a wider audience that attendance would constitute a powerful act of resistance against the status quo. We also leveraged the dual meaning of Powerhouse, referencing our Warriors as well as the museum itself.

The resounding success of Blak Powerhouse led to a commitment by the Powerhouse Museum to host it every year on January 26th, creating a safe and secure space for First Nations people to celebrate Blak pride.

When most creative teams are still predominantly composed of dominant groups, what should creative professionals and their clients grasp about the significance of diverse perspectives and representation to avoid dismissing alternative ways of knowing or worldviews?

You're right. For a long time, the most celebrated or emulated work coming out of the design community was created during the twentieth century by a monolithic group of white, mostly male, designers.

And it's not lost on me that I'm a white cis male from a privileged background. I do think it is important to acknowledge it. And then reinforce that, hopefully, by being in a position of privilege, you can be an ally—or better still, you can be an advocate. Ally to Advocate is inspired by Reni Eddo-Lodge's writing, explaining "Why I'm No Longer Talking to White People about Race." An ally stands there and acknowledges, and an advocate stands up and uses their voice to push back, to lift up, to move out of the way.

In an increasingly globalized world, where more businesses are beginning to acknowledge the role of brand and design in helping them resonate in different cultures, the need to make room for other narratives is so important. Creatives and their clients are responsible for embracing the significance of diverse perspectives and representation. The key lies in a holistic approach that begins with understanding how people interact with the product, service, or experience.

At R/GA, we've tried to be really intentional about designing for diversity. I've deliberately grown our creative and brand teams by hiring incredible people of different backgrounds: gender, age, race, ethnicity, religion, disability status, and sexual orientation—people with different backgrounds, personalities, life experiences, and beliefs.

This means there's no room or situation we can enter where we don't have that empathy or understanding of the person, perspective, or problem.

How can creatives and their clients be mindful of the potential impact of their work?

It starts with a recognition of the power of privilege. In my role as an industry leader, creativity is the potent force to influence the sector, and I aim to inspire other creatives to become business leaders themselves. The evolving landscape of the world underscores the increasing importance of creativity, taking on a nonlinear trajectory.

I deliberately look for opportunities with brands that hold the potential for significant social impact. Many organizations possess the means to create change, but not all share the same level of ambition. The true impact journey begins when the alignment of "means" and "ambition" occurs. This intersection becomes the catalyst for transformative and meaningful outcomes.

As an advocate or ally, you can't just be passive. This means sometimes having hard conversations with brand owners and C-suites. It sometimes means holding them accountable for their point of view and guiding them back into line.

How do you leverage advertising or branding to drive positive change?

The current landscape, particularly in Australia, is characterized by heightened polarization and fragility, moments of crisis, national debates, and misinformation. In response, businesses, brands, and organizations need to shoulder the responsibility of doing good. Gone are the days when the primary focus was solely on the bottom line and profit margins. Companies now have the opportunity to reassess their profit allocation, and those with a progressive, long-term approach are poised to outperform their short-term-focused competitors. This paradigm shift emphasizes the intrinsic link between profit and purpose, which Salesforce CEO Larry Fink famously coined.

The challenge lies in encouraging apathetic brands and advertisers to think deeper and recognize the advantages of societal impact. By adopting the triple bottom line framework—centered on people, planet, and prosperity—we can collectively drive measurable positive change. This sets in motion a virtuous cycle where everyone emerges victorious, creating a value exchange focused on societal impact that I hope lets us all sleep a little better. Failing to align actions with the notion that doing good is good for business raises the question of why we are persuading others. We have to wholeheartedly embrace the butterfly effect, committing to long-term, measurable impact and change. The key lies in discerning between a nice idea and actual impact. Brands and advertisers championing long-term change play a pivotal role in positively shifting the dial. Design, as a tool, becomes the bridge that connects gaps, fosters inclusivity, and shows the world that there can be a better way forward. And that has to be intentional.

It can't just be the young and progressive driving this change. It has to happen from the top down, regardless of what side of the political fence you sit on, where more seasoned leaders reevaluate their values and use their status (and deep pockets) to make change happen.

4.2 Museum of Chinese in Australia (MOCA). Client: MOCA; Creative Agency: R/GA Australia; Creative Director: Ben Miles, R/GA; Design Directors: Jane Duru / R/GA; Sam McGuinness / R/GA; Design Studio: PUSH Media Design Studio, Shanghai; Photographer: Daphne Nguyen, PUSH Media Design Studio

In recent years, there has been a disturbing rise in anti-Asian sentiment globally. This negative rhetoric, particularly surrounding the origins of the coronavirus, severely impacted Sydney's Chinatown. Once a vibrant community hub, the area became eerily quiet, with long-established businesses closing and tourism declining, putting Chinatown's cultural heritage at risk. In response to these changes, R/GA partnered with the Museum of Chinese in Australia (MOCA), a new museum in Sydney's Chinatown, tasked with accelerating their next chapter. The goal was straightforward: to celebrate the ingenuity, contributions, and resilience of Chinese Australians, past, present, and future.

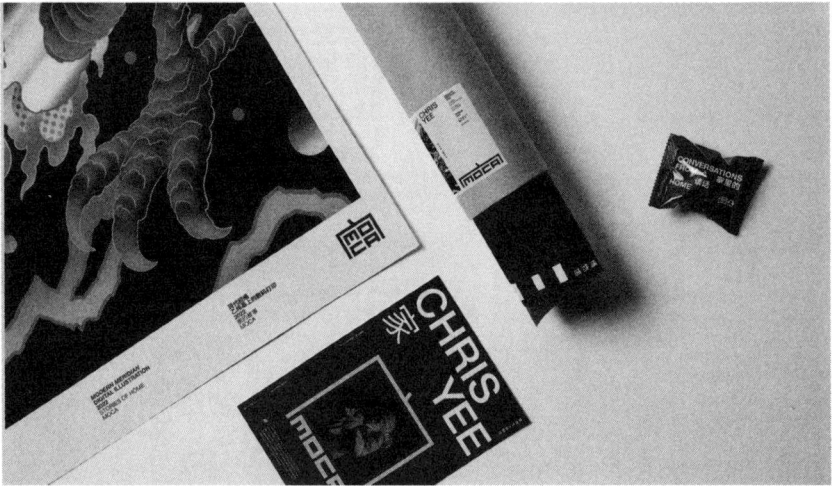

4.2 (*continued*)

4.3 G' AY Mate. Client: Cotton On Group Factorie; Creative Agency: Interbrand Australia; Executive Creative Director: Ben Miles; Designer: Henry Cook; Photographer: Tim Jones

G'day mate—the quintessential Australian greeting. When the debate on legalizing gay marriage took a negative turn, Cotton On Group incorporated this iconic phrase into the campaign to push back. G' AY MATE serves as a reminder of true Australian values: friendliness, a laid-back attitude, and giving everyone a fair chance.

4.3 (*continued*)

CHAPTER 5

DESIGNING BRAND IDENTITY

S tand out.

The designer's goal is just that: to create a brand identity that cuts through the noise by offering a unique and differentiated representation of the brand's construct and strategy across all touchpoints. Based on a design concept, a brand identity includes, but is not limited to, the logo, color palette, custom typography, imagery, website, motion, sound, haptics, and environments.

A designer must uncover a brand's "true self" by identifying what makes it unique, advises Lisa Smith, the global executive creative director at Jones Knowles Ritchie (JKR). She also adds: "Every touchpoint is an opportunity to authentically engage consumers."[1]

Visual Communication

Brand identity design centers on visual communication. It shapes how a brand construct and design concept are expressed through the thoughtful creation, selection, and arrangement of typography, imagery, and design elements, as well as related identity elements, including: sound (sonic) environments, haptics, copy (usually in the form of a descriptor, a phrase that aids in describing what the brand offers or defining the company's divisions or services), and tagline (a memorable phrase that captures the essence of the brand's promise or values).

A comprehensive identity design solution should forge a strong emotional connection, differentiate the brand, and be distinctive. Best practices leverage strategic creativity to build a brand that identifies, informs, engages, and conveys meaning with lasting impact. A prime example is Alexander Isley Inc.'s innovative identity, signage, packaging, and communication program for Philo Ridge Farm (figure 5.1), showcasing a fresh and thoughtful approach to holistic brand design (See the Focus: Alexander Isley for additional context on figure 5.1.).

Through the use of typography and imagery, identity designers:

- **Capture and convey the brand's essence**: Translate the core identity, personality, emotional associations, and values of a brand or entity into a distinctive visual language that resonates with audiences.
- **Ensure clarity and accessibility**: Make content and information easy to understand and navigate, ensuring it is accessible to diverse audiences, including those with varying needs and preferences.
- **Foster brand communities and advocates**: Design solutions grounded in strategy and audience insight to build connection and inspire trust, transforming customers into passionate supporters and self-appointed brand ambassadors.

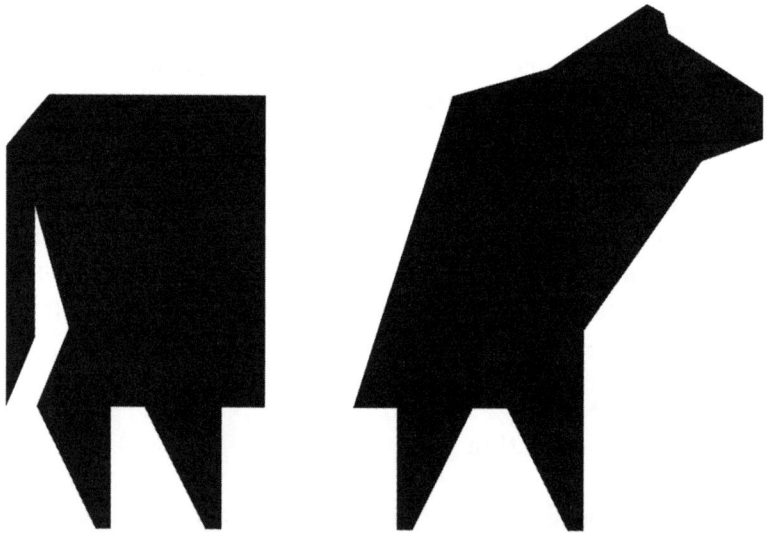

PHILO RIDGE FARM

5.1 Philo Ridge Farm, Charlotte, Vermont: *Comprehensive identity, signage, packaging, and communication program.* Studio: Alexander Isley Inc.; Creative Director: Alexander Isley; Designers: Matthew Kaskel, Shannon Stolting

5.1 (*continued*)

5.1 (*continued*)

5.1 (*continued*)

5.1 (*continued*)

5.1 (*continued*)

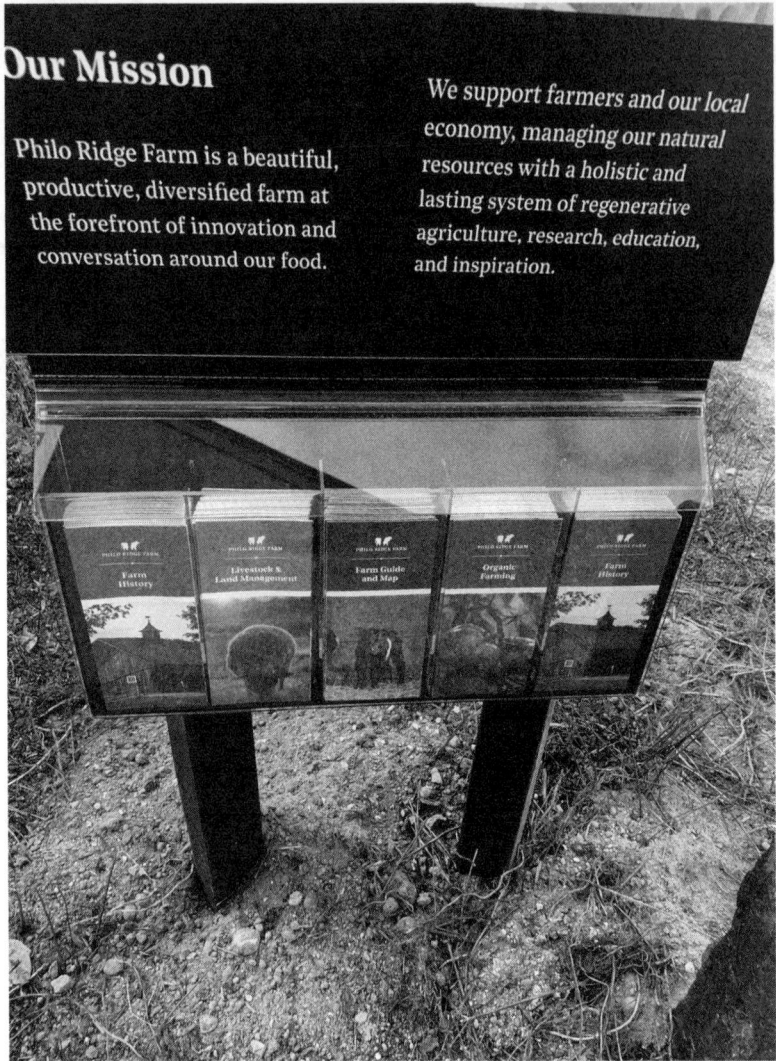

Our Mission

Philo Ridge Farm is a beautiful, productive, diversified farm at the forefront of innovation and conversation around our food.

We support farmers and our local economy, managing our natural resources with a holistic and lasting system of regenerative agriculture, research, education, and inspiration.

5.1 (*continued*)

- **Design intuitive digital experiences**: Develop user-friendly, functional, and engaging digital platforms, from websites and apps to virtual experiences, enhancing overall user interaction and satisfaction.
- **Craft multi-format experiences**: Design compelling tangible, digital, experiential, or hybrid engagements that cater to diverse formats and interactions, ensuring a seamless brand experience across all touchpoints.

The Logo System

Philo Ridge Farm
Identity Guidelines

Version 1.3
August 1, 2018

Page 2

The logo serves as the cornerstone of our visual identity. It informs and supports all aspects of communication and, through consistent use, establishes an identity that is truly reflective of the spirit, mission, offerings, and values of Philo Ridge Farm.

The logo is a combination of two elements; a stylized rendering of the iconic "Beltie" cow, coupled with a customized line of lettering.

We have developed three versions of the logo, two horizontal and one stacked. Any of these can be used; having a choice enables us to pick the one that fits best and has the most visual impact. (Refer to page 10 of this guide to see a range of sample applications.)

Whenever possible the "Primary" logo version should be used, to appear as black against white or light-colored backgrounds.

In the rare circumstances in which the black-on-light application won't work, the logo can be reversed out.

In certain situations the "Beltie" icon can be used as a standalone element. In those cases the viewer should be provided with enough information (the name is in adjacent text or they're standing inside the market, for example) to understand that this is a representation of Philo Ridge Farm. Avoid using a standalone reversed-out icon.

Always use supplied artwork for the logo and lettering lockups. Don't try to make them yourself: The configurations have been carefully prepared to be balanced and consistent.

[NOTE: Subcategory logo lockups to be added to this section once names are confirmed.]

Primary logo version

Secondary, reversed out logo version

PHILO RIDGE FARM

PHILO RIDGE FARM

Horizontal logo 1: "Big Beltie"

PHILO RIDGE FARM

PHILO RIDGE FARM

Horizontal logo 2: "Big Type"

PHILO
RIDGE
FARM

PHILO
RIDGE
FARM

Stacked logo

Standalone "Beltie" icon

5.1 (*continued*)

- **Develop socially impactful solutions**: Design solutions that address broader societal and environmental concerns, extending beyond promoting products or services to benefit the community and environment.
- **Shape cohesive social media campaigns**: Make sure visual elements and messaging in social media campaigns align with the brand's central narrative and identity, resonating effectively with the target audience and driving engagement.

Analyzing the Structure Behind Effective Branding

To communicate effectively, you must first capture your audience's attention. Unified compositions, striking imagery, and well-crafted typography engage people across various media channels. To maintain the audience's interest, creatives must present the content coherently and impactfully, ensuring the message is clear and meaningful.

Understanding the Principles of Design

The logo that caught your eye? It didn't happen by accident. A designer had to conceive the idea thoughtfully and craft the typography, imagery, and composition carefully to capture your attention and convey meaning. A brand's visual identity must differentiate it from competitors and express a unique look, feel, and essence to ensure distinctiveness.

A deeper understanding of design principles highlights their essential role in shaping impactful branding. Here's a short primer:

Composition refers to the spatial arrangement and structure of graphic components—such as type and images—in relation to each other and the format of the medium, whether it's a screen, printed page, or another substrate. To craft these visual compositions, designers and art directors use formal graphic elements, including line, shape, color, value, pattern, and texture. To achieve an effective and cohesive design, they apply key principles such as balance, emphasis, visual hierarchy, flow, rhythm, and unity.

Balance creates visual stability by evenly distributing visual weight across a composition. It ensures that no part of the design appears heavier than another, maintaining a sense of harmony and equilibrium.

Emphasis involves creating a focal point that draws attention to a specific element, component, or area within a composition, guiding the viewer's focus. For example, in a logo design, emphasis ensures that we first notice either the brand name or the symbol, as well-designed logos rarely give equal prominence to both. Designers achieve emphasis through several techniques, such as:

- Contrast: Differentiating elements using color, size, shape, or texture to make one stand out.
- Size and scale: Enlarging an element compared to its surroundings to draw attention.
- Color: Applying bold or distinct hues makes an element stand out.

- Placement: Strategically positioning an element in a central or prominent area.
- Typography: Highlighting words or taglines using purposefully selected typefaces, sizes, colors, or weights.

Strategic emphasis ensures the key message or focal point is easily discernible, helping the overall design communicate its intended message clearly and cohesively.

Visual hierarchy directs how the viewer's eyes scan by signaling a clear sequence of importance: "Start here, then move here," and so forth. Designers arrange images, typography, and design elements to guide the viewer's attention from the most important to the least significant parts of a composition. For instance, on an image-centric platform like Instagram, balancing the prominence of the image with other design elements is crucial.

Flow is the visual pathway that guides the viewer's gaze through a design. It means arranging elements such as type, images, and graphics to smoothly direct the viewer's attention from one area to another. Strategically designed flow ensures the viewer focuses on key elements, creating a coherent and engaging experience.

Rhythm in graphic design involves repeating or alternating design elements to create a sense of movement and harmony. You create rhythm through patterns, alternating or repeating colors, recurring shapes, and varying sizes. Rhythm establishes a visual tempo and structure, enhancing cohesiveness and evoking a specific response from the viewer.

Unity refers to the harmonious arrangement of elements within a composition, creating a sense of cohesion and completeness. It ensures that all parts of a design work together seamlessly, presenting as a unified whole rather than disparate, unrelated elements. Unity is essential to creating designs that are memorable and emotionally resonant with the audience. Key practices for achieving unity include:

- Consistency: Using a uniform visual language across the design, including color palettes, typefaces, and imagery styles.
- Repetition: Repeating elements such as shapes, colors, or textures to foster a sense of continuity and cohesion.
- Alignment: Positioning elements to establish a coherent and organized structure, for example, consistently aligning typography.
- Proximity: Grouping related elements to clarify their relationships and enhance the overall organization of the composition.
- Similarity: Using consistent shapes, colors, textures, patterns, sizes, or positioning so that the viewer perceives similar elements as related.

While unity aims for coherence, incorporating some variety can enhance a design. For example, in multi-page formats such as corporate websites or annual reports, introducing variation in layout, color, or imagery helps sustain viewer interest and engagement across multiple pages, screens, or sections. In a corporate annual report, for instance, designers typically establish a unified layout system through consistent grids, typography, and a cohesive color palette. To sustain visual interest across pages, however, they may introduce variety by incorporating accent colors or occasionally breaking the grid.

> I often compare branding to voice.
>
> The way someone speaks is distinctly individual. Song lyrics can conjure feelings of joy or solitude. Speeches can empower and embolden. Cheers and shouts can be a rallying cry. I think graphic design—and the visual bits of branding—can do the same things. A brand's colors can instill delight, its posters might sing, and its typography can summon a call to action.
>
> These graphic fundamentals (type, color, image, and movement, to name a few) paired with language and media merge and contribute to what a brand says and the tone with which it speaks.
>
> —Kelcey Gray, graphic designer, author of *Let's Make Letters!* and assistant professor of practice in design at The University of Texas at Austin

Building a Brand Identity: Key Considerations

To create a cohesive and impactful brand identity, a designer must consider interconnected factors, from purpose and audience insights to typography and tone of voice. The design shapes how the target audience experiences the brand. Key factors to consider include:

- **Purpose**: The core reason for the brand's existence beyond profitability, encompassing its mission and vision.
- **Values**: The fundamental principles and beliefs the brand upholds should align with internal stakeholders and the target audience.
- **Target audience**: A deep understanding of the audience is crucial. Demographics provide statistical data about groups based on factors such as age, gender identity, gender expression, income, education level, occupation, marital status, and geographic location. Psychographics delve into lifestyle habits, values, attitudes, and other traits that shape behaviors and preferences.

   Maya Dukes of Delta Air Lines, at Cannes Lions 2024, highlighted that traditional demographic segmentation often fails to capture the complexity of today's audiences. She urged brands to move beyond simplistic categorizations and embrace the multifaceted identities of their consumers. Dukes emphasized that while brands may still use demographic "boxes," they must be more nuanced to remain relevant. Consumers can detect when brands lack genuine understanding, which can lead to disengagement.[2]

- **Needs and values**: Crafting a brand identity involves expressing the brand's essence while addressing the target audience's needs, desires, aspirations, and core beliefs. The design should reflect what the audience seeks and values. See figure 5.2 for a compelling example.
- **Differentiation**: The visual identity should immediately and unmistakably convey how the brand stands out from competitors, creating a distinct emotional response, establishing a unique position in the market (see chapter 2 for a deeper exploration of differentiation).
- **Market position**: This involves understanding the brand's relative position in the market, including how it compares to competitors and how its perceived value, benefits, and unique attributes contribute to its standing.
- **Visual identity elements**:

  o *Name*: The primary verbal identifier of a brand, a name should be memorable, legally available, distinctive, easy to pronounce, and sonically engaging.
  o *Logo*: A unique, distinctive, and memorable mark that encapsulates the brand's essence and remains recognizable across various media channels. (Refer to the glossary in this chapter for types of logos.)
  o *Color palette*: A carefully chosen and distinctive set of colors that identify the brand, align with the brand's personality, and evoke the desired emotional response. (See the glossary for the full definition.)
  o *Typography*: Selected or bespoke typefaces that reflect the brand's concept and essence, ensuring readability across different media.
  o *Imagery*: The style and category of imagery—whether illustration, photography, mixed media, or motion graphics—should reinforce the brand's message and narrative, and resonate with the target audience.
  o *Tagline*: A short, memorable phrase that captures the essence of a brand's promise, personality, or positioning, crafted to reinforce brand recognition, evoke emotion, and communicate a core message in a succinct and impactful way.

- **Consistency across touchpoints**: Ensure uniformity in visual, written, spoken, motion, and sonic elements across online and offline media. Consistent application prevents confusion about the brand's portrayal and strengthens recognition.
- **Guidelines and standards**: Develop and adhere to a comprehensive brand guidelines manual to maintain consistency in the application and communication of the brand identity.

- **Brand voice**: Apply a consistent tone and style across all media channels and campaigns, aligning with the brand's personality, central narrative, values, and audience to maintain coherence.
- **Key messages**: Craft clear and compelling messages, such as a tagline, to effectively communicate the brand's core values and positioning.
- **Experiential design**: Create interactive, multisensory, and hybrid experiences that engage users and elicit an emotional response.
- **Brand experiences**: Ensure positive and engaging interactions with the brand across various media and environments, from virtual platforms to package design to social media and live events.
- **Emotional associations**: Establish no more than two strategic emotional connections that resonate with the audience across messages and touchpoints.
- **Flexibility and adaptability**: Design a brand identity that can be deployed on various media platforms and physical applications, allowing for evolution with market trends and business growth while retaining core elements.
- **Gather and refresh**: Continuously collect feedback and refine the brand to stay relevant, differentiated, and impactful.
- **Data**: Utilize quantitative and qualitative insights to refine visual and verbal brand elements. Data and visualization systems should be integral, not just supplementary. For further insights on data visualization, see the interview with Giorgia Lupi, partner at Pentagram, in chapter 6.
- **Competitive analysis**: Study competitors to identify gaps and opportunities and understand their positioning to better differentiate your brand. To judge a brand identity based on differentiation, familiarity, favorability, and relevance, use a Q Score (or Q rating): a metric used to gauge the popularity and likability of a brand. Compare the Q Score of your brand to that of competitors to understand relative performance.
- **Brand perception**: Collect qualitative data on how the audience receives and perceives various brand identity elements.
- **User experience (UX)**: Assess the overall experience users have when interacting with the brand's products or systems, focusing on user needs, behaviors, and pain points to create a seamless, enjoyable experience. Refer to insights from product designer Stuart Haury in chapter 6 for more on UX.
- **Usability testing**: Evaluate user interactions with branding elements across platforms, including websites and apps, to ensure a smooth and engaging experience.
- **Localization and personalization**: Leverage data to understand cultural preferences and regional differences, ensuring that the brand identity resonates effectively and responsibly in various markets and with different individuals.

FOCUS: ALEXANDER ISLEY

Alexander Isley is a Connecticut-based identity, communication, and environmental designer. He has taught at the School of Visual Arts, The Cooper Union, Rhode Island School of Design, and Yale, where he has been a lecturer and critic at their School of Art. He is past president of AIGA NY.

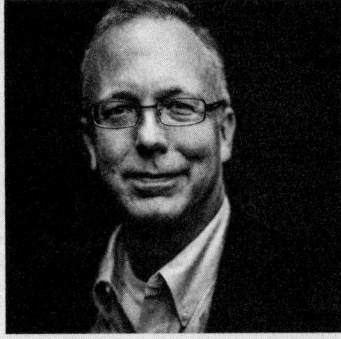

In 1995, Alex was selected as an inaugural member of the *I.D.* 40, a survey by *The International Design Magazine* (*I.D.*) of the country's most influential designers. In a recent *Graphic Design USA* magazine poll, Alex was named by his peers as one of the most influential designers of the past fifty years.

His work is in the collections of the Museum of Modern Art, the Smithsonian Institution, the Library of Congress, and the Museum für Gestaltung in Zurich.

In 1998, Alex was selected for membership in Alliance Graphique Internationale (AGI). He is an AIGA Fellow, and in 2014 was presented the AIGA medal, the industry's highest honor, in recognition of his body of work and contributions to the field.

Philo Ridge Farm is a diversified working farm, educational center, and restaurant that integrates livestock, orchards, gardens, and community events. Situated on 400 acres of pasture and woodlands in Charlotte, Vermont, the farm develops and implements practices founded in regenerative agriculture to aid in soil recovery and the strengthening of the ecosystem.

The farm sought our help in developing a brand platform, communication plan, and identity and communication materials to help spread the word of their mission to their community, partners, and visitors [see figure 5.1]. In developing the logo [see the logo system in figure 5.1], our goal was to create an arresting mark that suggests that Philo Ridge Farm has a unique and contemporary mission. The farm's distinctive Belted Galloway cattle are the inspiration for the logo. (As an added bonus, the cow incorporates a stylized map of Vermont.)

As part of our work, we developed a retail signage system for the café and market, including custom updatable menu boards, shelf displays, and informational signs. Templates were provided so that updates can easily be made in-house. The packaging is simple, honest, clean, and clear. The Philo Ridge Farm visual program includes signage for the buildings and grounds as well as the development of maps, printed literature, apparel, and educational materials.

—Alexander Isley

WREN

Women's Rights & Empowerment Network

5.2 Women's Rights and Empowerment Network (WREN), Columbia, South Carolina: *Comprehensive naming, branding, and communication program.* Studio: Alexander Isley Inc.; Creative Director: Alexander Isley; Designer: Angela Chen; Strategist and Writer: Georgann Eubanks

WREN is a South Carolina-based organization created to advance the health, economic well-being, and rights of South Carolina's women, girls, and their families. The organization works with its partners and supporters to advocate for laws and policies to enhance the status of women, contribute to the well-being of families, educate policymakers and the public, and empower South Carolinians to speak up and out for a better state.

We worked with the organization's leadership to create a comprehensive identity and communication program, giving them the tools to help refine and spread word of their mission. We started off by leading a naming initiative. Working in collaboration with our colleague, writer and strategist Georgann Eubanks, we explored a variety of approaches leading up to our recommendation of WREN, the Women's Rights and Empowerment Network. The acronym is short, memorable, and makes reference to the South Carolina state bird, known for its hardiness and persistent voice. Once the name was in place, we turned our attention to developing the visual program.

The idea of a multicolored nest as a logo appealed to us: A nest represents safety and security, nurturing, and the idea of a home. It's a place where the young are protected.

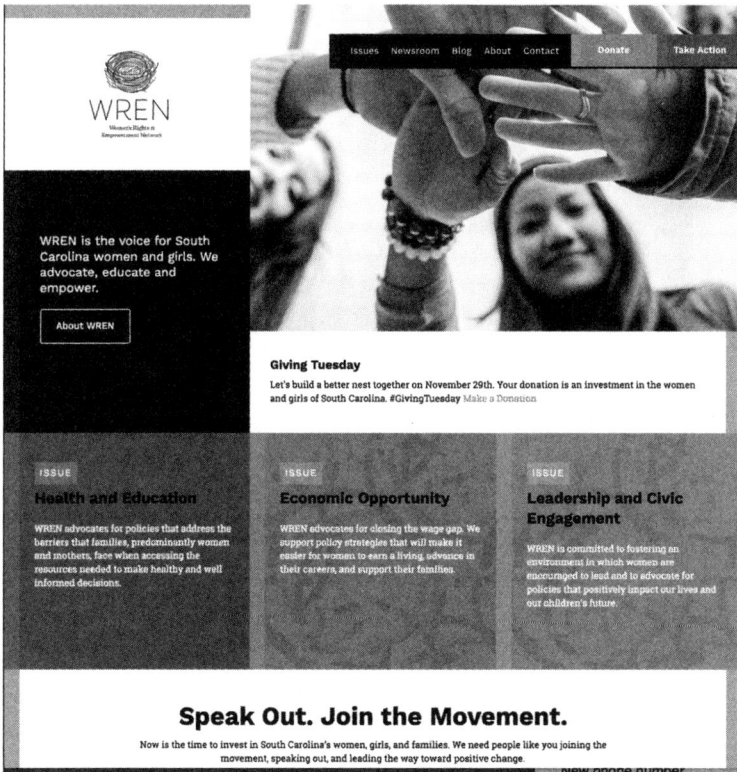

5.2 (*continued*) A nest is tightly woven, its strength coming from the intertwining of individual members. The "nest" icon is memorable, flexible, and can work in a wide variety of situations. And we like the idea of a fancy scribble serving as a memorable identifier.

5.2 (*continued*)

5.2 (*continued*)

Logo Components

The nest and lettering elements should be maintained as a consistent set of elements wherever possible. In some instances it is acceptable to use only the logo (the nest illustration and WREN lettering) so long as the descriptor line appears clearly in proximity to the logo (see samples on page 12 for reference).

Primary Centered Lockup

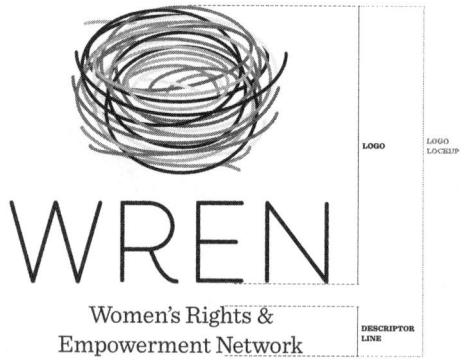

LOGO

LOGO LOCKUP

WREN

Women's Rights & Empowerment Network

DESCRIPTOR LINE

3

5.2 *(continued)*

Brand Identity Design Glossary

Brand architecture is the strategic framework that organizes a company's portfolio of brands, sub-brands, and products. It outlines the relationships and hierarchies among these elements, detailing how they interact and support each other. This structure helps companies manage their brands effectively, ensuring clarity, consistency, and coherent communication with their target audiences.

Branding is the process of developing and managing a distinct identity for a product, service, individual, company, or organization. It differentiates the entity from competitors and shapes specific perceptions and associations in the minds of consumers. Branding is the strategically creative use of visual, language-based, sonic, haptic, olfactory, and experiential elements to build recognition, establish credibility, and forge emotional connections with the target audience.

Brand identity encompasses a range of visual, language-based, and sonic elements that collectively represent and differentiate a brand in the marketplace to make it distinctive, also known as visual identity. Key components include:

- *Logo*: The visual symbol representing the brand, often the most recognizable aspect of its identity. Logos can take various forms:
  - *Wordmark*: The brand name designed in distinctive typography, also known as a logotype.
  - *Lettermark*: A logo using the brand's initials or a single letter.
  - *Pictorial mark*: An image representing a recognizable object or symbol.
  - *Abstract mark*: A visual that uses stylized or simplified forms, which may hint at recognizable objects, to evoke a particular feeling or idea.
  - *Non-pictorial mark*: A nonrepresentational design that does not depict real-world objects, composed of lines, shapes, colors, volumes, tones, textures, or patterns. (Often confused with abstract marks, which retain some reference to the natural world.)
  - *Emblem*: A design that combines text and imagery into a unified form, typically incorporating a symbol or graphic element with the brand name or initials.
  - *Dynamic mark*: A flexible and adaptable brand mark that can change or evolve across different contexts or media while maintaining core brand elements. Unlike static logos, dynamic marks offer variation in appearance based on usage and context.

Brand identity standards manual: This comprehensive guide outlines the guidelines and rules for consistently applying a brand's visual and verbal elements. It ensures the brand is represented accurately and uniformly across all channels and touchpoints. The manual serves as a reference for anyone working with the brand, from marketing teams to external partners, to maintain consistency and reinforce the brand's identity through standardized practices.

Brand name: This is the distinct word or combination of words used to identify and differentiate a product, service, company, or organization from others. It is a key element of the brand's identity, designed to be memorable, meaningful, and relevant to the brand's values, offerings, and sometimes its origins. A well-crafted brand name can evoke specific emotions, associations, and perceptions, helping to shape the brand's image and reputation among its audience.

Brand strategy: A comprehensive plan detailing how a brand will achieve its long-term goals and objectives through coordinated and deliberate actions. This strategy focuses on effectively connecting with the target audience and distinguishing the brand from its competitors.

Color palette: A set of colors consistently used across all brand materials. These colors cue the audience to recognize the brand and help create a strong association with the brand by evoking specific emotions and reinforcing brand identity.

Imagery: The style of visual elements—such as photography, illustrations, icons, and graphics—used consistently throughout the branding program to create a unified visual identity.

Package design: The design and appearance of a product's packaging, including materials, colors, structure, and surface-design elements. Effective package design reflects and reinforces the brand's identity while also appealing to consumers.

Rebranding: The process of changing or updating a brand identity or branding program, which may include creating a new name, symbol, visual identity, or combination thereof. The goal is to establish a differentiated identity in the minds of consumers, investors, competitors, and other stakeholders. Rebranding can range from a complete overhaul to a subtle update that retains brand equity and can apply to a company, product, or service.

Refresh: A more limited update or modification to the existing brand identity. It typically involves refining or modernizing elements such as the logo, color palette, typography, or messaging while retaining the core brand essence and elements. A refresh aims to keep the brand relevant and contemporary without altering its essential identity.

Signage: A system of visual displays employed to identify, communicate information, or provide directions within a physical space. This includes various formats such as printed, digital, carved, etched, painted, or illuminated signs, including labels, banners, plaques, and screens.

Sonic logo: A distinctive short sound or melody representing a brand, functioning similarly to a visual logo but in audio form, also known as a sonic tagline.

Tagline: A memorable phrase that encapsulates the essence of the brand's promise, positioning, and values. Also known as an endline, strapline, catch-phrase, or slogan, taglines are designed to be impactful and may change more frequently than the visual identity.

Tone of voice: The style and attitude of the brand's written and spoken communications. It defines how the brand engages with its audience and can vary from formal and authoritative to casual and friendly.

Typography: The typeface(s), commonly referred to as *fonts*, that are used consistently in branding materials. Typography should reflect the brand's personality and tone, contributing to its distinct identity.

Wayfinding: The process of directing people through physical spaces to help them reach specific destinations, which involves designing and implementing navigational elements such as maps, signage systems, directional signs, and landmarks to aid in orientation and navigation.

FOCUS: BOMBAS

"Bombas is a comfort-focused sock and apparel brand with a mission to help those facing housing insecurity. One purchased = one donated, always and forever. As Bombas grew beyond socks, they needed a more sophisticated brand system that could keep pace with their growing product extensions. We created a new color system, new typography, and a new graphic system to generate custom shapes, motion principles, art direction, and product systems.

We centered the brand direction around the concept of "Little Big Things." Little Big Things is the intersection of Bombas's product and mission. While socks, underwear, and tees are small, they can make a big impact on the world. Bombas has donated over 150 million items of clothing to those experiencing homelessness. Diving deeper into the name Bombas (Latin for bee), we were inspired by the way bees work together in a hive to make a big impact. The entire graphic system for the identity is built on the hexagonal shapes of the individual wax cells of a hive. Every hexagon has a distinct identity represented by the different glyphs in the brand. When all of these little pieces come together they create a larger system. The hexagon grid allows for system expansion to account for new product lines and future creative needs."
—& Walsh

(*continued on next page*)

(*continued from previous page*)

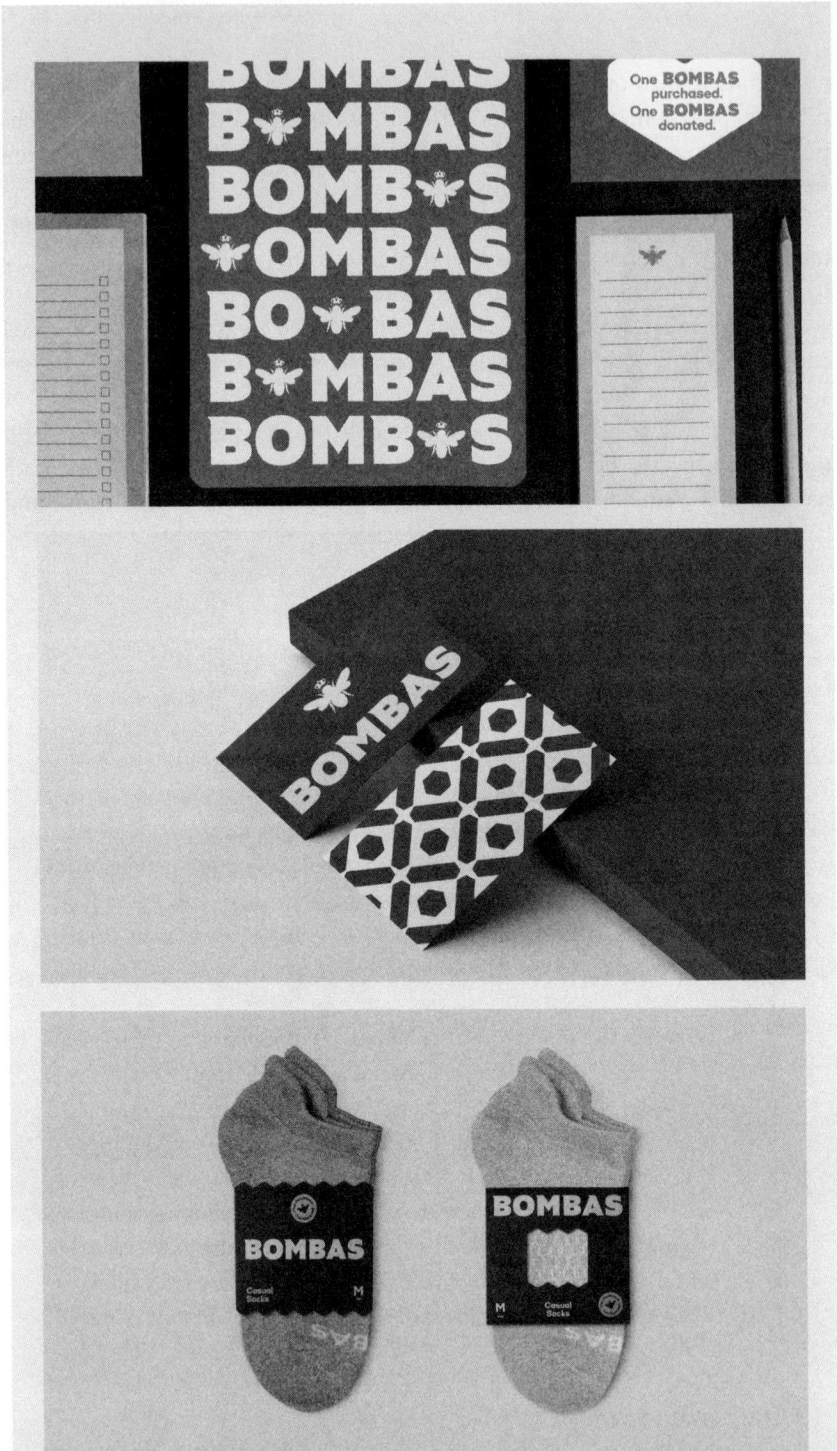

5.3 Bombas. Agency: &Walsh; Client: Bombas, Aaron Wolk, Randy Goldberg, Jessica Krantz; Creative Direction: Jessica Walsh; Strategy: Lauren Walsh; Production: Allison Raich, Evan Delp, Victoria Najmy, Kasia Sasinowska; Copywriting: Bombas,

5.3 (*continued*) Jessica Walsh, Lauren Walsh, Stephanie Halovanic; Lead Design: Carlos Bocai, Gabriela Namie, Sasyk Mihal; Design: Jeremy Rieger, Simoul Alva, Katyayani Singh, Julian Williams, Sergi Delgado, Alex Slobzheninov, Riisa Liao, Jess Gracia, Hayley Lim, Juanse Carvajal, Fabrizio Morra, Elinor O'Brien, Sofia Noronha, John Sampson, Lucas Luz; Animation: Soomin Jung, Lucas Luz, Heewon Kim, Jada Akoto, Daniel Zepeda. Courtesy of Bombas.

Interview: Joseph Han, Executive Creative Director, Collins NY

Joseph Han is an executive creative director at COLLINS NY. He has led a wide range of projects with organizations including Apple, Google, Facebook, Samsung, Equinox, Peloton, Harvard Graduate School of Design, the Institute of Design at the Illinois Institute of Technology (ID), the

AIA Center for Architecture, Yale University, the *New York Times*, Storefront for Art & Architecture, New York Botanical Garden, Verizon, Van Leeuwen Ice Cream, and Buffy. He was previously an associate partner at Pentagram and a design director at Base Design. His work has been featured by international organizations including the *New York Times*, WIRED, *Fast Company*, *Quartz*, It's Nice That, Type Directors Club, Gwangju Design Biennale, Counter Print, and GDUSA. Joseph was named to the 2023 GDUSA's People to Watch List. Joseph has given talks at the *New York Times*, Rhode Island School of Design (RISD), ID, MassArt, and Carnegie Mellon University. He graduated with honors from RISD and teaches at the School of Visual Arts (SVA).

How does branding impact culture?

The relationship between brands and culture is a dynamic and ever-evolving force, with each continuously shaping and influencing the other.

Brands are profoundly impacted by cultural shifts, particularly during moments of significant societal change. For instance, in the aftermath of George Floyd's death and the rise of the Black Lives Matter movement in 2020, there was a growing expectation that brands would take a stand on pressing social issues. Nike's decision to feature Colin Kaepernick, a figure who ignited a national debate on racial injustice, at the center of its campaign exemplifies how brands can not only reflect cultural moments but also actively shape and lead conversations around justice and equality. As a result, the ad not only achieved record-breaking engagement on social media, attracting an unprecedented number of followers and likes, but it also propelled Nike's stock to new all-time highs.

On the other hand, brands that fail to engage with or lead in cultural conversations risk alienation or even outright rejection. This was starkly demonstrated in 2020, when several food brands, including Quaker's Aunt Jemima syrup, faced backlash for perpetuating imagery deemed offensive and racist. The Aunt Jemima character invited a troubling narrative, encouraging a fantasy where enslaved individuals—and by extension, all of Black America—are depicted as submissive, self-effacing, and pacifying. This portrayal boxed in Black people as prepackaged and ready to satisfy, intertwining consumerism with racial overtones.

Joseph Han. Photography: COLLINS

In response to public outcry, Quaker retired the Aunt Jemima mascot after 130 years, rebranding the product as Pearl Milling Company. This example highlights the profound consequences for brands that are out of sync with cultural shifts, emphasizing their critical role in both reflecting and shaping societal values.

Conversely, culture is also deeply impacted by brands. A prime example is Apple's influence on modern communication and lifestyle. The introduction of the iPhone in 2007 did more than just release a new phone; it revolutionized how people interact with technology and each other. The iPhone popularized the concept of the smartphone, combining a phone, camera, internet browser, and media player into one device. This innovation fundamentally reshaped how we communicate, work, and consume media. And the way we communicated reshaped us in return.

As the iPhone and its ecosystem of apps became ubiquitous, they influenced numerous aspects of culture. The iPhone's integration with social media apps like Facebook, Instagram, and later Snapchat and TikTok transformed communication and content sharing, shaping social interaction and even language through the rise of emojis, GIFs, and memes. Additionally, the iPhone democratized photography, making high-quality cameras accessible to everyone, which significantly impacted visual culture and how we document our lives. Moreover, the iPhone has altered work culture, facilitating remote work and constant connectivity, and contributing to the rise of the gig economy.

Apple's design philosophy, which emphasizes simplicity, elegance, and user experience, has set new standards not just for technology but for broader consumer expectations across industries. The cultural impact of the iPhone is a clear example of how a brand can transform the way people live, work, and connect.

The interplay between brands and culture is both powerful and reciprocal. Brands have the ability to reflect and shape cultural values, while cultural shifts, in turn, influence how brands operate and evolve. This dynamic relationship underscores the importance of brands staying attuned to societal changes, as their impact on culture is profound and far-reaching.

What's the importance of differentiation in branding?

The essence of a brand is rooted in its ability to differentiate. Without differentiation, what remains is not a brand, but merely a commodity, indistinguishable and easily replaced by countless others.

Consider your most recent purchase. Take, for instance, a cup of coffee. Opting for a coffee simply because it's the most convenient—the nearest option to your doorstep—yields a vastly different experience from choosing one for its intricate flavor profile, the superior quality of its beans, and the skill of the barista who expertly crafts it. The former is a commodity; the latter is a brand that lingers in your memory, forging an emotional connection and securing a unique place in your mind.

Now, think of the first five brands that come to mind. It's highly likely that these brands have successfully differentiated themselves through cultural relevance, distinct personalities, shared values, unique experiences, consistent quality, and a profound sense of trust.

In branding, differentiation is not just important; it is paramount. It is the defining characteristic that elevates a true brand above the noise of mere commodities.

One of Brian Collins's design principles is, "Design is hope made visible," which emphasizes the role of hope as an "imagined, better reality." Could you describe how this concept of hope influences your design process?

Brian's mantra, "Design is hope made visible," guides every step of our design process.

Hope and design are deeply intertwined, each grounded in the anticipation of multiple futures—a concept Brian emphasizes to highlight the vast possibilities that lie ahead. They both seek to envision what could be and work toward actualizing that potential.

This forward-looking ambition compels us to constantly question the brief before providing solutions: What is the underlying intent behind the stated objective? How do we craft a narrative that resonates more sharply and on a larger scale? Who are the most meaningful customers our clients aim to reach? How do we position our clients not as the leader or the best—but as the *only*?

By beginning our design process with these probing questions, we gradually uncover the roots of hope. Our work then is to make that hope tangible and visible.

Given that many people understand the world through stories, how do you ensure your brand narratives are distinct, relevant, and inclusive?

The new brand COLLINS created with the Institute of Design (ID) is one example of how a powerful story—and how you frame that story—can help push for a new and surprising territory (figure 5.4)—in this case, for a historic institution originally founded as The New Bauhaus in 1937 in Chicago.

As we were invited to help evolve the school for the future—and build a new identity around their vision of the transformative power of design, it quickly became clear that ID does not view design as a tool for revolution or disruption. This is not about tearing down the old to make way for the new. Rather, design is used to identify possibilities, focus on the most promising, and refine the best. At ID, design is a dynamic process building toward positive impact.

The transformational idea of "The Evolutionary" led us to imagine a new voice and visual language that could itself evolve. Inspired by the founder László Moholy-Nagy's artistic experiments with geometry and ID's legendary director Jay Doblin's genius with complex systems, we crafted six foundational structures able to transform from abstract shapes into words and images. They, like design itself, move seamlessly from chaos to clarity.

The typography and the identity system, at first glance, might seem to break the convention of what a good typeface should do: be "easy to read." But we wanted the role of this typeface to be not merely a conveyor of a written message, but an embodiment of what the school has been doing for the past eighty-five years and is continuing to do: evolving what it means to be a designer in the world by bringing clarity out of chaos. Constructed strictly from only six modules, the entire typographic program perpetually shifts within the grid to signal that the school is always in the process of solving what's next.

As we collaborated with our clients at ID, we not only connected the story back to the pioneering history of the school but also emphasized the impact of the always-imperfect, unfolding state of its visual language. Milton Glaser explained the beauty behind the "I ♥ NY" identity: "The creation of a puzzle is one of the tools you have in communication to make people understand things. When they activate the mind to try to figure something out, the likelihood is that they will remember and respond to it more than if they are told something differently."

The shifting, dynamic nature of the ID identity fights against what is, inevitably, the eventual loss of power from endlessly repeated visual stimuli. We try to build operating systems that elevate brands far above the banal. So, our work with ID is an attempt to keep an identity system from slipping back into invisibility. You have to pay attention to it to understand it.

The dynamism of this system is ID's story, providing a voice and a canvas to show students, businesses, and *everyone* the extraordinary power of design to create possibilities that are both positive and impactful.

Number 11 of Brian Collins's 101 Design Rules is: "Are you going to tell a story? Then tell a big story. An enormous story. An epic story. Or tell no story at all."

5.4 Institute of Design. COLLINS: Joseph Han, Sanuk Kim, Jing Qi Fan, Eric Park, Tom Elia, Janet Ginsburg, Alex Blumfelder, Alex Athanasiou; Typeface Design: Joseph Han, Sanuk Kim, Jing Qi Fan, Ryan Bugden; Nucleus: Chelsea Carlson, Gena Cuba, Elizabeth Talerman; Microsite Development: Raphaël Améaume; Website: Self Aware; Photography: Mari Juliano, Celso Assunção; Institute of Design: Anijo Mathew, Kristin Gecan, Denis Weil, Ruth Schmidt, Judd Morgenstern, Matt Mayfield, Brandon Kinports, Arnold Fishman

5.4 (*continued*)

5.4 (*continued*)

CHAPTER 6

DESIGNING BRAND EXPERIENCES

C an an alphabet preserve a culture?

For languages without a digital script, the risk of extinction looms large.[1] Losing a language signifies the loss of knowledge passed down through generations—knowledge that encompasses ways of understanding the land, sea, sky, and their inhabitants. Rituals, recipes, myths, and memories vanish. For those speakers of the language, this means losing a part of their identity.[2] Moreover, governments lose valuable wisdom regarding the stewardship of marine and land resources in fragile ecosystems.[3]

Pulaar, the language of the Fulani people in West Africa, is spoken by over forty million people and is not in immediate danger of disappearing. Historically, however, Pulaar lacked an alphabet. As the Fulani increasingly engage in business, access information, and communicate through text on mobile devices, the need for a written form of Pulaar has become essential. Without an alphabet that accurately represents their spoken language, there is a risk that they may adopt other writing systems and, eventually, other languages.

Thirty years ago, Abdoulaye and Ibrahima Barry, two Fulani brothers, sought to reverse this trend. They created an alphabet that would one day spread across the global Fulani community and beyond. This alphabet became ADLaM, an acronym for the alphabet's first four letters, which stands for *Alkule Dandayɗe Leñol Mulugol*, or "the alphabet that protects the people from vanishing."

"Government communication is provided in a language that more than three quarters of the population does not understand. There is a purpose to that. Maybe you don't want people to understand the laws because you want to rule them in a certain way," said Abdoulaye Barry, cocreator of the ADLaM alphabet.[4]

In 2022, the Barry brothers and a team of typeface designers collaborated with Microsoft and creative agency McCann Worldwide to create ADLaM Display, a revised font. "While helping the Barry brothers to tell their story, we realized that access to the alphabet was as important as the alphabet itself. We learned that ADLaM adopters were connecting through online groups but didn't have access to a digital form they could all use. We thought, let's help the brothers take the alphabet where it needs to be. And that ended up meaning one billion devices," Christiano Abrahao, group creative director at McCann NY, told me.[5]

Released in 2023 as a free download on multiple platforms worldwide, this initiative promotes Pulaar literacy across West Africa, Europe, the Middle East, and the US. Microsoft's global integration of the Pulaar language into Microsoft 365 increased access to their products for this marginalized community and helped preserve a language that was nearly lost.

Culture is everything. It's what propels society forward and helps communities thrive. Advertising, branding, and design feed off of it. But it's symbiotic. At least it should be. The channels through which this symbiosis travels are greatly controlled by technology. Some technology can be a catalyst; sometimes it can hinder.

ADLaM was definitely in the former category.

We used technology and design to help unlock the potential of what the Barry Brothers (creators of ADLaM) had made their lifelong mission—to bring literacy to millions and stop their culture and language from disappearing. Their intention was to deeply connect their cultural heritage and how ADLaM showed up in the world by intrinsically linking the shapes and iconography of the Fulani people. Something that made this project so rich and impactful.

I believe the most impactful projects are conceived with a truthful impetus and a clearly thought-out purpose. The more we contribute to culture and respect it, the more we get out of it."

—Luke Flynn, creative consultant[6]

Designing Impactful Brand Experiences

Two projects—ADLaM, the design of an ancient language's alphabet; and the development of an Augmented Reality (AR) experience based on the film *Hidden Figures*—aim to preserve and promote underrepresented cultures and historical contributions.

The first, ADLaM, focuses on creating a written form for an ancient language, addressing the need to document and preserve linguistic heritage. The second, "Outthink Hidden" (figure 6.1), extends the *Hidden Figures* film by using AR technology to educate the public about the significant yet often-overlooked

6.1 "Outthink Hidden" AR. Creative director/Founder @ Fake Love: Layne Braunstein; Experience by: Fake Love Inc.; Partners: *New York Times*, NASA, and IBM; Place: Metaverse & Universe

"Outthink Hidden" explores the stories of the heroes from *Hidden Figures*, highlighting them alongside ten other innovators in the fields of science, technology, engineering, and mathematics (STEM).

contributions of African American women and underrecognized individuals in STEM fields at NASA during the 1960s. While the app features Katherine Johnson, Mary Jackson, and Dorothy Vaughan, all central figures from the film, it also expands the educational scope.

AR allows individuals to experience a physical environment through a different medium, such as a mobile device screen. It uses sensors to overlay a digital layer onto real-world space, enhancing it with visual elements such as 3D images, descriptive text, videos, and audio. This engaging AR app employs a location-based approach similar to Pokémon Go's PokéStops. Users visit more than 150 designated sites across the country, where they activate sensors to trigger AR renderings. Each location provides audio and visual narratives, accompanied by 3D models of influential figures in science, technology, engineering, and mathematics. (At the end of this chapter, you can read the interview with Layne Braunstein, who designed the experiential "Outthink Hidden.")

While commerce may center on transactions, how can brands infuse purpose and social good into the process? Creating an impactful brand experience begins with a keen understanding of what matters to the target audience. When grounded in audience insights and a genuine commitment to social purpose, dignity, and fairness, brands can make a positive impact. Given the significant profits corporations generate from their customers, it's only fair that they acknowledge their responsibility to give back and support the communities that contribute to their success.

Consider the following when conceiving brand experiences:

- **Bold initiatives**: Create work that inspires social sharing and sparks conversations, driving word of mouth.
- **Impactful design**: Deliver memorable, fresh, and engaging experiences.
- **Emotional resonance**: Offer experiences that deeply connect with the target audience, fostering strong brand affinity and encouraging action.
- **Genuine communication**: Be transparent in all communications and actions to build trust and credibility.
- **Audience involvement**: Actively engage people in the brand's narrative, promoting interaction and community building.
- **Feedback and agility**: Listen to customer feedback and adapt strategies to improve the experience.
- **Continuous evolution**: Embrace new ideas to stay relevant and exceed expectations.

Show, Don't Tell

Russian playwright and short-story writer Anton Chekhov once advised his brother Alexander on effective writing: "Don't tell me the moon is shining; show me the glint of light on broken glass."[7] This guidance has been distilled into the widely recognized principle of "Show, don't tell." While telling merely states facts, showing vividly illustrates and substantiates them. This principle is just as crucial in creating impactful brand experiences.

For example, if extreme heat had become the norm due to climate change, imagine how the Dutch Postimpressionist painter Vincent van Gogh might have portrayed the effects of prolonged temperature and weather pattern shifts on his wheat fields.

To explore this concept, World Wildlife Fund (WWF) Germany and creative agency Leo Burnett Germany collaborated with AI experts and climate researchers to process eight renowned landscape paintings. Using specially developed AI pipelines trained on the distinct styles of each artist and integrated with regional climate data from the World Climate Report, they transformed scenarios from the Intergovernmental Panel on Climate Change into vivid, impactful images. This innovative approach, showcased in the WWF's "Climate Realism" exhibition, offered a powerful visual representation of the potential consequences of climate change.[8] By merging art, technology, and climate science, the exhibition's web experience, physical galleries, and digital assets provided a fresh perspective on climate futures, generating significant attention, fostering richer discussions, and amplifying the urgency to address climate change.

FOCUS: MY JAPAN RAILWAY / DENTSU INC., TOKYO

Travelers celebrate Japan Railway for its practicality and punctuality. Dentsu's "My Japan Railway" campaign deepened this connection by offering two options for personal engagement: an interactive web app tailored for rail users and a book. This campaign successfully changed how people perceive the station. "Commuting turned into a small adventure, and stations became places with personal significance rather than just transit points," said Yoshihiro Yagi, executive creative director of Dentsu Japan.[9]

The initiative transformed the routine commuting experience into an engaging brand interaction, reshaping perceptions of the company and inspiring travelers to explore new destinations by rail. The campaign also encouraged creativity by featuring scenic attractions throughout Japan.

At the heart of the campaign were intricately illustrated digital stamps representing over 900 stations nationwide. Users could collect these stamps on their smartphones, with each stamp personalized based on the "stamping force" applied during screen presses. These woodcut-style stamps, inspired by seasonal changes, personal memories shared on social media,

(continued on next page)

(*continued from previous page*)

and tributes to trains and railway staff, added a nostalgic and analog touch to the digital experience. I asked Yagi why it is essential for a brand to have a conversation with its audience. He replied:

> Focusing solely on our technology has its limits when it comes to brand growth. We believe it's essential to explore the relationship between humans and the brand, engaging in meaningful dialogue with people.
>
> The railway in Japan has a 150-year history of transporting people faster, further, and in greater numbers. However, the era of merely pursuing technological advancements has come to an end. Now, we've contemplated what the railway can do next and shifted our focus from "technical infrastructure to emotional infrastructure." Emotional infrastructure means connecting people to each other and to the railway on an emotional level, creating touchpoints with stations that are felt rather than logically understood.[10]

6.2 My Japan Railway Use App. Creative Agency: DENTSU INC., Tokyo; Brand: JR GROUP, Tokyo; Executive Creative Director: Takuma Takasaki, DENTSU INC.; Creative Director: Yoshihiro Yugi, DENTSU INC.; Art Director: Hiroyuki Kato, DENTSU INC.; Art Director: Nanae Ishikawa, DENTSU INC.; Art Director: Asuka Yamamoto, DENTSU INC.; Copywriter: Mariko Fukuoka, DENTSU INC.; Copywriter: Mina Sugioka, DENTSU INC.; Creative Producer: Akiko Seino, DENTSU INC.; Account Executive: Naoto Ikegami, DENTSU INC.; Account Executive: Mami Umezawa, DENTSU INC.; Account Executive: Jun Maeda, DENTSU INC.

6.2 (*continued*)

(*continued on next page*)

(*continued from previous page*)

6.3 My Japan Railway Stamps. Creative Agency: DENTSU INC., Tokyo; Brand: JR GROUP, Tokyo; Executive Creative Director: Takuma Takasaki, DENTSU INC.; Creative Director: Yoshihiro Yugi, DENTSU INC.; Art Director: Hiroyuki Kato, DENTSU INC.; Art Director: Nanae Ishikawa, DENTSU INC.; Art Director: Asuka Yamamoto, DENTSU INC.; Copywriter: Mariko Fukuoka, DENTSU INC.; Copywriter: Mina Sugioka, DENTSU INC.; Creative Producer: Akiko Seino, DENTSU INC.; Account Executive: Naoto Ikegami, DENTSU INC.; Account Executive: Mami Umezawa, DENTSU INC.; Account Executive: Jun Maeda, DENTSU INC.

6.3 (*continued*)

(*continued on next page*)

(*continued from previous page*)

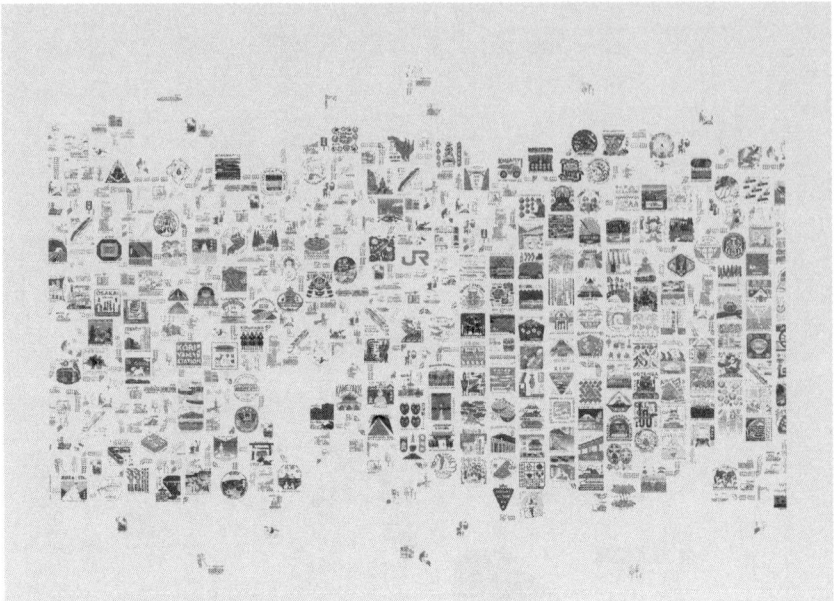

6.3 (*continued*)

6.4 My Japan Railway Book. Creative Agency: DENTSU INC., Tokyo; Brand: JR GROUP, Tokyo Executive Creative Director: Takuma Takasaki, DENTSU INC.; Creative Director: Yoshihiro Yugi, DENTSU INC.; Art Director: Hiroyuki Kato, DENTSU INC.; Art Director: Nanae Ishikawa, DENTSU INC.; Art Director: Asuka Yamamoto, DENTSU INC.; Copywriter: Mariko Fukuoka, DENTSU INC.; Copywriter: Mina Sugioka, DENTSU INC.; Creative Producer: Akiko Seino, DENTSU INC.; Account Executive: Naoto Ikegami, DENTSU INC.; Account Executive: Mami Umezawa, DENTSU INC.; Account Executive: Jun Maeda, DENTSU INC.

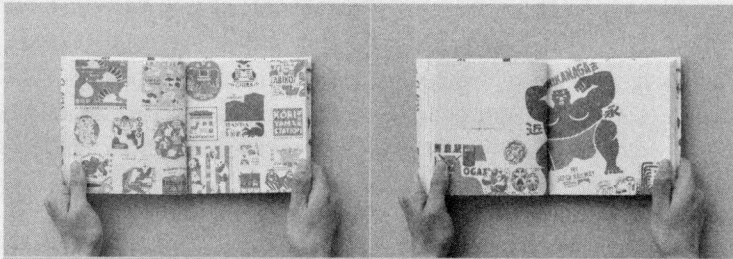

6.4 (*continued*)

FCB Chicago and Current Global partnered with the Digital Public Library of America (DPLA) to launch the "Banned Book Club." This digital library provides free e-books of banned titles to readers in regions across the US where access to those books has been restricted.

The campaign aims to combat threats to intellectual freedom by ensuring that all books remain accessible. It features virtual libraries in select US locations, specifically targeting areas with existing book bans through GPS-based geotargeting. To access the banned books, readers download the Palace e-reader app and choose "Banned Book Club" as their virtual library.[11]

Speaking of consequences from policies, did you know male trees produce allergenic pollen, whereas female trees don't? Female trees absorb the pollen. Despite this, in 1949, the United States Department of Agriculture recommended that cities plant only male trees to avoid the mess caused by fruit-bearing female trees, which led to a botanical imbalance, increased pollen levels, and record-high allergy cases. In response, allergy-relief brand Claritin—in collaboration with Energy /BBDO Chicago, CANJA Audio Culture, Coyne PR, and twelvenote—launched the "DiversiTree Project" not only to relieve seasonal allergies but also to help prevent them.

The goal was to create allergy-friendly environments by planting and distributing female trees across the US, to raise awareness of the issue among allergy sufferers, and to provide policymakers and city planners with new data to consider as part of the urban planning process. Simply by planting female trees, Claritin demonstrated that a future with reduced pollen is achievable.

In the program's first year, Claritin and partners planted over 200,000 female trees, reducing pollen levels by 25 percent. The initiative resulted in a 255 percent increase in branded searches for "Claritin" and "Fighting Pollen," and created more than 6.5 million square feet of allergy-relief green spaces.[12]

Three Things That Brand Experiences Have to Do

Hollywood films often glamorize creativity, portraying artists as having sudden bursts of inspiration that lead to success. This portrayal overlooks the extensive training and preparation that underpin those moments of insight. Exceptional creative work—produced by creative directors, art directors, copywriters, brand designers, and brand strategists—derives its value not just from inspiration or talent alone, but also from strategic creative thinking. The word "exceptional" is key here, since much commercial work may fall short due to factors such as team dynamics, focus group feedback, or client constraints.

Many people possess creativity and a capacity for imaginative thinking, often adding unique twists or offering fresh perspectives. Some can generate entirely original ideas. The following three actions help define what sets outstanding, strategically creative solutions apart.

For branding, brand experiences, or advertising to succeed, they must:

- **Grab attention**: Instantly capture the audience's interest
- **Hold attention**: Sustain engagement to convey and imprint the message
- **Call to action**: Motivate the audience to take the next step

A creative solution can perform many roles: branding, identifying, informing, locating, engaging, and conveying meaning. But if it doesn't first capture the consumer's attention, it fails to set the stage for action.

FOCUS: STUART HAURY, PRODUCT DESIGNER

Stuart Haury is a versatile product designer, currently immersed in the world of advertising and branding. With ten years of professional experience in all phases of user experience (UX) and human-centered design, he has worked with a wide range of clients, including Coca-Cola, Disney, Microsoft, Ford, and EMI. His passions include photography and exploring off-grid in the forests of the Pacific Northwest.

On the benefits/dangers of hopping-on culture:

"Everything on the internet is already old" is a saying that still holds, even though social media culture is drastically shortening the "oldness." When brands react to cultural trends, it often falls flat or backfires because it feels like a parent retelling a joke in a desperate attempt to look cool.

A better use of a brand's energy is to have a unique, philosophical approach of why they are doing what they're doing, regardless of which way the meme winds blow—which is the closest thing philosophically to "just be yourself, no one else is doing that."

Culture is what society deems important enough to remember. And brands are remembered for being authentic, not pretending they're "with

(*continued on next page*)

(*continued from previous page*)

it." The more authentic the philosophy is, the more customers want to be associated with that brand.

On how brands can best employ AR / VR / MR innovation to connect with consumers:

In my recent career shift from thinking about desktop and mobile devices to augmented and virtual reality, I constantly remind myself not to focus on the device, but to unlearn the device form factors and instead focus on the world-building and immersion of the experience. Focusing on spatial development, and prioritizing design and experiences that consider multiple dimensions and senses, forms the foundation of a truly successful experience.

There will always be creative constraints and limits to the latest tech that act as boundaries, but creativity can thrive within those boundaries if we embrace the restrictions. If the experience is engrossing enough, the user won't notice the technology, form factor, or budget and quality of the way it was built.

Innovation (in the true sense of the word) happens at the periphery and is more concerned with larger shifts in our culture and the world around us than it is about solving problems for specific brands. So, I have a hard time with the term innovation in its true form, when defined within the construct of a specific brand.

The other issue with innovation is that by definition it is not mainstream, and there's a learning curve for any new consumers or any new use for an established brand. Most corporations are lazy or afraid of new things, ideas, processes, cultural shifts, and technology, and would rather give consumers what they already understand and are familiar with—which is not innovating.

Brands—and the corporations that create brands—are made of people. And people are scared of what they don't understand. So, the catch-22 of trying to innovate with technology, specifically AR/VR/MR, is that people say they want new things, but then get scared and regress back to the same ideas and culture they already know, which isn't new. It takes a special kind of client or brand to put their trust in new thinking—not to be scared of the inevitable faults, missteps, and lessons that come with it, even without a guaranteed payoff, popularity, or financial return.

In recent years, the hype cycle around Web 3.0, virtual reality, augmented reality, and the misunderstood "metaverse" has given people the impression that these mediums are limitless in quality and bandwidth: we're told the shiny glossy future we've wanted for so long is here, and it's always sold to us as pixel-perfect. The problem is that, for now, these experiences are inherently low-fidelity; they have to operate on low bandwidth because of the limited processing capacity of our phones and average consumer devices. Powerful devices that can handle high-quality seamless experiences in multiple dimensions are expensive and hard to come by.

Luckily, the best state-of-the-art and cutting-edge examples of these experiences can be transmitted even via the simplest and lowest-fidelity medium. I've seen short animations with extremely crude illustration quality—and yet, because they were in virtual reality and I was immersed inside them, they've left me with lingering feelings of awe and a desire to want more. If the storytelling and the core reasons behind the experience are there, the user won't care about the lower-quality execution of the visuals. If they're engaged in the idea, the limits melt away.

On how UX design can best facilitate conversations between individuals and brands:

Listen to your customers. Actually listen. They made your product successful, and now you have to keep them coming back by making their lives better and easier. The minute your brand prioritizes shareholders, maximizing profits, and internal tensions over your customers' needs, they'll "fire" you and your brand and find a better solution.

UX tools can shape people's lives, yet it's individuals' unique experiences that ultimately dictate which tools are most effective for them. If your brand's UX isn't optimal for their needs, they will seek out better alternatives.

The latest state of AI/ML [machine learning] products and their horrible approach to UX—or complete lack thereof—is a perfect example. Brand/Product A may have the best technology around, but if Product B has an interface that's easier and more enjoyable to use, they'll easily win the race.

Once Product B establishes itself as the easiest and most preferred way for customers to solve problems or interact with the world around them, they have now set the lowest bar that all other products must meet at a bare minimum. Any brand's bar of quality for their product's UX is set by their customer's last best product experience.

On what constitutes an optimal user experience:

The unfortunate truth about being a user experience designer is that no one will notice when you do your job correctly. A product working and doing what the customer expects is the bar you must always meet, and there's no public acknowledgment of meeting the bare minimum. As soon as you don't deliver on the expectations and needs of your customers, people react with negative brand perceptions.

An optimal user experience is when you make your customers' lives easier and help them with problems they didn't know they had, or didn't think you could solve. When this optimal user experience is met, the payoff offers surprise, delight, and positive brand perceptions.

To mix the metaphors and philosophical approaches of Jobs Theory and the hospitality industry: when a customer hires you to solve their problems, and you solve them while treating them better than anyone has treated them before, congratulations—you've delivered an optimal user experience.

As Sean Thomas, executive creative director at Jones Knowles Ritchie, says: "Brand design lays the foundations for brands to grow on. We get things in order, reset the direction, find what made the brand special, and make it as distinctive and consistent as possible."[13]

Brand experiences:

- Make information and content easily accessible
- Capture and express the brand's essence in ways that resonate with the audience
- Build brand communities and foster engagement
- Take the form of practical and relevant brand applications, websites, experiences, and platforms across tangible, digital, experiential, sonic, olfactory, and hybrid formats
- Align with the brand's core narrative and value proposition
- Go beyond promotion to deliver solutions that benefit people, creatures, or the planet

Interview: Layne Braunstein, creative principal, ESI | NBBJ, & founder of Fake Love, a NYT Company

Layne is a seven-time Cannes Lions and two-time Clio Award winner, recognized for his groundbreaking work in creating next-gen immersive environments that push the boundaries of technology, storytelling, and design. A leader in the modern experiential movement, he blends high design, physical space, art, and social interaction to craft deeply human-centered experiences.

In his career of more than twenty-five years, Layne has led groundbreaking experiential projects for clients including Google, Twitter, Microsoft, IBM, Cartier, Samsung, Virgin, Lexus, Hermès, BMW, Star Wars, Coca-Cola, Marc Jacobs, Tiffany, and Nike.

He is also known for being a pioneer and spokesperson in the worlds of VR, AR, and XR, and has created some of the first-ever public projects in each of them for such clients as Google, IBM, and the *New York Times*.

As the principal creative at ESI Design, an NBBJ Studio, Layne sets the conceptual vision and tone for the Experiential Practice and its projects. He oversees the creative aspects—from market development to design strategy, production, innovation, and beyond—to ensure that everything ESI and NBBJ are involved with is future-forward, market-relevant, and culturally transformative.

Prior to joining ESI, Layne founded the internationally award-winning experiential agency Fake Love and served as its CCO. After just six years, he

sold it to the *New York Times*. This partnership allowed the *Times*—a company more than 165 years old—to re-imagine who they could be, from integrated experiential design to acclaimed launches with NYTVR and NYTAR.

Layne has spoken about innovation design at places like the Cannes Lions International Festival of Creativity, TEDx, Adobe 99U, Future of Storytelling, Collision, Design Matters, MIT, and Columbia University. He has been featured in publications including *Wired*, the *New York Times*, the *Wall Street Journal*, *Fast Company*, *Architectural Digest*, *Communication Arts*, *IdN*, and *Adweek*.

The agency has been recognized with numerous honors, including being named *Ad Age's* Small Agency of the Year and earning a spot on the Inc. 5000 list. It has received a Gold Clio for Experiential, seven Cannes Lions including a prestigious Grand Prix, and a One Show Gold Pencil. Additional accolades include multiple Clios, three Promax|BDA awards, a Rosoff award, and a nomination for Best of Show at SXSW. It was also honored by AIGA SEED and short-listed eight times for other Cannes Lions awards.

He currently lives in Brooklyn, New York. Give him a shout if you are around.

What do you mean by "True Experiential Design"?

In this "age of experience," every designer says they are an experience designer. It's seen by many as an adjective to describe a design in a modern way. It's true that the word *experience* itself is broad and can describe literally anything. In today's design world, I have seen it used for everything: from the interior design of a conference room to a branded web campaign to formal architecture. These designers aren't wrong—yes, people can "experience" these things, and actual experience designers do use aspects of these in their work. But here's the thing: Experiential design is an actual discipline in which designers like myself earn undergraduate and master's degrees. It takes decades to hone our understanding of this discipline. The fact that some designers just wake up in the morning and suddenly decide they are experience designers or describe what they are doing as "experience" disrespects this discipline and the people who work in it and study it. My mentor, Ed Schlossberg, has been doing this for over forty years, for example, and teaches experiential design at Columbia University.

A dream of mine is to see the development of some kind of formal certification license to practice experiential design—similar to the field of architecture.

Many of us have tried over the years to come up with a new word for what we do that is more ownable—transmedia, phygital, multimedia, immersive—but none of it sticks. So, in conversation, I generally use the term "true experiential design." This describes a design that has most of these aspects (and I say this differently every time):

1. Physical meets digital design—it's never fully analog, and never fully digital.
2. Interactive, not passive design—there needs to be an interaction where the audience can affect the resulting design in real time.

3. Multisensory—it should involve more than one sense through its output—and two at the minimum.
4. Artistic in its representation—A pure data viz is just a data viz. But if it's designed in a way that elevates it to art, it can be experiential.
5. Emotional Impact—designed to stir feelings in the audience that have a lasting emotional impact, long after they leave the experience.

This is still subject to interpretation, but I think achieving a good three out of five aspects should be the goal. I also tend to use the word *experiential* rather than *experience*. It further sets this up as a design discipline, rather than a philosophical design idea.

Please share some of your thinking about experiential audio in the built environment.

Audio is most often forgotten, or value-engineered out of experiential for the built environment because many people see audio as a disruptor, rather than an enhancer to a space. To me, assuming we only see the world, and don't hear it or touch it, is assuming we only experience the world in a single sense at a time. For a true emotional connection to occur for any type of experiential design, I would argue that you need to engage at least two senses, and ideally, one of them is auditory.

Furthermore, if given the choice between entering a space with sound or visuals, I will always choose sound. You can put sound in any space, regardless of the design, and it will immediately change the mood and feel of it. Visuals can't always do that, and often don't get seen at all, as people's eyes are usually taken up with their phones or finding their way to their destination. If you know me, you know that I can't sit in a room without some kind of music playing, or it just feels like a mausoleum to me.

But how I see the world is not how many people see it. For example, for individuals with hearing impairment, sound won't be as important for emotional impact—but touch and haptics (vibration) are. In this case, I would still use the rule of two senses by using touch/haptics and visuals in an experience. I did this for the *7UP Concert for the Deaf* with great success.

You've said that the metaverse pushes the boundaries of what's possible in experiential design. Please explain.

I am sort of retiring the word metaverse for now, as it's more marketing than anything else; I will refer to it as the "virtual space" for these purposes. The virtual space and experiential design share a common goal: to captivate users by immersing them in engaging and interactive experiences. They both overlap but are missing pieces from one another. One thing that experiential has been lacking is the ability to fully take over one's surroundings in a fully visual way. What I mean is filling a real space (meatspace) with visual objects all around you—basically holograms. Until we figure out how to bend light into realistic holograms, the next best option is pass-through VR, such as the Vision Pro or Augmented Reality.

In these technologies, the user sees a blend of virtual objects layered into the real world. The more this technology advances, the more the line between virtual and real becomes blurred. As an experience designer, we typically have boundaries in the physical space for what we can create—something goes on a wall there, a sculpture here, a kinetic structure there, or a transparent screen here. With pass-through virtual experiences, we can lift our art into the air and

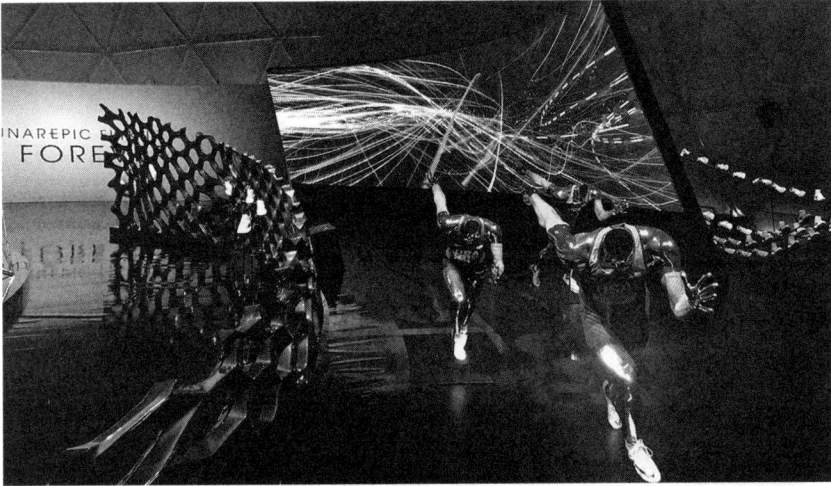

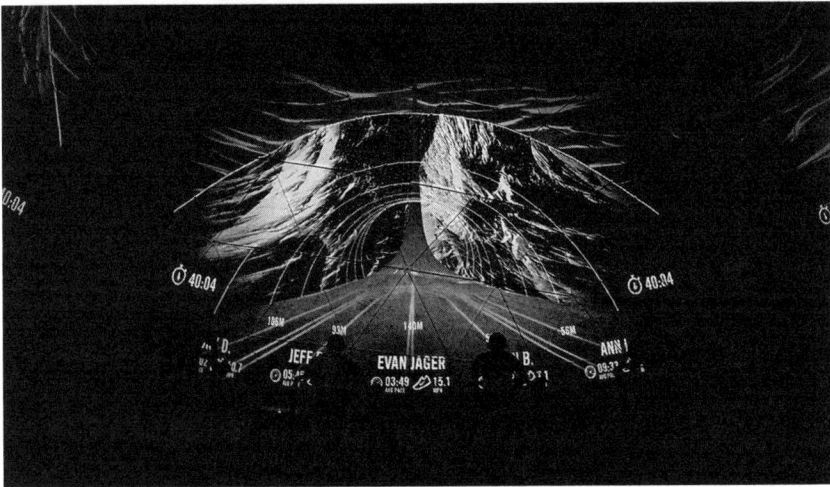

6.5 "Nike Olympics Track & Field." Creative director/Founder @ Fake Love: Layne Braunstein; Experience by: Fake Love Inc.; Partner: Nike; Place: Olympic Track & Field, Eugene, Oregon

"Two elite Nike experiences in a series of massive enclosed domes. Immerse yourself in an artistic data inspired Flynit experience; and then with a Flynit try-on, compete against virtual Olympians in a treadmill powered 360° surreal race." https://layneb.com/#/nikeolympics/

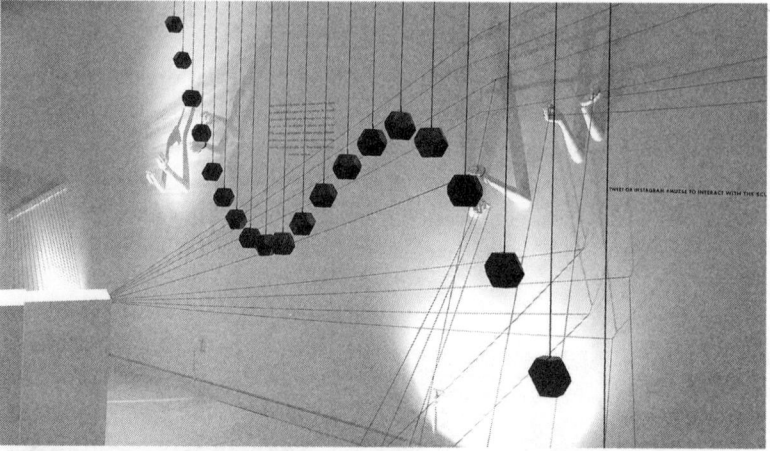

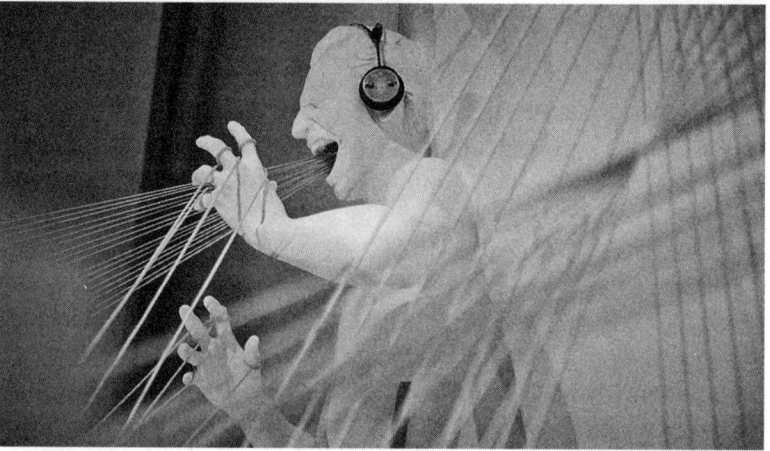

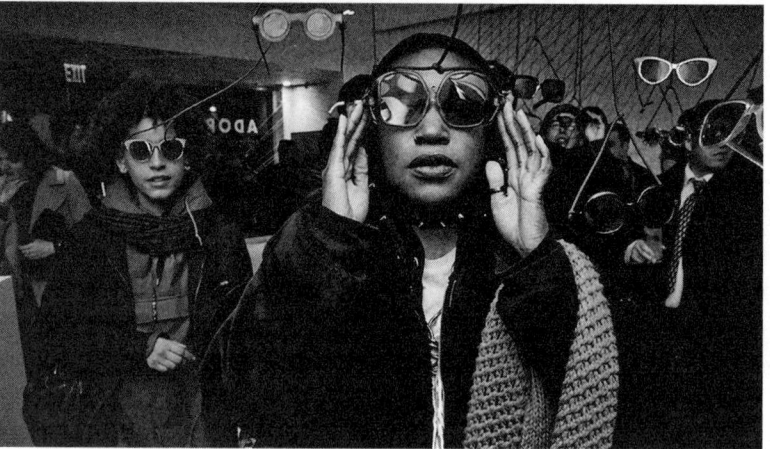

6.6 Intel, "Adorned." Creative director/Founder @ Fake Love: Layne Braunstein; Experience by: Fake Love Inc.; Partner: Milk Studios; Place: Chelsea, NYC

"Adorned" blends art with experience, intertwining the past and future of wearable technology."
https://layneb.com/#/adorned/

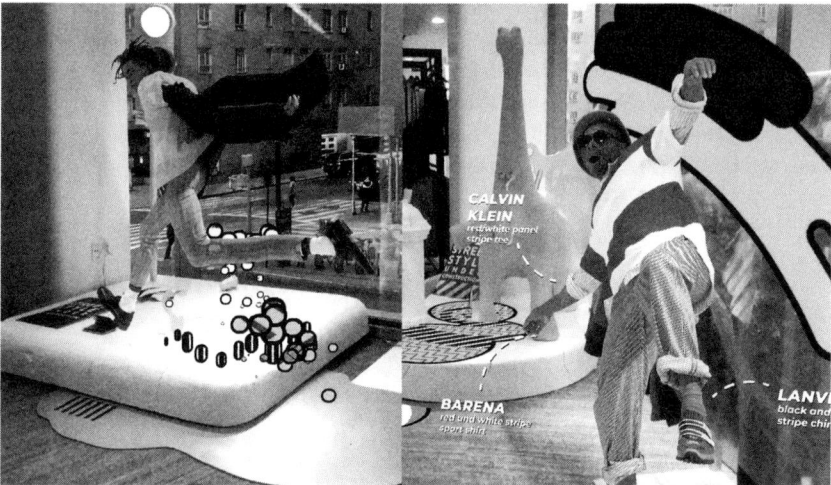

6.7 Nordstrom AR. Creative director/Founder @ Fake Love: Layne Braunstein; Experience by: Fake Love Inc.; Partner: Nordstrom; Place: Nordstrom NYC Flagship

For the launch of Nordstrom's Men's flagship store, this unique Augmented Reality activation pairs local street artists with models in a distinctive blend of virtual and physical elements. https://layneb.com/#/nordstrom/

have it flow wherever we want in space. Plus, these objects can be interacted with. Nothing I am saying here is new to interactive designers—in fact, it's a little old hat, as this tech has been around for decades in some fashion. But, particularly in the built environment, we haven't taken advantage of what a clever

6.8 "The Treachery of Sanctuary." Creative director/Founder @ Fake Love: Layne Braunstein; Experience by: Fake Love Inc.; Partner: The Creators Project / Vice Media, Chris Milk; Place: Dumbo, Brooklyn & San Francisco

Conceptualized by Chris Milk, "The Treachery of Sanctuary" is a large interactive triptych that guides viewers through three stages of flight using Kinect controllers and infrared sensors. The Unity game engine, combined with Microsoft Kinect and openFrameworks, delivered a highly immersive, realistic experience. At The Creators Project in San Francisco, there were three twenty-five-foot installations featuring a reflecting pool to maintain user interaction with the Kinect sensors. This setup offered a lifelike shadow experience, allowing participants to feel as though they were genuinely interacting with ravens.

James George, Aaron Meyers, and Brian Chasalow, "How It Works: Chris Milk's The Treachery Of Sanctuary," June 12, 2012, accessed September 7, 2024, https://www.vice.com/en/article/how-it-works -chris-milks-ithe-treachery-of-sanctuaryi/

6.9 Levi's "Station to Station." Creative director/Founder @ Fake Love: Layne Braunstein; Experience by: Fake Love Inc.; Partner: Levis; Place: Across the United States

"Station to Station" was a cross-country event that invited and challenged artists such as David Bowie and Patti Smith to collaborate and create. These artists had the freedom to board or exit a vintage train at any iconic stop on its journey across the United States. Inspired by the pioneers and artists who once used trains for travel and creativity, Fake Love reimagined authentic creative tools, transforming them into IoT-enabled devices capable of capturing new art and sharing it with a global audience.

Layneb.com, accessed September 7, 2024, https://layneb.com/#/levis-station-to-station/

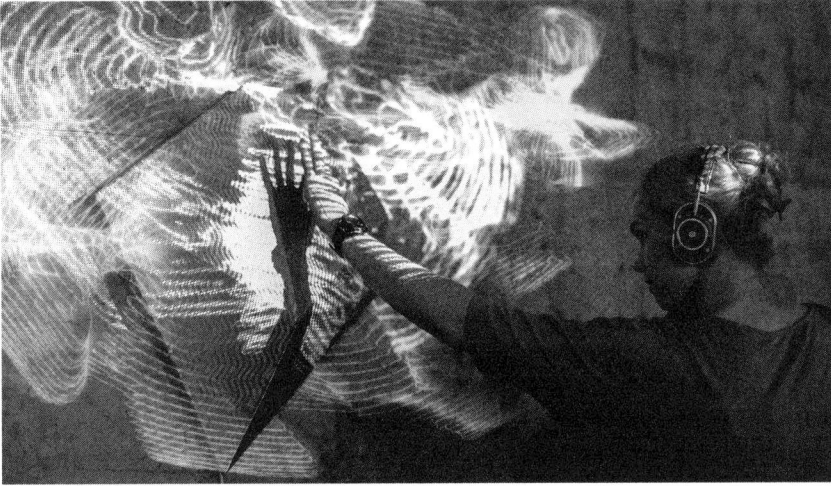

6.10 Master & Dynamic Brand Launch. Creative director/Founder @ Fake Love: Layne Braunstein; Experience by: Fake Love Inc.; Partner: Master & Dynamic; Place: NYC

To capture Master & Dynamic's "Sound is Creativity" philosophy, Fake Love designed a series of interactive sculptures for their launch event. These sculptures featured visual interpretations of the logo and product textures, and when activated, they produced distinctive sounds and holographic visuals.

"Master & Dynamic | Case Study," Layneb.com, accessed September 7, 2024, https://layneb.com/#/master-dynamic/

blend of the physical and virtual space can do. Currently, its only accepted use is for gallery, cultural, or temporary experiences. I am hoping that as our ideas on virtual spatial computing become commonplace, so too will our thinking around its creative applications in permanent experiential spaces.

Interview: Giorgia Lupi, Partner, Pentagram

Giorgia Lupi is an information designer and partner at the international design consultancy Pentagram. In her practice, she challenges the impersonality of data, designing engaging visual narratives that reconnect numbers to what they stand for: stories, people, ideas. Giorgia was born in Italy and earned her

Giorgia Lupi. Photographer: Jake Chessum

doctorate in design at Politecnico di Milano, where she focused on information mapping. In 2011, she cofounded Accurat, an acclaimed data-driven research, design and innovation firm with offices in Milan and New York. Her work is part of the permanent collections of both the Museum of Modern Art and the Cooper Hewitt, Smithsonian Design Museum, and her TED Talk on her humanistic approach to data has garnered over one million views. She has published two books: *Dear Data* (Princeton Architectural Press, 2016), which explores the details of daily life through hand-drawn visual data; and *Observe, Collect, Draw! A Visual Journal* (Princeton Architectural Press, 2018), a guided journal for collecting visual data.

You pioneered and popularized a philosophy of information design called "data humanism." Please tell us about data humanism.

Data humanism is my approach that sees data not only as cold numbers but as an abstraction of reality. Data is a filter we can use to see the world, one subject at a time, to better understand it. This approach only works if we include the human qualities found in data, however: context, missing data, imperfection, and uncertainty. Data is not perfect and is always subject to collection errors and interpretation, but through design data humanism comes alive. When we can render data visually, people are able to understand and experience it in a new, more human way.

How can design have a transformative impact on healthcare?

If we look through an information design lens, we can help to bring patients' needs to the fore. When people are reduced to numbers, their charts, their labs, we focus on those ranges or points and we dehumanize the people. We end up missing the big picture and the whole journey. I have personally been doing a lot of data collection on a medical journey I am going through, and my data tracking has helped me communicate with many different practitioners more effectively. I can show months (and years) of history to them in a few minutes, which helps get across the importance of my journey as a patient when I am not in the office. We can find tools in design to bring this journey forward. In a perfect world, all medical records would be connected so design could take all information into account and make the most helpful visualization possible. Dataviz can and should express the individuality of patient stories in a better way.

You are the 2022 recipient of the National Design Award from the Cooper Hewitt, Smithsonian Design Museum, and the first data visualization practitioner ever to be named in its communication design category. Please tell us about your work at the intersection of data visualization and communication design.

I am primarily a designer. I used to say that data was my favorite material to design with. As a designer, data is a narrative and communication tool just like type, images, words. With my team at Pentagram, we work in all different fields—healthcare, finance, tech, nonprofit, education—and we design all kinds of outputs. Sometimes they are for print, or for environmental graphics, digital apps, ad campaigns, brand identities, and even products like clothes or rugs with dataviz patterns that tell a story. I was honored to receive the National Design Award, and it's a testament to the value of information and data in how we consume new knowledge and relate to the world. Through the power of design, we can make so many experiences tangible for the first time.

You told Matt Alagiah of It's Nice That: *"It's a really interesting time to be working at the intersection of data, design and branding because there's so much potential for shaping the conversation between brands and customers through design, when it comes to data."*[14] *How do you utilize data in your branding process?*

Every current Pentagram client has a wealth of data representing internal goals, performance analysis, investment assessments, etc. They also gather data, which they use to communicate with their own customers. Data has become currency for every customer interaction. For our projects, we try to see data and visualization systems as a true extension of the brand and not as an afterthought. We not only stylize charts; we also build entire systems that take the brand to the next level, and then, through dataviz, we give it a unique signature that can be a central brand asset. We also design data-driven identities where logo, type, layout, or graphic patterns respond to stories found in data that are proprietary or that we find elsewhere. The data we employ can be related to the mission of the company, their value proposition, or any subject they care about.

How do you make data accessible and relatable?

Only through good visual communication are our minds able to interpret trends, rankings, statistics, etc. To make that data relatable, however, we have to include human stories. We, as humans, don't relate to aggregated big numbers. We can understand them intellectually; we can assess urgency as with climate change; but ultimately we change our behavior only when we learn how this data might affect us. We have to see ourselves in the stories. If we use climate change as an example, we see temperatures rising or emissions going up—but it's only when we see a chart or a poetic visualization about the cities that we will never be able to see again, or the bird songs we won't be able to hear anymore, that we gain true understanding and change our behavior. Only these visceral specifics lead to a true increase in empathy.

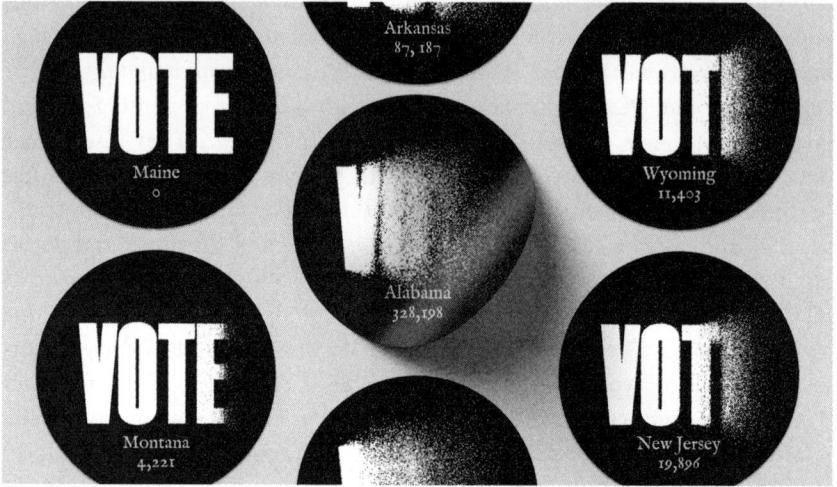

6.11 Campaign, Data Driven Design: "I Voted." Design: Giorgia Lupi, Partner / Pentagram; Client: *Fast Company*

Fast Company asked Giorgia Lupi and her Pentagram team to redesign the "I Voted" sticker to boost its impact. Lupi and her team focused on voting rights and disenfranchisement, using data from The Sentencing Project's report to highlight how felony convictions affect voting eligibility. The team created 50 custom buttons, each representing disenfranchisement rates by state, with the word "Vote" visually distorted according to the number of disenfranchised individuals, making the text less legible in states with higher rates. The stark black-and-white design, with neon yellow data labels, emphasized the issue's severity. They also developed a poster and additional concepts addressing voter apathy and repeat voting.

"I Voted," Pentagram.com, accessed September 7, 2024, https://www.pentagram.com/work/i-voted/story

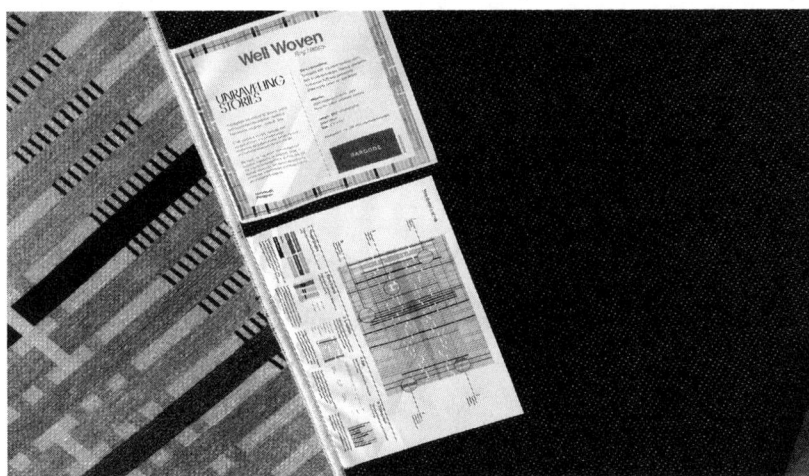

6.12 Data Driven Design: "Unraveling Stories." Design: Giorgia Lupi, Partner / Pentagram; Client: Well Woven

Lupi designed the "Unraveling Stories" rug collection for Well Woven, using data visualization to highlight endangered textile techniques worldwide. The rugs, available in multiple sizes and colors, feature bars representing data from fifty-nine distinct textile traditions. Inspired by the geometric nature of the loom and Anni Albers's modernist aesthetic, the design emphasizes the fragility of these techniques. Lupi's team researched endangered textiles, drawing data from UNESCO and other sources to create a visually striking collection that combines storytelling with everyday functionality, bringing awareness to the preservation of cultural heritage through craft.

Textiles have long played a vital role in human civilization, serving ceremonial, practical, and domestic purposes. However, many traditional textile crafts are now at risk of being forgotten as people become increasingly distanced from these practices.

"I love creating data art that people interact with daily," said Lupi. "A data-driven rug brings the story embedded in its design into your home. Seeing the world through data, I'm thrilled when these stories can touch others' lives. Collaborating with Well Woven has been incredibly exciting!"

"Unraveling Stories," Pentagram.com, accessed September 7, 2024, https://www.pentagram.com/work/well-woven/story

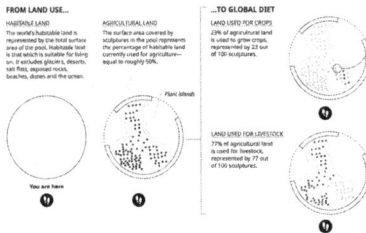

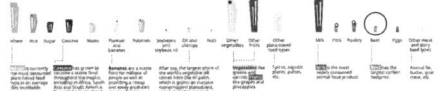

6.13 Exhibition Design, Data Driven Design: *Around the World's Table*. Design: Giorgia Lupi, Partner / Pentagram; Client: NYBG

Around the World's Table is an immersive data installation at the New York Botanical Garden (NYBG) conveying the global impact of food production and consumption; it is Lupi's first data-driven sculpture, reflecting her human-centered approach to data visualization and storytelling. Amid warnings of a global food shortage from the UN, the project examines how global land is used for food production and the environmental impact of our diets. "We wanted to highlight what we eat and where it comes from, aiming to foster a deeper understanding of food choices' effects," Lupi explains. "Ultimately, we hope to spark questions: Where does our food come from, and how do our choices impact the planet?"

The data installation was set in the reflecting pool of the Palms of the World Gallery at NYBG's Enid A. Haupt Conservatory. The pool serves as a metaphor for both the world and a dinner plate, featuring one hundred partially submerged metal totems representing major food groups, their share in the global diet, and their carbon footprint. The arrangement of the totems mirrors the proportion of the world's habitable land dedicated to agriculture, covering roughly half of the fountain.

"Around the World's Table," Pentagram.com, accessed September 7, 2024, https://www.pentagram.com/work/around-the-world-s-table/story

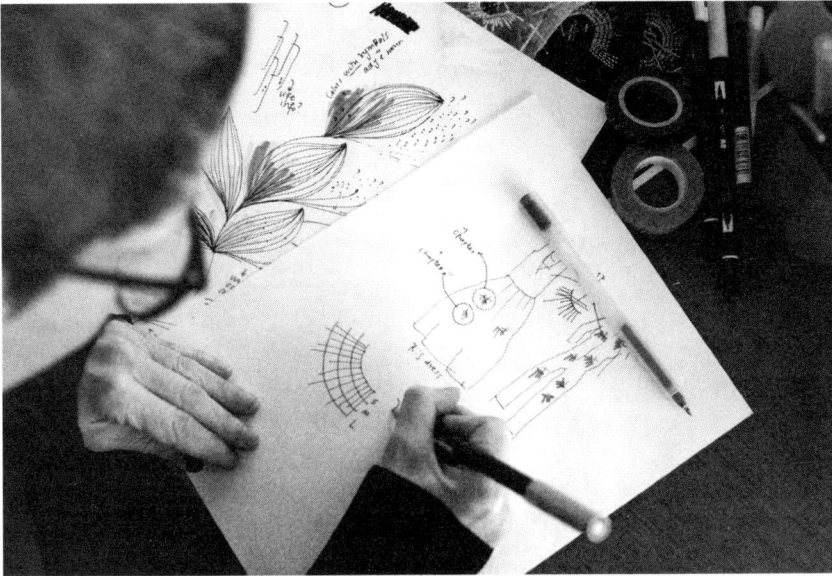

6.14 Data Driven Design: "Giorgia Lupi & Other Stories." Design: Giorgia Lupi, Partner / Pentagram; Client: & Other Stories

"Giorgia Lupi & Other Stories" is a data-driven fashion collection inspired by three trailblazing women in science.

Lupi aims to humanize data by revealing the stories behind numbers. In collaboration with the fashion brand & Other Stories, she created a ready-to-wear collection that brings data to life through wearable hand-drawn patterns. These designs are inspired by three trailblazing women: Ada Lovelace, "The Mathematician" and first computer programmer; Rachel Carson, "The Environmentalist" and pioneer of the environmental movement; and Mae Jemison, "The Astronaut," a former NASA physicist and the first African American woman in space.

This project aligns with Lupi's Data Humanism Manifesto, which redefines data as personal and approachable. Inspired by *Good Night Stories for Rebel Girls*, Lupi used the lives of Lovelace, Carson, and Jemison to create abstract data patterns that celebrate women's achievements in STEM, integrating them into the garments' design.

"Giorgia Lupi & Other Stories," Pentagram, accessed September 7, 2024, https://www.pentagram.com /work/giorgia-lupi-other-stories/story

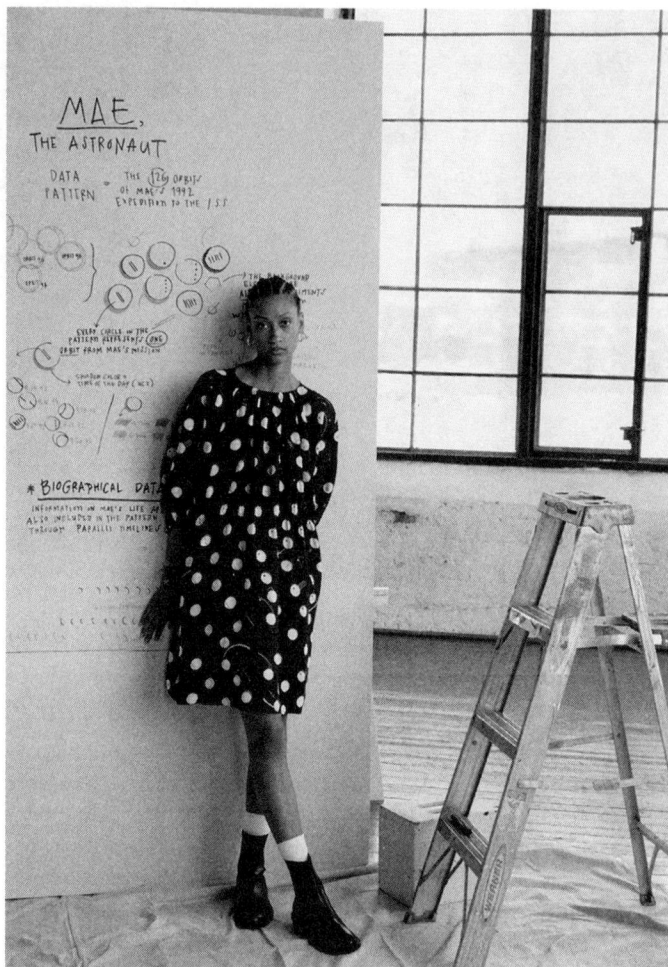

6.14 (*continued*)

CHAPTER 7

A BRAND IS A PROMISE KEPT

For the first time ever, a blind person commentated a basketball game. Live. On TV.[1]

Because of its rapid pace, basketball has always presented a unique challenge for people who are blind or visually impaired. Michelob ULTRA's tagline "It's Only Worth It If You Enjoy It" exemplifies the brand's journey to redefine the limits of accessibility in sports. That's why they've pioneered accessibility technology, enabling individuals who are blind or visually impaired to immerse themselves in the game using haptic feedback, spatial audio, artificial intelligence, and refreshable Braille.[2]

Blind since birth, Cameron Black pursued his passion for sports and became a local sports journalist in Kansas. Yet one dream remained seemingly out of reach: becoming a sports broadcaster. That changed when Black made history as the first blind basketball commentator on television, shattering barriers.

"DreamCaster," the initiative developed by FCB New York, empowered Black—an ardent Kansas City Chiefs fan—to experience basketball through cutting-edge technology. Utilizing haptic feedback vests and wearables, alongside generative artificial intelligence that translates game data into refreshable Braille, DreamCaster aims to provide profoundly immersive basketball experiences for individuals who are visually impaired. Black's commentary during a New York Knicks game, broadcast on MSG, showcased this new technology. Michelob ULTRA partnered with Black to create technology that lets fans who are blind or visually impaired experience every nuance of basketball.[3]

Michelob ULTRA's promise: "We remain unwavering in our advocacy for responsible drinking and making every experience with beer a positive one."[4]

A Brand Is a Promise Kept

"Because I'm worth it."

Four words from L'Oréal Paris helped redefine women's perception of personal care. "When actress Joanne Dusseau first uttered the now-iconic phrase in the early 1970s, it was the first time an advertisement [sic] campaign claimed beauty for oneself, not for men. The tagline became a rallying call that voiced the shifting place of women in society."[5]

When I purchase a box of L'Oréal hair color, I expect beauty care with proven effectiveness.[6] A brand must consistently deliver on its promises, offering tangible and emotional benefits—like those provided by hair color—that distinguish it from competitors. Effective brand building depends on reliably fulfilling these promises, providing a strategic framework that directs and motivates all company efforts. Customers rely on the brand to keep its promises and meet or exceed expectations. As the State Farm website states, "Our business is based on a promise. We've made it a century because we take that promise seriously in everything we do."[7]

Initially, a brand promise draws people in. As their awareness grows, they come to prefer the brand for its consistent ability to deliver value and meet their needs and desires. As Brian Collins, cofounder of renowned brand consultancy COLLINS, says, "A brand is a promise performed consistently over time."[8]

The following attributes enhance positive brand perception and help build a strong, lasting relationship between the brand and its customers:

- **Delivering consistently high-quality** products or services reinforces reliability and trust.
- **Creating positive emotional experiences** at every touchpoint strengthens the connection with customers.
- **Sharing engaging, entertaining, or informative stories** that resonate with the audience fosters emotional bonds and enhances brand value.
- **Upholding brand integrity on social media**, where it is continuously under scrutiny, is crucial to fostering trust.
- **Consistently communicating** and embodying the brand's mission and vision across all channels and actions helps avoid perceptions of performative behavior. Genuine actions show the brand is truly "walking the talk."
- **Committing to environmental and social causes** reflects a brand's dedication to issues that resonate both with its core values and those of its audience.

- **Transparency around business practices**—such as product sourcing, fair labor, and animal testing—fosters trust and enhances credibility.
- **Engaging stakeholders** helps them understand and embrace the brand's values, empowering them to serve as authentic, active brand ambassadors.
- **Actively connecting with people** through social media, customer service, community involvement, and experiential design—whether informative or entertaining—cultivates belonging and appreciation.
- **Strengthening emotional connections** enhances brand salience.
- **Adding value** to a brand enriches people's experiences and sparks greater interest and engagement.
- **Promptly addressing customer concerns** builds trust and can turn negative experiences into positive ones, encouraging loyalty. Satisfied customers often share their experiences, organically drawing others to the brand. This responsiveness offers valuable insights for improvement and strengthens the brand's reputation and credibility.

The Holistic Brand Promise

People expect brands to do more than simply deliver on product or service promises. Consumers, especially Gen Z, are increasingly seeking out companies that actively contribute to the betterment of people, creatures, and the planet.[9]

As awareness of environmental and social impacts increases, consumers expect brands to adopt a comprehensive approach to their promises.[10] With 93 percent of people acknowledging climate change as a serious and imminent threat, brands must address these concerns to stay aligned with contemporary public values.[11]

By embracing a holistic brand promise, companies can meet evolving consumer demands and showcase their dedication to making a positive impact:

Sustainability and environmental responsibility: Consumers increasingly prioritize brands that commit to sustainable practices. Nearly 85 percent report experiencing the disruptive impacts of climate change, prompting 46 percent to seek more sustainable products to reduce their environmental footprint.[12] This includes efforts such as reducing carbon emissions, minimizing waste, using eco-friendly materials, and adopting renewable energy sources. Brands that genuinely embrace environmental stewardship can attract and retain customers passionate about protecting the planet, moving beyond perfunctory-grade corporate responsibility.

Corporate Social Responsibility (CSR): Consumers expect brands to engage in ethical behavior beyond environmental concerns, which includes fair labor practices, gender pay and promotion equity, support for farmers and the labor force, ethical sourcing, community engagement, and advocacy for social causes. Brands actively involved in CSR initiatives can build trust and generate interest among people who value ethical and socially responsible practices.

Transparency and accountability: Brands face intense scrutiny and the public expects them to be transparent about their practices and policies. Consumers demand clear information on how companies use personal data and advance their sustainability and social responsibility goals. Brands that openly disclose these details and demonstrate accountability are likelier to build trust and credibility with their audience, fostering a stronger connection and a positive reputation.[13]

Aligning with consumers' values: Kantar MONITOR tracking in the United States shows that nearly two-thirds of consumers prefer brands that align with their personal values. Globally, 80 percent make an effort to support companies that advocate for causes they care about.[14] Many consumers prioritize social conscience and are more inclined to support brands committed to social justice, environmental sustainability, and ethical practices.[15]

Long-term value and impact: Consumers recognize that their spending power can drive meaningful change. Choosing brands that prioritize sustainability and social responsibility contributes to efforts benefiting future generations, making every purchase more impactful.

Environmental sustainability is a critical concern for Gen Z and millennials, with about 60 percent voicing concern about climate change. They expect businesses to adopt sustainable practices. The 2024 Gen Z and Millennial Survey, which includes 23,000 respondents across forty-four countries, identifies environmental protection as a major societal challenge where companies can make a significant difference, shaping business practices through consumer choices.[16]

Building A Brand Connection Through Audience Engagement

"Brand is a promise PERFORMED," said Brian Collins at Cannes Lions.[17]

When choosing between brands, whether corporate or nonprofit, consumers often ask, "What's in it for me?" Addressing their concerns, challenges, pain points, and aspirations fosters more resonant connections and improves outcomes. How do a brand's offerings provide solutions, assistance, relief, or hope?

To effectively integrate insights into the brand promise, it's crucial to understand the target audience's aspirations and needs (see chapter 9 for more on audience insights). A brand's value lies in its ability to meet these needs and desires now and in the future by delivering solutions that align with its promises.

The relationship between a brand and its audience is intricate, shaped by a dynamic interplay in which it's often unclear whether the audience shapes the brand's promise, or the brand's offerings shape the audience's desires. Ideally, a brand strikes a balance where its offerings consistently reflect its values while also effectively meeting its audience's evolving needs and aspirations.

Refining the Brand Promise

To refine a brand promise effectively, pinpoint and address the specific issues the brand resolves for its audience while consistently excelling in those areas.
Define Your Target Audience(s):

- Primary Audience: Identify the core customer group central to your brand's success.
- Secondary Audience: Map out supporting audience segments, including occasional users or peripheral stakeholders.
- Potential Users: Recognize other potential audiences who may engage with your brand in new or emerging ways.

Understand your audience's needs, desires, and aspirations. To forge a meaningful connection, consider their perspectives, values, and lived experiences. Start by identifying their immediate needs, preferences, and short- and long-term goals. What problems are they trying to solve? What drives their engagement with your brand? These insights enable you to create tailored solutions and messaging that resonate personally, enhancing relevance and trust.

Address challenges and pain points. Investigate the specific obstacles and frustrations your audience faces. What keeps them up at night? Continuously gather customer feedback to stay updated on your audience's evolving needs and pain points. Study how competitors address similar issues and identify opportunities for differentiation. Brands that effectively alleviate customer challenges build stronger connections and trust.

Understand motivations and drivers. Beyond addressing pain points, delve into what motivates the audience to seek out the brand's solutions. Consider how the product or service integrates into their life or business. Develop messaging that addresses their needs and resonates with their deeper motivations, creating a substantive relationship between a brand and its audience.

Craft tailored messaging. With a clear grasp of the target audience's needs, challenges, and motivations, develop personalized messaging that directly speaks to these factors. Tailored communication makes the audience feel seen and valued, fostering interest and engagement. Always respect data privacy and use insights responsibly and transparently.

Articulate the problem the brand solves. Define the core value the brand offers. Instead of focusing solely on features, emphasize how the product or service improves the customer's life or business.

Continuously evaluate and keep the brand promise. The needs and aspirations of your audience evolve, and so should your brand's benefits or offerings. Regularly review your brand promise and adjust messaging as market conditions change. Ensure your brand remains aligned with its audience, consistently fulfilling or exceeding its commitment.

Brand Promise Statement Example:

For our target audience facing [specific challenge] and seeking [desired solution], our brand is committed to delivering [specific functional or emotional benefit]. This commitment sets us apart and ensures we consistently uphold the promise of _____.

Key actions:

- Identify the core elements that define the brand, including its purpose, mission, values, and the key attributes of its products or services.
- Determine the brand's unique differentiators. (See chapter 2 for more on differentiation.)
- Outline all potential emotional benefits associated with the brand.
- Aim to create a strategic emotional connection that aligns with the brand's essence, benefits, and creative platform.
- Highlight the brand's functional benefits, emphasizing the value these advantages deliver to consumers.
- Emphasize benefits over features, highlighting the value and advantages consumers will gain. For example, people don't choose an electric car for its battery specs—they choose it to save money on fuel and reduce their environmental impact.

Building a Brand Promise

Purchasing a leading brand anywhere in the world should guarantee a consistent experience: quality, service, and reliability. This expectation underscores the critical role of the brand promise, a principle that signifies a brand's unwavering commitment to its customers and stakeholders, thereby shaping its reputation. A brand's promise must align with its actions, necessitating the maintenance of quality, core values, guiding principles, and identity across all interactions with consumers, customers, employees, and stakeholders.

For instance, Dole's website declares their commitment: "Our promise to **People, Planet and Prosperity** is inspired by the spirit of 'Sampo Yoshi,' a Japanese philosophy that views the well-being of society and business as interdependent, ensuring the business is beneficial to all three—the seller, the buyer and the community." Dole also asserts: "We are doubling down on our mission to do business differently and joining forces with strategic partners to work toward the Sustainable Development Goals (SDGs) outlined by the United Nations to better our world today and for future generations to come."[18]

One way Dole fulfills its commitment is through their Piñatex® initiative. The United Nations Industrial Development Organization highlights leather production as one of the most polluting sectors globally, second only to oil. Seeking a sustainable solution, Dole, a major pineapple producer, has partnered with Ananas Anam to transform pineapple leaves, typically discarded after harvest, into Piñatex®. This innovative material serves as a vegan, cruelty-free alternative to leather, aiming to mitigate environmental impact by repurposing waste and reducing methane emissions from decomposing leaves.

Elements of a Remarkable Brand

A company delivers on its brand promise through several key elements: the quality of the product or service, the effectiveness of communications (including branding and advertising), and the audience's perception of its value, personality, and uniqueness. These elements must work together seamlessly, striving to stand out and be remarkable while staying relevant to individual needs and contemporary contexts.

The seven essential factors that support a brand promise are quality, consistency, authenticity, relevance, differentiation, brand communications, and adaptability. Additionally, the audience's perceptions, reactions, and reviews play a crucial role in shaping the brand's reputation and overall standing.

Quality and consistency: Upholding the quality of products, services, processes, and organizational practices is essential for honoring a brand promise and building customer relationships. Key metrics such as reliability, durability, and craftsmanship contribute to how consumers evaluate quality. Consistently meeting or surpassing these standards fosters trust and earns goodwill over time.

Authenticity and **transparency** are crucial to earning consumer trust and credibility. A brand must align its stated values with its actions to build a reputation for reliability and commitment. This alignment creates genuine connections with consumers who value integrity and honesty, reinforcing the brand's dependable and transparent image.

Relevance and differentiation: A brand endures when it aligns with people's lives, work, or beliefs. Without that connection, it risks fading into irrelevance. By aligning with its audience's needs, desires, and values, a brand fosters stronger emotional bonds and drives engagement. Staying relevant also involves adapting to evolving circumstances, ensuring sustained interest and growth.

As discussed in chapter 2, differentiation is key to constructing a distinct and memorable brand identity. It sets a brand apart from competitors, captures attention, and provides a competitive edge. A well-differentiated brand clearly defines what it represents and why it matters, compelling consumers to choose it.

Communications: Branding extends to every touchpoint, encompassing a comprehensive visual identity program and advertising; each consumer interaction helps shape perception and plays a crucial role in driving brand success. Design components such as logos, typography, color palettes, and imagery convey the brand's values and personality. Consistency in these components enhances recognition, distinctiveness, and memorability, reinforcing the brand's identity.

Advertising campaigns should articulate the brand promise, emphasize its unique value proposition, and engage consumers within individual ads and throughout a campaign. Brand campaigns can inform, raise awareness, promote, or entertain, creating memorable experiences and fostering emotional connections with the audience.

Adaptability: The market landscape is continually changing due to technological advancements, shifting consumer preferences, economic fluctuations, and social and political changes. An adaptable brand responds swiftly to these changes, ensuring its offerings and messaging remain relevant and aligned with current demands. This flexibility allows brands to stay attuned to societal values, economic conditions, emerging trends, and new technologies, maintaining audience interest and engagement.

In the realms of sustainability and corporate social responsibility, adaptability is crucial. Brands that evolve their practices to enhance sustainability and social responsibility improve their image and align with consumer expectations.

Adaptability also fuels ongoing research and development, enabling brands to introduce innovative products, services, or experiences that resonate with their audiences and keep the brand promise fresh.

Various factors, including the product, service, or entity itself, brand interactions, branding, advertising, company reputation, social media content, press coverage, and direct experiences, shape audience perception. Effective brand management involves actively shaping and understanding these perceptions to ensure alignment with the brand's intended positioning, benefits, and values. Cultivating positive perceptions should be a primary focus to reinforce the brand's image and credibility.

FOCUS: HONEST EGGS CO.'S "FITCHIX" / VML

Choosing eggs in the supermarket can be confusing due to the labels companies use, such as free-range, open range, barn-laid, and cage-free. Consumers often struggle to identify the most ethical and sustainable options. Honest Eggs Co., an Australian egg farming brand, addresses this challenge with a commitment to complete transparency and high animal welfare standards. Their eggs are produced through regenerative farming practices, allowing chickens significant freedom—less than 30 chickens per hectare, in stark contrast to the government-regulated free-range limit of up to 10,000 chickens per hectare.

Honest Eggs Co. aims to showcase the benefits of regenerative farming for chickens and the environment, encouraging consumers to rethink their egg-purchasing decisions. Partnering with creative agency VML, the brand introduced "FitChix," a step counter designed for chickens. This device tracks the steps and movements of the hens as they wander the farm, helping the company gain insights into their health and nutritional requirements. Honest Eggs then prints the hens' step counts on their eggs to show how freely and healthily they live. They use the devices intermittently, not continuously.[19]

Roger Boyd, General Manager of Honest Eggs Co., emphasized: "Our goal is to revolutionize egg farming. With FitChix, we monitor our chickens' health and demonstrate the advantages of regenerative farming for hens, eggs, land, farmers, and communities. In a complex market, Honest Eggs Co. distinguishes itself through transparency and honesty. We invite consumers to visit our farms and see firsthand our commitment to openness."[20] By inviting people to book tours directly on its website, the brand underscores its commitment to transparency and authenticity.

Interview: Juliana Constantino, Group Creative Director, Dentsu

Prior to joining Dentsu, Juliana Constantino was an executive creative director at Pereira O'Dell and spent over eight years at Meta leading global creative product for the Instagram Creative Lab. Most notably, in 2017, she

Juliana Constantino

led the go-to-market strategy for innovative products at Instagram, tasked with driving engagement and excitement for new offerings, including Reels, Stories, and IGTV. She played a pivotal creative role in connecting brands with creators, generating ideas and content to introduce these new platform tools for the first time. Her work has won over twenty international creative awards at Cannes Lions, One Show, and the CLIO Awards. She was formally recognized as Digital Communication Professional of the Year by the Brazilian Advertising Association and as Professional of the Year for Brand Content at the Share Awards.

You are known for your ability to connect data and creativity. Why is understanding this vital to understanding how people consume information and entertainment?

For many years, advertising was unidirectional and often synonymous with TV spots. Even back then, understanding the audience's mindset was essential. The fragmentation of attention—amplified by social media and second-screen behavior—makes this task more complex. Marketers now need extensive knowledge of various channels and the right ways to craft messages for each one.

Of course, this wealth of data, when used effectively, helps us make well-informed decisions about our campaign strategies. However, there is no Super Bowl every day, which brings three different approaches to consider when working on an idea:

1. The solution for your brief might be something other than a TV spot.
2. What is the best channel for this message? Where is your audience?
3. How is the audience going to react? This is particularly important to anticipate. Regardless of the channel used to spread the message, the audience will always find a way to express their opinions, especially if they don't like it or feel offended.

Please tell us about maker culture and how you employ it.

Maker culture is the heartbeat of innovation and, at the same time, a return to the roots of creative work, where ideas and the creator's craft skills come together. It's all about embracing creativity, resourcefulness, and hands-on exploration to bring ideas to life. From prototyping new designs to crafting unique experiences, we infuse the spirit of making into every aspect of our work. Whether it's through DIY projects, collaborative workshops, or simply encouraging our team to tinker and experiment, we're constantly pushing boundaries and redefining what's possible.

Please explain the interdependence between branding and advertising. How do they complement each other to deliver a cohesive message and build a strong brand identity?

Branding and advertising? They're like peanut butter and jelly—great on their own, but even better together. Branding sets the vibe, personality, and tone of your brand, while advertising shouts it out loud to the world. When they're in sync, it's like music to your audience's ears, creating an irresistible vibe that makes sense. It's the key to building a brand that people love and can't get enough of.

Only a solid brand identity provides the right ammunition for a successful advertising campaign. Conversely, only constant and consistent advertising efforts can keep the brand solid.

You've said you admire "creative work when it taps into an unquestionable human truth and reveals something so obvious that everybody feels terrible for not thinking about it that way before." How do you uncover insights about your target audience? What methodologies or approaches do you employ to understand their motivations and behaviors?

There has never been a time in history when we've had so much access to data. Yet, uncovering those hidden gems of human truth requires diving deep into the psyche of our audience. It's not just about having data for its own sake; it requires viewing this information through very human lenses. It starts by embracing empathy: putting ourselves in their shoes and seeing the world through their eyes. It is very personal.

We don't stop at surface-level insights when we're on a mission to uncover those compelling truths that make people say, "Wow, how did they know?" and that allow the message to be fully understood in the audience's mind. That's why we shouldn't shy away from getting a little unconventional with our research approaches. Maybe it involves spending a day shadowing our audience, immersing ourselves in their world. Or perhaps it's leveraging the power of social media to listen in on their conversations.

But always respect the individual's privacy. It's important to differentiate between using information to understand an audience profile and violating their privacy.

What key considerations or best practices do you recommend for brands aiming for purpose-driven branding and storytelling?

It is important to distinguish between purpose-driven branding and purpose-driven campaigns.

Purpose-driven brands embody a social mission integral to their business, going beyond mere advertising to actively support their cause. This genuine connection to their purpose ensures that when they share their story, it feels authentic and resonates deeply with audiences.

On the other hand, some brands jump on social issues for short-term campaigns without a genuine commitment to the cause. These efforts can come across as insincere or opportunistic, especially when their actions don't align with their promises. In today's hyperaware consumer landscape, these discrepancies are often quickly noticed and can erode trust.

The authenticity and ongoing commitment of purpose-driven branding set it apart from short-lived, opportunistic campaigns. It's not just about joining a conversation; it's about living your brand's values every day.

CHAPTER 8

PLANET-FIRST BRAND BUILDING

W hat compels a cat food company to invest in the preservation of coral reefs?

Sheba, a cat food company, asked: "How can a cat food brand help the planet?" Their answer was the Hope Reef initiative, marking the start of a global effort to restore coral reefs worldwide. Without coral reefs, 25 percent of marine life would lose their habitat.[1] Since the project started, coral growth at Hope Reef has surged from 2 percent to 70 percent, fish populations have risen by 260 percent, and there has been a 64 percent increase in the number of fish species. Sheba is now extending these efforts by collaborating with Kuleana Coral Reefs, an ocean protection organization in Hawaii led by a diverse team of locals, including divers, fishermen, and scientists.[2]

Given the potential for significant adverse impacts, the corporate sector must adopt a planet-first approach. Brands must move beyond transactional relationships and embrace a broader vision that places environmental health at the forefront. To genuinely affect the planet and culture, brands and their parent companies must actively engage in public welfare initiatives, which involve advocating for urgent causes, taking clear stances, and forming partnerships to address issues at local, state, national, and international levels.

Moving beyond transactions means supporting well-funded, long-term projects that drive systemic change for the betterment of the planet. Companies and brands go beyond profitability by raising awareness and positively impacting societal and environmental issues. By harnessing the strategic and creative power of branding, advertising, and design, they can champion meaningful causes, shape culture, and advance collective well-being.

Planet-First Thinking

Brands don't need to get consumers onboard. We already are.

Consumers overwhelmingly respond positively when asked about buying environmentally and ethically sustainable products. Over 60 percent of respondents said they would pay more for products with sustainable packaging. A recent NielsenIQ study also found that 78 percent of US consumers consider a sustainable lifestyle necessary.[3]

Planet-first branding, design, and advertising are vital for fostering a sustainable economy, which means adopting policies and production methods prioritizing sustainability, managing supply chains responsibly, and utilizing eco-friendly materials and processes. By focusing on resource efficiency, renewable energy, and green innovation, companies can create sustainable environments and preserve natural resources.

Creative professionals can help companies adopt green business models that integrate environmental considerations into their operations. These models pursue economic success while reducing environmental harm and actively contributing to our planet's well-being. For a brand to truly embrace sustainability, environmental protection should be central to its values.

Brands like Patagonia and Eileen Fisher exemplify this approach. They focus on environmental stewardship by promoting circular economy models—repairing, recycling, and reselling products to extend their lifecycle. Seventh Generation also follows this path with household and personal care products made from sustainable, biodegradable ingredients. Their mission reflects their commitment: "For over thirty years, we've been on a mission to transform the world into a healthy, sustainable, and equitable place for the next seven generations—and beyond."[4] By adopting such principles, brands can lead the way towards a more sustainable future.

Driving Meaningful Impact with Green Business Models and Branding

Consistent, action-oriented initiatives—not just performative gestures—create real impact. A brand must be both remarkable and eco-conscious to stand out. To be considered meaningful, a brand should excel in six key areas:

1. *Environmental relevance*: Does the brand prioritize environmental sustainability in its practices? Is there a consistent commitment to improving the planet's well-being and preserving ecosystems? Are sustainability principles embedded in its production, materials, manufacturing, and distribution processes?

Actions to take:

- o Obtain and prominently display relevant environmental certifications (e.g., B Corp, Fair Trade, Organic) to build credibility.
- o Invest in technologies and methods that minimize environmental impact.
- o Develop and implement products, processes, and practices that significantly reduce environmental harm while enhancing sustainability.
- o Collaborate with environmental organizations to amplify impact.
- o Communicate the brand's sustainability efforts clearly and transparently to consumers and all stakeholders.

2. *Practical relevance*: Does the brand provide tangible benefits, such as useful products, valuable information, education, or entertainment, all while maintaining a green business model? Do customers consider the brand reliable and integral to fulfilling their needs and aspirations?
   Actions to take:

- Ensure that products or services are eco-friendly, of high quality, and deliver effective solutions.
- Regularly assess and improve sustainability practices to address environmental challenges and stay ahead of regulations.

3. *Emotional relevance*: Does the brand build a strong emotional connection with its audience through a genuine commitment to eco-conscious values? Does its dedication to environmental sustainability foster customer interest and a sense of belonging?
   Actions to take:

- Share authentic stories and testimonials that showcase the brand's impact on the environment and on communities.
- Create platforms or communities where like-minded individuals can connect, share experiences, and support the brand's eco-conscious mission.
- Engage personally with customers to build relationships, showing appreciation for their support and reinforcing shared values.
- Ensure all brand communications consistently reflect a genuine commitment to sustainability and environmental stewardship.
- Launch campaigns that highlight the positive impact of sustainable practices on the planet and future generations and evoke strong emotional responses.
- Acknowledge and reward customers for their sustainable choices, strengthening their emotional connection with the brand.

4. *Personal relevance*: Does the brand align with consumers' interests and spark a sense of desire? Does it reflect and uphold consumers' values of sustainability

and environmental responsibility? Is the audience able to identify with the brand's eco-conscious actions?
Actions to take:

- Conduct in-depth market research to understand the target audience's specific interests and values related to sustainability.
- Tailor marketing messages to resonate with consumers' values and desires, highlighting the brand's commitment to eco-conscious practices.
- Collaborate with influencers, content creators, and brand ambassadors who share values and advocate for sustainability to enhance relevance.
- Highlight how the brand's sustainability and environmental stewardship efforts resonate with its audience's values and lifestyle choices.
- Use experiential design solutions—like eco-friendly challenges, immersive pop-ups, or community events—to create interactive experiences that engage consumers and deepen their connection to the brand's mission.
- Regularly gather consumer feedback on sustainability initiatives and adapt practices to align with evolving values and interests.

5. *Community relevance*: Does the brand demonstrate a genuine and meaningful commitment to sustainability and environmental stewardship? What is the tangible impact of these efforts on the greater good?
Actions to take:

- Develop educational programs and workshops to raise community awareness about sustainability and the brand's initiatives.
- Publish detailed reports on the brand's sustainability efforts and their impact to ensure transparency and build trust.
- Collaborate with local communities, NGOs, and other organizations on sustainability projects that deliver visible, meaningful results.
- Encourage community participation in sustainability initiatives through volunteer opportunities, events, and campaigns.
- Create channels for community feedback on sustainability efforts, enabling the brand to adapt and enhance its approach based on input.

6. *Actionable impact*: Are the brand's sustainability efforts substantial and credible, rather than just performative? Are commitments to environmental responsibility and green practices genuinely upheld?
Actions to take:

- Integrate sustainability into the core value proposition of the brand's offerings, ensuring eco-friendly products are both functional and desirable.

- Maintain transparency in all communications about sustainability efforts to uphold honesty and avoid greenwashing (when companies falsely market their products or services as environmentally friendly or sustainable, exaggerating or fabricating their environmental efforts). See chapter 13 for more on insincere efforts by brands.
- Create resources that provide actionable tips for sustainable living, such as reducing waste, conserving energy, and making eco-friendly choices. Integrate these tips into product packaging, promotional materials, and online content.
- Create channels for customer feedback to continuously refine product utility and sustainability practices.
- Proactively adapt practices to exceed environmental standards, not just meet them.
- Regularly update stakeholders on the brand's sustainability initiatives and progress to build trust and demonstrate commitment.

Global Goals

The United Nations' 2030 Agenda for Sustainable Development presents a unique opportunity for brands to align their strategies with global imperatives. The 17 Sustainable Development Goals (SDGs) serve as a comprehensive framework encouraging all sectors, including businesses, to contribute to a more sustainable and equitable world. This agenda underscores the urgent need for collective action and provides a roadmap for brands to embed sustainability into their core practices to drive meaningful impact.[5]

The 17 Sustainable Development Goals (SDGs) are:

Goal 1: No Poverty · Goal 2: Zero Hunger · Goal 3: Good Health and Well-Being · Goal 4: Quality Education · Goal 5: Gender Equality · Goal 6: Clean Water and Sanitation · Goal 7: Affordable and Clean Energy · Goal 8: Decent Work and Economic Growth · Goal 9: Industry, Innovation and Infrastructure · Goal 10: Reduced Inequalities · Goal 11: Sustainable Cities and Communities · Goal 12: Responsible Consumption and Production · Goal 13: Climate Action · Goal 14: Life Below Water · Goal 15: Life on Land · Goal 16: Peace, Justice and Strong Institutions · Goal 17: Partnerships for the Goals.[6]

Eradicating poverty and addressing deprivations requires a holistic approach that simultaneously improves health and education, reduces inequality, and fosters economic growth, while also tackling climate change and preserving oceans, forests, and their ecosystems.[7]

To combat climate change, businesses can play a pivotal role by committing to reduce their carbon footprints, adopting eco-friendly practices, and investing in renewable energy sources. For instance, companies such as Samsung and United Airlines have set ambitious targets to achieve net-zero emissions by 2050. Moreover, over 400 companies participating in the RE100 initiative are dedicated to sourcing 100 percent of their electricity from renewable sources. "RE100 is the global corporate renewable energy initiative bringing together hundreds of large and ambitious businesses committed to 100 percent renewable electricity."[8]

FOCUS: AMERICAN AIRLINES AND GOOGLE'S "CONTRAILS"

Contrails, short for condensation trails, are the line-shaped clouds you often see trailing behind airplanes. They form when water vapor in the atmosphere condenses around tiny particles of soot and other pollutants released by airplane engines.[9]

Contrails can remain as cirrus clouds for minutes or even hours, depending on the conditions. Typically, the side of the Earth not facing the sun releases heat overnight. At night, natural clouds and airline contrails trap this heat. During the day, these clouds also reflect incoming sunlight and warmth. Nighttime contrails have a greater warming effect than daytime contrails because they only trap heat without reflecting incoming sunlight, leading to a net warming effect. A recent IPCC report (Intergovernmental Panel on Climate Change) indicated that clouds formed by contrails contribute to about 35 percent of aviation's global warming impact.[10]

A notable example of innovative collaboration is Google's partnership with the airline industry to mitigate the effects of contrails, which account for over a third of aviation's climate impact and contribute significantly to global warming. In collaboration with American Airlines and Breakthrough Energy, Google utilized AI and satellite imagery to gather extensive data, including satellite images, weather conditions, and flight paths. They developed contrail forecast maps, enabling pilots to choose routes that avoid creating contrails.[11]

Google Research's Climate AI teams are leveraging their expertise to reduce the climate footprint of its users, partners, and itself. This initiative addresses both a significant climate opportunity and a major AI challenge.[12]

Addressing Global Goals

Here are examples of innovative initiatives that advance various United Nations Sustainable Development Goals in order to foster a more resilient and equitable future.

Global Goal No. 11, "Sustainable Cities and Communities," aims to foster inclusive and accessible urban environments. In response, creative agency Grey and the cement company Sol Cement developed "Sightwalks," a series of numbered cement tiles designed to assist visually impaired individuals. These tiles allow users to identify nearby businesses such as banks, grocery stores, hospitals, bus stops, and pharmacies by feeling the tiles from left to right with their walking sticks. This initiative enhances inclusivity and promotes independent navigation in urban spaces.

The project, refined over nearly two years, involved a collaborative effort between industrial designers, engineers, and leading associations for Peruvians with visual impairments. This teamwork ensured the tactile tile system's effectiveness and usability.

What distinguishes Sightwalks is its open-source approach; Sol Cement has made the tiles a copyright-free invention. This decision encourages cities, organizations, and individuals worldwide to adopt the tiles, enhancing urban accessibility for people who are visually impaired.

Before its successful implementation in Miraflores, extensive collaboration with blind associations across Peru was instrumental in validating and testing the tactile tile system. This project exemplifies how thoughtful design can significantly contribute to societal well-being.[13]

Global Goal No. 14, "Life Below Water," aims to conserve and sustainably use the oceans, seas, and marine resources to support sustainable development. [14]

Clean energy company Fortum partnered with Fishheart, an independent Finnish company, to tackle a longstanding environmental challenge by creating a hydraulic fishway system that allows migratory fish to bypass dams and reach their natural spawning grounds upstream. This innovation not only helps restore biodiversity but also supports local fishing communities. The system uses AI to detect fish and collect real-time data and photos of their migration. To date, more than 13,300 fish from 22 species have been safely transported upstream, and 20 countries have adopted this unique solution.[15]

Driven by its eco-friendly initiative "Change for Good," French footwear and apparel brand TBS draws inspiration from the sea for its collections. In partnership with creative agencies Change and FCB Global, they launched the "RockSeeds" project to protect oceans and address climate change. This initiative focuses on restoring kelp forests, which are crucial for biodiversity and CO_2 absorption. By using seabed stones to cultivate kelp trees in controlled environments before transplanting them to open waters, TBS is making an environmental impact.

TBS has also initiated reforestation programs in Norway, French Polynesia, and the Loire Estuary in France, with progress monitored in real time via underwater cameras. If scaled globally, their RockSeeds method could sequester 47 million tons of CO_2.[16]

Global Goal No. 15, "Life on Land," aims to protect, restore, and promote the sustainable use of terrestrial ecosystems, manage forests sustainably, combat desertification, and halt biodiversity loss.[17]

According to the Food and Agriculture Organization (FAO), Colombia wastes 6.1 million tons of food annually, with 40 percent being fruits and vegetables. In response, Makro Supermarkets, in collaboration with creative agency Grey Colombia, introduced "Life Extending Stickers" to reduce waste and educate consumers on food preservation. These stickers, integrated into the traditional practice of labeling fresh produce, reflect the color changes of fruits and vegetables as they ripen and offer recipe suggestions for each stage. For example, a banana's sticker transitions from green to black, providing ideas for using the fruit in dishes such as ice cream, tempura, and cupcakes.

This campaign has extended the average lifespan of produce purchased by Makro customers and reduced food waste in stores and at home. Generating over 85,000 interactions on social media and reaching an audience of 264 million through organic articles across more than 25 countries, the campaign effectively changed perceptions of ripeness and encouraged consumers to make more sustainable choices.[18]

The Amazon rainforest faces a critical juncture, with rapidly escalating deforestation rates. Surprisingly, local communities drive much of this deforestation, as 95 percent of jobs in these areas are linked to land clearing. The challenge is introducing agroforestry—a sustainable farming method—to these isolated communities, encouraging a shift from harmful practices to ones that support both their livelihoods and the environment.

For the "Seeding Songs" project, FarFarm, a consultancy specializing in supply-chain networks, collaborated with creative agency VML, local farmers, music producers, and artists to create educational songs outlining the three stages of agroforestry. These songs leverage the oral tradition's core elements: rhythm for coordination, harmony for enjoyment, and lyrics for education. By broadcasting these songs via local radio stations and community leaders, FarFarm and VML aimed to integrate innovative agricultural practices into farmers' routines, blending tradition with sustainability.

The initiative has strengthened community resilience and made significant contributions to rainforest preservation. This initiative has regenerated over 120 football fields of land, increased family incomes by 50 percent, and preserved more than 10,000 hectares of forest. Additionally, farmers have sold all cotton produced using agroforestry practices, and 188 new families have adopted these sustainable methods.[19]

Putting the Planet First

Putting the planet first highlights the critical connection among environmental sustainability, business success, and brand reputation. By prioritizing sustainability, businesses protect the environment, strengthen their resilience, enhance their brand value, and secure long-term success in an eco-conscious market.

- **Business sustainability**: As progress on the UN Sustainable Development Goals (SDGs) lags, integrating sustainable practices into business operations has become urgent. This involves responsibly sourcing materials, minimizing waste and emissions, and adopting renewable energy solutions. These actions support environmental conservation while boosting operational resilience and cost-effectiveness over time.
- **Risk mitigation**: Prioritizing environmental responsibility helps companies manage risks by anticipating regulatory changes, reducing dependence on finite resources, and fostering positive stakeholder relationships. Ignoring ecological issues can lead to reputational damage, regulatory challenges, and operational disruptions.
- **Brand integrity and reputation**: Embracing sustainability reflects a commitment to ethical values and responsible management. Consumers are increasingly attracted to brands that demonstrate environmental and social accountability. Companies that actively support environmental causes can enhance their reputation, build consumer trust, and appeal to environmentally conscious customers and stakeholders.

Consumers are looking to businesses and institutions to play a leading role in encouraging them to adopt more environmentally sustainable practices. Specifically:

- 53 percent would appreciate enhanced initiatives to reduce plastic and packaging.
- 46 percent seek more explicit instructions on disposal and recycling.
- 35 percent support stricter regulations requiring companies to improve consumer options.
- 31 percent expect increased government intervention to make low-emission transportation modes more accessible and affordable.[20]

Research by industry consultancy Deloitte UK shows that over half of consumers believe a company's commitment to climate change and sustainability impacts their trust. Specifically, 34 percent of consumers said their trust would increase if an independent third party recognized brands as ethical or sustainable providers. Additionally, 32 percent would have greater confidence in brands whose supply chains are transparent, accountable, and socially and environmentally responsible. Furthermore, 27 percent of consumers would trust brands more if they pursued net-zero goals through direct carbon emission reductions rather than relying solely on carbon offsetting.[21]

Marketers know that engaging their audiences is key, but making a real impact also requires a commitment to protecting the planet. Planet-first thinking is essential for advancing a sustainable economy. This approach weaves environmental responsibility into every aspect of business, from product development and operations to ecosystem stewardship and policy advocacy. It calls for a collective shift toward planet-first business models, emphasizing environmental stewardship and adaptability to evolving challenges and opportunities. Embracing this mindset ensures that our actions benefit people, the planet, and all living beings, driving meaningful, lasting impact.

Interview: Pancho González, Co-Founder and Chief Creative Officer, Inbrax, Santiago, Chile

Pancho González studied advertising at the Universidad de Santiago in Chile and earned his MBA from the Berlin School of Creative Leadership at Steinbeis University, Germany. Currently, he is the chief creative officer at Inbrax Chile, board member and VP at IAB Chile, marketing circle member at Icare, and board member of Cámara de Empresas Creativas (Chilean Chamber of Creative Businesses).

He has served as a juror at: Cannes (2007–2021), the Clio Awards, D&AD, One Show, the New York Festivals, the Art Directors Club, LIAA, Dubai Lynx, Caples, the Global Best of the Best Effie, the Webby Awards, Ad Stars [now MAD Stars], the PIAF Awards, the Grand Jury at Cresta, FIAP, FICE, the Effie Awards, Mobius, the Echo Awards, the Golden Awards of Montreux, the Cristal Festival, AdForum, El Ojo de Iberoamérica, and ACHAP (Chile), among many others. He has also chaired the juries of the AME Awards, *The Drum*, and WINA. He has been a speaker in Argentina, Brazil, Chile, Costa Rica, Czechia, Germany, Guatemala, Japan, Mexico, Peru, Russia, South Korea, Sri Lanka, and the United States.

González has also received more than 250 national and international awards, including: Cannes, ADC, LIA, One Show, New York Festivals, *Comm Arts*,

FIAP, Ojo de Iberoamérica, Effie, Grand Effie, Webby Awards, Echo Latam, Grand Prix FICE, *The Drum*, Caples Awards, AME Awards, Young Guns, Epica Awards, Cristal Festival, *Creativity*, Cresta Awards, *Graphis*, PHNX, AdForum, Eagle, AdStar, IAB Mixx Awards, WINA Awards, ACHAP, Archive, The Indie Summit Awards, Creativepool, Fepi, Eagle Awards, Summit Creative Awards (Best of Show), A'Design Awards, and Never Zapping Festival.

He was ranked among the Top 25 Worldwide CCOs and as one of the Top 100 Worldwide Influencers by Creativepool (London) in 2017, 2018, 2021, 2022, and 2024. He was also named Top Creative Director, Top 10 ECD, and Top 10 Creative Agency at Bestadsontv.com in 2017 and 2021. Additionally, he was nominated for MKTG BEST as Chief Creative Director in Chile in 2018, 2021, 2022, 2023, and 2024. He was named Chile's Top Copywriter of the Decade and his agency was ranked Top 2 Agency of the Decade, both by *Lüerzer's Archive*. His agency also won Agency of the Year at the WINA Festival in 2020, 2021, and 2022. In 2020, 2023, and 2024, he led the Digital Agency of the Year and Indie Agency of the Year at ranking TopFICE. He was ranked in the Top 10 Crema Ranking by Adlatina in both 2014 and 2020, and was included in the 40 Over Forty list in 2020.

González has served as a mentor and coach: he has mentored at Acción Emprendedora and Female Foundry, as well as at Red de Mentores, and coached at LIASON (2021, 2022) and D&AD (2021, 2022). He is an MBA professor at both Miami Ad School and Universidad de Santiago de Chile. Additionally, he has presented at the IAB Chile Seminar on "New Normal Digital" and at CRECHI (the Chilean Congress for Creativity). He is the host of the podcast #IABDigitalTalks.

Throughout his career he has worked for local and global brands and is happily married and partnered with Carolina, with whom he has a son named Caetano.

How do you leverage advertising or branding to drive positive change?

To leverage advertising and branding for positive change, we support our brands to authentically align with meaningful causes and values, inspiring audiences to take action. We help our brands to communicate their commitment to social responsibility, sustainability, or any other social issue; brands not only foster trust but also encourage consumers to make informed, responsible choices. Positive storytelling, transparency, and engagement can empower brands to become catalysts for positive change, amplifying their impact and contributing to a more socially conscious and sustainable world. To do this, we use Conscious Marketing strategies, to which I will refer later.

You've chaired and served on many awards juries and your work has garnered innumerable awards. What criteria do you use when creating and judging work?

When creating and judging work in advertising, key criteria typically include creativity, effectiveness, relevance, impact, storytelling, and originality. Creative campaigns should stand out, capture attention, and engage the audience while effectively conveying the intended message. Relevance to the target audience and the context is crucial, as is the measurable impact of the campaign. Effective storytelling and originality can elevate an advertisement, making it memorable and resonant. These criteria help ensure that advertising not only captures attention but also achieves its intended goals and leaves a lasting impression. But the criterion that I like most is purpose—beyond originality and execution, if there is no positive impact, there is nothing; the work won't move forward.

How do you foster a sense of shared purpose between a brand and the audience?

To foster a sense of shared purpose between a brand and its audience, it's essential to authentically communicate and demonstrate the brand's values and purpose. Consistent messaging, transparent actions, and meaningful engagement help build trust and alignment with the audience's beliefs and aspirations. Brands can actively involve their audience in shaping the brand's purpose, co-creating content, and supporting causes that resonate with both parties. This collaborative approach deepens the connection, making the audience feel like active participants in the brand's journey and shared purpose. To do this, we have to consider active social listening to keep our purpose constantly aligned with the audience.

How do you drive a brand's role in culture? And how do you make sure it's responsible and responsive?

Driving a brand's role in culture involves authentically connecting with the values, interests, and aspirations of its target audience. This can be achieved through relevant and impactful content, engaging in meaningful conversations, and supporting causes that align with the brand's purpose. To ensure responsibility and responsiveness, brands must maintain a commitment to ethical practices, diversity, and inclusivity. They should actively listen to audience feedback, adapt to cultural shifts, and be prepared to address any concerns or controversies with transparency and integrity. A brand's role in culture should be a dynamic and evolving relationship, grounded in respect and genuine engagement. In a nutshell, brands need to be part of the culture if they want to be part of the conversation; this forces a strategy where brands have to be involved in all the cultural issues related to the brand's purpose, and not show up simply because they have to be aware.

When we shape brand marketing and branding according to the cultural context of the target audience, how can we ensure we're being respectful and mindful of people's cultures and communities (and not appropriating)?

Respecting and being mindful of people's cultures and communities when shaping brand marketing and branding in a specific cultural context requires careful consideration and sensitivity. It's crucial to conduct in-depth research to understand the cultural nuances, values, symbols, and traditions of the target audience. Engaging with members of the culture and seeking their input and feedback can provide valuable insights. Avoiding stereotypes, caricatures, or the commodification of cultural elements is essential. When incorporating cultural elements, do so with authenticity, transparency, and respect for the culture's significance. Be open to criticism, listen to concerns, and be willing to adjust your approach if it is perceived as appropriative or disrespectful. Ultimately, the key is to approach cultural context with humility and a genuine desire to engage respectfully, ensuring that your branding efforts enhance cultural understanding rather than perpetuating harm or offense.

How do you approach cross-cultural branding or advertising?

Approaching cross-cultural branding or advertising necessitates a nuanced and culturally sensitive strategy. I love conducting thorough research to understand the target cultures, including their values, norms, preferences, and taboos. I usually do ethnographies to track this cultural approach. Then we have to craft the messaging, imagery, and tone to resonate with each specific culture while avoiding stereotypes or cultural appropriation. Collaborating with local experts or teams who have a deep understanding of the target culture to ensure authenticity could be one tactic. Be flexible and open to adapting your campaigns based on cultural feedback and have an always-on dialogue with your diverse audience to foster inclusivity and relevance. Cross-cultural branding should reflect a genuine commitment to respecting and appreciating the diversity of your global audience while promoting the core values of your brand.

Some brands have become cultural conversation innovators. Should marketers and designers rethink their focus and strategies to establish cultural relevance?

Absolutely, in today's dynamic and diverse cultural landscape, creatives must continually rethink their focus and strategies to establish cultural relevance. Brands need to be part of the conversation. Being a cultural conversation innovator means actively engaging with evolving societal values and trends. This requires staying updated about cultural shifts, listening to audience feedback, and being open to adaptation all the time. Brands that foster inclusivity, embrace diversity, and address pressing cultural issues are better positioned to resonate with their audience and stay relevant. By placing a premium on authenticity, empathy, and social responsibility, creatives can create content and campaigns that not only capture attention but also contribute positively to the cultural conversation and improve people's lives as well.

Social media has transformed how culture works. What should creative professionals, businesspeople, and clients understand about how brands create cultural impact on social media?

Social media revolutionized cultural impact, and it's essential for brand strategists, creative professionals, businesspeople, and clients to understand what's going on out there. First, authenticity and transparency are paramount: audiences can quickly detect insincerity. Second, engagement and dialogue are vital: brands must actively listen and respond to their audience to build meaningful connections. Third, relevance is dynamic: brands need to stay agile and adapt to shifting trends and conversations. Finally, social responsibility is crucial: brands should use their influence to promote positive change and address societal issues, aligning their values with those of their audience for a more significant cultural impact. Actually, brands can create cultural movements (as we saw with Nike's campaign featuring Colin Kaepernick).

What are the best-practice considerations for purpose-driven branding and storytelling?

In the realm of purpose-driven branding and storytelling, authenticity reigns supreme. It is imperative for brands to wholeheartedly embrace values that align with their chosen cause and maintain complete transparency about their endeavors. The bedrock of trust is constructed upon a foundation of consistent messaging and actions, while the application of captivating storytelling techniques serves as a potent means to effectively communicate the brand's dedication. Furthermore, fostering engagement with the audience, inviting them to be part of the journey, and demonstrating tangible impact are pivotal elements in crafting a purpose-driven narrative that is both profound and motivational.

What role does courage play in brand storytelling, and what would you say to encourage bravery from other marketers or brands?

Courage within brand storytelling embodies a readiness to venture into the unknown, challenge established norms and confront pressing societal concerns. It entails unwaveringly upholding your brand's principles, even when met with controversy, and fearlessly striving to effect tangible change. I urge marketers and brands to acknowledge that authenticity and audacity often forge deeper bonds with their audience. Embrace the potency of your brand's distinctive perspective, use storytelling as a catalyst for positive transformation, and bear in mind that bold storytelling not only distinguishes you but also has the potential to ignite and mobilize your audience in support of your mission. In today's socially conscious landscape, taking a principled stance and narrating impactful stories with conviction can wield significant influence for the greater good.

As consumers expect more from the brands they engage with, how is Inbrax able to connect with them so effectively?

To effectively connect with today's consumers, advertising agencies must undergo a transformation to align with shifting expectations and behaviors. At Inbrax, our first priority is gaining a deep understanding of the target audience, harnessing data and insights to craft highly tailored and personalized strategies. Next, authenticity is at the core. To achieve it, we track the values of our audience and craft purpose-driven storytelling. Our third priority is to stay at the forefront of emerging trends and technologies, such as social media, AR, content creators, and interactive content, to meet consumers on their preferred platforms. Building trust through transparency, ethical practices, and open two-way communication is vital. At Inbrax, we adapted the 3G model from Robin Landa, which we use to establish positive impact campaigns so that we can genuinely bridge the gap between brands and society and craft compelling and relatable narratives that resonate with the audience's aspirations and values.

Why is the Corporate Social Responsibility (CSR) component important to Inbrax and the brands you collaborate with?

CSR has evolved beyond a mere public relations tactic; it has become a foundational element of contemporary business for Inbrax and the brands we collaborate with. CSR initiatives enable brands to showcase their dedication to positive social and environmental impacts, aligning seamlessly with the values of a progressively conscientious consumer base. Actually, it is closely linked to Inbrax's purpose: making a better world with ideas. The incorporation of CSR into campaigns offers a compelling narrative and an opportunity to forge profound connections with audiences. Additionally, it sets brands apart from their competitors, cultivates trust and loyalty, and aids in mitigating risks associated with societal and environmental concerns. In essence, CSR represents a mutually beneficial endeavor, enhancing both a brand's reputation and society at large. Advertising agencies play an indispensable role in conveying and amplifying these commendable efforts.

As technology has radically changed content consumption and creation, what are the constants of great brand storytelling that you feel have remained unchanged?

Despite technology revolutionizing content consumption and creation, the fundamental elements of effective brand storytelling have remained remarkably consistent. Authenticity remains the linchpin: developing a compelling narrative firmly rooted in a brand's true values and clear mission that resonates powerfully across different mediums.

Forging emotional connections continues to be vital; stories that evoke strong emotions leave enduring imprints. Staying relevant to audience needs, desires, and values remains an enduring principle. Above all, storytelling's enduring capacity to inspire, educate, entertain, or empower persists; brands that provide value through their narratives continue to captivate and engage audiences in a continually evolving digital landscape. While technology may change how stories are delivered, the foundational principles of storytelling endure.

Does Inbrax have a philosophy about how consumer brand affinity is achieved through authenticity?

We believe in Conscious Marketing, a methodology that uses four steps to trace the positive impact of a strategy. This philosophy involves the following steps: 1) Identifying a social issue that is closely aligned with the core business; 2) understanding that social issue in depth; 3) sharing the values learned from that social issue throughout the entire organization; and 4) demonstrating social leadership to sustain the strategy in the long term, including setting the budget and ensuring its alignment with the business strategy.

This social focus led Inbrax to launch a spin-off called Belong Lab, the first Chilean communication lab dedicated to diversity, equity, and inclusion (DEI) strategies both within organizations and in the broader community. Stay tuned!

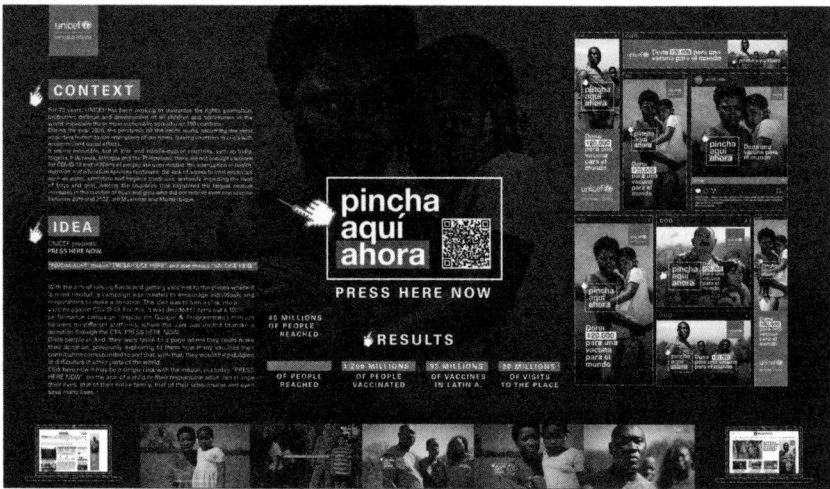

8.1 Campaign: "Press Here Now" (Pincha Aquí Ahora). Client: Unicef Chile; Creative Agency: Inbrax Chile; Chief Creative Officer: Pancho González; Creative Director: Cristián Chávez; Art Director: Carlos Fuentes, Cristián Chávez; Copywriter: Matías Maldonado, Pancho González; Planning Director: Ricardo Álvarez; Account Executive: Elizabeth Gallardo; Post Producer: Sebastián Vega; CEO: Carolina Pinheiro; Chief Marketing Officer: Carlos Heredia; Production Company: La Motoneta; Sound Production: Miranda & Tobar; Partner Agency: Adrenaline Advertising, South Africa

For seventy-five years, UNICEF has been working to guarantee the rights, promotion, protection, defense, and development of all children and adolescents in the world, especially those most vulnerable, spread over 190 countries.

It seems incredible, but in low- and middle-income countries, such as India, Nigeria, Indonesia, Ethiopia, and the Philippines, there are not enough vaccines for COVID-19 and millions of people are unprotected; the interruption in health, nutrition and education services continues; the lack of access to vital resources such as water, sanitation and hygiene continues, seriously impacting the lives of boys and girls. Among the countries that registered the largest relative increases in the number of boys and girls who did not receive even one vaccine between 2019 and 2022 are Myanmar and Mozambique.

With the aim of raising funds and getting vaccines to the places where it is most needed, a campaign was created to encourage individuals and corporations to make a donation. The idea was to turn a click into a vaccine against COVID-19. For this, it was decided to carry out a 100 percent performance campaign (display on Google & Programmatic) through banners on different platforms, where the user was invited to make a donation through the CTA: PRESS HERE NOW. Once people clicked, they were taken to a page where they could make their donation, previously explaining to them how many vaccines their contribution corresponded to, and with that, they would help children in difficulties in other parts of the world.

"Click here now" once meant a simple mouse click, but today, "PRESS HERE NOW," on the arm of a child or their guardian, can change their lives, that of their entire family, that of their schoolmates, and even save many lives.

Results: 40 million people reached; 1.2 billion people vaccinated; 93 million vaccines in Latin America; 20 million visits

Pancho González email correspondence with the author, October 18, 2023.

CHAPTER 9

AUDIENCE-FOCUSED BRAND BUILDING

As a teenager, my maternal grandmother immigrated to the United States and learned English. Although she became fairly fluent, like many immigrants, she faced challenges as an adult when navigating crucial conversations with native speakers, communicating with healthcare providers, and completing paperwork. As a first-generation North American in her early teens, my mother often served as my grandparents' translator, even attending "parent"-teacher conferences for her younger brother. My mother's experience is familiar to many immigrant families.

Produced by creative agency McCann Worldgroup, *Translators* is a documentary film in a slice-of-life style that delves into the lives of three bilingual children from immigrant families. These children serve as the primary English speakers in their predominantly non-English speaking households, helping their families navigate daily life through language. U.S. Bank, in collaboration with filmmaker Rudy Valdez, brings forth the narrative of these young interpreters and addresses a significant cultural and generational issue within Hispanic/Latinx communities. The film resonates with U.S. Bank's mission to empower individuals and ensure accessible banking for all.[1]

When U.S. Bank introduced Asistente Inteligente, the first Spanish-language virtual assistant offered by a US financial institution, it addressed the significant language barrier faced by Hispanic/Latinx Americans. This service also underscored a common solution within many families: relying on bilingual children to translate essential daily communications, including banking documents. Remarkably, while only 23 percent of first-generation immigrants from

Spanish-speaking countries are proficient in English, this proficiency reaches a highly significant 94 percent among their grandchildren—a lesser-known aspect of life for Hispanic/Latinx Americans, particularly outside their community.[2] That insight revealed a chance to tell this untold story through the documentary *Translators*.

Insights Into the Audience and Brand

Whether launching a new venture or promoting an established one, an essential step for building a resonant brand is connecting with the audience meaningfully. A thorough understanding of the individuals you aim to influence or inform, often rooted in consumer insights, forms the basis of this connection.

A consumer insight reveals the target audience's unmet needs, beliefs, or collective mindset, uncovering their thoughts, emotions, and previously unrecognized behaviors. It should fundamentally shift how creative and marketing teams view the audience's interaction with the brand and category, fueling idea generation, branding strategies, and storytelling. Unlike surface-level observations (e.g., general preferences), a true insight reaches beyond the obvious, highlighting a hidden frustration, a cultural shift, an emotional need, or an unspoken aspiration.

Similarly, insights about a product, service, or entity can highlight unique benefits, market positioning, competitor strategies, industry norms, or underlying consumer concerns, guiding more effective and impactful branding and advertising efforts.

Despite the rise in body positivity, there has been a notable resurgence in the focus on weight loss. Web searches for "weight loss exercises" and "quick weight loss" have surged, accompanied by a significant increase in media content about methods for "fat burning" and "quick weight loss." In contrast, discussions about the importance of exercise for emotional health remain much less common.[3] In response, ASICS and creative agency Golin launched the "15 Minute Weight Loss" campaign, featuring videos that initially appear as typical weight loss content but reveal that just fifteen minutes of exercise can alleviate mental stress. Partnering with fitness and body positivity influencers, ASICS aims to shift the focus from physical weight loss to the mental benefits of exercise.[4] Professor Brendon Stubbs of King's College London led a global study showing that just fifteen minutes and nine seconds of physical activity is sufficient to begin experiencing positive mental benefits—an insight that informed the campaign.[5]

Strategically creative thinkers use insights to achieve meaningful outcomes, rather than pursuing creativity for its own sake. For example, Golin discovered that people often avoid hearing tests for up to ten years due to the fear of hearing loss. They transformed one of the most famously misheard songs into a mass hearing test to initiate a new, less intimidating dialogue about hearing health. By re-recording Rick Astley's "Never Gonna Give You Up" with intentionally mis-heard lyrics, they orchestrated a nationwide "Rick-Roll." This unique campaign to promote Specsavers' audiology services, known as "The Misheard Version," sparked widespread conversation about hearing loss. The song garnered twenty million plays in just eight hours, and the story received coverage in 95 percent of the UK's major media outlets. As a result, Specsavers saw hearing test bookings soar by a record-breaking 1,220 percent above their target.[6]

Uncovering consumer insights requires research and keen observation. "Tap into something that's really hot in culture . . . It needs to represent [the] values of the brand, a strategy and link to a product benefit," advises Aaron Stark-man, Rethink's global chief creative officer.[7] But a brand or entity—and its creative agency—need the right cultural conditions to be part of a community: They need to understand and respect the target audience's cultural context to build genuine relationships and be accepted as part of the community. Steadfast respect is critical.

Insights also can be discovered within cultural trends. For instance, *Xinzhongshi*, or "New Chinese Style," has permeated the lives of mainland Chinese consumers, emphasizing the culture, presentation, and branding of products that reflect traditional Chinese heritage. This trend manifests in var-ious forms, such as bubble tea served in bamboo cups or home decor with traditional Chinese elements. The excitement surrounding New Chinese Style stems from a combination of modern China's history of moving away from tra-ditional customs and the recent rise of the *Guochao* trend, which celebrates and revitalizes Chinese cultural identity. Chinese fast-food brand Tastien has capi-talized on *Guochao*, as have other fast-food chains such as Mr. Rice, by offering dishes that closely resemble traditional Chinese foods.[8] Social media has played a significant role in boosting the popularity of Zhang Ying's new Chinese-style clothing online with more customers discovering her brand through Douyin (the most popular short-video app in China).[9]

Assessing whether a cultural trend or event presents a creative engagement opportunity for a brand or poses a real reputational risk is paramount. The goal is to transform potential challenges into meaningful engagement. However, any cultural insight or trend must align with the brand's purpose and actions to maintain authenticity. Additionally, the brand must establish credible authority within its chosen purpose space.

Insights often arise at the crossroads of various factors: culture, technology, demographics, trends, economic conditions, social movements, and data. For instance, learning that 94 percent of grandchildren of Spanish-speaking indi-viduals are fluent in English led to the creation of U.S. Bank's *Translators* doc-umentary. The key questions are: What can we create to add value to people's lives? How will their lives change after they've engaged with the brand?

On-site interventions can provide valuable insights, such as observing consumer behavior in supermarkets or conducting "social listening" on social media to gauge sentiments. Analyzing discussions about competitors also helps illuminate consumer preferences and perceptions. "Recycle Me" features images of the Coca-Cola logo on crushed cans, visually representing the recycling process. To achieve unique distortions of the iconic logo, they employed various techniques, including mechanical presses and vacuums, to replicate the different ways people crush their cans before recycling.[10] The insight behind Coca-Cola's "Recycle Me" campaign stemmed from a common behavior: people often crush their cans before recycling them. By pairing striking visuals with the "Recycle Me" call to action, the campaign emphasizes the importance of recycling and encourages consumers to recycle their Coke cans immediately after drinking. Developed by Ogilvy, New York, and Open X, WPP's dedicated creative agency for Coca-Cola, "Recycle Me" underscores the brand's sustainability commitments. Coca-Cola has pledged that by 2030 it will be using all-recyclable packaging and will also recycle a bottle or can for each one sold.

The company Contagious interviewed Islam ElDessouky, Coca-Cola's Global Vice President of Creative Strategy and Content, to explore the insight behind the campaign:

> From a regulation perspective, recycling plants prefer it if you do not crush the can, they want to collect all the cans as an authority and [then] crush [the cans] themselves . . . But we decided that even still, the symbolism opportunity was huge because it's very human and intuitive to you to crush the can. We're showing that Coca-Cola is dead serious about recycling because we're crushing it on our real estate too—our logo. Then when we go into print and OOH [Out-of-Home advertising], that's money we're spending to convey that message, so people say, "Oh, they're really serious about this."[11]

FOCUS: "THE INFLATION COOKBOOK" / DENTSU CREATIVE CANADA

Skip (formerly SkipTheDishes), a Canadian online food delivery service, tackled the impact of inflation on food costs by launching The Inflation Cookbook, an AI-powered grocery shopping tool. This innovative tool uses real-time pricing data for over 400 ingredients across 100 major retailers to forecast weekly price drops. It then suggests seven nutritious recipes

(*continued on next page*)

(continued from previous page)

based on the most affordable items, helping Canadians find economical and wholesome ingredients for home-cooked meals.

Alongside The Inflation Cookbook, Skip introduced a charitable initiative, pledging to donate all excess food from its twenty-three Skip Express Lane fulfillment centers to local food banks nationwide. They also committed $100,000 to Food Banks Canada, providing 200,000 meals to those facing food insecurity. This effort is part of their ongoing monthly food donations throughout the year. Developed in collaboration with Dentsu Creative Canada, the campaign encourages individuals to explore The Inflation Cookbook via its dedicated website.

Steve Puchala, former Interim CEO of Skip, commented on the campaign, stating:

> As a proud Canadian company, we understand the important role we play in creating positive change for our industry, our communities, and our environment. And, in the face of rising food costs in Canada, Skip is committed to continuing to fight food insecurity by expanding our partnership with Food Banks Canada to help provide hunger relief from coast-to-coast. We're also proud to provide the Inflation Cookbook as a meal-planning tool that all Canadians can use to source affordable groceries for less.[12]

Ways to Find Insights

Creative marketers can utilize the following methods to better understand their target audiences and craft more effective brand strategies and marketing campaigns.

Experimentation and observation on social media: Strategic experimentation on social media can reveal what truly resonates with the target audience. While successful for some brands, this approach requires careful monitoring by skilled and agile teams to avoid pitfalls, clichés, or potentially offensive content. The goal is to identify the content that garners the most attention, providing valuable data to inform future initiatives.

Social media platforms are ideal for this strategy. By consistently creating, testing, and managing engaging content designed to stand out in users' feeds, marketers can gain immediate insights. Early successes should be identified and built upon. Short-lived and cost-effective, ephemeral content allows for rapid content creation and deployment, offering continuous learning opportunities.

This type of content facilitates real-time, consistent brand engagement, similar to interactions with social media influencers, creators, or podcasters. Unlike traditional TV commercials or YouTube videos, ephemeral content blends seamlessly into users' online experiences, without feeling overly intrusive.

Content categorization: Consider content in two main categories: ephemeral marketing content and big-budget brand-building projects. Most content is ephemeral—brief and not frequently shared; creative agencies design certain pieces for instant engagement, including social media posts, reels, and novelty items like memes. In contrast, larger-scale projects aim to captivate audiences over extended periods—such as when the internet went wild for McDonald's and creative agency Wieden+Kennedy's "Grimace's Birthday"; Burger King's now-classic "Subservient Chicken" campaign by creative agency Crispin Porter + Bogusky, which went viral; or Red Bull's extreme sports ventures distributed online.

Preparedness: Marketers must be at the ready to manage both the controllable and the unforeseen, ensuring they can respond effectively to any situation that arises. Such agility safeguards the brand and enables confident leadership during uncertain moments, including consumer backlash and product recalls.

Entertain rather than market: Instead of relying solely on traditional marketing, prioritize entertainment. If your audience enjoys humor, irreverence, or expects to be entertained, delivering authentic, original content—whether developed in-house, by creative agencies, or through collaborations with creators and partners—can effectively engage them and grow a brand's social media following. By embracing the principles of engaging entertainment, a brand can capture and hold its audience's attention, fostering sustained engagement and stronger connection. The ultimate goal is to deliver memorable experiences that resonate and cultivate lasting brand affinity.

> Humor is all about connection. Humor cuts through the noise. We live in a state of constant assault on our senses, but if something is funny, you'll seek it out. It doesn't mean we shy away from tough stuff—humor is one of the best ways to deal with rough things going on in the world.
>
> —Kenan Thompson, actor, producer, comedian, and cast member of *Saturday Night Live*, speaking at Cannes Lions 2024[13]

The era of relying solely on demographic-based audience targeting has passed. Today, successful campaigns demonstrate precision by directly addressing audiences' passions, fears, and concerns on social media. Kantar reports that 67 percent of successful ad campaigns exhibit this surgical precision in reaching the ideal audience on platforms such as YouTube.[14]

Adele Reeves, global development lead at Makers, cautions: "Audiences are media-savvy and can discern between when they're being entertained and when they are being sold to. Brands' growing interest in entertainment projects requires producing content that feels natural and not overly commercial."[15]

"If a brand uses humor 80 percent of people are more likely to buy from the brand again; 80 percent are more likely to recommend the brand to family and friends; 72 percent of people are more likely to choose the brand over the competition; and 63 percent of people will spend more with the brand." Moreover, 41 percent would walk away from a brand if it didn't make them smile or laugh regularly.[16]

Examples of entertaining unique content include:

- Sydney Opera House's "Play it Safe": Created by The Monkeys and Accenture Song Sydney, "Play it Safe" is a mini-musical featuring Australian comedian, musician, and songwriter Tim Minchin. Crafted to celebrate the 50th anniversary of the Sydney Opera House, this piece is a witty and daring tribute to taking risks and honoring creativity.[17]
- *Skittles Commercial: The Broadway Musical*: Instead of opting for a traditional Super Bowl commercial, Skittles produced a Broadway-style musical performed live during the game, starring Broadway veteran and TV actor Michael C. Hall. Skittles donated the proceeds from the ticket sales to Broadway Cares/Equity Fights AIDS.
- Metro Trains Melbourne's "Dumb Ways to Die": This animated musical campaign humorously highlighted various life-threatening scenarios to deliver a powerful public safety message. The campaign went viral on YouTube, becoming one of the most widely shared social media campaigns globally at the time. Its success led to the creation of "Dumb Ways to Die 2: The Games," which has since achieved over 130 million downloads and two billion unique plays worldwide.[18]
- e.l.f. Cosmetics Challenge on TikTok: Launched by creative agency Movers+Shakers, this campaign embodied the brand's ethos—"e.l.f. is for every eye, lip, and face." With a custom music track inspired by current hits, the challenge quickly became TikTok's fastest-growing campaign, with nearly five million user-generated videos and seven billion views. The campaign attracted numerous unsponsored celebrity participants, including Ellen DeGeneres, Reese Witherspoon, Kevin Hart, and Jessica Alba. Beyond TikTok, Movers+Shakers fueled the campaign's virality by distributing the track to DJs globally, leading to its rise on Spotify's viral charts. The success garnered the attention of Republic Records, resulting in a music video release on Vevo and YouTube.[19]

Utility over marketing: Consumers prioritize brands that offer more than just products or services, seeking additional value that benefits them, their families, and their communities. Brands that go beyond their core offerings to provide tangible benefits build goodwill and strengthen their reputation.

Power outages can severely impact small businesses. Brands that step in to help during such events not only improve their brand image but also foster community support. A notable example is Dat Bike, a Vietnamese electric motorcycle manufacturer.

During Vietnam's Tết festival, a critical trading period, Dat Bike addressed power outage issues by creatively using their e-bikes as emergency power generators for small businesses in Ho Chi Minh City. During blackouts, they provided free charging sessions to local rice plate shops and grocery stores. Dat Bike owners, equipped with the brand's chargers, delivered a practical solution to a pressing problem by offering one to three hours of charging whenever power was lost. This initiative highlights Dat Bike's commitment to corporate social responsibility and showcases its advanced charging and battery technology. By involving local Dat Bike owners in supporting their communities, the brand reinforced a spirit of mutual aid and underscored its dedication to innovation and social impact.[20]

> "Playing it safe isn't really a strategy for creative. . . . Every once in a while, you will have a screwup. But I'd rather have one of those a year . . . than everything at a just-playing-it-safe level."
> —David Mogensen, VP of Marketing, Uber[21]

Challenge category conventions: To gain meaningful insights into a category, it's essential to examine and challenge its established norms. Conventional approaches often fail to capture attention, so breaking away from these norms and aligning with audience interests is vital for engagement. Extraordinary strategies, rather than ordinary ones, are what truly capture attention.

In industries such as pharmaceuticals and health, where brands often look and behave similarly, there's an opportunity for disruption. By breaking away from conventional practices and aligning with the brand's authentic identity and audience values, you can reshape the category. "Challenger" brands typically lead disruptions that focus on human-centric innovation and leverage digital technologies to explore new avenues for product distribution and service enhancement.[22]

The most significant risk is playing it safe. Research by System 1, eatbigfish, and Peter Field reveals that "dull" ads—those failing to evoke emotional responses—require significantly higher spending to achieve the same market share growth as more engaging advertisements. For instance, US brands would need to spend an additional $228 billion, and UK brands an extra 10 million pounds. Notably, System 1 found that 50 percent of UK ads performed worse than a video of a cow chewing grass.[23]

Vaseline's partnership with Ogilvy Singapore led to the development of Transition Body Lotion, the first clinically proven skincare product for transgender women. Recognizing the unique skin challenges during the transitioning process, Vaseline conducted two years of research to create a solution tailored to this demographic in Thailand, which has a significant transgender population.

Philips also challenged industry norms with its "Better Than New Refurb Editions" initiative in Germany, addressing the high return rates of online sales and the environmental impact of returned electrical products. By offering refurbished products with extended warranties, Philips raised awareness through an Earth Day campaign, a pop-up store, and augmented reality activations. The campaign resulted in the sale of 52,000 refurbished products, preventing 185 tons of e-waste and avoiding approximately 277 tons of CO_2 emissions.[24]

Monitor social media: Regularly tracking social media platforms allows you to observe discussions, mentions, and emerging trends, providing insight into public sentiment and evolving topics.

An effective customer insights system operates as a self-reinforcing cycle. As customers grow to trust and value your brand, they become more willing to share their feedback and engage with you. This engagement offers valuable insights into their needs and preferences. When you act on these insights, enhancing experiences, refining products, and improving services, you strengthen trust and deepen engagement. Over time, this builds a continuous loop of momentum known as the flywheel effect, where each interaction fuels the next, driving sustained growth.[25]

Using Conventional Market Research to Uncover Insights

Focus groups: Engaging a diverse group from your target demographic can yield qualitative insights. Conducting these sessions before finalizing strategies, along with creating campaigns to extract valuable feedback, ensures that insights will enhance rather than compromise creative efforts. *Caveat:* Focus groups may sometimes favor conventional thinking and are not always the best tool for evaluating bold, fresh ideas. It's best practice to avoid relying on focus groups when testing standout concepts as their input can dilute bold ideas.

Surveys and interviews: Surveys enable the collection of quantitative data on consumer preferences, behaviors, psychographics, and demographics. Personalized interviews delve deeper into individual attitudes and motivations. Minimizing survey bias and involving expert oversight are crucial to ensuring honest and accurate responses.

Customer feedback, reviews, and ratings: Analyzing customer feedback from e-commerce platforms, social media, and other channels helps identify recurring praise or criticisms. Recognizing areas for improvement or gaps in competitors' offerings can guide more effective strategies and product enhancements.

A notable example from a few years ago is Domino's, which addressed widespread customer dissatisfaction with its pizza. Complaints had likened the crust to cardboard and the sauce to ketchup. Acknowledging the need for improvement, Domino's launched a campaign promising to enhance its pizza. The initiative gained traction when morning shows conducted taste tests, reigniting customer interest. By humorously acknowledging its past shortcomings and replacing stylized food images with authentic depictions, Domino's successfully rebuilt trust and showcased its commitment to genuine improvement. It worked.

Collabs and Partnerships

A brand collaboration and a brand partnership represent strategic alliances between companies but differ significantly in scope, duration, and objectives. Collaborations are generally short-term and project-specific, while partnerships are long-term and strategic, aimed at achieving sustained mutual growth.

Not all collaborations are conventional; insights into audience desires for novelty and excitement fuel some unusual alliances. These insight-driven collaborations are fueled by creative ideas and innovation, resulting in unique, limited-edition offerings. For example, the collaboration between e.l.f. Beauty and Chipotle illustrates how tapping into a specific demographic's desire for unexpected variations can lead to successful and engaging product innovations.

"We're always looking for opportunities to lead culture and make authentic connections with Gen-Z alongside brands that share similar values," said Tressie Lieberman, vice president of digital marketing and off-premise operations at Chipotle. "Following our first launch with e.l.f., which sold out in less than four minutes last spring, we've taken our collab to the next level with beauty products celebrating our real ingredients in totally unexpected ways."[26]

Jenna Drenten, associate professor of marketing at Loyola University Chicago's Quinlan School of Business, highlights that in today's digital consumer culture, audiences exhibit an "attention deficit." "Consumers get very bored with the existing offerings on the market," says Drenten. "Having unexpected, unconventional collaborations between brands is a way to revitalize the brand quickly, without a lot of effort on the brand side."[27]

For brand collaborations to succeed, both companies must stay aligned with their mission, values, and purpose while demonstrating a profound understanding of their shared target audience.

- **Get reacquainted with your customer**: Consistent customer engagement provides valuable insights into their evolving needs, preferences, and behaviors. This ongoing interaction ensures your strategies stay relevant and aligned with what truly matters to your audience.
- **Identify unmet needs**: Market gaps or unmet needs present valuable opportunities. By actively listening to customer feedback, conducting thorough market research, and observing emerging trends, brands can uncover these opportunities and develop solutions to meet underserved demands effectively.
- **Identify areas of disinterest**: Identifying and understanding which aspects of products, services, or features fail to engage consumers provides valuable insights. Brands should avoid allocating resources to areas with low consumer interest or demand and instead focus on developing offerings that genuinely align with customer needs, desires, and preferences, ensuring their efforts create value where it matters most.
- **Move at the speed of culture and adapt swiftly and strategically**: Staying responsive to shifts in societal norms, consumer behaviors, the economy, and market trends is crucial for brands aiming to move at the speed of culture. Continuously evolving strategies, products, and messaging ensure relevance and resonance with the audience in a rapidly changing environment. This agility enables brands to seize opportunities and navigate challenges effectively, maintaining a competitive edge, just as Philips responded to the German market.

  At the Cannes Lions 2024 session "Courage to Let Culture Lead," marketers explored how to build genuine connections with audiences to foster brand interest and community in an ever-evolving industry. Advocating for diversity in the decision-making and creative processes, Maya Dukes, managing director of global brand strategy and creative and social media for Delta Air Lines, highlighted the importance of including diverse voices in the creative process. She emphasized that actively involving individuals who shape culture ensures content reflects inclusivity and connects authentically with the audience.[28]
- **Embrace your core strengths**: Understanding and embracing a brand's unique identity, values, and capabilities is essential. By confidently focusing on these core strengths and aligning activities accordingly, you foster authenticity and build trust with your audience. Delivering consistent value and distinctive content rooted in these strengths ensures your brand stands out in the marketplace.
- **Leverage your difference**: Whether in innovation, values, or customer experience, highlighting the unique aspects that differentiate your brand is necessary. Emphasizing these distinguishing qualities attracts and

retains individuals who resonate with them. This approach offers a competitive edge and fosters meaningful connections with your target audience, ensuring your brand stands out and gets noticed.

- **Data mining**: Utilizing AI capabilities to anticipate competitors' actions can provide a strategic advantage through advanced, AI-driven insights. Information extraction systems can efficiently uncover insights from publicly available documents such as annual reports, quarterly financials, press releases, statements, and social media posts. Combining this data with human interpretation and market expertise allows you to gain visibility into strategic relationships and competitive dynamics, giving your company a valuable edge.[29]
- **Influencers (or not)**: Instead of focusing solely on A-list celebrities, some brands collaborate with creators and individuals who genuinely embody the brand's values. These partnerships foster organic brand awareness and build a more authentic connection with the target audience.
- **Assess potential threats**: Identifying and evaluating factors that could impact your brand—such as competitive actions, shifts in consumer preferences, economic downturns, regulatory changes, technological advancements, or reputational risks—ensures its resilience. This proactive approach helps safeguard your brand against potential threats, positioning it to adapt and thrive.
- **Craft the brand's obituary**: Analyzing factors contributing to a brand's downfall offers valuable insights and helps avoid similar pitfalls. Understanding the causes of a brand's demise provides critical lessons for refining future strategies and decision-making.

Interview: Teresa Barreira, Global Chief Marketing and Communications Officer, Publicis Sapient

Teresa Barreira is a global C-suite leader with over twenty-five years of experience building and leading teams in both large and small companies. She was born and raised in Northern Portugal and emigrated to the United States as a teenager prior to attending the University of Massachusetts Amherst. As a

Teresa Barreira

young Hispanic student, she was inspired by the US education system and the opportunity it gave her to explore multiple disciplines. Barreira pursued a Master of Business Administration at Northeastern University following completion of her undergraduate degree.

Teresa began her career at IBM, where she spent over ten years working in various parts of the organization. Over the years she has held leadership positions in multiple leading Fortune 500 organizations from Accenture to Deloitte. She is now the global chief marketing and communications officer at Publicis Sapient where she leads a rapidly growing team of more than 150 members across more than seven countries.

Teresa's passion is empowering the next generation of leaders. Whether through her day-to-day role at Publicis Sapient, where she instills a "test-and-learn" mentality across her team, or in the expansive work in local communities she is committed to, she is focused on inspiring youth at the high school and college levels. Her commitment to enabling and building future talent pools via internships and immersive learning experiences is evident. Teresa believes that giving young people access to explore future career paths beyond those they encounter daily and inspiring them is an important component of advancing DEI and empowering the next generation.

Teresa is based in Boston, and resides in Toronto, Canada, with her two teenage sons.

You've said that "brands must provide solutions both to individuals and to society at large." Could you elaborate on what this means?

Every problem is a human problem. By addressing human/individual problems, brands are also solving societal problems, small and large. For instance, we digitally transformed an organization in North Carolina that provides assistance to renters. We didn't start by asking them, "What does your organization need?" We started by asking, "What does your customer need?" It turns out what those customers needed was for their applications to be processed much faster. And so by centering our entire solution around solving that customer need, we not only created better business results for our client but we also had a material impact on the lives of their customers, which in turn impacts their entire community. This was the subject of our film *Never Done*, which tells the story of one of these customers: a single mother named Kersten.

Corporate social responsibility is a nice, lofty goal, but orienting your entire point of view and solutions around solving human problems is the best way for a brand to drive both "business growth" and "people impact." I don't view this as brands needing to do two separate things. They need to do one thing, which is to solve customer pain points, and they need to do it really well. If every problem is a human problem, then making a positive impact on the world begins by putting people at the center of everything we do, big and small.

4.2 Museum of Chinese in Australia (MOCA). Client: MOCA; Creative Agency: R/GA Australia; Creative Director: Ben Miles, R/GA; Design Directors: Jane Duru / R/GA; Sam McGuinness / R/GA; Design Studio: PUSH Media Design Studio, Shanghai; Photographer: Daphne Nguyen, PUSH Media Design Studio

In recent years, there has been a disturbing rise in anti-Asian sentiment globally. This negative rhetoric, particularly surrounding the origins of the coronavirus, severely impacted Sydney's Chinatown. Once a vibrant community hub, the area became eerily quiet, with long-established businesses closing and tourism declining, putting Chinatown's cultural heritage at risk. In response to these changes, R/GA partnered with the Museum of Chinese in Australia (MOCA), a new museum in Sydney's Chinatown, tasked with accelerating their next chapter. The goal was straightforward: to celebrate the ingenuity, contributions, and resilience of Chinese Australians, past, present, and future.

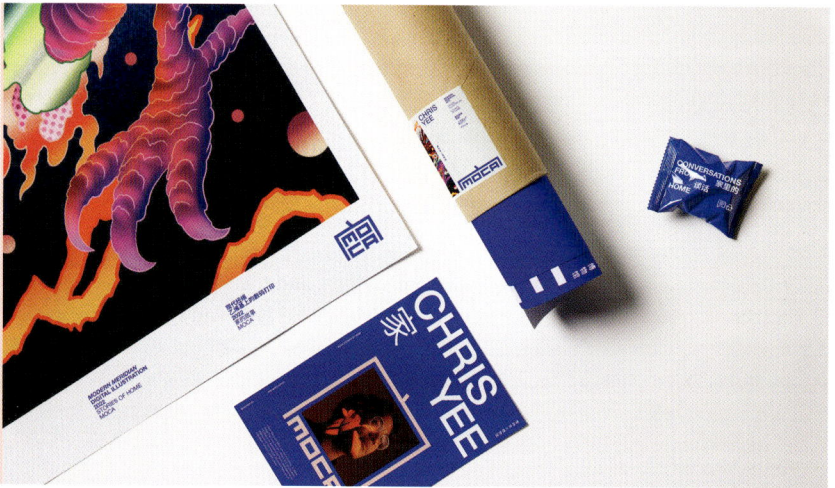

4.2 (*continued*)

WREN

Women's Rights & Empowerment Network

5.2 Women's Rights and Empowerment Network (WREN), Columbia, South Carolina: *Comprehensive naming, branding, and communication program.* Studio: Alexander Isley Inc.; Creative Director: Alexander Isley; Designer: Angela Chen; Strategist and Writer: Georgann Eubanks

WREN is a South Carolina-based organization created to advance the health, economic well-being, and rights of South Carolina's women, girls, and their families. The organization works with its partners and supporters to advocate for laws and policies to enhance the status of women, contribute to the well-being of families, educate policymakers and the public, and empower South Carolinians to speak up and out for a better state.

We worked with the organization's leadership to create a comprehensive identity and communication program, giving them the tools to help refine and spread word of their mission. We started off by leading a naming initiative. Working in collaboration with our colleague, writer and strategist Georgann Eubanks, we explored a variety of approaches leading up to our recommendation of WREN, the Women's Rights and Empowerment Network. The acronym is short, memorable, and makes reference to the South Carolina state bird, known for its hardiness and persistent voice. Once the name was in place, we turned our attention to developing the visual program.

The idea of a multicolored nest as a logo appealed to us: A nest represents safety and security, nurturing, and the idea of a home. It's a place where the young are protected. A nest is tightly woven, its strength coming from the intertwining of individual members. The "nest" icon is memorable, flexible, and can work in a wide variety of situations. And we like the idea of a fancy scribble serving as a memorable identifier.

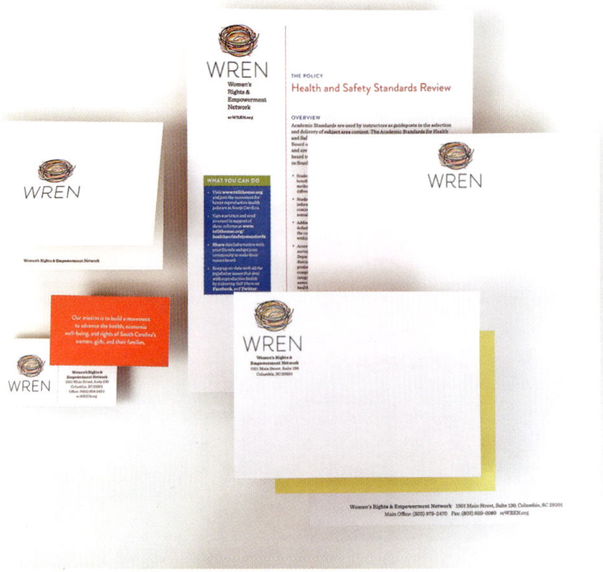

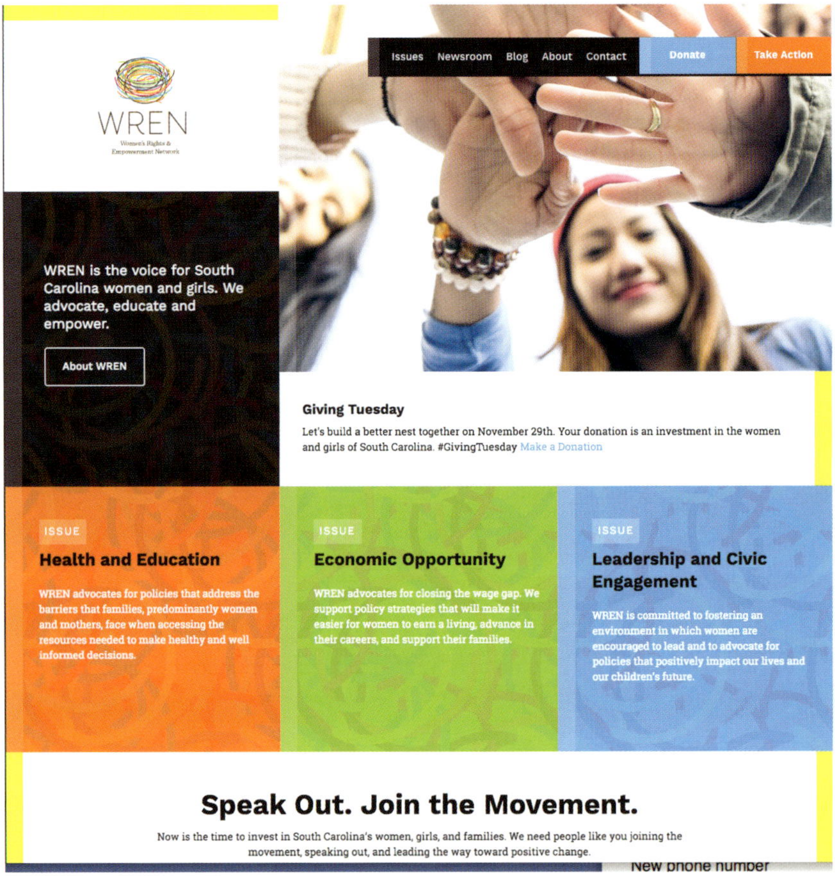

5.2 *(continued)*

5.2 (*continued*)

5.2 (*continued*)

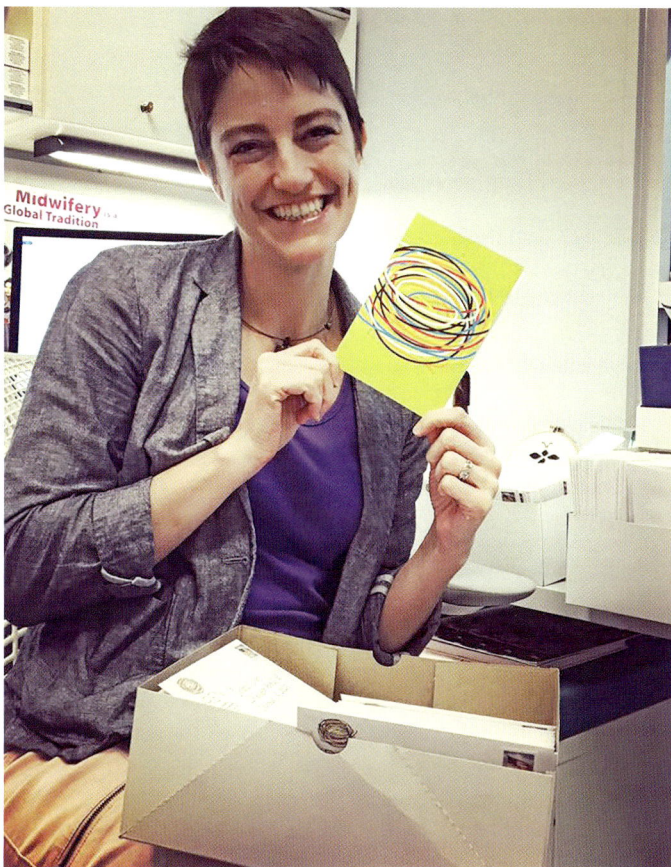

Logo Components

The nest and lettering elements should be maintained as a consistent set of elements wherever possible. In some instances it is acceptable to use only the logo (the nest illustration and WREN lettering) so long as the descriptor line appears clearly in proximity to the logo (see samples on page 12 for reference).

see samples on page 12 for reference

Primary
Centered Lockup

WREN

Women's Rights &
Empowerment Network

LOGO

LOGO
LOCKUP

DESCRIPTOR
LINE

3

5.2 *(continued)*

5.3 Bombas. Agency: &Walsh; Client: Bombas, Aaron Wolk, Randy Goldberg, Jessica Krantz; Creative Direction: Jessica Walsh; Strategy: Lauren Walsh; Production: Allison Raich, Evan Delp, Victoria Najmy, Kasia Sasinowska; Copywriting: Bombas, Jessica Walsh, Lauren Walsh, Stephanie Halovanic; Lead Design: Carlos Bocai, Gabriela Namie, Sasyk Mihal; Design: Jeremy Rieger, Simoul Alva, Katyayani Singh, Julian Williams, Sergi Delgado, Alex Slobzheninov, Riisa Liao, Jess Gracia, Hayley Lim, Juanse Carvajal, Fabrizio Morra, Elinor O'Brien, Sofia Noronha, John Sampson, Lucas Luz; Animation: Soomin Jung, Lucas Luz, Heewon Kim, Jada Akoto, Daniel Zepeda. Courtesy of Bombas.

5.3 (*continued*)

6.2 My Japan Railway Use App. Creative Agency: DENTSU INC., Tokyo; Brand: JR GROUP, Tokyo; Executive Creative Director: Takuma Takasaki, DENTSU INC.; Creative Director: Yoshihiro Yugi, DENTSU INC.; Art Director: Hiroyuki Kato, DENTSU INC.; Art Director: Nanae Ishikawa, DENTSU INC.; Art Director: Asuka Yamamoto, DENTSU INC.; Copywriter: Mariko Fukuoka, DENTSU INC.; Copywriter: Mina Sugioka, DENTSU INC.; Creative Producer: Akiko Seino, DENTSU INC.; Account Executive: Naoto Ikegami, DENTSU INC.; Account Executive: Mami Umezawa, DENTSU INC.; Account Executive: Jun Maeda, DENTSU INC.

6.3 My Japan Railway Stamps. Creative Agency: DENTSU INC., Tokyo; Brand: JR GROUP, Tokyo; Executive Creative Director: Takuma Takasaki, DENTSU INC.; Creative Director: Yoshihiro Yugi, DENTSU INC.; Art Director: Hiroyuki Kato, DENTSU INC.; Art Director: Nanae Ishikawa, DENTSU INC.; Art Director: Asuka Yamamoto, DENTSU INC.; Copywriter: Mariko Fukuoka, DENTSU INC.; Copywriter: Mina Sugioka, DENTSU INC.; Creative Producer: Akiko Seino, DENTSU INC.; Account Executive: Naoto Ikegami, DENTSU INC.; Account Executive: Mami Umezawa, DENTSU INC.; Account Executive: Jun Maeda, DENTSU INC.

6.3 (*continued*)

6.3 (*continued*)

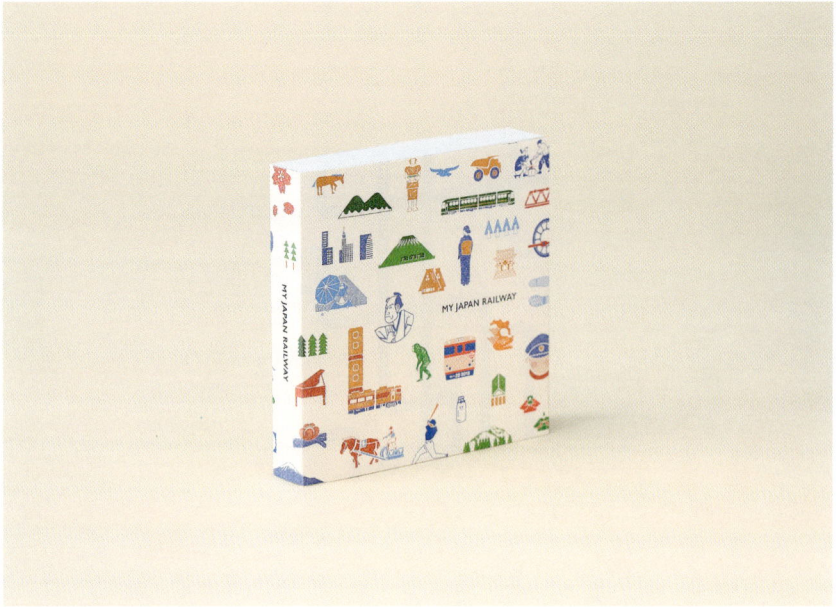

6.4 My Japan Railway Book. Creative Agency: DENTSU INC., Tokyo; Brand: JR GROUP, Tokyo; Executive Creative Director: Takuma Takasaki, DENTSU INC.; Creative Director: Yoshihiro Yugi, DENTSU INC.; Art Director: Hiroyuki Kato, DENTSU INC.; Art Director: Nanae Ishikawa, DENTSU INC.; Art Director: Asuka Yamamoto, DENTSU INC.; Copywriter: Mariko Fukuoka, DENTSU INC.; Copywriter: Mina Sugioka, DENTSU INC.; Creative Producer: Akiko Seino, DENTSU INC.; Account Executive: Naoto Ikegami, DENTSU INC.; Account Executive: Mami Umezawa, DENTSU INC.; Account Executive: Jun Maeda, DENTSU INC.

6.4 (*continued*)

8.1 Campaign: "Press Here Now" (Pincha Aquí Ahora). Client: Unicef Chile; Creative Agency: Inbrax Chile; Chief Creative Officer: Pancho González; Creative Director: Cristián Chávez; Art Director: Carlos Fuentes, Cristián Chávez; Copywriter: Matías Maldonado, Pancho González; Planning Director: Ricardo Álvarez; Account Executive: Elizabeth Gallardo; Post Producer: Sebastián Vega; CEO: Carolina Pinheiro; Chief Marketing Officer: Carlos Heredia; Production Company: La Motoneta; Sound Production: Miranda & Tobar; Partner Agency: Adrenaline Advertising, South Africa.

In an article, you mentioned, "The biggest threat to brands today is irrelevance." Would you elaborate on what you mean by this?

Until now, most brands have existed to inform and help consumers when it's time to make a decision.

But today we live in a world of unlimited choices. Switching between brands has become frictionless. And generative AI will accelerate this trend because consumers will no longer need to rely on the brand to make a choice. If an autonomous agent can compare insurance plans, cross-reference claim-to-complaint ratios, and negotiate the best rate on one's behalf, what role will an insurance company's brand play in their purchase decision? It will be irrelevant. And so, every brand leader should be asking themselves, "Why does my brand exist?" The brands that can't answer that question aren't just in danger of being irrelevant, they already are irrelevant. To maintain relevance, brands must prove their role and place in people's lives time and time again. This requires continuous evolution of your product and services. But most importantly, it requires understanding the business you are in because who you are is not what you do. Ralph Lauren believes they are not in the fashion business or the apparel business—they are in the business of creating dreams. Knowing this enables Ralph Lauren to enact "dreams of luxury" through their products and experiences. As companies continue to evolve their "what," the "why" should never change. Knowing "why" they exist will anchor all decisions in their purpose and will keep them relevant.

Your company has created non-branded content that expands reach and trust by avoiding self-promotion. Why should brands engage with the public organically instead of pushing their brand aggressively?

Marketers should never forget that people are mission-critical for their business. Customers are individuals with multiple interests, and we don't sell to targets or personas, we sell to people. Take me, for example: Yes, I'm a chief marketing officer (CMO). But I'm also a mother, a friend, a sister, and an immigrant. If brands compete for an ever-shrinking slice of my attention by focusing only on the context of my role as a CMO, they ignore opportunities to reach me in all those other contexts. Non-branded content is a way to reach people—not in the boardroom, but in the living room—because it's not self-promotional. It elevates the brand and builds trust with the audience.

It invites the audience to take a step forward, to come in and engage with the brand in a very authentic way. Non-branded content is content that people actually want to watch because it entertains, engages, and inspires. It is about engaging people who may not have paid attention to the brand previously. Think of it as a coat of primer that helps the paint stick better. Just like the primer, it can help the brand message stick better and last longer by conditioning the audience to be more attuned to the brand message. Ultimately, non-branded content forces the brand to lead by influence instead of force—the brand leads from behind versus from the front. Of course, with non-branded content, you need to find ways to tie it back to your brand, but that's done with the surrounding activities, not within the content itself.

How will generative AI transform marketing?

I'm incredibly optimistic about the potential of generative AI, but I also think that most marketers are thinking about it in the wrong way—as a companion, versus an augmentation or superpower.

AI will force the marketing function to be completely reimagined and will fundamentally change the way we do everything. If you look back at the evolution of marketing over the last forty to fifty years, it has gone from being process-focused to engagement-focused. The difference today is that, unlike what we saw with the advent of the internet and mobile and social apps, AI will not simply add another marketing channel. It will become embedded in all that we do. It will be more like electricity powering everything we use in our daily jobs. And, as a result, it will give marketers a superpower that makes us smarter, more creative, and more strategic. This transformation will force marketers to become more multidisciplinary and work on cross-functional teams, thus helping us understand more than one craft. Marketing skills will be blended, and will require a hybrid team that includes a technologist, data scientist, ethical guardian, and creative thinker. This will ultimately force marketers to act more like interpreters rather than creators. Overall, we will become amazing orchestrators and conductors of artificial intelligence with human ingenuity.

Some brands have become cultural conversation starters. Should marketers and designers rethink their focus and strategies to establish cultural relevance?

"Awareness" is no longer enough to fend off irrelevance. Up until now, size, resources, and scale have been seen as a competitive advantage for established brands. Whether their products were good or bad, culturally relevant or not, they could use their scale to buy their way into a consumer's consideration set and culture. Now, the media landscape is fragmenting more and more, making large-scale "awareness" campaigns harder and harder to achieve. Generative AI is allowing small brands to compete with bigger rivals through hyperefficient spending, speed, and agility. What all of this means is that you can no longer mask a bad product with a good campaign or culture. To thrive, established brands must embrace a challenger brand mindset that challenges the status quo and favors evolution and innovation, aiming for fame versus awareness or acceptance. This means leaning into intelligent naivety—asking questions others won't, taking a strong point of view, sacrificing some things to overcommit to others, and embracing rejection over indifference. Brands that want to become culturally relevant need to replace awareness strategies in favor of fame.

Interview: Christina Carey Dunleavy, VP of Entertainment Brand Solutions, Disney CreativeWorks, and Multicultural & Inclusive Solutions, Disney Advertising

Christina Carey Dunleavy. Photographer: Disney/Yolanda Perez

Christina Carey Dunleavy is the vice president of Entertainment Brand Solutions, Disney CreativeWorks, and Multicultural & Inclusive Solutions at Disney Advertising. In this role, Dunleavy is responsible for the long-term Multicultural Strategy, the business operations of Disney CreativeWorks, as well as entertainment-based client solutions across The Walt Disney Company's entertainment and sports offerings through linear, digital, social, audio and ad-supported streaming businesses, including ABC, ABC News, Disney Channels Worldwide, Disney Digital, ESPN Networks, ESPN+, Freeform, FX, National Geographic, Hulu, Disney +, and its eight ABC-owned local stations. At the helm of the Multicultural & Inclusive Solutions Division, Christina is leading Disney Advertising Sales's continued investment in diversity, equity and inclusion, with a focus on engaging growth audiences through campaigns that have even greater relevance and authenticity.

Prior to her current role, Dunleavy served as vice president of Portfolio Integrated Marketing and Partnerships at Discovery, where she was responsible for developing and executing multi-platform integrated marketing solutions to maximize revenue across the company's portfolio of networks. Before joining Discovery, Dunleavy served as vice president of Client Partnerships at NBCUniversal, where she was responsible for the development, positioning, and packaging of multi-platform solutions.

Dunleavy began her career with Disney in 2001 at Walt Disney Television, eventually rising to the role of creative director before pursuing her MBA at the UCD Smurfit School of Business in Dublin, Ireland. Following her time abroad, Dunleavy returned to Disney as director of ESPN CreativeWorks, where she managed the development and execution of contextually relevant custom creative and branded programs distributed across all ESPN platforms.

Christina Carey Dunleavy earned a B.S. in Management Science and Marketing from Kean University prior to earning her MBA and is currently a doctoral student at Hampton University working towards her PhD in Business Administration and Marketing. Dunleavy is also certified in Diversity and Inclusion from Cornell University and has completed a course in Disruptive Strategy through Harvard Business School. As of 2024, she is an adjunct professor in the Department of Marketing, Global Business, and Economics at Kean University.

To fully leverage Disney's vast content portfolio, how can you harness its emotional resonance to engage its varied audiences?

The audience always comes first, and to deliver on that promise, we need a deep understanding of what best resonates with our audience and why that is the case. We tap into our arsenal of research, data, and marketplace dynamics—and of course our gut instinct (the great marriage of art and science)—to guide the strategy that ultimately drives impactful multifaceted campaigns. The result of going deep with our audience is that we know which levers to pull to best connect with them—whether through in-show integration, custom content, social-first strategies, and/or streaming—along with the use of talent, IP inclusion, contextual relevance, storytelling, tone, music, voiceover, location, aesthetic, etc. Essentially, we have all the ingredients needed (insights, strategy, creative, and distribution) based on Disney's extensive portfolio, and with considered intention, we build meaningful outcomes that reach the target audience in a way that drives engagement/action.

How does Disney approach the intersection of branding and cultural influence, especially in today's diverse and rapidly changing world?

By remaining incredibly mindful of the world in which we exist, the populations we serve, the importance of cultural fluency, and ultimately the impact we want to have across all facets of our business.

As I've mentioned, we are committed to our audiences, and we do this by speaking authentically in everything we do, creating audience-based strategies for our advertisers, and amplifying underrepresented voices.

Across all our brands and every major pillar of our company, we are dedicated to super-serving all audiences no matter how they interact with us: on our streaming platforms, at our parks, through our networks. It all comes down to driving systemic change with an engaged effort to understand and reflect culture, mindsets, and behavior.

How does Disney Advertising collaborate with diverse creators and communities to ensure authentic representation and cultural relevance in its initiatives?

We drive relevance for brands through creativity, connection, and collaboration. Our goal is to meet all audiences where they are, across The Walt Disney Company, and to show up in meaningful ways that deliver impact.

We are making a measurable difference through:

o Creativity—with inclusive stories that bring our creators' voices to the forefront, we empower future generations of storytellers and innovators while advancing authentic representation in streaming, sports, and entertainment.

o Connection—our stories and our platforms are the vehicles that connect you and your brand's goals to our viewers. We provide innovative solutions curated to our audiences across all dimensions of life.

o Collaboration—our work does not stop with a successful media campaign. Disney also engages in:

- Advancing education and cultural fluency
- Supporting initiatives, like Project Elevate, that support small businesses through access to creative and business resources
- Partnering with research and measurement companies that specialize in multicultural insights
- Driving impactful collaborations and making strategic community and media investments

What is the best practice for navigating multi-platform branding and advertising?

When you start with Disney, the advertiser is placed at the center—not simply of creativity and innovation, but also in the space where insights and expertise translate into action and, ultimately, make an impact.

§ Disney has one hundred years of storytelling, as well as an immense library of fan-favorite shows that bolster the viewing experience with all types of content the audience wants.

§ No matter the content category—scripted, reality, documentary, sports, music, classics, specials, news, adult animation, live moments, or Disney Vault—no other company can deliver the scale, nostalgia, or cultural moments like the Disney portfolio.

§ No matter where a show or series originates, it almost always has windowing on our streaming platforms—either same-day, next-day, or as part of our streaming-first originals.

§ With all these distribution vehicles, we reach advertisers' audiences at scale, and each screen delivers an incremental or unduplicated audience set.

§ Our content and audiences are unified through innovative, built-for-streaming technology that delivers seamlessly across every screen, bringing targetability, performance, and transparent measurement to an advertiser's brand.

CHAPTER 10

━━━━━━

BRAND BUILDING: FORGING EMOTIONAL CONNECTIONS

I found myself crying during a television program.

It was not over the main character's breakup with her fiancé, but during a Subaru commercial titled "Baby Driver." In the spot, a father hands the car keys to his daughter as she sets off to drive alone for the first time. Through the father's eyes, we initially see "his little girl" in the driver's seat, which then transitions to his teenage daughter taking the keys. As a parent of a daughter who has just learned to drive, and as the daughter of a father who once handed over his car keys to me, this commercial deeply touched me. I felt like the ad agency creatives at Carmichael Lynch in Minneapolis knew me.

Not only did "Baby Driver" resonate with me emotionally, but it also made great sense for Subaru—a brand strongly associated with family. At the end of "Baby Driver," the father's voiceover says, "We knew this day was coming. That's why we bought a Subaru."

And if you believe in the power of emotional connections, consider this tagline: "Love. It's what makes Subaru, Subaru."

How do you stand apart when your competition is spending literally billions of dollars? By connecting with what's truly important to your audience—not just features they might like, but the life that they love. Their families. Their pets. The great outdoors. Even the venerable old Subaru they've been driving forever. In 2007, we introduced the "Love" campaign. In the years since, sales and market share have more than tripled and love has spread to every level of the brand.—Carmichael Lynch[1]

10.1 "Subaru Loves Learning." Brand: Subaru. Courtesy of Subaru

"Subaru of America, Inc. volunteers help support students in high-needs schools in partnership with AdoptAClassroom.org® through the Subaru Loves Learning® initiative as part of the Subaru Love Promise®."—Subaru of America, Inc.

Driven by insights that Subaru owners value "love," active lifestyles, and community contributions, Subaru launched the Subaru Love Promise®, which includes initiatives like the Subaru Loves Learning® program (as shown in figure 10.1) and the Share the Love Event. Unlike their competitors, who relied on discounts, Tom Doll, former CEO of Subaru America, and Subaru pioneered a different strategy: offering customers a $250 donation to their chosen charity instead. Initially controversial with their parent company and retailers, these efforts eventually resonated deeply with customers, distinguishing Subaru from its competitors.

Subaru continues to donate $250 for every vehicle sold during select months each year, allowing buyers to choose the charities that receive the funds. This initiative has made Subaru the leading corporate donor in the automotive sector to organizations such as the National Park Service, ASPCA, Meals on Wheels, and Make-A-Wish.

Doll underscored Subaru's ethos of contributing beyond car sales, fostering a sense of purpose among employees and customers alike.[2]

The Role of Emotional Experiences in Brand Building

When asked, "Why are memories attached to emotions so strong?" René Hen, PhD, professor of psychiatry and neuroscience at Columbia University Vagelos College of Physicians and Surgeons, replied, "It makes sense we don't remember everything. We have limited brain power. We only need to remember what's important for our future well-being."[3]

Hen's insight applies directly to branding, design, and advertising that strive to create lasting impressions. By evoking strong emotions, brands can make their messages and experiences memorable and impactful.

As Dan Wieden, the cofounder of Wieden+Kennedy, said: "It's been the same since people gathered around the campfire to hear a story. Are you a good storyteller or a bad storyteller? Make me laugh, make me cry, make me do something. Whether you do it on the Internet or on a balloon floating above me, I don't care. *Just move me, dude* [my emphasis]."[4]

Emotional branding taps into Hen's principle and Wieden's directive, crafting experiences that resonate deeply with consumers, thereby enhancing brand recall. Analysis has confirmed the relationship between brand attachment and consumers' emotional well-being, demonstrating that people use brands to improve their emotional health. Ultimately, emotional connections forged through branding capture attention and align with individuals' inherent drive for well-being.[5] A strong brand framework can leverage emotions in memory to forge impactful connections with consumers.[6] This elevates the brand beyond mere transactions, resonating in an emotional realm that transcends the product or service's basic utility. Subaru's Love Promise® campaign fosters emotional benefits by creating a sense of belonging, trust, and shared values among customers. By focusing on community involvement and helping support causes like education and animal welfare, the campaign strengthens the emotional bond between the brand and consumers. Customers feel valued, knowing their purchase contributes to initiatives that align with their values of love and compassion, enhancing their sense of purpose and well-being as part of a community making a positive impact.

As a foundation for crafting a brand, we should ask: "How do we want people to feel when they encounter this brand?" This question precedes all brand executions, including visual identity, and centers on the emotional impact we aim to achieve. The priority is to evoke a stirring response from the target audience, ensuring you preserve emotional resonance when conveying messages, showcasing visual identity, and executing advertisements or activations. In some cases, the emotional response becomes the message itself, making the communication memorable—or, if mishandled, forgettable.

Emotional Associations

Emotional events create our most powerful and enduring memories.[7] In a recent study published in *Nature Human Behaviour*, Joshua Jacobs, PhD, associate professor of biomedical engineering at Columbia University School of Engineering and Applied Science, and his team identified a neural mechanism in the human brain that associates information with emotions to enhance memory. Their research revealed that high-frequency brain waves in the amygdala (crucial for emotional processing) and the hippocampus (vital for memory formation) significantly strengthen memories tied to emotional stimuli.[8]

In branding and advertising, evoking emotional responses—whether awe, excitement, joy, or even negative emotions like disgust—is crucial for creating a memorable brand experience. By tapping into core emotional motivations, brands transcend functionality, reaching a deeper emotional connection that product or service features alone cannot achieve. Understanding these emotional drivers is key to shaping consumer desires and behaviors.

Consider the common factors that fulfill a sense of belonging: Membership clubs, niche online communities, team sports, gaming groups, social media platforms, and cultural institutions all offer connection and community. Identifying and leveraging these emotional ties can significantly enhance brand engagement. For example, we might ask: What motivates someone to buy life insurance to secure their family's future? Does coloring one's hair boost one's self-esteem? Would joining a niche forum on Reddit fulfill a need for belonging? Does the shared experience of experiential advertising strengthen interpersonal connections?

Kantar, a marketing data and analytics business, tested over 10,000 ads for their clients and found that "making the viewer feel something wins engagement for the ad, bypassing the natural tendency to screen out advertising. It also has positive effects on the brand's emotional associations."[9]

Emotional Profile

A brand's emotional profile refers to the specific set of affective experiences it attempts to consistently evoke in its audience through its messaging, design, advertising, and overall experiences. For example, Skittles always amuses; Subaru offers a "love promise"; Duolingo is playful; and Cadbury is associated with joy.

A well-defined emotional profile can:

- Forge an emotional bond with consumers through strategically emotive and creative experiences
- Stimulate engagement

- Enhance brand recall and preference
- Drive purchase decisions through emotional connections[10]

"Emotions are the key drivers of campaign effectiveness," according to Ian Forrester, CEO of DAIVID, the creative effectiveness measurement platform. One study looked at "39 distinct emotional responses to ads and revealed that the strongest creative [work] is most frequently connected with "intense positive emotions (59.2 percent)."[11] Leading emotional traits in prize-winning content included admiration (15.1 percent), hope (10.6 percent), and awe (8 percent).[12]

Key Aspects of a Brand's Emotional Profile

A brand's emotional profile helps shape how consumers perceive and relate to the brand.

Core emotional experiences refer to the primary emotions a brand aims to elicit. A brand should focus on a narrow range of closely related emotions—for example, happiness (a broad feeling of well-being and contentment) and joy (an intense burst of positive emotion) are closely related. Maintaining this focused emotional range is foundational; straying too far can confuse the audience. For instance, Skittles' emotional profile revolves around generating feelings of playful absurdity. The creative teams and company consistently aim to amuse their target audience through their TV spots, package design, and ventures such as their postmodern *Skittles Commercial: The Broadway Musical*. In his review of *Skittles Commercial: The Broadway Musical* for *New York Magazine, Vulture* critic Jackson McHenry wrote:

> Brilliant and frustrating, *Skittles Commercial: The Broadway Musical* had beaten me to that point, and many others. During the song "Advertising Ruins Everything," when the crowd turns on Michael C. Hall, he describes Skittles as "fruit flavors that are deliciously surprising, the perfect treat for this anti-capitalist uprising," to which the people around him sing, "Oh my God, he's still advertising!"[13]

It's important to note that a branded film or TV spot can take viewers on an emotional journey, incorporating a range of emotions, such as eliciting anger during a conflict, only to have it resolve into happiness. However, the overall emotional experience should still align with the brand's promise and personality, ensuring a cohesive and authentic connection with the audience.

FOCUS: WHATSAPP DOCUMENTARY WE ARE AYENDA

The WhatsApp documentary *We Are Ayenda* is a half-hour documentary that recounts the journey of the Afghan Girls National Football Team and their daring escape from Afghanistan following the Taliban's rise to power in 2021. The film blends poignant interviews with gripping archival footage and real text messages that the teenage players exchanged in their WhatsApp group as they covertly planned their escape. It highlights the courage of these young women and their unwavering commitment to the sport they love.[14]

"They are looking for us," reads one WhatsApp message shown in the film. "We need to get out." The Meta-owned messaging service was especially valuable due to its privacy features, which were crucial at a time when the Taliban was closely monitoring public social media posts. "My life depended on my phone and on my privacy," one of the athletes says in the film's trailer.[15]

Entertainment Lions jury president Geoffrey Edwards, managing director, creative at Gale US, said: "We follow how they navigated their escape during the Taliban takeover of the capital city of Kabul in 2021 by using the safety features on WhatsApp. The film represents hope and demonstrates a perfect marriage of narrative storytelling with the brand playing a central and critical role. Stories like this represent the power that brands and entertainment have to impact real change in the world."[16]

Consider the following aspects when building an emotional profile.

Emotional differentiation: Differentiation is always paramount, and emotional differentiation is no exception. A brand's emotional appeal must set it apart from competitors, contributing to its unique identity. Emotional differentiation can make a brand stand out.

BMW's "'Sheer Driving Pleasure' slogan delivers positive emotions and does exactly what a claim should," states Joachim Blickhäuser, head of corporate and brand identity at the BMW Group. The word "Freude," meaning "joy," "fun," or "pleasure," first appeared in BMW advertisements in the mid-1930s. A 1936 billboard for BMW cars and motorcycles declared, "Kraftfahren muss Freude bereiten!" (Driving should be a pleasure!).[17]

"'Sheer Driving Pleasure' describes the essence of the brand, which is very robust, resilient and future-oriented. The pleasure a person derives from their car has nothing to do with its drive technology—or whether it's driven autonomously or not. Joy is universal. It is a human emotion that binds us all together. So I think it will remain just as relevant in the future as it is now," states Blickhäuser.[18] BMW has been consistent in claiming driving pleasure.

Consistency and cohesion: To maintain its unique identity and differentiation, a brand must consistently evoke related core emotions across all touchpoints. For the audience, this consistency ensures that the emotional experiences remain stable. However, to avoid predictability and keep the audience engaged, the brand should also incorporate elements of surprise and innovative thinking, making each experience feel fresh and exciting.

Emotional resonance: A deep understanding of the audience is indispensable. When a brand's emotional appeal truly resonates with its target audience, it can lead to transformative outcomes. Think of the success of brands with stable and clearly expressed emotional appeals, such as Dove, Coca-Cola, John Lewis (UK), Disney, or Liquid Death. Effective emotional resonance strengthens consumer engagement, fostering a more consequential connection.

Emotional triggers: Key brand assets—such as the logo, imagery, tone of voice, tagline, sonic logo, and narratives—should evoke the desired emotions in individuals. For instance, the aforementioned Subaru commercial "Baby Driver" resonated so deeply with me that it brought me to tears. The creative team carefully crafted the concept to connect with a parent figure. Evoking emotional responses from viewers enhances engagement with the advertisement, bypassing their inclination to ignore advertising.[19] This approach also reinforces positive emotional associations with the brand.

Key Emotional Benefits

Key emotional benefits play a vital role in shaping current and potential users' brand preferences and choices. A robust brand strategy identifies these key emotional needs and aligns the brand's attributes to address them effectively. These emotional benefits are integral to the brand's construct and strategy, manifesting in its commitment to social good, messaging, branded experiences, key associations, legacy, origins, ambassadors, advertising, imagery, typography, and the memories they evoke.

- **Compassion**: Fulfilling a proactive desire to help others, creatures, or the planet
- **Joy and happiness**: Providing moments or associations of pleasure and delight
- **Security or safety**: Feeling protected and reassured (related to peace of mind)

- **Peace of mind**: Offering reassurance and reducing anxiety (related to security or safety)
- **Status or prestige**: Elevating one's social standing, often linked to luxury brands, high-end fashion, or exclusive services, however, also linked to premium value or accessible luxury brands that offer high quality or desirable products at prices that, while not inexpensive, are still within reach for a broader audience (related to achievement and success)
- **Achievement and success**: Contributing to personal accomplishments and recognition (related to status or prestige)
- **Belonging and social connection**: Fostering a sense of community and inclusion
- **Empowerment**: Boosting self-esteem and confidence
- **Nostalgia or comfort**: Evoking warm, familiar feelings, often associated with childhood memories or classic products
- **Freedom and independence**: Enhancing personal autonomy and self-reliance
- **Inspiration or creativity**: Stimulating imagination and artistic expression or associated with creative types
- **Love and affection**: Strengthening relationships and expressing care
- **Purpose and meaning**: Helping consumers feel their purchases are making a difference
- **Adventure and excitement**: Offering thrills and new experiences
- **Trust and reliability**: Building confidence in consistent quality and performance
- **Relaxation and stress relief**: Easing tension and promoting calm

Distinctive Brand Assets

Activating emotions—those that elicit a response—are more likely to foster engagement and drive action. Brands that create intense emotional experiences build lasting associations in consumers' minds.[20] Positive emotional motivators can influence consumers' brand choices during the decision-making or purchasing process.[21] Therefore, it is essential for brands to have distinctive assets that not only differentiate them but also evoke positive emotional responses, serving as emotional cues that streamline the decision-making process. Additionally, brands should consistently create emotional experiences across all touchpoints, especially those that are interactive (two-way engagement), experiential (whether immersive, real-world, virtual, hybrid, gamified, or personalized), and participatory (involving audience co-creation or contribution).

Distinctive brand assets—including logos, color palettes, taglines, jingles, mascots, sonic branding, package design, films, advertising, social media presence, and unique branded experiences—facilitate instant recognition and salience. When well-designed and executed, these assets can evoke positive associations and create emotional connections without consciously retrieving specific past experiences. They are shortcuts to desired emotional responses, like Coca-Cola's script logotype, Duolingo's owl mascot Duo, or Tiffany's blue box.

Consistent use of these assets strengthens emotional connections over time, acting as powerful memory triggers that signal the brand's presence and promise. During purchasing decisions, these cues quickly evoke the brand and its associated positive emotions, often influencing choices subconsciously.

Distinctive and well-designed brand assets play a crucial role in differentiation. They capture attention and ensure that the positive emotions associated with a brand remain distinct from those of competitors. While chapters 5 and 6 explore design in more depth, it is important to highlight the significance of professionally conceived and crafted brand identities and touchpoints. Expertly designed logos and packaging use design principles such as balance, proportion, rhythm, and unity to subconsciously communicate positive attributes and emotions, thus enhancing brand perception. Similarly, well-thought-out brand names, such as Kayak, created by branding agency Wolff Olins, contribute to a brand's success and memorability.

Consider the Coca-Cola logo and its iconic red color, which evoke happiness due to the brand's long-standing association with joyful moments, memorable taglines, and nostalgic connections. When you design brand assets to spark specific, predominantly positive emotional responses such as happiness or excitement, they create strong and lasting connections with target audiences.

Interview: Ari Halper, Global ECD and Head of Creative Excellence, R/GA

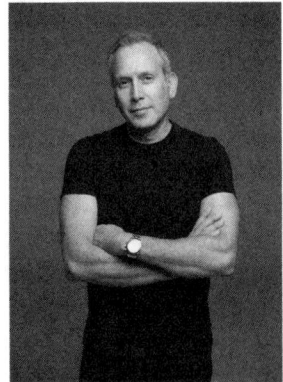

Ari Halper. Photographer: Julia Kuper

Ari Halper is currently a global executive creative director and the head of creative excellence at R/GA. In his first two years at the company, he helped lead it to consecutive record-breaking performances in 2021 and 2022, with work such as Reddit's "Superb Owl," Nike Synch, and Auditorial for Google.

Prior to joining R/GA, Ari served as the chief creative officer of FCB New York, where he helped to turn around the agency with work such as the "Whopper Detour" for Burger King, the single most awarded idea in the industry for 2019.

Before that, Ari spent 13 years at Grey New York as an executive creative director, where he contributed, in no small part, to the agency's turnaround, helping it earn Agency of the Year honors in 2013 and 2015.

Other career highlights include fathering the E*TRADE Baby, Canon's "Long Live Imagination" campaign, switching people from cable to DIRECTV, intercepting the Superbowl for Volvo, helping the Democrats to the best mid-term election performance in 90 years, and repeatedly tackling the issue of gun safety in the United States through initiatives such as "Guns with History," which earned a Gold Clio.

Ari's work has received awards at every major show in the industry, including an Emmy and a shortlist at the Oscars.

Every major show in the industry has awarded your work, including an Emmy and a shortlist at the Oscars. How do you conceive such strategically creative ideas?

I have had both the pleasure and the good fortune of working with some very brilliant strategists who were smart enough to look deeper, and brave enough to push their clients out of their comfort zones, which helped unlock some of the most famous work I've ever done.

You were the chief creative officer at FCB NY for one of the GOAT campaigns, Burger King's "Whopper Detour," which exemplified creative thinking, a deep understanding of the client's audience, and strategic use of technology, e.g., geofencing. How do you and your teams generate such innovative concepts and bring them to life?

It starts with a diversity of skill sets and mindsets. Case in point, it was the strategist who mined the data to uncover an inspiring insight (that most people had to drive past a McDonald's to get to a Burger King). A tech-savvy creative who flipped geofencing on its head. A brave client, strong storytellers, scrappy producers, etc. And everyone was involved from start to finish, furiously collaborating over WhatsApp for an entire year (clients included)!

You've overseen and actively contributed to impactful campaigns for social causes. How do you leverage advertising to drive positive social change?

When I was just starting out in the industry, I went to see Oliviero Toscani speak about the controversial work he was doing at the time for Benetton, featuring images of genocide and individuals living with AIDS, which was obviously a very strange approach for selling clothes. But it was working. And even better, it was opening people's eyes.

And when I asked Toscani why he chose to take this approach with Benetton's advertising, he said something I will never forget: "Advertising is the most powerful medium in the world. You have more money being spent per second and square inch than on anything, anywhere else on the planet. So why on earth would I waste such power just to sell people a pair of sweatpants they don't need?"

This stuck with me for a very long time. But I never truly knew what to do with it, until . . . the Sandy Hook Elementary shooting, which hit incredibly close to home, just thirty minutes from my house, and at the time, my son was close to the same age as those young victims. At that point, I knew I had to do something more with this "power" that Toscani had spoken about and decided to make it my mission to push for safer gun laws. Over the years, this led to work such as "Ed," "Toys," "Guns with History," and "Student Body Armor."

For your clients, you have "repeatedly broken sales records, crushing KPI's, and benchmarks while managing to win every award in the industry [including fifty-seven Cannes Lions across sixteen different disciplines], including the Emmy and even a shortlist at the Oscars, proving that award-winning work can also win at the register." What are the best practices for aligning creative strategy with a client's business objectives?

It might sound like a "duh" response, but I always ask myself the same question, "Will it actually work?" And it is the ability to be brutally honest with yourself when you answer that makes all the difference. So, if the client wants 500k app downloads, will the idea I'm presenting get at least that or more? And then: If they want sales? Impressions? Views? Whatever it be, I always ask . . . "Would I actually watch it? Share it? Click it? Do it?" Now, obviously, I'm not always the target, so it means having a great deal of empathy, putting yourself into the mindset of others. But you'd be surprised how similar we are when it comes to our basic motivations.

You've said that one vital skill for a creative director is adaptability. Please tell us why.

One of my favorite lessons in business and in life comes from Darwin: "It's not the strongest species that survives. Or the smartest. Or even the fastest. It's the most adaptable." Which I firmly believe is one of the things that separates some of the most successful people in the industry today from the rest (who are over 40, of course).

Because many of us grew up in an industry that was dominated by TV, radio, and print/OOH [out of home media]. But with the arrival of the internet, those who embraced social media, mobile, web, and technology solutions maintained their relevancy. And it's about to happen all over again with AI.

Even beyond the disruptions of innovation, adaptability is just as vital in your day-to-day work, as you go from assignment to assignment, client to client, employee to employee, and even from meeting to meeting. Because you need to be able to bring different skill sets to different situations.

Your title at R/GA is unusual, and yet it makes complete sense. What are some of the initiatives you are leading to ensure creative excellence at the agency?

My remit is to help make the work as strong as possible, throughout the network and at all stages of a work's lifecycle, which means, at times, I'm brought in as early as the pitch or during the ideation phase. Other times, I'm brought in mid-production, and other times, I'm brought in once the work is complete, whereby I help to tell the story of that work in the most compelling way possible.

As a result, I have helped to launch a number of initiatives at R/GA to increase success rates. First, by simply streamlining their case study process.

One of the biggest initiatives we built at R/GA is a system and a tool for both viewing and benchmarking the work as a network. We do this upstream—before the work has even been made, as well as with work that's already been produced—to help identify priorities, support, PR needs, case studies, and awards. And while other global agencies have something similar, most are basically numerical scales where the highest number equals the best work. The trick was to create something ownable and unique to R/GA and the different types of work we do—work that isn't quite like that done at a lot of other agencies. The tool is also backed by data, data visualization, and an ever-growing digital database that will be a resource at R/GA for decades to come.

When You Find Me, *a short film you worked on with Ron Howard was shortlisted at the Oscars, and* Inspired *won an Emmy, both created for Canon as part of the same campaign. How does storytelling differ when you have twenty minutes compared to the more limited thirty- or sixty-second timeframe of a commercial spot?*

As for how storytelling differs, when you only have thirty to sixty seconds, it really becomes an exercise in simplicity. The trick is to say one thing *really* well—whereas long-form content affords you the freedom to have different motifs, subplots, and richer character development, including backstory and the like.

That said, both always benefit from commonalities, such as great writing, acting, filmmaking, music, etc. In other words, attention to craft.

You're a creative LIAison coach. What does that role entail?

When the London International Advertising Awards asked me to be a LIAison, it took me all of about two seconds to say yes, because one of my favorite things to do at this point in my career is give back. To give younger talent the guidance and mentorship I wish had been available when I was coming up through the industry, which is exactly what I did for the three art directors who selected me specifically as their first choice. Something I found quite interesting, because I'm actually a writer by trade. But upon meeting with each of them, I found that it didn't really matter—after all, I've mentored dozens of art directors over the years in my career.

With each art director, I had an initial thirty-minute meeting to get to know them, and the types of questions they would want to cover in a one-hour session to follow. Some were about career guidance, others about process, or trends and predictions in the industry. In between, I went over their websites to familiarize myself with their work and also reflect on their various questions, so that we could get the most out of each session.

With the surge of misinformation and disinformation on social media, there's a notable effect on democracies worldwide. Do advertising, branding, and design bear a responsibility in addressing this issue, and if so, what steps can creatives and their clients take to mitigate it?

Social media is far and away the greatest culprit when it comes to the pro-liferation of falsehoods—using algorithms to ensure clicks and profits, while disregarding the collateral damage it creates. And while that's not exactly news, they wouldn't be doing it if brands refused to continue feeding them.

That's why I think it's incumbent upon brands, agencies, and clients to exhibit some sort of moral compass that supersedes their bottom lines—whereby they take an active stance against disinformation, its sources, and even the tolerance of it on platforms, which could and should be done a bit like corporate respon-sibility messages. It can also be done by simply boycotting and/or divesting from the perpetrators, which many brands do, but certainly not enough.

Any brand or entity can embrace a social mission or cause, but how can adver-tising or branding make a real contribution?

The misguided use of "goodvertising" is a real problem in our industry, done too often just to win awards or drive brand affinity, or both. But the most successful ones out there are the ones that actually try to fix or make a dent in the issue—to educate and enlighten people. And they don't just do it once a year, on a specific day or month devoted to that cause, because authenticity is as important as the message itself. So, it needs to come from the right brand, and not just when it's convenient and they want to sell something.

Throughout your career, you've had experience with some of the largest global brands. Why is it especially crucial for these influential brands with prominent voices to share relatable and inclusive stories?

I'm not so sure that it's "especially crucial" for large brands, any more than it is for smaller brands to share stories that are relatable and inclusive. Sure, more people are likely to see them, which makes it important, but in truth, every brand needs to connect with people on an emotional, insightful level—because that's how we build our strongest relationships—and make no mistake, consumer-brand is definitely a relationship, like any other.

How do you foster a sense of shared purpose between a brand and the target audience?

First, it has to come from a place of authenticity. Ideally rooted in the DNA of the brand. However, it can also come from something in the zeitgeist as long as the brand is willing to commit to that purpose as its mission for years to come. Regardless of which path they take, it has to come from a truth, from an insight—into the audience, brand, category, or culture—that resonates and is earnest.

How do you drive a brand's role in culture? And how do you make sure it's responsible and responsive?

I hate to use the same word again but . . . authentically. Culture is fickle. And it's not something you can fake. Therefore, if a brand wants to align itself with culture, it needs to be relevant to that culture, first and foremost—either by association, integration, or amplification. But whatever it may be, it should feel as if the brand is making things better, more interesting, or more enlightening. Otherwise it's just appropriating culture without bringing anything of value to the party.

How does having individuals with divergent points of view and from underrepresented communities on your creative teams fuel advertising's cultural impact?

Talent is great, but it's no substitute for the diversity that can only come from lived experiences, be it from underrepresented communities or countless other points of view that are far less promoted. And within them lie such incredibly rich insights, learnings, and understanding that make for some of the greatest storytelling of our time. Not just in advertising, but in all forms of storytelling: from music, to film, to books and beyond. Because it gives us a magical gift: being able to see the world through another person's eyes.

What is the responsibility of creatives when hopping on cultural moments?

Again . . . authenticity.

Some brands have become cultural conversation starters. Should marketers and designers rethink their focus and strategies to establish cultural relevance?

Only if it makes sense for the brand. Otherwise, it risks coming off as an insincere attempt to glom on.

Social media has transformed how culture works. What should creative professionals, businesspeople, and clients understand about how brands create cultural impact on social media?

I think the obvious answer is for the brand and agency to have a keen understanding of the behaviors that are taking place on each social media platform, because there are subcultures and trends that can be very specific to one, and completely irrelevant to another.

The thing that is less obvious, however, is that a brand shouldn't lose its sense of self in order to appeal to the audiences on these respective platforms. Instead, they need to find a way to bring their brand narrative to life in a way that feels harmonious with the trends taking place on each channel. Otherwise, the brand risks coming off as a "tryhard," or even worse, schizophrenic.

CHAPTER 11

BRAND BUILDING: MANIFESTOS

"We're just a funny beverage company who hates corporate marketing as much as you do. Our evil mission is to make people laugh and get more of them to drink more healthy beverages more often, all while helping to kill plastic pollution."[1]

With its unconventional manifesto, Liquid Death channels the rebellious spirit of DDB's creative revolution in advertising. In 1959, DDB's "Think Small" ad for Volkswagen broke convention by winking at consumer skepticism: "We know you get it, so let's skip the sales pitch."

Brand manifestos often borrow the rebellious tone and provocative ideas of sociopolitical manifestos to challenge norms and galvanize audiences. By employing provocative, declarative language, these manifestos aim to move beyond profit-driven strategies by forging deeper ideological and emotional connections with consumers. They present the brand not just as a product, but as a catalyst for change and a champion of specific ideals.

This approach aligns brands with progressive or avant-garde movements, appealing to consumers who prioritize authenticity and marketing that feels genuine. By leveraging unconventional creative choices, brands cultivate a distinctive voice and identity that resonate with their audience's values.

Liquid Death's CEO Mike Cessario emphasizes that a charismatic brand offers people a compelling reason to engage beyond the product's functional aspects. As he told Bloomberg, "If you have a valuable brand, it means that people have a reason to care about you beyond the small functional difference."[2]

Liquid Death's website states: "Plastic is not technically recyclable anymore because it is no longer profitable to recycle. Most recycling facilities simply send plastic to landfills because they would go out of business trying to recycle it. . . . But of all the aluminum produced since 1888, over 75 percent of it is still in current use. #DeathToPlastic"[3]

Jacob Stern writes in *The Atlantic* that when it comes to selling water, "the brand is what's important; the brand is all there is." Stern further emphasizes that "the advertisement is the product."[4] Cessario underscores the wider truth of this: "Like every truly large valuable brand, it is all marketing and brand because the reason people choose things 98 percent of the time is not rational. It's emotional," he told *The Washington Post.* "People often bring up that the marketing is so important because it's water, but it is important for every single product that exists."[5]

Manifesto as Signifier

Before Johnson & Johnson (J&J) went public, General Robert Wood Johnson, chairman from 1932 to 1963 and a founding family member, crafted "Our Credo." This document articulated the company's commitment to corporate social responsibility well before brand manifestos became mainstream. It served as a "moral compass" and a blueprint for achieving business success. According to J&J, "Our Credo" remains the cornerstone of the company's principles, guiding every aspect of its operations.[6]

The 1943 version of "Our Credo" opens with:

We believe our first responsibility is to the patients, doctors and nurses, to mothers and fathers and all others who use our products and services. In meeting their needs everything we do must be of high quality. We must constantly strive to provide value, reduce our costs and maintain reasonable prices. Customers' orders must be serviced promptly and accurately. Our business partners must have an opportunity to make a fair profit.[7]

J&J's current statement includes their responsibility to all stakeholders: "We are responsible to our employees who work with us throughout the world. . . . We are responsible to the communities in which we live and work and to the world community as well. . . . Our final responsibility is to our stockholders."[8]

The decision by General Robert Wood Johnson to craft "Our Credo" just before Johnson & Johnson (J&J) went public underscores the importance of publicly affirming a company's principles and mission. This document, akin to a brand manifesto, serves as more than a guiding statement—it is a declaration of the company's commitment to corporate responsibility and its blueprint for achieving business prosperity.

A manifesto brings emotional clarity and purpose to a brand, helping foster substantive connections with all stakeholders. Clearly articulating the brand's values and goals enhances engagement and aligns the brand with its audience's beliefs.[9] Initially intended as an internal motivational tool, manifestos are increasingly used externally as an outward brand expression. Brands today leverage manifesto marketing to align their public narratives with their core beliefs, extending this approach beyond traditional advertising into channels like social media and package design, as in figure 11.1.

FOCUS: BRAND IDENTITY: LULULEMON MANIFESTO / PENTAGRAM

11.1 Lululemon Manifesto. Client: Lululemon; Design Studio: Pentagram; Partner & Lead Designer: Eddie Opara; Designers: Brankica Harvey, Ken Deegan, Pedro Mendes, Xinle Huang

11.1 (*continued*) "The lululemon manifesto is a graphic representation of the core values of lululemon athletica, one of the world's leading activewear brands. The company goes beyond retail to function as a holistic lifestyle brand for a devoted following of consumers who apply its vision of wellness to their everyday practice of yoga, running, working out, self-care and mindfulness."

Pentagram partner Eddie Opara and his creative team developed this . . . "new version of the manifesto for lululemon's typography-covered shopping bags and other applications, including environmental graphics for its headquarters and stores, and a special line of apparel that allows adherents to literally wrap themselves in the motivational language of the brand."—Pentagram

"Lululemon Manifesto: Brand Identity," Pentagram.com, accessed September 6, 2024, https://www.pentagram.com/work/lululemon-manifesto/story

(*continued on next page*)

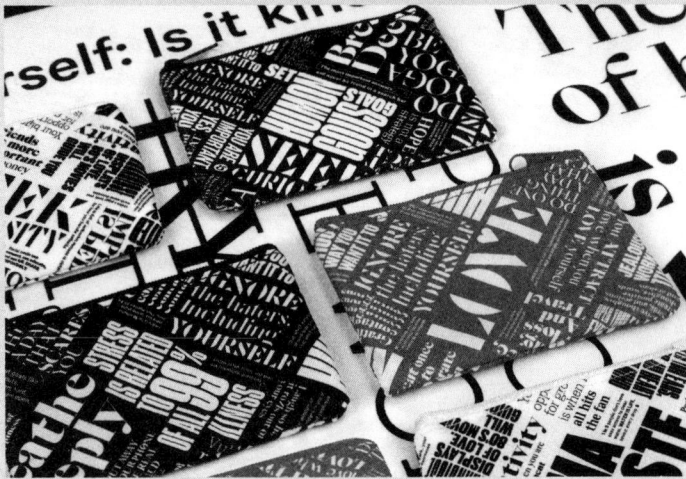

11.1 *(continued)*

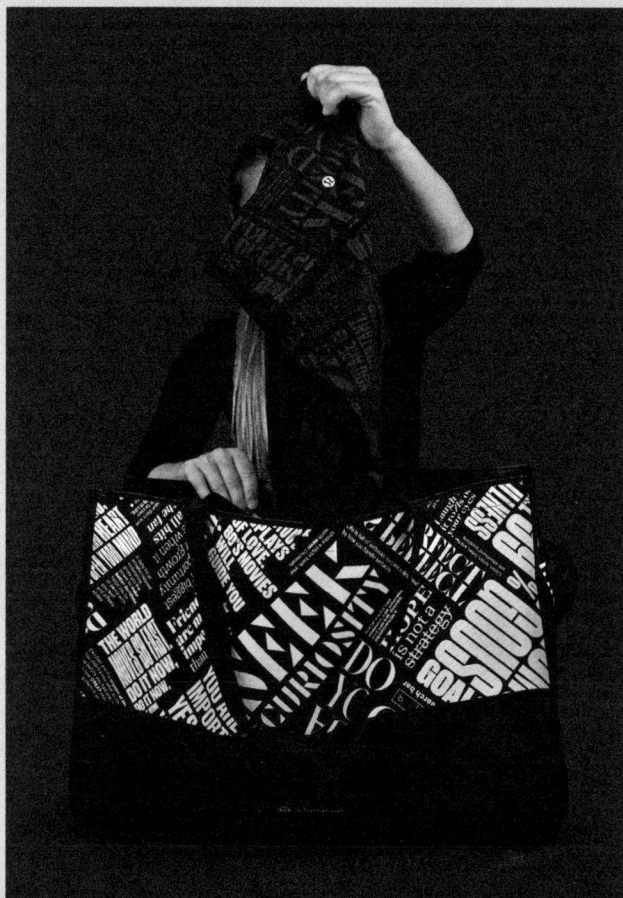

11.1 (*continued*)

(*continued on next page*)

(*continued from previous page*)

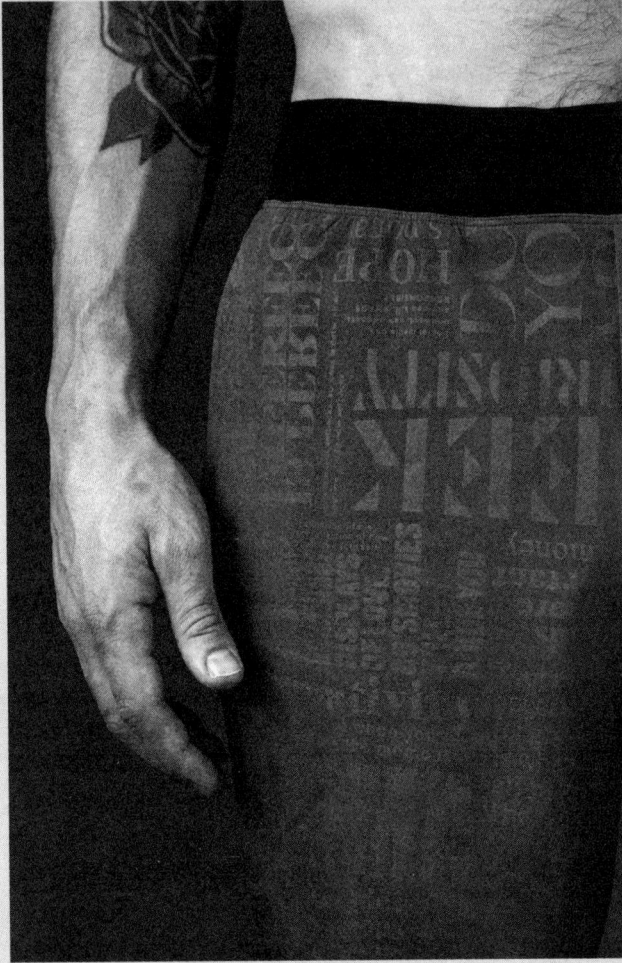

11.1 (*continued*)

A brand manifesto is vital to brand building for internal alignment or external communication. It reveals the brand's core philosophy, defining its purpose and unique proposition.

"Brand manifestos are foundational and serve as the brand's voice and North Star," says Melissa Grady Dias, Cadillac's Global Chief Marketing Officer. "At Cadillac, our brand strategy informs everything we do—from writing briefs and creating content to selecting partners." Dias also notes that while campaign manifestos are deeply rooted in the brand, they are often tied to specific moments, such as launches or reveals. "Campaign manifestos are more tactical, focusing on eliciting an emotion or driving an action, whereas the brand manifesto transcends these immediate objectives, guiding the brand's overall direction and identity."[10]

Manifestos take various forms—written statements, spoken-word videos, reels, or integrated into packaging and advertising. They convey core values, spark action, and create a lasting emotional impact like the Lululemon manifesto (see figure 11.1).

Regardless of its specific use, a brand manifesto captures the brand's promise and purpose-driven goals. It outlines commitments to stakeholders and its cultural aspirations, reinforcing its role as a market leader and a cultural participant.

A brand manifesto is an inspirational statement that encompasses:

- **Brand essence or DNA**: The core identity and foundational elements that define the brand
- **Cultural relevance**: The brand's alignment with cultural values and trends
- **Contributions to society**: The brand's impact on individuals, communities, creatures, or the planet
- **Enhancement of well-being**: The brand's role in improving quality of life, well-being, or productivity
- **Brand values**: The principles and beliefs that underpin the brand and their significance
- **Core brand purpose**: A cohesive articulation of the brand's functional benefits, emotional resonance, and social relevance, genuinely embraced from within to ensure authenticity
- **Purpose with emotional resonance**: The brand's "why"—its purpose articulated in a way that resonates emotionally with its audience. It can also highlight the specific emotional benefits the brand offers

Manifesto Components

A brand manifesto can exert significant cultural influence by aligning with its corporate mission and the values of its target audience. To deepen this connection, it should address relevant societal issues that resonate with consumers who share similar beliefs, particularly if the brand holds credibility in that space. Crafting a persuasive manifesto involves considering key factors, which are:

Audience: The manifesto must resonate with the target audience by addressing their unique needs and aspirations, reflecting an understanding of what matters most to create relevance and foster connection.

Value: The brand should deliver an emotional, symbolic, or experiential advantage that fosters lasting connections built on generosity and reciprocity.

Emotive tone and clarity: The tone should evoke a specific emotional response. This tone influences how people experience the message, inspiring warmth and belonging or driving action and commitment.

Differentiation: The manifesto should emphasize the brand's unique qualities with humility, avoiding self-aggrandizement. Nick Sonderup, chief creative officer at StrawberryFrog, advises that differentiation is key.[11]

Brand stories: The manifesto should contribute to and help define the brand's unique narrative, including its origin, purpose, mission, essence, and key differentiators. It should highlight how the brand's actions and values benefit individuals, society, or the environment, providing a compelling reason for its existence.

Voice: The voice should be focused, emotionally resonant, and perhaps philosophical, effectively conveying the brand's core message and fostering a connection with the audience. It symbolizes the bond between the brand and its audience, capturing the brand's essence and setting the stage for the tagline. This voice can reflect various personas—whether the consumer's, the brand's, or another relevant figure—and may use provocative language to challenge norms, creating urgency or significance around the brand's message.

Crafting a compelling brand voice is essential for effective storytelling. This voice serves as the narrative thread connecting audiences with the brand's unique personality, identity, and values. A distinct voice has the ability to captivate the audience, grab their attention, and communicate in a way that fosters a lasting relationship with consumers. Through carefully cultivated stories, a brand's voice becomes the fabric for building emotional resonance, trust and loyalty."[12]

—Dr. Kristen Schiele, associate professor of marketing
at the University of Southern California

Symbolism and Imagery: Symbolic visuals or imagery can evoke strong emotions and associations, enhancing the manifesto's message and making it memorable.

Structure: The opening sentence sets the tone and captures attention, while the concluding sentence leaves a lasting impression. A strong manifesto engages readers from beginning to end, encouraging them to consider the message.

Declaration: It is a concise, heartfelt mission statement outlining the brand's purpose and the positive change it seeks to create. Bold, clear statements about the brand's purpose, values, and vision help differentiate it from competitors.

Values: It should reflect the brand's ethical stance and align with audience expectations, guiding its purpose and the promises made to stakeholders.

Vision: By outlining the brand's long-term goals and role in a dynamic future, the manifesto reinforces its guiding ideals and aspirations.

Call to Action: The manifesto invites consumers to join a movement, support a cause, or align with the brand's mission. Rather than pushing for a direct purchase or short-term response, it fosters a sense of purpose and participation—aiming to build a lasting emotional connection.

The Greater Branding Program and Manifesto Relationship

A well-crafted brand manifesto offers significant benefits both internally and externally. Internally, it unites employees by clarifying the brand's core values and mission, thereby strengthening corporate culture. Externally, it provides the target audience with insight into the brand's essence, fostering emotional connections beyond mere transactions. The manifesto's core message is often integrated into marketing and communication materials, effectively conveying the brand's identity and purpose to a broader audience.

The key is maintaining coherence between the brand narrative presented in the manifesto and the overarching branding strategy. For example, as Lululemon states on their website: "Our manifesto is one way we share our culture with the community. It's an evolving collection of bold thoughts that allow for some real conversations to take place. Get to know our manifesto and learn more about what lights our fire."[13]

On X (formerly Twitter), Lululemon's post stated, "They're more than words, rather a collection of mindful, motivating and moving statements that make what we call our manifesto—and ultimately reflect our 20-year journey."[14]

A manifesto provides a platform to articulate a brand's aspirations regarding its impact on the world and cultural influence. Many brands use manifestos to express their cultural values, aiming to connect with consumers through shared principles and convictions. This strategic approach fosters a deeper bond between the brand and its audience.

Interview: Kristie Malivindi, Creative Director, Jones Knowles Ritchie (JKR)

Kristie Malivindi: Photographer: JKR

Kristie Malivindi is a creative director at global branding agency Jones Knowles Ritchie (JKR). With over two decades of experience, Kristie has been instrumental in building brands. Her expertise includes creating the new fashion brand Kate Spade Saturday, as well as guiding established brands in making impactful changes, such as the Burger King Meltdown. Additionally, she has helped legacy brands like M&M's and The Coca-Cola Company own and enhance their iconic status. Originally from Boston, she is a graduate of MassArt and currently resides in London.

Social or cultural impact and purpose should not be performative but instead be part of a brand's values. How do you incorporate this into your branding process at JKR?

To create authentic social or cultural impact, brand purpose must be: 1) built from a core brand truth; and 2) backed with action. Purpose can't be invented or changed to chase trends. In fact, it shouldn't be fundamentally changed, full stop. While values can evolve over time, a brand's purpose should be intrinsically linked to the brand's philosophy, products, or services—its reason for being. Then, of course, action with tangible proof points must be demonstrated.

Take Patagonia—a best-in-class example—who are "in the business to save our home planet." While it's a big, bold statement for a commercial brand to make, it's undeniably and credibly who they are. Since day one, Patagonia has created products to facilitate people's love of and appreciation for the great outdoors. Authentic link to products: check. As for demonstrative action? Take your pick—from ongoing external platforms like Worn Wear (repair-and-recycle program) or 1 percent for the planet, to internal shifts like creating new, organic cotton supply chains—Patagonia lives and breathes its beliefs.

At JKR, our branding philosophy is summed up perfectly in what's often called an Oscar Wilde quote, "Be yourself. Everyone else is already taken." Being authentic and acting with integrity are imperative to resonating honestly in culture. As strategic, creative partners we consult, we steer, and we can have honest, direct conversations with our clients to that effect.

What role does a brand manifesto play in a comprehensive branding strategy and program?

A manifesto, by definition, is meant to inform and inspire. I find them invaluable in the process of brand-building—as the first stepping-stone from strategy to creating the outward brand expression.

A well-crafted manifesto conveys tone, character, and personality, while outlining the essential aspects of the brand. It is easily the cheat sheet that a designer can pick up to begin brand creation. However, an exceptional manifesto evokes emotion and serves as a valuable tool for aligning and rallying internal teams and agency partners behind the scenes.

Branding is intended to last for several years. How does that modify your thinking when working in a complex consumer landscape?

I agree with the premise that branding is a long game. I think if we start there, putting the complex landscape to the side for a moment, the ambition when creating a brand is always: recognition and relevance (or timeless + timely) to create a meaningful connection.

Recognition is timeless. To achieve this, you need distinct assets and behaviors deployed consistently. Relevance is where you can flex to be timely. For this, you need enough built-in agility to adapt—to ever-increasing ecosystems across ever-growing lists of touchpoints, to new technologies, to new needs of new consumers. Finally, connection is the development of relationships, the emotional pull, the brand in the mind. It's what people think and feel when they think of a brand, what compels them to engage.

So, to oversimplify, you should make every brand asset as ownable and meaningful as possible. Use them consistently until they're known, then start playing and flexing to keep things interesting and stay part of the wider cultural conversation.

Adapt. Evolve. Stay true to yourself, but never stand still.

What should be integral to creative brand strategy? And how do you keep the brand promise?

Creative brand strategy: there are so many models out there. Every company, every agency, everyone has their preferred terms, their houses or keys or pyramids or golden circles or onions. Design idea or behavioral idea, creative platform, or campaign idea . . . Is it the promise, or the purpose, or the "why"? However you want to define it, you stay true by always referring to your North Star—always check that your creativity is in service of what is authentic and true to your brand.

What is integral? Whatever the model, keep it succinct: if you're repeating yourself within your chosen chart, you're either doing it wrong or you've got too many boxes to fill in (so try a more straightforward model). Make it simple: the strategy should inspire solutions, not try to solve one. Make it specific, based on a pointed insight or a brand truth—it has to have a point of view.

How do you drive a brand's role in culture? And how do you make sure it's responsible and responsive?

First, and most importantly, you have to start from a place of authenticity. Clearly define what your brand stands for and what it delivers, setting the foundation for genuine purpose. Next, determine your key messages and identify your target audience, meeting them where they are.

Responsibility involves mindfulness and thorough research, utilizing internal networks, focus groups, and diversity, equity, and inclusion advisors to ensure the impact of your work aligns with your intentions. For responsiveness, agility is essential. Having essential infrastructure to promptly respond to cultural changes, combined with the confidence to genuinely articulate a point of view, is crucial.

CHAPTER 12

BRAND BUILDING: THE POWER OF STORIES

You are not enough.[1]

Approximately 80 percent of Chinese university students report experiencing mild symptoms of social phobia or social anxiety disorder, making it one of the most widely discussed topics on mainland China's social media platforms.[2]

In response, Apple produced *Little Garlic*, a film created by TBWA\Media Arts Lab Shanghai, shot entirely on iPhone, as part of its annual "Shot on iPhone" Lunar New Year campaign. It tells the story of Wei, a young girl grappling with insecurities who discovers her power to shape-shift. The narrative asks: What's more powerful: becoming someone else or embracing yourself?

Written by Chinese screenwriter Pan Yiran and directed by Marc Webb, *Little Garlic* stars Chinese actor Fan Wei. Its timely message resonated globally, affirming "You are enough."

After seven years of Lunar New Year films, Shot on iPhone continues as a product demonstration. *Little Garlic* went beyond, delivering a poignant story and timely message that garnered 306 million views in 72 hours, surpassing Super Bowl attention. Online reception was overwhelmingly positive, generating over 1700 press articles with nearly quadruple the online buzz.[3]

Apple has consistently showcased its products as catalysts for creativity, not mere devices. A resonant brand doesn't just tell a story; it embodies the story itself.

Every corporate action, message, and touchpoint shapes how we perceive a brand over time. How a company and its teams conceive, create, distribute, and manage these elements crafts the brand's narrative and defines its purpose and benefits in the audience's mind. Just as a story unfolds through its plot points, a brand evolves from its past and present actions, as well as the narratives it shares.

As a brand recounts its origins, purpose, and impact, it undergoes continuous evolution, embodying an ongoing process of becoming. The brand narrative and its sub-stories shape perceived benefits and reinforce its identity. Thus, a brand acts as a collective narrative, one that evolves through the contributions of both its creators and audience, underscoring the critical role of storytelling. This dynamic nature underscores the need to rethink how we approach brand storytelling.

"Storiestelling"

Even in an era of active consumer engagement and critique, a brand must start by crafting its own story. To do this effectively, companies and creative agencies enlist talent, directors, creative teams, and marketing professionals to develop and produce these narratives. For a mass audience to relate and see themselves in these stories, creative, production, and marketing teams must be diverse and inclusive, capable of representing a wide range of perspectives.

Brand storytelling must evolve into "storiestelling," an inclusive practice that reflects identities across race, ethnicity, socioeconomic status, gender expression, age, and disability. Excluding diverse voices is unethical and a missed opportunity to connect with a broader audience. Such omissions can be seen as a form of marginalization, overlooking the unique needs and narratives of diverse groups.[4] Despite progress, many overestimate the advancements in representation within branding, design, and advertising.[5] According to a recent 4A's Diversity in Agencies Survey, 90 percent of ad agency executives are white.[6] Kantar research shows that while visibility has improved—32 percent of ads feature people with diverse skin tones or ethnicities, and 80 percent feature women—only 4 percent show women in aspirational roles.[7]

The World Health Organization reports that 16 percent of the global population lives with some form of disability, yet advertisers represent this group in fewer than 2 percent of advertisements.[8] Additionally, people aged 65 and older, who comprise a growing demographic, appear in just 3.5 percent of ads.[9] The underrepresentation of older women is especially pronounced.[10]

Authenticity relies on diverse and inclusive representation. Without it, narratives lack depth and fail to reflect the broad spectrum of human experience. Stories should amplify voices from various backgrounds and life experiences, elevating historically marginalized perspectives while rejecting dehumanizing or stereotypical portrayals.

Brand as a Facilitator

Fuzzy Feelings is a four-minute short film that follows a young woman struggling with her grumpy boss. To cope, she creates a stop-motion film on her iPhone featuring a puppet version of her boss in comical mishaps. As time passes, her treatment of the boss puppet becomes increasingly harsh. However, when her boss surprises her with a gift in real life, she sees him in a new light and decides to show kindness by using the gift to craft a dog. The animation concludes with a heartwarming resolution that reflects real-life transformations. Combining live action and stop-motion, created entirely using an iPhone and Mac, and set to George Harrison's "Isn't It a Pity," the short film has garnered over 31 million views, with an average watch time of two minutes and 23 seconds and a 65 percent completion rate. Praised worldwide, it topped holiday ad lists, generated over 300 headlines across 35 countries, and increased Harrison's streaming by 25 percent. Internet reviews celebrated it as a work of art, emphasizing its inspiring message of kindness.[11] In line with Apple's brand story, the animation illustrates how creativity can shift perspectives and make holidays more meaningful. By presenting Apple products as tools for creativity and fostering deeper human connections, this heartwarming Christmas story reinforces the idea that "you make the holidays" and evokes warm, festive feelings. Apple received the 2024 Emmy Award for Outstanding Commercial for *Fuzzy Feelings*, marking the first time a brand has won the award consecutively for two years.

FOCUS: ARIEL'S "SEE THE SIGNS, SHARE THE LOAD" / BBDO INDIA

Ariel, a leading laundry brand in India, continues its "Share The Load" campaign with its latest installment focusing on unconscious gender-role biases. In its sixth year, the campaign explores how unequal distribution of laundry duties contributes to relationship problems. Research shows that 65 percent of women in India feel emotionally distant from their spouses, often leading to communication breakdowns. The new campaign, "See the Signs, Share The Load," emphasizes how imbalanced chore distribution affects relationships.

Using a problem-solution format, Ariel aims to create happier households where men and women "Share The Load" equally.[12] This four-minute film portrays a woman's growing disconnection from her husband due to the overwhelming burden of household work. It follows a mature couple whose relationship has changed over time. The husband comes to recognize their silent separation and learns from their daughter that the mother's unshared responsibilities for child-rearing and household chores have contributed to their widening distance. Realizing his role in this separation, the husband takes steps to rebuild their relationship. The film concludes with the couple happily sharing a cup of tea, while the washing machine runs in the background.

Josy Paul, chairman and chief creative officer at BBDO India, describes this edition of "Share The Load" as an eye-opener for married couples and younger generations, revealing a hidden truth about relationship neglect.

Sharat Verma, chief marketing officer of P&G India and vice-president of fabric care for the Indian subcontinent, explains that the campaign aims to drive change by sparking meaningful conversations, "With Ariel 'Share The Load,' we want to engage with consumers, join their conversations, and amplify them to promote meaningful dialogue."[13]

The Impact of Brand Stories

A brand story typically begins with a protagonist in a stable situation, until an inciting incident disrupts their world and challenges the status quo. This event sets them on a journey toward growth or resolution, with the brand playing a pivotal role in guiding that transformation and ultimately improving the protagonist's life.

Brands impact consumers' lives in several significant ways:

Problem solving: Brands meet specific needs by offering products or services that address practical requirements or emotional desires, providing tailored solutions that align with consumer aspirations.

Community building: Many brands foster communities around shared interests, values, or lifestyles, offering platforms where like-minded individuals can connect and engage. Examples include Twitch, Reddit, and other niche networks that thrive on user participation and common purpose.

Experiential engagement: Brands create physical, virtual, and hybrid environments—such as retail spaces, websites, social media, and events—to provide spaces for meaningful interactions and connections with consumers.

Innovation and influence: Brands drive industry innovation through research and development, introducing new ideas and technologies that shape consumer behavior and market trends. For example, Klick Health Toronto and KVI Brave Fund's "Voice 2 Diabetes" uses voice samples for diagnostics, a pioneering approach recognized by Diego Machado, Cannes jury president for the Innovation Lions and global chief creative officer at AKQA Global. Machado remarked, "In a few years, perhaps by 2034, we'll look back and recognize this as the first use of voice for medical diagnosis. This isn't just a significant advancement for this brand but also paves the way for innovations in other fields."[14]

Connection and communication: Brands build authentic relationships by clearly expressing their values and personality across all consumer interactions. When messaging stays consistent, people connect with the brand's purpose and not just its products.

Identity and self-expression: Brands allow individuals to express their affiliation with specific groups or tribes, known as brand tribes.[15] A brand tribe is a community of people who collectively identify with a brand and share common values and beliefs about it. This affiliation fosters a strong sense of belonging and reinforces a shared identity among members. For example, when a group adopts a particular footwear brand, it signals shared values and strengthens their collective identity.

FOCUS: ON'S DOCUMENTARY "THE RIGHT TO RACE" / HUNGRY MAN PRODUCTIONS

Swiss sportswear brand On released *The Right to Race*, a documentary that follows Dominic Lokinyomo Lobalu's journey from stateless refugee to elite athlete. Premiering on World Refugee Day, the film celebrates untapped potential and delves into themes of identity, representation, and belonging.

Directed by Richard Bullock and produced by Hungry Man Productions, the documentary traces Lobalu's path from the war-torn regions of South Sudan to the athletic tracks of Switzerland. It follows his struggle to represent his new country at the World Athletics Championships, despite being excluded from official refugee teams and facing a decade-long wait for Swiss citizenship.[16]

Lokinyomo Lobalu said, "I was born in South Sudan in a small village called Chukudum. When the war started we lost everything. We lost our parents. At nine years of age, I was forced to run away from my country to Kenya to look for a better life. Because I was the only boy in my family, my sisters didn't have a chance to go to school. They are all looking to me. So they have all their hope in me."[17]

It's Not About the Brand

While the brand is important, the primary focus should be on the audience.

A brand's role is often to facilitate meaningful transformation. To craft a compelling narrative, it is crucial to understand the audience's issues, challenges, desires, and aspirations for a better present and future. This understanding should encompass their hopes for themselves, their families, their communities, and the planet. By demonstrating genuine compassion and insight, brands can create stories that inspire action, convert individuals into advocates, and encourage engagement.

Jonathan Bond and Richard Kirshenbaum, founders of ad agency Kirshenbaum Bond & Partners (now KBS), articulated their philosophy in *Under the Radar: Talking to Today's Cynical Consumer*. They argue that "persuasive marketing should be invisible," because once we recognize a message as marketing manipulation, it loses its persuasive power. Their creative agency's tongue-in-cheek motto captured their point of view perfectly: "Your strategy is showing."[18]

Their emphasis on subtlety left a lasting impact on me. I strive to capture and hold audience attention by avoiding conventional advertising tactics, steering clear of overt selling, and eschewing typical ad-speak. I often compare effective advertising to the aroma of freshly baked pie—enticing, inviting, and impossible to ignore. It doesn't push; it pulls you in.

MAKE IT SHAREWORTHY

Focus on resonance: Tell stories your audience genuinely connects with. Focus on meaning and engagement rather than promotion to spark emotional impact.

Ensure relatability: Address the audience's needs, desires, and aspirations so they can see themselves in the story. Make it relevant and personal to enhance its impact, as personalization is crucial in today's market.[19]

Evaluate shareability: Determine whether the story is compelling enough to share. If it wouldn't inspire you to share it, refine it until it becomes more engaging.

Distribute effectively: Select distribution channels based on where your audience is most active, and tailor the story to each channel's format and expectations. As Greg Braun, retired deputy global chief creative officer at Commonwealth/McCann, points out in our book, *Shareworthy: Advertising That Creates Powerful Connections Through Storytelling*, some stories are better suited to

(continued on next page)

(continued from previous page)

specific formats—for example, a layered, character-driven narrative like *Succession* works far better as a TV series than as a PowerPoint presentation.

Create emotional impact: Develop an original story with the right emotional tone to inspire your audience to feel or act. Ensure that the emotional resonance aligns with the story's message and purpose.

Respect Your Audience: Show respect for your audience and those featured in your story. Doing so builds trust and strengthens the credibility of your narrative.

Interview: Yousuke Ozawa, Creative Director, Ultrasupernew K.K., Tokyo

Yousuke Ozawa. Photography: Mariko Ozawa

After graduating in 2003, Yousuke packed his bags, said goodbye to Tokyo, and headed off to New York to learn how to become a creative. His first role was at Dentsu New York where he learned art direction. Then, with a taste for the finer things in life, Yousuke was drawn first to an in-house creative role at fashion house Coach New York, and then to beauty brand Elizabeth Arden New York. Creative roles at Ogilvy Tokyo, Weber Shandwick Tokyo, and Havas followed, where he worked on award-winning campaigns for IBM, American Express, DAZN, and Sony Music. This eventually led to a position at the independent creative hotshop UltraSuperNew, where he sprinkles some creative magic for clients such as SKYN, Cloudflare, and HP. Well acquainted with international recognition, Yousuke has proudly received awards from Cannes Lions, D&AD, Clio, The One Show, AD Stars (now MAD Stars), Spikes Asia, The Webby Awards, FWA, the Effie awards, and the Tokyo Copywriters Club. When Yousuke is not creating commercials and brand communications, he likes to write short stories and spend lots of time with his wife and kids.

When you're not creating commercials and brand communications, you're writing short stories. What are the common characteristics of impactful storytelling in brand communications and short fiction?

The most important thing when writing short stories is to keep it simple and right to the point. But most importantly, betray expectations.

A really good way of assessing if you're on the right track is to verbally tell a story to someone and see if they would yawn. You might want to reconstruct the story if they do.

If that works, ideally, the story should resolve full circle and end with something that inspires the readers.

You've worked on both the brand and agency sides. How does that inform your creative thinking?

For creatives, our real client is the consumers. Whoever is watching the advertisement is the client. Most people are busy —at times lazy. They have no obligation or interest in what you are selling. So, holding that viewpoint is critical when coming up with the plot.

The question, "how do we get people to stop skipping and scrolling?" makes writing stories much more interesting. For that reason, most of the time, I don't even know where the story is headed or when it will resolve . . .

You've said to do great work that moves business forward, three strong elements are essential—a great relationship, great vision, and a great creative solution. Please tell us more.

Yes, and I still believe that.

It is not a "chicken or the egg" situation, but a pyramid to me.

At the foundation, there is a "great relationship." Built upon that is a "great vision." Finally, at the very top, is a "great creative solution."

Every business or industry is merely a collection of people. And the glue that connects everyone together is, quite simply, trust. Over time, the bond with someone gets stronger and naturally we become partners. Sometimes, even family. Clients obviously feel at ease and open to suggestions with that mindset.

So, no matter how groundbreaking and innovative the creative idea, if there is no trust between the client and us, we will be wasting time. We rarely buy things from someone we don't trust or don't know. We buy from someone we trust, respect, or aspire to be.

The middle part of the pyramid is "great vision." That is strategy.

Once trust is established with clients, we can work on selling their product/services. We want to create an impact with a limited budget. So, most of the time, finding the right strategy is necessary.

The other reason why we need a great strategy is to convince all internal stakeholders. Not everyone works directly with the creative agency, so the presentation deck will be passed around, sometimes via email. If the strategy is bulletproof (insightful, clever, efficient, inspiring, or charming), we get to the fun stuff—the creative solution.

As fun as it seems, this is the hardest part. Because now you must take all that into account, and crystallize it into something people find entertaining and exciting. It's a battle between logic and art, emotion and information, common and uncommon. Yet, when you find the right idea, it will penetrate the market like a giant arrow, sneaking into people's subconscious, giving them a strong feeling about that brand.

As a leading authority on brand communications and someone who has spent a number of years living in Japan and the United States, how do you approach cross-cultural brand communications? Can an advertising or branding solution actually be cross-cultural?

Yes, it can. I grew up in the US, Singapore, and Japan, and used to hate not having any roots when I was younger. Every time we relocated, a chunk of my history disappeared for the time being. So, it was harder to be on the same page as everyone else. Kids are very cliquey, so not knowing specific things in pop culture definitely affected the way kids interacted with me.

But still, I had a lot of friends. I believe it was because I knew people were the same wherever I went. There were always cool people and people I could look up to. When I see a great advertisement, I have the same feeling. Old campaigns like Avis's "We Try Harder," P&G's "Thank You, Mom," or Queensland's Islands campaign "Best Job in the World," all have strong human insights that connect beyond borders. How the execution is worded and positioned requires cultural knowledge, but campaigns can definitely be cross-cultural.

What strategies or approaches do you use to consistently innovate and push creative boundaries year after year within the industry?

First, continue being interested in great advertising and people. It takes a lot of energy to come up with an idea that breaks through the clutter; the creative process can be very messy and chaotic. But when you find that special idea, you'll be as happy as can be.

For the juniors who are reading this: Trust me, it's the best feeling.

(You just have to think more than your peers.)

I study great campaigns from the past that moved me emotionally and try to dissect them. Then I see how that thinking can be applied to the brief. If nothing pops into my head, I research the product/service even more so I can understand it on a deeper level, hoping I will find something new.

It's also important to capture the essence of the brand, especially the feeling, because people are busy and don't have the capacity to remember a lot of things. But feelings are subconscious and will be anchored in our long-term memory.

Secondly, think of yourself as the consumer.

It is important to set the target personality as a busy, cynical, lazy version of yourself. It will make the idea simpler, more engaging/authentic, and get you off the couch. And I always study the content that makes me stop what I am doing.

I tell younger creatives when they are doing something else during work hours, they should at least "commit to it." When they are watching something on YouTube, or hanging out with friends (this is not ethical, btw), they have to put their full attention to it, because they might find something interesting, or more importantly, an idea.

12.1 Short film: *Meeting Again For The First Time*. Client: SKYN; Annie Hou, Associate Director—Sales & Marketing—MAM LifeStyles; Creative Agency: UltraSuperNew; Creative Director: Yousuke Ozawa; Producers: Daiki Shimizu & Alexander Tatsuki; Web Producer: Mana Shigeki; Art Director: Rebecca Chen; Copywriter: Noga; Production Company: Amana; Director: Tomokazu Saito

SKYN condoms aimed to help long-term couples rediscover the initial excitement and affection they felt when they first met, which often fades over time. They also wanted to encourage couples to reflect on why they're still together and what sparked their journey as partners.

Meeting Again For The First Time involved an intriguing social experiment captured in a short film, posing the question, "Can a couple rekindle their feelings for each other if they met again as strangers?"

Haruka and Chiaki Hatakeyama, married for ten years, volunteered to be hypnotized individually, with the goal of making them forget each other entirely. After the hypnosis, they were introduced to each other as if meeting for the first time, with no memory of their shared past. Initially awkward, the couple eventually connected emotionally, revealing their softer sides. When asked if they wanted to meet again, both said "Yes."

Annie Hou of SKYN explained that the brand has always focused on fostering deep connections between couples, and this campaign aimed to remind them of the core reason they stay together: because they genuinely like each other. Though there were initial doubts about the hypnosis working, the successful outcome left the team in awe.

"2023 One Show: Meeting Again For The First Time," Oneclub.org, accessed August 14, 2024, https://www.oneclub.org/awards/theoneshow/-award/47671/meeting-again-for-the-first-time

12.2 Short Film: *Real Blind Date.* Client: SKYN; Annie Hou, Associate Director—Sales & Marketing—MAM LifeStyles; Creative Agency: UltraSuperNew; Creative Director: Yousuke Ozawa; Producer: Daiki Shimizu; Web Producers: Mana Shigeki, Alexander Watanabe; Assistant Producer: Alex Schmidt; Art Director: Sayu Fujii; Art Director: Rebecca Chen; Art Director: Yusuke Suzuki; Copywriter: Kohei Okamura; UX/UI Designer: Yerai Zamorano; Creative: Yan He; Production Company: Geek Pictures; Director: Takuya Kawasaki; Producer: Satoshi Ootake

SKYN condoms redefined the concept of a "blind date" by organizing a unique romantic encounter where a single man and woman, both seeking partners, met while blindfolded. Created by UltraSuperNew Tokyo, social campaign "Real Blind Date" challenges superficial judgments based on appearance, which often hinder the dating process and the potential to find genuine love and intimacy.

12.2 (*continued*) Hannah, 23, and You, 20, were paired through an audition, despite their usual preferences being quite different—Hannah typically dates older men with long hair, while You is usually drawn to introverted women. Blindfolded throughout their date, they spent time together, and they grew emotionally closer. Their initial guardedness faded into genuine enjoyment of each other's company. By the end of the date, both admitted, with some shyness, that they were attracted to each other.

Yousuke Ozawa added, "Although 'looks' plays an important role, we wanted to emphasize the importance of interpersonal compatibility, which tends to be ignored sometimes. What was interesting is, during the experiment, the more they spent time with one another they were visibly and emotionally getting close to each other. We also made some ground rules, where they couldn't talk about certain topics, like age and occupation, just so the conversation can focus on understanding who they both are."

"UltraSuperNew: SKYN Gives a Whole New Meaning to the Term 'Blind Date' in New Christmas Campaign," *Little Black Book*,
November 11, 2023, accessed August 14, 2024, https://lbbonline.com/news/
skyn-gives-a-whole-new-meaning-to-the-term-blind-date-in-new-christmas-campaign

12.3 Campaign Hero film: *Soft Love, Brings Us Closer.* Client: SKYN; Annie Hou, Associate Director—Sales & Marketing—MAM LifeStyles; Creative Agency: UltraSuperNew; Creative Director: Yousuke Ozawa; Art Director: Rebbecca Chen; Copywriters: Nobuaki Nogamoto, Ryo Motooka; Producer: Daiki Shimizu; Web Producer: Mana Shigeki; Production company: Amana; Director: Akinori Kajima

When couples share a deep love, a unique bond forms. This connection allows them to identify each other, even without sight.

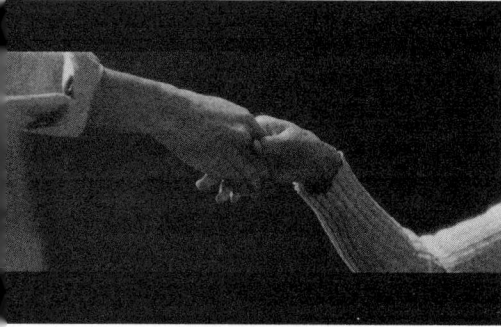

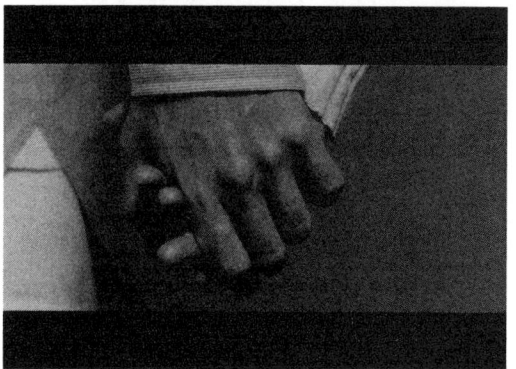

12.3 (*continued*) In this latest campaign, SKYN and agency UltraSuperNew explored whether partners could recognize one another solely by the touch of their hands.

"Soft Love Brings Us Closer," Ultrasupernew.com, accessed August 14, 2024, https://ultrasupernew.com /work/skyn

For example, I went for a full body checkup just the other day. It required everyone there to not eat for 10 hours prior to the checkup. Everyone was starving. For some reason I couldn't stop thinking about sandwiches . . . Then I noticed, Subway sandwiches is conveniently located across the street and the Subway sign was the first thing everyone saw coming in and out of the health checkup.

Whether intentional or not, I thought that was a great strategy. And it made me think, "What if we made an advertisement for a restaurant, targeting hospitals that do health checkups. Could we influence people to go to the restaurant?" It could be quite impactful for immediate conversion. So, I kept that idea in my back pocket and am still waiting for the right time, and the right client . . . Any takers? (just kidding!)

Interview: Emma Robbins, Chief Creative Officer, M&C Saatchi Melbourne

Emma Robbins is the Chief Creative Officer at M&C Saatchi Melbourne, where after 30 years' experience in Australian advertising, she's helping to build a National creative agency to help serve clients wanting to create great work with a positive impact on the people and communities they serve. Emma has built a career that is extremely rare in this industry. It's a career that has stared down discrimination, forged in the furnace of adversity, and thrived on the combination of talent, tenacity, kindness, and the lifting up of others. Emma's leadership, talent, and humanity has shone through in a male dominated industry. Having leadership responsibility thrust upon her as Clemenger BBDO's first ever female Executive Creative Director at the age of 32. Having had a significant experience in behavior change programs working with State and Commonwealth Government—Family Violence, Respect Women to name a few, Emma is highly motivated to make "meaningful work" a backbone of her current creative agency. Caring about people and our community, Emma led the creative pitch for the Victorian Government COVID-19 Communications response, working directly with The Department of Premier and Cabinet, Multiple Government Ministers and the Premier's Private Office. Creating the platform "Staying Apart Keeps Us Together" with bespoke communications programs for diverse (CALD) audiences and Aboriginal and Torres Strait Islander members of our community. Emma leads new business, has enormous experience in guiding communications for large corporations and public sector

Emma Robbins. Photographer: Chris Budgeon

programs, and has a passion for creating behavior change programs that support people, whilst building a culture of people who care and have a big heart. Emma is a mentor to young women in advertising through The Aunties Program, a lecturer and tutor of up-and-coming creative talent through AWARD School—Australia's premier course for aspiring creatives. She has been invited to judge at numerous local, national and international advertising award shows. She has been named Melbourne Advertising's Creative Leader of the Year, is a regular advertising public speaker locally and nationally. She's married to an artist, is a parent to two children, and loves Victoria's biggest and smallest galleries and events, is a mad Tigers fan, a lover of eating out, design, theater, live music, traveling, and family.

You've served on many industry awards juries and your work has garnered innumerable awards. What criteria do you use when creating work and judging work?

I look for ideas, first and foremost, that make me feel something. Generally, the amazing ones give me goosebumps, a cold chill up the back of my neck, a laugh that just bursts out, or sometimes, a green tinge of envy. After that, it's looking at that idea again from a craft point of view, a strategic point of view, and of course an "is it real" point of view.

How do you foster a sense of shared purpose between a brand and the audience?

Shared purpose from brands with their customers comes when brands don't behave like corporations but just like people. Sounds simple, but it's not for so many brands who continue to talk about themselves, their products, and how amazing they are. It's when brands think, speak, and act customer first, that their values feel shared with people. People to people is the place brands succeed from.

Diversity of racial representation and underrepresented groups (e.g., members of the LGBTQ+ communities) in advertising campaigns authentically reflects society. Why is it important to have diverse and inclusive creative teams as well?

For exactly the same reason. The advertising world must reflect the real world. To create ideas that resonate and that are relevant to all cultures, those ideas need to be created and crafted by diverse thinkers. Gone are the days when an advertising idea is created by a two-person creative team in a lush corner office. Now, ideas belong to many—to integrated thinkers from many disciplines—from strategic thinkers, data experts, designers, researchers, social and PR experts, as well as traditional advertising teams. No one owns the idea. The best ideas come from all kinds of minds, belonging to all kinds of thinkers from all kinds of cultural and diverse backgrounds.

Is there an insight about brand storytelling that you would like to share?

The best brand storytelling happens when a brand is telling the story of their customer. Their customer's need, their customer's life, their customer's success.

Not their own. Brands can appear arrogant and unapproachable when they tell a "we" story. We're the biggest. We're the most awarded. We're the most popular. People don't care about that. They care how being the biggest will help them feel. How being the most awarded will make them feel safer. Telling a brand's story is only relevant if it's about how customers will benefit from it.

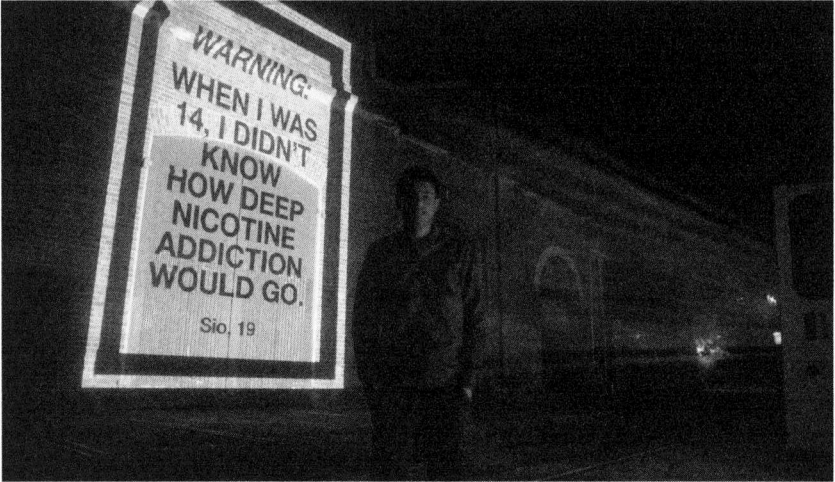

12.4 Anti-Vaping Campaign: We Are The Warning (https://www.uncloud.org/). Client: Minderoo Foundation; Creative Agency: M&C Saatchi Australia; Chief creative officer: Cam Blackley; Executive Creative Director: Emma Robbins; Creative Director: Chris Cheeseman; Art Directors: Codee MacDonald, Tristan Cornelius; Copywriters: Daniel Borghesi, Tessa Midgley, Jason Leigh

"Young Australians, whose mental and physical health has been affected by vaping, write the warning labels they were never given. Spearheaded by UNCLOUD where you can get the facts, get help, and share a warning of your own.

Created in tandem by minds across the M&C Saatchi Group, from public policy, creative, data, media, PR and social. The work seeks to create lasting behavioral and legislative change."—M&C Saatchi

"Minderoo Foundation: We Are The Warning," accessed August 11, 2024, https://mcsaatchi.com/change/work/minderoo-anti-vaping-campaign

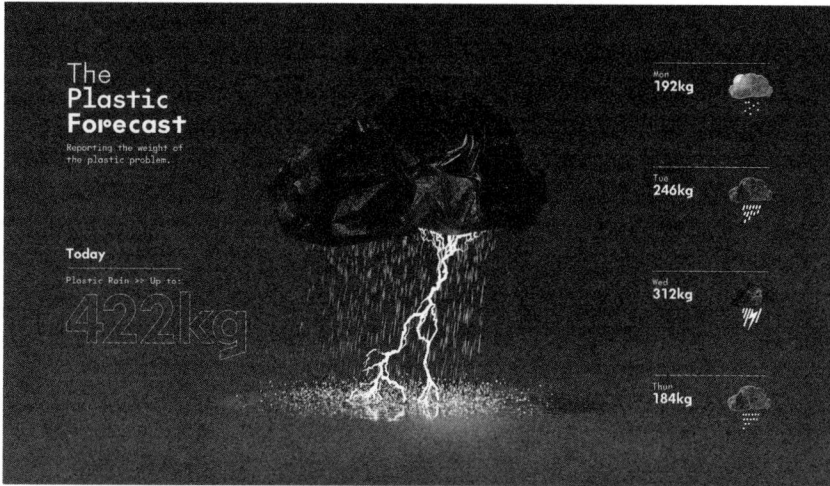

12.5 Data Visualization: The Plastic Forecast (https://plasticforecast.com/). Client: Minderoo Foundation; Creative Agency: M&C Saatchi; Chief Creative Officer: Cam Blackley; National Executive Creative Director: Emma Robbins; Creative Directors: Andrew van der Westhuyzen, Chris Cheeseman, Russel Fox; Senior Copywriter: Daniel Borghesi

Plastic production is inflicting severe environmental damage and is projected to triple by 2060. In response, the Minderoo Foundation and MC Saatchi have launched "The Plastic Forecast," a novel weather metric unveiled in Paris ahead of the UN's Plastic Treaty negotiations (INC-2) at UNESCO headquarters. Developed in collaboration with scientists from the Minderoo Foundation, this initiative estimates daily plastic precipitation using atmospheric research and weather data. The data is visualized through 3D plastic clouds created by Collider. The aim is to lobby UNESCO members to take action against the growing issue of plastic production.

Dr. Tony Worby, director of the Planet Portfolio at Minderoo Foundation, refers to The Plastic Forecast as a pivotal realization for anyone concerned about human and environmental health, "Because many plastic particles are so tiny, you cannot always see the plastic waste and pollution that plague this planet. The Plastic Forecast highlights this fact and will undoubtedly strike a chord with the general public. We believe this will be a powerful tool moving forward to generate widespread public support for an ambitious plastics treaty that puts a stop to unsustainable plastic production."

"Minderoo Foundation: The Plastic Forecast," accessed August 11, 2024, https://mcsaatchi.com/change/work/the-plastic-forecast

CHAPTER 13

SOCIAL IMPACT

I love ice cream.

When it's time to indulge, I reach for Ben & Jerry's. It's not just for the uniquely named flavors; it's because the founders, Ben Cohen and Jerry Greenfield, created a values-led business genuinely committed to advocating for social causes. Their values align with mine, and their commitment to making a positive social impact is long-term; they are not chasing trends or jumping on the flavor-of-the-month social issue. The founders and brand earned my trust by consistently working to make the world a better place.

Although they sold the brand to Unilever, Ben and Jerry's social mission continues: "We have a progressive, nonpartisan social mission that seeks to meet human needs and eliminate injustices in our local, national and international communities by integrating these concerns into our day-to-day business activities."[1]

Ben & Jerry's identifies five pillars to address the shortcomings of the US economic system, whose lack of equal opportunity has led to a widening wealth gap. The brand's "focus is on children and families, the environment, and sustainable agriculture on family farms," and it aims to:

- create economic opportunities for the underserved and promote sustainable economic justice models;
- strive to minimize the negative impact of manufacturing and the waste it creates;
- support sustainable and safe methods of food production that reduce environmental degradation, maintain the productivity of the land over time, and support the economic viability of family farms and rural communities;

- seek nonviolent paths to peace; and
- show deep respect for human beings inside and outside the company, and for the communities in which they live.[2]

Cohen and Greenfield pursued a double bottom line—profits and people—a philosophy they called the "double dip."

Positive Social Impact As a Guiding Principle

In a polarized climate, research shows a decline in trust in the institutions responsible for steering us through change and toward a more promising future. By contrast, according to a study, the public trusts the business sector far more than institutions such as the media and government.[3] Valid or not, for some, business is now the only institution perceived as both competent and ethical. At the same time, some view government as unethical and incompetent.[4] Big business can step up to fill the voids left by governments. With their larger platforms, louder voices, and immense influence, corporations can attempt to drive change on social justice issues more effectively than activists working alone. Given the many devastating issues affecting cultures and countries worldwide, we need brands to take a stand now more than ever.

Ben & Jerry's is a socially driven brand that makes prioritizing social impact and ethical practices integral to its mission and operations. Thankfully, they are not alone. Brands such as Dove, its parent company Unilever, Orange, Mastercard, Renault, Patagonia, Subaru, and Sheba, among others, share similar commitments. Altruistically driven brands are committed to creating positive societal change by addressing issues such as environmental sustainability, social justice, equity, and community development. They integrate values emphasizing the well-being of the planet and its inhabitants into their products, services, and policies, and strive to balance profit with social purpose.

In contrast, prosperity-driven brands prioritize financial growth and profit maximization above all else. Their primary focus is increasing wealth for executives, shareholders, and stakeholders, often emphasizing efficiency, market expansion, and revenue generation. While they may undertake corporate social responsibility initiatives, these are typically secondary to their primary goal of economic success. Prosperity-driven brands do not inherently prioritize social or environmental impacts in their core mission or business model.

Focusing on social impact should not be a mere marketing strategy. Companies can thrive by doing good and embracing the triple bottom line—planet, people, and prosperity—rather than focusing solely on profit. To drive positive change and achieve a meaningful impact, an organization's core mission must inform its decisions regarding products, services, policies, stakeholder relationships, and collaborations with branding, design, and advertising agencies.

This alignment ensures that their values and mission resonate with the issues they champion, the partnerships they form, and their adherence to core brand principles. Key areas of focus include:

- Social stances
- Access and equity
- Environmental stewardship and sustainability
- Community support
- Education and future generations
- The arts
- Partnerships with other brands, community leaders, activists, nonprofits, NGOs, and governmental organizations for a unified effort

A socially driven company can positively impact its customers, communities, and the world while reaping business benefits. However, maintaining a genuine and authentic presence in the social impact space is crucial. People quickly grow weary and skeptical of brands that profess to be purpose-driven but whose long-term actions fail to align with their stated values or messaging.

Regardless of the stance or social issue, a company may face criticism or even a boycott. Advocating for social issues or demonstrating allyship is increasingly essential for brands seeking to engage with Gen Z and socially conscious Millennials, Gen Xers, and Boomers. For instance, many brands, including Bud Light, Pepsi, and Target, have faced backlash for supporting various movements, such as Black Lives Matter. Bud Light's collaboration with transgender influencer Dylan Mulvaney sparked a notable backlash from some conservatives, resulting in widespread calls for a boycott. This example underscores the delicate balance brands must navigate in their social advocacy efforts.

A recent article in *Harvard Business Review* noted that "few anticipated the sustained decline in sales that Bud Light experienced" as a result of the boycott.[5] The authors attribute its severity to several factors, noting that consumers are more inclined to act on a boycott "when a product is more substitutable, when it is more visible, and when consumers feel psychological 'ownership' over it."[6] This "buycott" made some CEOs reluctant to engage with hot-button social issues.

Yet, in *Forbes*, Alan Schwarz observes that "more than ever, customers are valuing what brands stand for beyond the products themselves. Despite recent reports of decreasing corporate and public support for companies' environmental, social and governance (ESG) initiatives, *Forbes*' Best Brands for Social Impact list suggests that consumers might actually be considering companies' efforts more than they have in the past."[7] Interestingly, it's not just consumers who value brands that take a stand. "By a 4:1 margin, workers in the U.S. want to be a part of a business that promotes social justice."[8]

FOCUS: JONATHAN DANIEL, BRAND AND INNOVATION STRATEGIST

Jonathan Daniel is a strategist specializing in brand, product, and innovation. With a background in the social sciences, he takes a psychologically rooted approach to better understand what drives human and consumer behavior.

He is passionate about using creativity/innovation to solve challenges for business across tech, ESG, retail spaces, and much more. He also has a passion for using innovation to create change in the world. When he's not doing strategy, he enjoys staying up on new trends, traveling, and discovering both old and new films.

Jonathan Daniel. Photographer: Kenneth Brandon

In today's world, we're exposed to a variety of advertising and marketing content through traditional media, digital, print, and out-of-home channels, all from brands that are competing for prime real estate to increase visibility, engagement, and profit.

In the advertising space's crowded market, it's important that brands not only stand out, but also have a solidified brand strategy that effectively communicates their core values, mission, and purpose across their ads, products, and offerings to consumers.

It's also important for brands to unlock PURPOSE beyond profit, such as by investing in Diversity, Equity, and Inclusion (DEI). A 2019 Adobe study showed that 61 percent of consumers value diversity in marketing and advertising efforts. Since the social unrest in 2020, brands have made more strides to integrate DEI initiatives within their branding and marketing; however, remaining authentic and consistent are the most important factors to drive REAL change moving forward.

I believe there are two strategies companies can use to market their brands while making sure to remain authentic:

On Improving Brand Communications:

Companies can shift how they articulate their dedication to diversity and inclusion through proper visual and verbal representation. One way of doing so could be to integrate people of color (POC) in visual

(*continued on next page*)

(*continued from previous page*)

ad campaigns and use wording in ad messaging that promotes community. I think representation matters to diverse consumers because it allows them to be "seen and heard," which can result in increased customer loyalty.

On Long Term Commitment:

To me, nothing is more intentional than when companies proactively commit to DEI for the long term—not just across their brand and inside the workplace, but in the world as well. This could be a multi-year initiative with programs aimed at increasing employee diversity, such as enhanced hiring and retention of POC, as well as the creation of internal communities for employees of color. I think brands can commit by investing in programs that champion equity and inclusion, such as Apple's HBCU partnerships, which create a talent pipeline for Black engineers, or Apple's Creative Studios, which serve as a conduit for creativity in underrepresented communities and cities.

Consumers ultimately want to see that brands don't just talk the talk, but actually walk the walk and inspire change. I believe that by taking these small steps, companies can improve their DEI marketing efforts and drive true social transformation.

Acting in the Purpose Space

Deceptive or insincere efforts by brands or organizations to promote themselves as socially responsible or environmentally friendly, while their actual practices do not align with those claims, are unfortunately common. This phenomenon, often called "washing," involves companies or organizations adopting the appearance of supporting a cause without taking substantial actions to back those claims. Such performative activism can erode consumer trust and undermine the causes themselves. Here's a breakdown of the most common types:

Greenwashing occurs when companies falsely market their products or services as environmentally friendly or sustainable, exaggerating or fabricating their environmental efforts.

Bluewashing, akin to greenwashing, involves making exaggerated claims about corporate social responsibility, charitable initiatives, or affiliations with international organizations (for example, the UN) to create an illusion of accountability. This practice is also known as "rightswashing" or "ESG-washing" (where ESG stands for action in the environmental, social, and governance realms).

Pinkwashing refers to companies or organizations that position themselves as advocates for LGBTQ+ rights, particularly during events such as Pride Month, without taking concrete steps or implementing policies that genuinely support the community; also known as "rainbow-washing." Companies that exploit minority groups for profit without taking genuine action to address their concerns or providing tangible benefits are acting unjustly and opportunistically. Pinkwashing also is used to describe companies that *claim to* support breast cancer research.

Purplewashing involves companies asserting their support for gender equality, particularly women's rights, while failing to tackle deeper systemic gender issues within their own operations. This includes advocating for the feminist movement or for pay or promotion equity without taking concrete actions to dismantle barriers such as the "glass ceiling."

Wokewashing is when companies use social justice themes in their marketing to project a progressive image while failing to align their actions or policies with the values they claim.

Businesses face heightened scrutiny when addressing societal issues. At the same time, stakeholders expect companies to lead on key social justice matters, making this the new norm. They now expect organizations to engage actively in these initiatives, even when they are not explicitly labeled as such, including climate justice, democracy, economic inclusion, racial justice, gender equity, LGBTQ+ inclusion, caregiving, unionization, and community impact.[9]

To be credible in the purpose-driven space, consider the following:

- **Authentic behavior**: Ensure the social cause aligns with the company's mission, manifesto, and values.
- **Funding integrity**: Support words with actions through long-term, substantial initiatives.
- **Consistency**: Demonstrate ongoing commitment to social causes, avoiding the appearance of merely jumping on the latest trend.
- **Differentiation**: Take bold stands, craft unique messaging, and develop brand assets ready to respond to cultural shifts. (Integrating social issues into a brand's identity can strengthen its appeal to specific audiences, while risking alienation of others.)
- **Fulfilling expectations**: Align the brand's values and mission with the target audience's expectations regarding stances, purpose, and meaningful action.
- **Information and disinformation**: Be vigilant in verifying sources, data, and research. Social media platforms and online forums can amplify

disinformation, making it harder to distinguish reliable information from misleading claims. Promoting media literacy and critical thinking is essential. Governments, organizations, and individuals must work together to verify information, combat falsehoods, and elevate trustworthy sources in the public domain.

When I interviewed Ari Halper, global executive creative director and the head of creative excellence at R/GA, I asked: "With the surge of misinformation and disinformation on social media, there's a notable effect on democracies worldwide. Do advertising, branding, and design bear a responsibility in addressing this issue, and if so, what steps can creatives and their clients take to mitigate it?" While the full interview with Halper is available in chapter 10, here is his response to this specific question:

> "Social media is far and away the greatest culprit when it comes to the proliferation of falsehoods—using algorithms to ensure clicks and profits, while disregarding the collateral damage it creates. And while that's not exactly news, they wouldn't be doing it if brands refused to continue feeding them.
>
> That's why I think it's incumbent upon brands, agencies, and clients to exhibit some sort of moral compass that supersedes their bottom lines—whereby they take an active stance against disinformation, its sources, and even the tolerance of it on platforms, which could and should be done a bit like corporate responsibility messages. It can also be done by simply boycotting and/or divesting from the perpetrators, which many brands do, but certainly not enough."[10]

ADVOCATING FOR TRUTH: NINE CONSIDERATIONS

Companies and brands that advocate for truth and combat disinformation contribute to a healthier information ecosystem by upholding accountability and prioritizing trust, credibility, and civil discourse. Their efforts enhance their reputations and benefit society by promoting factual public messages and safeguarding public trust in institutions and information sources.

Here are key aspects to consider:

- **Distributing reliable information**: Companies can help disseminate accurate information by ensuring that their external and internal communications materials are factually sound. Partnering with credible sources, such as academic institutions, research organizations, or independent fact-checkers, can help verify information before the companies share it with the public.

Opinions are not facts.

In times of crisis or when misinformation spreads rapidly, brands can play a critical role in providing accurate updates, reassuring stakeholders, and preventing the spread of falsehoods.

- **Data usage**: Researchers must gather data ethically, ensure accuracy, and follow established protocols to prevent manipulation or misrepresentation. Companies must be transparent about data collection methods and clearly communicate the scope and intent of their research.
- **Educational campaigns**: Brands can launch educational initiatives to raise awareness about critical thinking, media literacy, and how to identify credible information. These campaigns, aimed at consumers and employees, help equip people to recognize and combat misinformation.
- **Supporting media integrity**: Brands can bolster media outlets committed to ethical reporting standards and factual accuracy. This support can take the form of brand partnerships, funding investigative journalism, or advocating for policies that safeguard press freedom and uphold media integrity.
- **Transparency and accountability**: Companies demonstrate transparency by openly sharing their information sources, data collection methods, research methodologies, and potential conflicts of interest. They uphold accountability by promptly correcting misinformation and publicly acknowledging errors.
- **Digital responsibility**: Brands should adopt responsible digital practices by combating bots and fake accounts, promoting responsible online behavior, ensuring responsible oversight of AI, and supporting initiatives to counter online hate speech and harmful content.
- **Advocacy**: Companies can take a proactive stance by advocating for policies and regulations that promote truth in advertising, combat digital misinformation, and uphold ethical communication standards.
- **Collaborating with governing bodies**: Businesses can work with governments to build consensus and implement solutions that foster a more just, secure, and prosperous society.
- **Leveraging a powerful voice**: As one of the most trusted sectors, business has the platform to shape public discourse and drive solutions to challenges such as climate change and pay inequity. To foster trust and reduce polarization, companies must invest in fair compensation, workforce development, and community support.

Social Responsibility Checklist

All stakeholders in branding, advertising, and design have a duty to honor the diversity of society, including differences in age, race, ethnicity, socioeconomic status, religion, beliefs, gender identities and expressions, sexual orientations, disabilities, and living situations. Responsible messaging is crucial because poorly conceived branding, advertising, and design can unintentionally perpetuate systemic inequality by influencing cultural representations and shaping perceptions. Perpetuating exclusionary narratives carries substantial risks in mediums designed to persuade or inform broad audiences.

On Truth:

- Does the brand distribute and promote reliable information?
- Does the brand support media outlets that adhere to ethical reporting standards and prioritize factual accuracy?
- Does the brand support educational initiatives that promote critical thinking, media literacy, and recognizing credible sources?
- Does the brand demonstrate transparency by disclosing its sources of information and data, use of AI-generated outputs, research or reporting methodologies, and any conflicts of interest?
- Does the brand hold itself accountable by correcting misinformation promptly and publicly acknowledging errors?
- Does the brand ensure human oversight of AI, environmental sustainability, privacy protection, security safeguards, continuous monitoring, stakeholder engagement, and regulatory compliance?
- Does the brand take a proactive stance by advocating for policies and regulations that promote truth in advertising, combat online misinformation, and uphold ethical standards in communication?
- In times of crisis or when misinformation spreads rapidly, does the brand help ensure information accuracy, reassure stakeholders, and prevent the spread of falsehoods?

On Power:

- Who wields power in the representation? Are the creative solutions deliberately exclusionary or do they marginalize some communities?
- Have you considered how individuals from diverse groups might perceive a creative solution?
- Does the solution reinforce stereotypes or established power dynamics?

- Could any group feel excluded or marginalized by the representation or message?
- Have you considered how intersecting identities influence power dynamics?
- Does the portrayal empower or undermine people?
- Does the work center on white Eurocentric ideals and standards? Does it overshadow diverse cultural perspectives and values?

On Storyline and Settings:

- Are gender stereotypes being perpetuated in roles and settings? Are stereotypes being reinforced in areas such as culinary roles, housing, or mental health?
- Are you applying an intersectional lens?
- Does the casting reflect diverse representation across various identities? In casting, could real families be used instead of constructed ones?
- Does the selection of metropolitan, suburban, or rural settings accurately reflect the diversity of socioeconomic backgrounds among your audience?
- Are there any instances of derogatory or discriminatory language, such as using terms like "inner city"?

On Interrogating Ideas, Stories, Images, and Copy:

- Have you examined all aspects of the content—idea, story, images, and copy—for stereotypes, tropes, or underlying messages?
- Does the casting and representation in the story, imagery, and copy reflect diverse groups from the broader population?
- Is the portrayal respectful and free from denigration, dehumanization, or tokenism?
- Does the content avoid caricature, offensive historical depictions, or distortion?
- Have you tested the imagery or messaging by swapping in representations of different identities, ensuring appropriateness and the absence of stereotypes?
- Have you sought diverse perspectives to gauge how different communities might perceive or identify with the content?
- Are immutable human characteristics treated appropriately and sensitively?
- Have multiple perspectives, including those of intersecting identities (e.g., BIPOC individuals who are transgender or disabled), been considered and integrated?
- Have you considered the ages of the people portrayed? Do the ages accurately reflect your audience and the population?

On Appropriation:

- Is another narrative or culture being appropriated without appropriate permission or consultation?
- Does the idea, representation, or copy diminish or devalue cultural significance?
- Are the traditions and customs of another culture respected, especially those considered sacred?
- Does the portrayal suggest one culture is more advanced or superior?
- If drawing from a narrative or culture other than your own, have you conducted thorough research and consultation?
- Is it reasonable to assume that members of the depicted culture would represent themselves and their customs similarly and would they approve of this portrayal?
- Are any aspects of the culture depicted out of their original context or stripped of their original meaning?
- Does the narrative or content appropriately credit the culture or community it draws from?

Interview: Karen R. Baker, CEO, Seven Concepts, DC

Karen R. Baker. Photograph: Kea Taylor, Imagine Photography

Karen Baker (she/her) is a nationally recognized thought leader, award-winning innovator, and dynamic entrepreneur with over twenty-seven years of experience leading work at the intersection of business, design, and social impact. Named by *Forbes* in 2024 as one of "3 Women Breaking the Glass Ceiling in the Male-Dominated Tech Industry," she has guided transformation across public, private, and academic sectors. Her expertise spans industries including media, arts and entertainment, higher education, spirits, technology, nonprofit work, and community development.

Karen served as CEO of Seven Concepts for twenty-three years before taking a three-year sabbatical to launch and lead the Washington, DC office of Boathouse Group, Inc. from 2021 to 2024. As founder and president, she spearheaded campaigns centered on corporate social responsibility and advocacy. A signature achievement was leading the American Diabetes Association's Project Power campaign, which screened four thousand Black and Brown individuals for Type 2 diabetes and earned recognition from the CDC Chief Medical Officer in 2023.

Her strategic vision has supported clients such as Pernod Ricard, Black Entertainment Television, the National Park Service, the Minority Business Development Agency, and the DC Commission on the Arts and Humanities. Karen's work has been featured in *Harvard Business Review, DMI Journal, AdAge, Campaign US, Axios, Technical.ly, Black Enterprise, Philanthropy News, AdWeek*, and the *American Urban Radio Network*. She consistently delivers measurable results by aligning creative thinking with organizational development.

An alumna of Howard University, Karen has pursued advanced studies at George Washington University and the Savannah College of Art and Design. She is currently working toward a PhD at the University of Kentucky's College of Fine Arts. Her academic pursuits reflect a lifelong commitment to learning, leadership, and arts advocacy.

Karen is the co-founder of Social Art and Culture, an award-winning arts organization, and a former professor with sixteen years of experience in higher education. She is a strategy subject matter expert known for connecting bold ideas to actionable solutions. With a passion for social entrepreneurship and design thinking, she continues to shape conversations around equity, culture, and innovation.

Her affiliations include the Design Justice Network, AIGA, Arts Education Partnership Council, Design Management Institute, American Education Research Association, and the African American Intellectual History Society. These connections reflect her dedication to inclusive design and systemic change. In every role, Karen brings clarity, conviction, and creativity to entrepreneurship.

You are an expert in design thinking, among other areas. What is the value of design thinking in business?

Having a background in business and marketing, I sought to adapt the design thinking methodology to ensure its effective implementation. Initially, there was some difficulty as many in the business realm were unfamiliar with its concepts and application. However, I found that design thinking is versatile, as it aligns with various practices because of its embedded principles. One significant stage in design thinking is empathy, which I frequently utilize.

In the realm of marketing, I've noticed that people's reluctance often arises from a desire to bypass the ideation phase; they don't want to fight through the ambiguity of ideation. They prefer to skip the process and move directly to what they perceive as the necessary concrete steps for execution.

Design thinking saves both time and money. Recently, a colleague made an insightful observation, saying, "Design thinking reduces the risk," and likening it to a bell curve. When discussing this with individuals in a business context, they may not grasp the concept of design thinking, but they do understand the concept of risk. By explaining that employing this methodology reduces the risk of investing significant resources only to discover it doesn't work, or having to repeat the execution process, or even going back to reassess and redo it multiple times, you can make a compelling case for design thinking's value.

Design thinking can really improve solutions because the process will reduce risk, if not mitigate the risk, before you start to implement and execute.

How can design thinking play a role in promoting design justice?

Design justice addresses the issue of marginalized communities not having a voice in design conversations. Often, products, systems, and technologies are developed without considering their needs and experiences. This practice emphasizes the importance of inviting these communities to the table and genuinely listening to them, rather than simply facilitating discussions.

The combination of design thinking and design practice forms a powerful approach. Designers trained in design thinking understand the value of stepping back, observing, and allowing people to express themselves—a process known as ethnography. This information is then used to inform the design process. This can be a challenge for marketers accustomed to constantly generating and executing ideas without pausing for reflection.

Design thinking may face resistance from marketers because it involves a thorough five-phase process, which includes rigorous testing and refinement before implementation. However, this meticulous approach ultimately reduces or even eliminates risks associated with introducing products or campaigns to any community, especially marginalized ones.

What is the significance of creative professionals, business professionals, and their clients addressing historical and structural injustices and striving for a fairer and more equitable society through design, branding, and marketing?

In my pursuit of a doctorate, it has become evident that individuals who grasp the potential of design often focus primarily on aesthetics, neglecting the crucial aspect of user experience and the foundational stages of research and idea formulation.

Design possesses the dual capacity to elevate or undermine. This is particularly evident in the realm of AI. Both design and AI wield this potential, yet this perspective is not as commonly acknowledged. While this perspective might be more prevalent in academic circles, it's not as frequently discussed in broader contexts, such as in business and everyday life.

Design is often seen through a creative lens, but its role in execution, especially in the initial phases of a project, is sometimes overlooked. Questions like "What are we trying to achieve?" and "How are we planning to implement it?" should be integral parts of the conversation. Design can act as a positive disruptor or can lead to disruptions of a less favorable nature. It's essential for people to gain a comprehensive understanding and appreciation for the invaluable contributions that designers bring to the table. This recognition is a crucial step forward.

What's the role of corporate social responsibility in marketing and branding?

When it comes to corporate social responsibility, we need major brands to step up. They're the ones with the visibility, the history, and often, the financial resources to make a significant impact. If we have more socially responsible businesses taking a leading role, it will drive conversations about the need for diverse creative directors to deliver socially responsible campaigns. You and I both understand that a diverse range of perspectives is crucial for such campaigns to truly resonate. Without that diversity of thought, the message won't hit the mark. That's a given.

In my research, particularly when it comes to incorporating social impact as a service, big brands consistently come to the forefront. They have the track record and resources to fulfill their commitments. However, it's essential to scrutinize whether they're genuinely delivering on their promises, especially in terms of who they aim to serve. Nonprofit organizations and mission-driven entities deliberately set out to make a positive impact, but it's important to engage with the recipients to ensure they're genuinely benefiting.

In the broader research landscape, the notable players are these major brands—the top fifteen or twenty—that have demonstrated their commitment to their responsibilities. I believe they deserve credit for their efforts, but they may need to amplify their voices more, emphasizing their dedication to social responsibility. This will help ensure that their endeavors are widely recognized and that others are inspired to follow suit.

Dominant groups in design, branding, and advertising can marginalize or erase certain groups or communities of people. How can the practice of design justice prevent misrepresentations, negative representations, stereotypes, and tropes?

In the creative industries, achieving diversity can be challenging due to the low percentage of representation. It's important to acknowledge that building a diverse team won't be a straightforward task. This realization was reinforced for me when I saw data highlighting the issue. Some of my colleagues and I have actively sought out diverse talent, but it's disheartening that the problem persists. I remember having a conversation about this three years ago, and it's disappointing to see that the issue is still prevalent today.

There is a wealth of talented individuals of color who possess the formal education to excel in the industry. This presents an opportunity for the industry to take proactive steps toward addressing the problem. It's crucial for companies to recognize that hiring people who share similar backgrounds and perspectives doesn't foster innovation. True innovation and creativity arise when a team is comprised of individuals with diverse lived experiences.

It's vital to value and respect the input of team members who bring a different perspective, especially when it comes to understanding specific communities and cultures. This can significantly enhance the quality of the work produced.

Furthermore, there are specialized search firms that can assist in finding candidates who will contribute to a more diverse and inclusive work environment. It's crucial to approach this issue with a focus on diversity of thought and inclusive thinking, recognizing that it enriches the creative process and ultimately leads to better outcomes.

Interview: Sadie Red Wing, Assistant Professor, Faculty of Design, OCAD University, Toronto

Sadie Red Wing is a Lakota/Dakota graphic designer and advocate from the Spirit Lake Dakota Nation. She received her Bachelor of Fine Arts in New Media Arts and Interactive Design from the Institute of American Indian Arts and her Master of Graphic Design from North Carolina State University. Her research on cultural revitalization through design tools and strategies created a new demand for tribal competence in graphic design research. Red Wing urges Native American graphic designers to express visual sovereignty in their design work, and also calls on academia to incorporate Indigenous perspectives into design curricula.

How can designers and other creative professionals and their clients be mindful of the potential impact of their work?

Graphic design is a powerful practice. Graphic designers visually show *something* exists by visually communicating the identity of the *thing*. Graphic designers show people what their language looks like, and what their nationality is. Visually communicating an identity of a language or a government is a large responsibility that requires respect and accuracy from the graphic designer. A graphic designer cannot fabricate visual identities. Many times, graphic designers will fabricate Indigenous languages and identities without realizing it. I would suggest designers and creatives who are tasked to visually communicate the identity of a culture to be mindful of misrepresenting Indigenous nationalities and their forms of documentation.

Please tell us about the importance of the practice of visual sovereignty and the fight against stereotypes.

North America does not express the nationalities of all its sovereign nations other than the three largest countries: Canada, United States, and Mexico. All the Indigenous nations that have sovereign governments, or federal

recognition, located in the United States are not seen as countries. The visual sovereignty of the United States overshadows the visual sovereignty of the Indigenous nations.

A problem many Indigenous nations share is the portrayal of being an "invisible" country. A solution to combating invisibility is providing the visual identity of an Indigenous nationality, or visual sovereignty. The graphic designer is the person who will create visual sovereignty for Indigenous nations.

The competency level of Indigenous sovereign rights is low in the continent of North America. Currently, the dominant imagery that showcases Indigenous nations is stereotypes. Stereotypes are exaggerations of identities that are not appropriate or accurate when demonstrating the visuals of nationalities. The importance of practicing visual sovereignty for Indigenous nations is to communicate a visual representation of a nationality to increase the cultural competency of Indigenous governments on the continent of North America.

Why is it critical to decolonize a land-based identity in visual communication?

To understand how to decolonize a land-based identity, the definition of decolonization needs to be defined accurately. As a design educator, and an enrolled member of the Spirit Lake Dakota Nation who experiences present-day colonization by the United States government, I define decolonization as an independent nation overtaking the land of a region to exploit the resources.

The United States government continues to exploit the resources of the Great Plains, or traditional grasslands, with corn fields, cow farms, and oil extraction. The harm of these colonization tactics destroys the resources indigenous to the Great Plains. Tribal nations located in the Great Plains will utilize the resources indigenous to the prairie terrain to invent forms of documentation with the use of grass blades and roots, buffalo leather and bones, dye and paints from plants and egg whites, porcupine quills, etc.

The mechanics of the resources are used in forms of weaving, threading, and drawing pictograms that depict significant events, important family histories, and knowledge passed down from elders that demonstrate the cultural values of the tribe. When creating visuals with natural resources, like weaving various colors of porcupine quills in a loom-formation to create a representation of an animal, the visual communicates as a symbol due to the geometric output from the looming grid. The geometric symbolism resulting from the grid provides a visual language that shares qualities of a pattern and shape formations that look like Nintendo 8-bit images that can be seen in traditional Great Plains adornment, like beadwork and quillwork.

It is critical to decolonize tribal identities because Indigenous nations are **governments**. A government needs a national identity that demonstrates the land they steward. If the land stewarded by the tribal nations is destroyed by colonization, the visual identity of the tribe will be destroyed too.

In the realms of design, branding, and advertising, we often encounter instances where the unique elements of a particular culture, including technologies, symbols, artifacts, genres, or aesthetics of marginalized communities, are appropriated by more dominant groups. What key insights should we gather about cultural appropriation?

Generally speaking, the general competency level of Indigenous visual languages in the continent of North America is low. When many of the citizens of the United States cannot recognize a pattern-based visual language tied to a specific tribe, harmful appropriation often occurs—such as miscommunicating the nationality of Indigenous peoples in branding, decorations, and other graphic design materials. When a non-Indigenous designer targets an Indigenous audience but wants to avoid using any tribal patterns or symbolic motifs, I suggest incorporating land-based imagery specific to the sovereign nation being targeted, such as flowers or other icons that demonstrate a land resource.

As a graphic design professor, I define three words to help students decipher actions when working with Indigenous visual languages: appropriation, adaptation, and fusion. To appropriate is to take an idea or invention without any acknowledgement, reference, or citation to the origin of the idea or invention. To adapt is to provide an acknowledgement, reference, or citation of where the idea or invention originated, and how the invention or idea is used to influence an action. When fusing two ideas or inventions together, both opposing ideas and inventions are acknowledged, referenced, and cited. (Great examples of fusion can be seen in contemporary food culture, like *pho burritos.*) By understanding these three definitions, designers can better understand their actions when creating projects that incorporate culturally inspired imagery.

What is crucial for creative professionals and clients to understand about the importance of diverse perspectives and representation—especially when creative teams are predominantly made up of individuals from dominant groups—to avoid dismissing alternative worldviews or ways of knowing?

When I am participating in conversations within the design community around diversity, inclusion, and equity, I feel many designers lack a strong understanding and competency of design practices, strategies, and inventions that are indigenous to the continent of North America. As an Indigenous designer with a unique perspective amongst non-Indigenous creatives, I feel the most crucial thing to grasp is knowing more global design histories outside of European design history.

In the United States, citizens are taught very little about the design histories of the continent of North America before the year 1500. One factor contributing to the lack of Indigenous design knowledge in creative practices is the low number of resources and curricula included in schools, starting at the elementary level. I feel creative professionals will benefit from design spaces with more education on resources indigenous to the North American continent before colonization, including the historical trade routes between North and South America.

Other than trade routes, another important topic for professionals to understand is the various timelines of how colonization impacted specific regions of the world. Countries in North America, like the United States, are still young in comparison to other countries around the world. When understanding the diverse timelines of colonization around the world, the acceptance of diverse perspectives and representation will flourish.

13.1 **Lakȟóta + Dakȟóta Visual Essay**. Designer: Sadie Red Wing

CHAPTER 14

ADVANCING EQUITY

F ewer than 6 percent of image-based search results show skin conditions on people of color.[1]

Systemic racism and longstanding healthcare inequities in the United States contribute to misdiagnoses and untreated conditions. With its brand promise of "Equitable Skincare for All," Vaseline® sought to address the lack of diversity in dermatological imagery. This is more than a user experience problem; it is an equity issue.

The lack of representation in dermatological imagery contributes to lower dermatologist visit rates and higher mortality rates among Black and Latinx individuals, especially for conditions such as skin cancer. In response, Vaseline partnered with creative agency Edelman to create See My Skin, the first database tailored to skin conditions in people of color. The campaign aims to raise awareness of racial biases in search algorithms, ensure accurate representation, deliver equitable healthcare, and improve visibility for underserved communities. In collaboration with VisualDx and HUED, Vaseline developed this unique platform over three years, assembling a vast medical image library. See My Skin allows users to access resources and connect directly with dermatologists, with an upload tool to expand the database in real time, addressing historical biases and promoting more equitable skincare practices.[2]

To advance its mission of making skin healthcare more accessible for people of color, Vaseline brand launched "Mended Murals," an initiative using art to highlight the need for greater access to skin health resources for underrepresented communities. The initiative showcases how, without proper resources, murals that once vividly reflected the culture and people of their communities can fade over time. The brand commissioned mural restorations from artists in the US cities of Baltimore, Brooklyn/NYC, and Hartford, embedding QR codes that link to SeeMySkin.com for skin health resources. Vaseline pledged $250,000 to charitable health clinics in each city with restored murals. Additionally, the brand also invites communities to submit significant murals for a chance at restoration by the original artist, with funds to support a local health clinic for each mural restored.[3]

In an interview about the See My Skin campaign, Kate Endeley, former vice president and strategy director at Edelman, told Contagious: "In the purpose space, action is the differentiator—what are you actually doing for the cause? A lot of the backlash that other brands have got has been because people can't associate any action behind what they are doing."[4]

Benchmarking Tool for Evaluating Branding, Graphic Design, and Advertising

What does it take to be an ally? Advocate? Activist?

Footwear manufacturer Havaianas deepened its commitment to the LGBTQ+ community by donating 7 percent of its Pride product sales. Motivated by the exclusion of sexual orientation and gender identity from the Brazilian government's national census, Havaianas intensified its support for the community and public welfare.

When the Brazilian government omitted questions about sexual orientation and gender identity from the national census, Havaianas launched the Pride Research initiative to increase visibility for the LGBTQ+ community. Collaborating with DataFolha and All Out, Havaianas spent eight months traveling to over 150 cities across Brazil. The initiative culminated in a seventy-eight-page report acknowledging over 15.5 million Brazilians as LGBTQ+ for the first time in history.[5] That initiative is not performative—it is proactive.

People perceive genuine ally brands more positively than performative ally or neutral ones (those that remain silent), particularly among Black consumers. Research shows that this favorable perception boosts self-esteem and deepens the emotional bond between the consumer and the brand.

Brands have little to gain from being performative allies, especially among communities most impacted by social injustice.[6]

Let's consider two fundamental brand strategies—one focused primarily on economic outcomes and the other on broader societal contributions. A prosperity-driven model is an economic-value approach that leverages marketing strategies to enhance profitability, brand equity, and market presence. Its goal is to drive economic benefits and competitive advantage for the brand or entity. In contrast, an altruistically driven model adopts a societal impact approach, prioritizing branding efforts that aim to generate positive cultural and environmental change. This model emphasizes sustainability, community support, social issues, and equity, focusing on making a meaningful impact beyond financial gains.

Prosperity-driven refers to initiatives, actions, messaging, and creative solutions that primarily focus on advancing the interests and success of a brand or an entity. This approach prioritizes objectives such as increasing profit, gaining notoriety, enhancing credibility, ensuring longevity, raising awareness, and expanding reach. While fulfilling their brand promise and meeting the needs and expectations of their target audience, prosperity-driven strategies center around achieving measurable business outcomes and enhancing the entity's market position and competitive advantage. Examples include branding strategies focused on driving sales and increasing revenue; initiatives aimed at increasing brand recognition and visibility, such as the sponsorship of high-profile events, celebrity endorsements, or large-scale advertising campaigns; market expansion efforts; rebranding efforts to differentiate the brand from competitors; activities focused on building and maintaining a positive public image, and so on.

Altruistically driven refers to a company's initiatives, actions, messaging, and creative solutions that prioritize social good and the well-being of people, communities, creatures, and the planet. This approach addresses and contributes to broader societal issues and values, such as responsible production, economic growth, peace, climate justice, democracy, financial inclusion, racial justice, gender equality, pay equity, LGBTQ+ inclusion, accessibility and inclusion for people with disabilities, sustainable cities and communities, decent work and wages, and community impact. Altruistically driven strategies aim to create positive cultural or environmental change and foster a sense of community and responsibility, often collaborating with nonprofits, community organizations, and other stakeholders.

To determine whether branding, graphic design, or advertising content is prosperity-driven or altruistically driven, assess how closely the brand's mission and values align with its initiatives, messaging, and creative solutions. Additionally, consider the audience's perspective, ensuring that the content resonates with their values and expectations and reflects a genuine commitment to economic gain or broader societal impact.

Assessing Brand Intent: Prosperity-Driven vs. Altruistically Driven Content:

Initiatives And Actions

Focus: Are the brand's initiatives aimed at societal or environmental impact (e.g., community support, sustainability), or are they primarily commercially driven?

Partnerships: Are these initiatives supported by partnerships with nonprofits, local communities, or advocacy groups?

Measurable outcomes: Are there clear, measurable results demonstrating societal or environmental benefits?

Example: The LEGO Group collaborated with artist Hebru Brantley to develop Fly Away Isles, an innovative play installation in the center of West Harlem in New York City. The vibrant imaginations of the community's children inspired this project.[7]

- **Missed opportunity**: Overlooking broader societal contributions, a brand that focuses solely on sales promotions —without acknowledging or acting on behalf of the community—risks appearing out of touch and inauthentic.

Messaging

Tone and language: Does the messaging advocate for social good and raise awareness of societal or environmental issues, or is it primarily promotional?

Inclusivity: Is the messaging inclusive, respectful, and aligned with the brand's values rather than just commercial gains?

Example: Barbie, a brand by Mattel, partnered with the American Foundation for the Blind to create a Barbie doll that authentically represents individuals who are blind or have low vision. This collaboration ensured that every detail— from the doll's face sculpt and fashion to the accessories, packaging, and e-commerce communication—was designed to accurately reflect the experiences of people with visual impairments.

- **Missed opportunity**: Messaging that centers solely on product features without acknowledging or addressing substantive issues.

Creative Solutions

Focus: Is the content centered on societal or environmental stewardship rather than just the product?

Content: Do the ideas and visual elements reflect environmental or societal themes and inclusion?

Respect and authenticity: Are stereotypes avoided, and do the portrayals represent cultures and identities authentically?

Example: For Bodyform (known as Libresse outside the UK), creative agency AMV BBDO created the film "Never Just a Period," which uses a mixed-media technique to offer a bold and candid critique of how society has historically denied women and girls basic body information.[8]

- **Missed opportunity**: A marketing approach that showcases a product's features or appearance without tying it to a larger story, purpose, or pressing issue. The imagery lacks depth and fails to connect with the audience emotionally or intellectually, missing an opportunity to resonate more deeply by addressing relevant themes or values. Imagery or branding that either perpetuates problematic or reductive portrayals of certain groups (stereotypes) or focuses only on showcasing the product without connecting it to a broader, more meaningful narrative (e.g., merely highlights the product without meaningful context). (For more on this, see the Social Responsibility Checklist in chapter 13.)

Evaluation Criteria

Weighting system: Assign importance to each criterion in the evaluation. For instance,

- Initiatives and actions: 34 percent
- Messaging: 33 percent
- Creative solutions: 33 percent

Feedback mechanism: Develop a process to gather audience feedback, such as:

- Surveys/questionnaires: Collect diverse audience feedback.
- Focus groups: Evaluate specific campaigns.
- Social media monitoring: Track reactions.

Regular review: Set a schedule to ensure the criteria remain relevant:

- Quarterly reviews: Engage stakeholders.
- Annual audits: Assess against standards and societal shifts.
- Continuous adaptation: Update based on feedback.

Implementation Example

Complete Evaluation Forms: Use weighted scores for a thorough assessment. Initiatives and Actions Evaluation Form:

- Initiative name:
- Description:
- Community impact: (Yes/No)
- Partnerships: (List any involved organizations)

- Measurable outcomes: (Describe the impact)
- Score (0–10):

Messaging Evaluation Form:

- Content title:
- Language inclusivity: (Yes/No)
- Tone: (Inclusive/Neutral/Exclusive)
- Focus: (Societal impact/Commercial gain)
- Score (0–10):

Creative Solutions Evaluation Form:

- Idea:
- Visual description:
- Equitable representation: (Yes/No)
- Stereotypes: (Present/Absent)
- Focus: (Societal or environmental themes/Product-centric)
- Score (0–10):

Cultural Engagement Spectrum

People increasingly expect businesses and brands to address societal and environmental issues, taking clear stances on justice, equality, and environmental stewardship. Brands can position themselves along the Cultural Engagement Spectrum, ranging from allyship to activism.

In their insightful article "When a Brand Stands Up for Racial Justice, Do People Buy It?," Geeta Menon and Tina Kiesler provide a valuable framework for assessing brand actions. They propose a four-part framework that distinguishes between corporation-oriented and societally-oriented actions, and between passive allyship and action-oriented advocacy. Menon and Kiesler contend that the most authentic brand actions actively support societally-oriented, anti-racist initiatives, even if they risk the corporation's business goals.[9]

The following section adopts a similar framework to examine various levels of brand engagement, providing examples and evaluation criteria for each.

Allyship: Demonstrates support for societal issues through visible but relatively passive measures. The brand or entity communicates its backing for social causes in its messaging without leading initiatives or making substantial investments.

Evaluation Criteria:

- Visibility: Is the support prominently displayed?
- Depth of involvement: Is the engagement mostly symbolic rather than substantive?
- Impact: Does the content raise awareness without driving significant action?

Example: Displaying a rainbow flag during Pride Month.

Supporter: The brand actively engages with societal issues through meaningful actions beyond symbolic gestures.

Evaluation Criteria:

- Visibility: Are the actions clearly communicated to the audience?
- Depth of involvement: Do the efforts extend beyond surface-level messaging to include meaningful action or sustained engagement?
- Impact: Does the brand provide tangible support, such as financial investment, educational programs, or volunteer initiatives?

Example: Spanish brand Chocolates Valor ran a campaign featuring sixty-six-year-old actor José Coronado to challenge stereotypes about aging.

Advocacy: The brand actively promotes societal or environmental issues, motivating its audience to engage and act.

Evaluation Criteria:

- Visibility: Is the advocacy effort clearly communicated and widely understood?
- Depth of involvement: Are there proactive campaigns with explicit calls to action?
- Impact: Are there measurable outcomes in audience engagement and awareness? Does the brand's advocacy contribute to meaningful change in communities, societies, ecosystems, or cultural contexts?

Example: McDonald's UK removed the smile from its Happy Meal boxes as part of a mental health initiative developed by creative agencies Ready10 and Leo Burnett UK. In collaboration with BBC Children in Need, the campaign addressed a study showing that over half of UK children feel pressured to appear happy. Limited-edition emotion stickers allowed children to express their true feelings on the boxes.[10]

Champion: The brand advocates for and leads substantial environmental or societal initiatives with significant impact.

Evaluation Criteria:

- Visibility: Is the brand widely recognized as a leading advocate or influential voice in advancing the cause?
- Depth of involvement: Are there sustained, large-scale initiatives and investments?
- Impact: Are there notable and measurable outcomes?

Example: Patagonia exemplifies this approach through its profound commitment to environmental conservation. Instead of selling or going public, founder Yvon Chouinard and his family transferred ownership of the $3 billion company to a specially designed trust and nonprofit organization. These entities ensure the company remains independent, with profits—approximately $100 million annually—dedicated to combating climate change and protecting undeveloped land globally.[11]

Activism: The brand takes a bold stance by investing in and leading initiatives aimed at driving meaningful positive change.

Evaluation Criteria:

- Visibility: Are the brand's activism efforts highly visible and widely publicized?
- Depth of involvement: Are there substantial, long-term commitments and investments?
- Impact: Do the brand's actions drive significant environmental or societal changes?

Example: Ben & Jerry's "Make Some Motherchunkin' Change!" campaign epitomizes brand activism by driving engagement for societal betterment. The campaign encourages activism in various forms, from advocating for racial justice to boosting voter participation. It underscores the idea that grassroots efforts can be a potent force for positive change, with messages such as: "Progress comes in many flavors! This is your call to harness your creativity and passion to join the fight for a sweeter world—one where everyone can thrive." It continues: "There's never been a better time to make your voice heard for a sweeter world! Surf a wave for racial justice. Plant a garden for healthy communities. Shake your groove thing to get people to the ballot box. If it excites you, it can be a powerful tool for change. We believe in scooping up some joy on the journey to justice."[12]

FOCUS: THE FEMALE COMPANY'S "THE TAMPON BOOK" / SCHOLZ & FRIENDS, BERLIN

The Tampon Book campaign creatively addressed societal injustice by challenging the high tax rate imposed on menstrual products in Germany. Tampons were classified as "luxury goods" and taxed at 19 percent, a higher rate than luxury items such as caviar. To contest this classification, The Female Company, an online retailer specializing in women's health products, partnered with the Berlin-based creative agency Scholz & Friends to create The Tampon Book. This product, containing fifteen organic tampons packaged inside a forty-six-page book, qualified for the lower 7 percent tax rate applied to essential items.

Beyond tampons, The Tampon Book featured stories and illustrations about menstruation. The initial print run sold out in one day, followed by another sellout within a week. The campaign drew significant attention from German lawmakers, with many female politicians distributing the book to their constituents. A Change.org petition supporting a tax reduction gathered over 175,000 signatures. As a result of this campaign and other protests, Germany reduced the tax rate on female sanitary products from 19 percent to 7 percent.

Inclusive Transformation: The brand actively challenges and dismantles Eurocentric norms by promoting diverse perspectives and values.

Evaluation Criteria:

- **Visibility**: Is the brand's commitment to inclusive representation clear, consistent, and visibly integrated across its messaging and actions?
- **Depth of involvement**: Are substantial structural changes and policies in place to foster long-term inclusivity?
- **Impact**: Does the brand's content show a measurable shift in representation and storytelling, reflecting progress toward more inclusive and authentic narratives?

Example: Google launched the "All In" inclusive marketing toolkit, providing comprehensive resources to drive industry-wide progress. This toolkit offers guidance on hiring and empowering underrepresented talent, integrating inclusivity into marketing and creative processes, setting measurable goals, and tracking progress. Co-created with organizations such as ADCOLOR, the Geena Davis Institute on Gender in Media, and GLAAD, it includes audience guides that ensure authentic, positive representation of historically underrepresented groups.

Making Amends: The brand acknowledges past mistakes or shortcomings related to cultural or environmental issues and takes concrete steps to address and rectify them.

Evaluation Criteria:

- **Visibility**: Is the acknowledgment and apology communicated publicly with transparency?
- **Depth of involvement**: Are substantive actions being taken to address and correct past actions?
- **Impact**: Are the brand's corrective efforts resulting in measurable, positive outcomes?

Example: Following widespread anti-racism protests in 2020, Mars Food renamed its Uncle Ben's rice products to Ben's Original and removed the imagery of an older Black man from the packaging—a portrayal that had been widely criticized for perpetuating harmful racial stereotypes rooted in the antebellum South. This rebrand addressed decades of concern about racially insensitive marketing and represented the company's attempt to reckon with its problematic brand heritage.[13]

Appeal through Allyship or Advocacy: The brand seeks to attract customers by positioning itself as an ally or advocate for societal issues.

Evaluation Criteria:

- **Visibility**: Is the brand's commitment to social causes communicated clearly, consistently, and with transparency?
- **Depth of involvement**: Does the brand demonstrate authentic, sustained engagement, or does it risk coming across as superficial or performative?
- **Impact**: Does this approach resonate with the target audience and result in meaningful engagement and measurable change?

Example: The General Mills foundation emphasizes agricultural sustainability and the protection of natural resources, demonstrating a genuine commitment that extends beyond profit-driven marketing.

Application of the Cultural Engagement Spectrum Tool

1. Evaluate Content:

- *Messaging*: Does the language reflect support (e.g., Advocacy) or address past mistakes (e.g., Making Amends)?
- *Images*: Are visuals inclusive (e.g., Allyship) or promoting change (e.g., Activism)?
- *Actions*: Are initiatives focused on support (e.g., Allyship) or driving change (e.g., Activism)?

2. Measure Impact:

- *Audience engagement*: Monitor social media interactions, comments, shares
- *Reach*: Track impressions and shares
- *Tangible outcomes*: Evaluate funds raised, volunteer hours, etc.
- *Brand perception*: Assess survey results, focus groups, Q Scores, etc.
- *Social media tracking*: Monitor platform analytics, sentiment analysis, hashtag performance, and share of voice
- *Media coverage*: Measure the extent and sentiment of coverage
- *Partnerships*: Analyze effectiveness and outcomes of collaborations
- *Long-term impact*: Track changes in societal issue metrics and Q Scores

Evaluation Form (exemplar):

- **Content title:**
- **Category**: (e.g., Allyship, Supporter, Advocacy, Activism)
- **Visibility**: (Score 1–10)
- **Depth of involvement**: (Score 1–10)
- **Impact**: (Score 1–10)
- **Comments:**

Impact Metrics:

- **Audience engagement**:

  o Interactions:
  o Comments:

- **Social media reach**:

  o Impressions:
  o Shares:

- **Tangible outcomes**:

  o Funds raised:
  o Volunteer hours:

- **Brand perception**:

  o Surveys:
  o Focus groups:

- **Earned media coverage**:

  o Organic unpaid mentions:
  o Sentiment:

- **Partnerships/Collabs**:

  o List:
  o Outcomes:

- **Long-term impact**:

  o Changes in metrics:

FOCUS: ALISON PLACE, ASSOCIATE PROFESSOR OF GRAPHIC DESIGN / UNIVERSITY OF ARKANSAS SCHOOL OF ART

Alison Place is a designer, educator, and writer whose work explores the intersection of design and feminist theory as a space of critical making and radical speculation. She is the author of *Feminist Designer: On the Personal and the Political in Design* (MIT Press, 2023), which illuminates design as a feminist practice through essays, case studies, and dialogues. She is an associate professor of graphic design at the University of Arkansas School of Art, where she also serves as the director of the graphic design program.

Alison Place. Photographer: Novo Studio

(continued on next page)

(continued from previous page)

Understand visual stereotypes and tropes relating to gender.

There is a long and well-known history of the sexist portrayals of women in advertising and media, from peddling vacuums and washing machines to housewives, to exploiting women's bodies by pandering to the male gaze (and wallet). We tend to think of these insidious clichés as historical accounts of eras gone by, disconnected from the ways that we perform and understand gender today. But harmful gender stereotypes in media have not been eradicated; they've simply evolved and adapted along with mainstream culture. In our scramble to avoid stereotypes about women as housewives and sex objects, we've landed on updated alternatives like the supermom or the carefree working woman who has it all. These modern tropes might seem more normalized, but they are just as problematic because they place unrealistic expectations on women. Stereotypes that capitalize on assumptions or negative portrayals of marginalized people's identities operate as a tool to reinforce their inferior position in society, both in day-to-day interactions and in broader power structures. Portrayals of gender in the media aren't simply a reflection of mainstream views; they are also channels through which we negotiate our own beliefs and behaviors around gender in a society. They have the power to belittle women and invoke violence, or, if implemented responsibly, to change views and advance equality.

Be wary of "femvertising" and "empowertising"—pandering to women's issues without addressing the root cause of them.

In 2018, Ann Friedman, cohost of the feminist podcast "Call Your Girlfriend," coined the term "millennial pink-washing"—when a brand "takes a feminist concept and drapes it in pink startup branding and sells it off to . . . any company that's selling women's fitness, beauty products or corporate advancement under the guise of empowerment." Years later, millennial pink seems to have run its course, but the exploitation of women's issues remains. Often referred to as "femvertising" or "empowertising," feminism is often co-opted by capitalism to pander to women's social and political problems without ever addressing their root cause. Corporations use it to appear culturally engaged and "values-centered," despite doing little to address gender inequality within their organizations, like closing the gender pay gap or providing paid family leave. Products and advertising aimed at women shouldn't merely highlight the challenges they face in a patriarchal society; they should explicitly acknowledge and address the larger power structures that marginalize them in the first place.

Cultural Impact Scale

> The opposite of courage is not cowardice. The opposite of courage is conformity.
> —Brian Collins, cofounder of renowned brand consultancy COLLINS.[14]

To measure the impact of branding and advertising effectively, similar to the effectiveness scales used by agencies such as FCB and Leo Burnett, organizations can implement a structured framework that evaluates creative efforts against strategic goals, ensuring maximum potential for success.

HARMFUL: Content that causes significant damage to individuals, a community, or the brand.

- **Indicators**: Offensive stereotypes, disinformation, or promotion of harmful behaviors with high potential for backlash, reputational harm, and negative societal impact.
- **Questions**: Does the content perpetuate harmful stereotypes or spread disinformation? Could it provoke an adverse reaction or contribute to public harm?

OFF-BRAND: Content that strays from the brand's mission, voice, or overarching narrative.

- **Indicators**: Misalignment with brand values, tone, or strategic goals; disconnect from the brand's core identity.
- **Questions**: Does the content align with the brand's core values and messaging? How well does it support the overall brand strategy?

CONFORMIST: Conventional content that lacks originality, resulting in minimal impact.

- **Indicators**: Imitative of existing ideas or trends without offering a fresh perspective or added value, struggling to capture attention or differentiate the brand.
- **Questions**: Does the content offer something new, or does it simply follow familiar patterns? Does it stand out in a crowded landscape or blend in with the noise?

NOTICED: Content that aligns with the brand's mission and messaging but lacks significant influence on audience behavior.

- **Indicators**: Effectively communicates the brand's purpose or values but generates limited engagement, emotional response, or measurable action.

- **Questions**: Does the content align with the brand's strategic objectives? Does it capture attention in a way that prompts action or a stronger connection?

BRAND BUILDING: Content that reinforces the brand's identity and contributes to long-term brand equity.

- **Indicators**: Consistently reflects the brand's values and personality, strengthening recognition and trust, even if it doesn't lead to immediate behavioral change.
- **Questions**: Does the content enhance the brand's reputation or visibility? Does it effectively reinforce core brand values and positioning over time?

PROVOKE: Content that encourages thought, conversation, and sharing, with the potential to influence behavior or perception.

- **Indicators**: Sparks meaningful dialogue, invites audience reflection, and encourages sharing or response.
- **Questions**: Does the content provoke thought or stimulate discussion? Is it likely to be shared, commented on, or debated?

CULTURAL FORCE: Content that significantly impacts culture, drives behavioral change, and elevates long-term brand value.

- **Indicators**: Aligns with or shapes cultural trends, sparks widespread sharing, garners favorable earned media coverage, and contributes to brand building and societal impact.
- **Questions**: Is the content culturally transformative or influential? How extensive is its impact and visibility across media, communities, or conversations?

Implementation Exemplar

- **Content title**:
- **Category**: (e.g., Harmful, Off-brand, Conformist, etc.)
- **Description**:
- **Visibility**: (Score 1–10)
- **Originality**: (Score 1–10)
- **Engagement**: (Score 1–10)
- **Impact**: (Score 1–10)
- **Comments**:

Evaluation Criteria

- **Visibility**: Does the content stand out?
- **Originality**: Is the content fresh and distinctive, or does it rely on familiar conventions and recycled ideas?
- **Engagement**: Does the content spark discussion, sharing, and interaction with the audience?

Leslie-Ann Noel, PhD. Photographer: Niamh Brennan

Interview: Lesley-Ann Noel, PhD, Dean, Faculty of Design, OCAD University, Toronto, Canada

Lesley-Ann Noel is a designer, researcher, educator, author of *Design Social Change*, and coeditor of *The Black Experience in Design*. She holds a BA in Industrial Design from Universidade Federal do Paraná in Brazil, an MBA from the University of the West Indies in Trinidad and Tobago, and a PhD in Design from North Carolina State University. She was awarded honorary doctorates for service to the field of design by the University of the Arts London and the Pacific Northwest College of Art. She is the new Dean of Design at OCAD University (OCAD-U). Prior to OCAD-U, she taught at North Carolina State University, Tulane University, Stanford University and the University of the West Indies.

You practice design through emancipatory, critical, and anti-hegemonic lenses, focusing on equity, social justice, and the experiences of people often excluded from design research. Please tell us about your work.

It's sometimes difficult to describe my work. When I was an undergrad in Industrial Design, one professor gave us some gems of advice: 1) the design professions we would end up in probably did not yet exist, and 2) we'd change professions a gazillion times in the forty or so years of our careers. I started off as an industrial designer, but perhaps I'm in social design today, and I'm probably most comfortable in design for social impact conversations. I landed here through some opportunities that I pursued in design for development projects, and the questions that I had about that type of practice made me stay to see how I could possibly make this work better.

Why is it essential to decolonize design, branding, and advertising?

Design, branding, and advertising are fields that can really feel hostile to people who are perceived to be minorities or at the margins. These industries are built around Eurocentrism, patriarchy, white supremacy, and modernity; if you are not white, male, young, and from the Global North, you can feel very insignificant in these fields. Decolonizing design, branding, and advertising means unlinking them from white Eurocentric ideals and standards, since the effects of colonialism and white supremacy mean that these ideas are often viewed as universal all over the world. Colonialism and colonization play significant roles in the value we place on many things, and intentionally decolonizing design would mean disrupting traditional thinking of which values are the norm and understanding whose point of view is privileged. It could mean an acceptance of new or alternative research methods and different worldviews and ultimately challenging the ideas that suggest that knowledge from one place or group is superior to others.

When a majority of creative teams still are predominantly composed of dominant groups, what should creative professionals and their clients grasp about the significance of diverse perspectives and representation in order to avoid dismissing alternative worldviews or ways of knowing?

The first thing that creatives and their clients should know is that diverse teams that reflect the societies we serve will better understand societal needs and create better outcomes. If your teams are not diverse, you are not "doing it right," and your team will need some tweaking to serve people better. Diverse teams will have a more complex understanding of the world and also have to develop an awareness of the care needed to work across differences. Therefore, there is the potential for them to work more respectfully and slowly as they navigate working across differences.

Designers must respectfully and thoughtfully meet the needs, perspectives, and expectations of multicultural audiences. How can we expand our understanding of design and its potential to address and validate divergent ways of thinking and designing?

It is useful to remember that design is a universal ability and that the field of design is very porous. With this in mind, it shouldn't be difficult to expand our understanding of design, as many people make design decisions daily, even if they weren't formally or traditionally trained in the field.

How can creatives and their clients be mindful of the potential impact of their work?

We can't always predict the impact of our work, but there are tools and strategies to make us more aware of both the positive and negative impacts. The first is individual and collective reflection—what worked well, what didn't, and how could this have gone differently? The second is merely asking for feedback throughout and at the end of a design process, whether through focus groups, discussions, surveys, or other informal conversations. Systems-thinking approaches help us understand the systems that we are working within that we intentionally or unintentionally support as we do our work. Finally, intentionally looking for unintended consequences before, during, and after the design process can help us be more aware of the impact of our work.

How do you leverage design to drive positive change?

I've adopted equity as a guiding principle in all the work that I do now. Having guiding principles makes it easier to know which questions to ask, which types of opportunities to forego, and which conversations to have with a client. One technique I've been trained to use to drive positive change is to center the needs of the most impacted stakeholder. I encourage every designer to reflect on and sign on to the Design Justice Principles [https://designjustice.org/read-the-principles] as a way of focusing on equity and justice in their work.[15] In my book *Design Social Change* [Ten Speed Press, 2023], I prompt readers to build a critical awareness of the world. This is one of my pedagogical guiding principles, inspired by the work of Paulo Freire. This critical awareness makes us see the world with its good and bad. Savoring the good while challenging the bad, and in this challenge, we can make positive social change. Finally, as a designer, when you ask yourself, "So what can I really do to drive positive change?," remember that there are many roles for changemakers. Deepa Iyer created a beautiful diagram about many social change roles in times of crisis.[16] Designers have the skillsets for many roles, such as storytelling, disrupting, experimenting, visioning, and building. And we can really lean into the last two roles—our expertise as visionaries and worldbuilders, to support other people to make social change.

Please tell us about The Designer's Critical Alphabet.

The Designer's Critical Alphabet was created soon after I did my PhD in design, and I was trying to apply a lot of the theory that I had recently read during my studies to my practice in general, and was also trying to make the theory understandable and relevant to other designers. I created the first few cards for a specific class that I was co-teaching at the Hasso Plattner Institute of Design at Stanford University (the Stanford d.school). Each card introduces a bit of theory and a question that makes the theory practical and applicable to designers. During that year at the d.school, I was experimenting with information formats and many different ways of sharing information, including games, flashcards, and mad libs. I had just written three articles for my dissertation but had no idea who would ever read them, so I was trying out a lot of other formats and the alphabet worked.

14.2 The Designer's Critical Alphabet. Made by PluriversalDesignLab "The Critical Alphabet (and the corresponding apps) is but one tool that people in design can use to remember to grapple with social issues, and should be considered a challenge to others to also engage with difficult and critical topics in their work."

Each card presents a theory corresponding to its letter, followed by a question or comment designed to bridge the theory with design practice.

Lesley-Ann Noel, "A Designer Teaches People How to See Others Who Are Not Like Them," November 17, 2020, Hyperallergic.com, accessed September 8, 2024, https://hyperallergic.com/601804/a-designer-teaches -people-how-to-see-others-who-are-not-like-them/

CHAPTER 15

BRAND BUILDING: ARCHETYPES

I need a hero.

His name is Chris Nikic.

Introducing Runner 321, an adidas initiative urging the world's largest marathons to reserve bib number 321—symbolizing Trisomy 21, or Down syndrome—for neurodivergent athletes. Launched on World Down Syndrome Day, this campaign seeks to enhance visibility and representation in sports for individuals with Down syndrome. It features Chris Nikic, the triathlete and marathon runner who became the first Ironman with Down syndrome, racing in the Boston Marathon with bib number 321.

Andrew MacPhee, executive creative director at FCB Canada, explains, "The initial spark came from our desire to create visibility and representation for neurodivergent people in running. We wanted to create a beacon for others to see what's possible."[1]

By sponsoring Nikic, adidas reinforces its commitment to diversity in sports and its mission to dismantle barriers for marginalized communities and demonstrate that "impossible is nothing." Runner 321 aims to integrate neurodivergent athletes into mainstream events, challenging the notion that they should be restricted to separate competitions.[2]

Just as Michael Jordan's iconic number 23 or Jackie Robinson's 42 symbolizes athletic excellence, Runner 321 aspires to become a symbol of perseverance and defiance of societal expectations for neurodivergent athletes. The campaign launched with a video featuring Nikic and a landing page inviting other races to participate, complete with a Runner 321 toolkit offering race instructions and social media resources.

We All Need Heroes

I need heroes.

Their names are Remie Akl and Nour Arida.

Creative agency Leo Burnett Beirut, in collaboration with the gender equality organization ABAAD and artist Remie Akl, created *Dirty Laundry*, a powerful film addressing the stigma faced by women who have survived rape in Lebanon. The film exposes the societal pressure on survivors to hide their "dirty laundry" to preserve family honor, forcing them into silence.

This narrative reflects ABAAD's findings that 60 percent of women who experience sexual assault in Lebanon do not report the crime due to shame or family pressure. *Dirty Laundry* aims to reveal the true extent of the crime and is part of the UN Women's #NoShameNoBlame initiative during the 16 Days of Activism. The campaign advocates for stricter penalties for sexual offenses. Additionally, popular Lebanese model and influencer Nour Arida hosted a web series featuring four courageous survivors who shared their personal stories.[3]

The #NoShameNoBlame campaign by ABAAD addresses sexual violence in Lebanon through data-driven research, advocacy, and awareness. The campaign has garnered significant backing, with Lebanese parliamentarians showing a promising commitment to legislative reform. "No longer should women in Lebanon be at the mercy of laws that shift the blame on survivors rather than on the assaulters. These laws are grotesque, unimaginable, and unfortunately, real," said Danielle Howayek, founder and legal advisor of ABAAD.[4] This movement has sparked critical discussions across the Arab world and beyond, marking an essential step toward securing women's rights and safety in Lebanon.[5]

• • •

I need a hero.

Her name is Lisa LaFlamme.

When workplace ageism and sexism became prominent issues in Canada, Dove took a stand with the #KeepTheGrey campaign. This initiative followed the controversial dismissal of Canadian news anchor Lisa LaFlamme, which many perceived as related to her choice to keep her hair gray. The incident highlighted broader issues of ageism and double standards in the workplace.

Dove, known for its commitment to gender equality and challenging beauty norms, aimed to support women facing age-based discrimination. With legal protections against ageism and sexism often inadequate, Dove's campaign sought to raise awareness and drive meaningful change. They turned the brand's iconic gold logo gray to symbolize solidarity and challenge societal expectations.

The campaign featured older women with gray hair in grayscale imagery, accompanied by Dove's new gray logo and the hashtag #KeepTheGrey. Launched on Dove's social media platforms, it encouraged others to join by updating their profile pictures to grayscale. Influencers amplified the message, and Dove donated $100,000 to Catalyst, a global partner dedicated to advancing women in the workplace.

The #KeepTheGrey campaign became the most talked-about in Dove Canada's history, significantly raising awareness about ageism and sexism. Ninety percent of viewers felt the campaign highlighted a crucial issue, 61 percent were more likely to purchase Dove products, 89 percent had a positive impression of the brand, and 83 percent wanted to see more such initiatives. Due to the campaign's success, Dove became the first beauty and consumer packaged goods brand to join the Ontario Human Rights Commission board, to continue advocating for women's rights and combating ageism in Canada.[6]

• • •

I need a hero.

His name is Colin Kaepernick.

Nike's "Dream Crazy" campaign, featuring Colin Kaepernick, is a now-classic example of leveraging activism in branding. In 2016, Kaepernick, then a quarterback for the 49ers, sparked national controversy by kneeling during the national anthem to protest racially motivated police brutality and risked his career in the process. Two years later, his courageous stance made him a fitting choice for Nike's campaign, in which he transitioned from athlete to civil rights icon.

The campaign elicited polarized responses. Some hailed Nike as a champion of social justice. In contrast, others criticized the brand for elevating Kaepernick, who had begun a movement of NFL players kneeling to draw attention to racial inequities.[7]

> Believe in something. Even if it means sacrificing everything.
> —Colin Kaepernick and Wieden+Kennedy for Nike's "Dream Crazy"

The backlash included calls to boycott Nike, with some posting videos of themselves burning Nike products in protest. Nike anticipated such reactions and used them to their advantage. Following the campaign's launch, Nike's stock surged, increasing the company's value by over $6 billion within two weeks.

Some view celebrity as superficial, but athletes, broadcast personalities, and influencers often serve as role models. Brands frequently capitalize on this admiration, using these figures' public heroism to elevate their image and appeal.

The Heroes We Promote

Psychiatrist Carl Jung pioneered the concept of psychological archetypes through his exploration of cultural mythologies. He observed that myths and legends from various cultures often feature common characters, which he believed arose from universal, unconscious symbols embedded in the human psyche. Jung defined these recurring figures as "archetypes," describing them as "forms or images of a collective nature that appear universally in myths and as individual manifestations of the unconscious."[8]

Derived from the Greek word "archetypos," meaning "original pattern," an archetype refers to a fundamental image, character role, or motif that recurs often enough to be considered universal. Jung's theory suggests that individuals inherit a collective unconscious—a shared pool of symbolic imagery and archetypes—beyond their personal experiences. While widely influential in psychology and the arts, this concept remains theoretical and is not empirically proven.

In branding and marketing, archetypes are powerful, universally recognized character types that, when applied effectively, can form the core of a brand's identity and narrative. While archetypal heroes can inspire empowerment and strength, it is essential to apply this framework inclusively, ensuring representation across a broad range of communities, ages, and genders, while avoiding narratives that reinforce dominance or exclusion.

Assessing how closely a brand's image aligns with an individual's identity is essential. Consumers often form strong connections with brands that reflect or reinforce their self-perception, creating a sense of self-congruity. It's essential, however, to be mindful of stereotypes or exaggerated portrayals that may be mistaken for archetypes.

Brands that skillfully leverage archetypes can forge stronger connections with their audience, as these archetypes tap into shared cultural ideals. However, we must consider evolving perceptions. For example, recent research on masculinity highlights a disconnect between traditional portrayals in advertising and modern consumer preferences, revealing that men and women often view masculinity differently.[9]

Interview: Nijel Taylor, Creative Director

Dedicated to inspiring meaningful change through design, Nijel Taylor has spent the last decade guiding the evolution of major brands across a spectrum

Nijel Taylor

of industries. As a highly accomplished creative director, designer, and strategic thinker, Nijel excels at translating insightful ideas into compelling brand narratives and strategic frameworks. His creative direction encompasses logo design, color strategy, photo art direction, illustration, typography, and 2D animation. Driven by a collaborative and empathetic approach, he partners with clients to craft exceptional brand experiences from initial vision to tangible reality. A firm believer in the power of diverse perspectives, Nijel champions inclusive design processes that foster curiosity, balance, and efficiency, leading to impactful and enduring brand solutions. He passionately sees design as a crucial tool for connecting with audiences and driving meaningful progress, consistently aiming to create work that resonates broadly and pushes the creative boundaries of branding.

His impactful collaborations include work with renowned creative agencies such as Lippincott, Trollbäck+Company, Superunion, and Siegel+Gale, contributing to the transformation and reimagining of iconic brands like Taco Bell, MTV International, and Sesame Workshop.

Nijel's foundation in design was solidified at The University of the Arts, where he graduated valedictorian with a BFA in Graphic Design. He has also shared his expertise as a Motion Design instructor at Kean University and actively mentors emerging talent. His work has been celebrated in esteemed design publications such as *GDUSA*, *Logo Lounge*, *Graphis*, and Robin Landa's *Graphic Design Solutions*, 6th edition, and *Strategic Creativity*. In 2022, he had the distinct honor of being a design jury member for The One Club for Creativity: Young Guns 20.

Nijel lives in Philadelphia, PA. He shares his life with his partner Connor and their dog Reese, finding creative fulfillment in writing alongside his brand leadership.

How do you design for emotional impact and brand authenticity?

Of course, most projects come fitted with a client's brief, but almost always, as creatives we are solving for an emotional solution as much as we are solving for a practical one. I like to start by asking myself and my team members: "How do we want the intended audience to feel?" It's a simple but effective question that sparks several other questions and opens up multiple lines of thinking.

A described feeling can often tell you plenty of what you need to know to create emotional impact, but feeling alone is not enough. When a brand embodies a feeling that is authentic to their identity, and at the same time embodies a feeling that is real to its audience's experience: *this* is when a brand becomes truly authentic.

I recently answered that question on a project, and the word I arrived at was "optimistic," because the intended audience is people struggling with a serious disease. Once that feeling was established as a goal, it afforded us several design approaches we could take to solve the branding challenge the client laid out for us. The colors could be bright, the typography could be human and approachable, and the logo could become a beacon that resonates with the audience and immediately telegraphs the word "optimistic."

What are the best-practice considerations for purpose-driven branding and storytelling?

Purpose-driven branding and storytelling are rooted in simple truths people share and can believe in. When defining a solution for a strategic foundation or a design solution, it is important to define the "so what" for the audience. A good example of this done well is Walmart's tagline, "Save Money. Live Better." It both defines the brand's role in helping the consumer and articulates the better outcomes the brand aspires to achieve. When brands understand simple truths in the context of a moment in time, they can unlock powerful stories that will resonate with consumers of the brand. In 2007, one of the worst U.S. recessions in history began, which was when Walmart launched its "Save Money. Live Better" tagline. It both encapsulated a simple truth and gave folks a reason to shop at a brand whose prices were affordable at the time.

What role does a brand play in building the right cultures in organizations?

Branding must go beyond marketing tactics for internal employees. I say that because while external audiences can appreciate a great brand, the internal organization and employees see everything that goes into making a brand great. Therefore, it is important to establish not just a strong brand idea and visual expression but also experiences that benefit employees internally and perhaps have a brand hook to them. I find that most leadership teams at organizations sometimes push too hard for their people to be brand advocates. If you need to convince someone to love something, is it worthy of love in the first place? But when you create experiences that honor your colleagues and are attentive to their goals, needs, and career ambitions, it often motivates them to engage with the brand in ways that fit their interests. A healthy organizational culture honors its people's interests and individual strengths, and aligns those advantages with the brand to create meaningful experiences that benefit everyone.

You've worked on several of the world's biggest brands throughout your career. Why is it vital for big brands with prominent voices to tell relatable and inclusive stories?

Brands inherently are a part of the cultural fabric of society. In today's media era, they simply can't hide, just like the rest of us. Their every word and every silence are noticed, so brands, whether they like it or not, must plant a flag and state their values. They must talk about the causes they champion and how they are doing more than just trying to sell stuff to clients and customers.

Since 2020, almost every brand has crafted a DEI statement. Every brand has a cause or commitment that they now advertise. This is not groundbreaking when you consider the conversation centered around inclusion was mainly sparked by the massive protests and unprecedented civil unrest in response to the murder of George Floyd. Neighborhoods and businesses shouldn't have had to burn down for brands to begin to care about social justice issues, but this is where we are today.

It is important that brands, no matter their size, tell relatable stories centered around inclusion because they reflect the world we live in. I can't state it more clearly than that.

Why is it critical to have diverse representation on creative teams, where underrepresented groups have a voice in the conversation and a seat at the table?

Diversity, equity, and inclusion are more than a commitment. It is real work that real people contribute to every day. When a team is not actively working to build diversity and equity amongst their ranks, they do the work and their clients a disservice. Underrepresented voices, mine included, can shed a lot of light—not just through better ideas, but also better collaboration processes, better ways to lead, and often better ways to build teams. We, as diverse creatives, are not often given the space or power to shape our own work environments and working conditions. Due to this, our role at organizations is sometimes significantly minimized and forgotten about. If companies are committed to advancing DEI in the world and not just in the walls of their companies, they should promote diverse candidates to impactful leadership roles. It's important not only to say you're committed but also to become the change you are promoting.

CHAPTER 16

CONNECTING TO CULTURE(S)

My connection to Mattel's Barbie was profound.

At the age of ten, I came home to find my beloved doll gone. Thinking I'd outgrown toys, my mother had given her away along with the handmade clothes I'd designed. Barbie was more than a toy; she was my surrogate, embodying my dreams and future self.

When Greta Gerwig's film *Barbie* (2023) debuted, it reminded me of a conversation from my early days working at an advertising agency. Over lunch, I had suggested the idea of a "Barbie" movie to a male colleague, a strategist. Initially, I imagined a romance—Barbie falls for a bad-boy type but soon realizes the merits of nice-guy Ken. Later, my vision evolved into a film that would celebrate the doll's role in representing overlooked girls, such as the original Black Barbie® from 1980, designed by Louvenia "Kitty" Black Perkins, or "Share a Smile Becky," the wheelchair-using doll introduced in 1996.[1] My colleague dismissed the idea outright, insisting Mattel would never stray from Barbie's traditional narrative, let alone create a live-action version portrayed by an actor.

When Gerwig's film premiered, I shared my long-ago idea and my colleague's skepticism on social media. On Facebook, a male acquaintance's pointed response was: "Let's see how *Barbie* performs at the box office."

Perform, it did. At last count, Gerwig's vibrant fantasy-comedy *Barbie* grossed over $636 million at the North American box office and $1.45 billion globally, making it the highest-grossing debut for a film directed by a woman.[2]

"Barbiecore" fever demonstrated the immense power of brand content rooted in cultural relevance. As Nancy Crimi-Lamanna, chief creative officer at FCB Canada, shared with me (see chapter 3), one essential criterion for creating and evaluating outstanding creative work is relevance. She explained that truly relevant work "addresses current and relevant cultural issues by providing insights and driving engagement for positive change."

A cultural moment can align so perfectly with the zeitgeist or a group identity that it transcends logic, creating a shared emotional connection. The *Barbie* film exemplified this, capturing the collective mood and making a significant cultural impact—proving it was the perfect time for Barbie to transform into a full-blown phenomenon and persona on screen.

While it may be evident to some that *Barbie* did not resonate with everyone—the universal appeal of a brand being inherently unfeasible—it undeniably struck a cultural chord with many at just the right moment. Timing is always a critical factor, much like a slot machine jackpot, where all the cherries must align perfectly to hit the win. For a brand or cultural moment to truly resonate, all the elements—timing, relevance, and execution—must come together seamlessly. In his interview in chapter 1, I asked Gaëtan du Peloux, chief creative officer and co-chief executive officer of Marcel Paris, how to make a brand matter or increase its value to people. He shared an insightful perspective, and I'd like to spotlight one key aspect:

> My goal is to do honest work for our clients, ensuring they stay relevant by connecting them with the current times. Timing is crucial—our WoMen's football campaign, for instance, might not have had the same impact if released three years earlier or later. Brands must resonate with the present, finding their legitimate space and relevant topics to engage with. This approach adds value to the brand.

And then you have Duolingo's mascot, Duo the Owl, walking the pink carpet at the *Barbie* film premiere in Los Angeles. Duolingo leverages AI to keep up with significant pop-culture moments, utilizing a scraper tool to track social media trends and employing ChatGPT to forecast which TV shows would gain popularity in global markets.[3]

From the Super Bowl to crashing Taylor Swift's *Eras* Tour phenomenon to attending a K-Pop concert, as well as participation in countless internet trends in between, Duolingo's lime-green owl mascot, Duo, seems to pop up and pop in everywhere. From Duo's witty comments on viral videos to creative takes on TikTok trends amassing millions of views—and even live appearances at major events—Duolingo, primarily known as a language-learning platform, has brilliantly established its mascot as a cultural icon of the internet.[4] By aligning itself with cultural phenomena—whether it's Comic Con, Charli XCX and Troye Sivan's "Sweat Tour," or playing *Squid Game* with Netflix's tie-up—Duolingo's Duo strategically integrates into the cultural conversation, positioning itself as an active and invested participant in the community—perhaps a surrogate for us. This mischievous and ubiquitous approach allows the brand to amplify its visibility and relevance by associating with the shared excitement and passion of these cultural epicenters. In doing so, Duolingo not only taps into existing cultural momentum but also strengthens its identity as a brand that understands and contributes to the moments that matter most to its audience. Douglas B. Holt, CEO and cofounder of the Cultural Strategy Group, former professor at Harvard Business School, and L'Oréal Chair in Marketing at Oxford, might refer to this as "coattailing," a postmodern marketing technique premised on the brand as an authentic cultural resource.[5]

Duolingo's humorous approach to promoting learning and unhinged media appearances attracts fans, users, and global growth. Duolingo's partnership with Netflix's *Squid Game* promotes Korean language learning through an immersive, one-of-a-kind campaign, including an update to its Korean course. "We saw a 40 percent increase in Korean learners just after *Squid Game* Season 1, underscoring the powerful connection between entertainment, culture, and language learning," said Manu Orssaud, CMO of Duolingo. "This campaign allows us to continue that momentum in a way only Duolingo can—with humor, intensity, and a bit of chaos! We hope fans will accept Duo's challenge to learn Korean and immerse themselves in the experience."[6]

Ad Age recently named Duolingo the Marketer of the Year. "All the stunty, buzzy marketing we talk about—especially the social stuff—has a pretty direct correlation with business growth," Katherine Chan, Duolingo's senior director of brand marketing, told *Ad Age*. "We ask people 'How'd you hear about us?' when they sign up as a new user, and, actually, a lot of people say TikTok or YouTube. . . . We have a playbook where it really starts with social, and we see that when we put dedicated resources into social, it helps grow the app significantly."[7]

Duolingo celebrates April Fools' Day with playful pranks each year, from announcing *Duolingo on Ice*, a four-hour multilingual skate-dancing extravaganza, to unveiling a fake Peacock reality TV show, *Love Language*.

When Duolingo planned its first Super Bowl ad, its in-house team focused on understanding what resonated with its audience. With only a few seconds of airtime, they turned to social listening tools to identify the most popular Duolingo memes and images, while steering clear of some of the more unconventional pop-cultural content created by users. It quickly became evident that Duo's butt was a surefire attention-grabber. On users' home screens, it had already gone viral. The team hoped their commercial would achieve the same level of impact.[8]

In a quirky five-second regional Super Bowl spot titled "Do your lesson, no buts," Duo the owl takes center stage. The spot begins with Duo turning away from the camera, seemingly showcasing the aftermath of a peculiar procedure.

Suddenly, the owl's rear inflates and bursts, accompanied by Duolingo's signature "Correct" chime. A new green owl emerges from the explosion, adding a humorous twist to the message.[9] According to Orssaud, in an interview with *Ad Age*, the spot playfully referenced online chatter about one of the eccentric illustrations on Duolingo's smartphone widget.[10] To complement the spot, a push notification was sent to four million users in the regional markets where the ad aired, perfectly timed to its five-second broadcast window.

Brands that align with the zeitgeist and address societal tensions go beyond selling products—they create cultural connections, trends, or moments of pop-culture transformation. As Kristie Malivindi, creative director at Jones Knowles Ritchie (JKR), shared with me in chapter 11, "Being authentic and acting with integrity are imperative to resonate honestly in culture." Cultural relevance involves understanding, influencing, and anticipating changing consumer preferences while consistently reflecting the spirit of the times in fresh ways. Achieving this requires a more flexible and evolving marketing strategy than traditional advertising or branded content typically provides.[11] People seem to eagerly consume what entertains or moves them. Recent data reveals that over half of US consumers favored advertisements that entertained them with humor, while nearly 50 percent appreciated ads that delivered motivational and inspiring messages.[12]

While *Barbie* captured the imagination of a global audience, Duolingo promotes language learning worldwide with pranks, shenanigans, and an influencer owl, and as you will read next, e.l.f. Beauty shows that even bold, controversial messaging can make a lasting impact by addressing a pressing cultural issue.

Culture-First Messaging

As e.l.f. Beauty sees it, America's corporate boardrooms have an issue: "So many Dicks."

There are more men named Dick (including variations like Richard, Rich, and Rick) on US public corporate boards than individuals from entire underrepresented groups.[13] In its latest chapter of the "Change The Board Game" initiative, e.l.f. Beauty aims to address corporate board inequity by promoting diversity and profitability in the boardroom. The "So Many Dicks" campaign, created by agency Oberland, highlights striking statistics, such as: "There are twice as many men named 'Dick' on publicly traded boards as there are Hispanic women, regardless of their name."[14] The campaign leads to a landing page where users can explore the link between boardroom diversity and improved business performance.

At a time when some corporations and universities are scaling back diversity initiatives, you might argue that the timing of this campaign was less than ideal.

Yet, the "So Many Dicks" campaign made a powerful impact, amassing 2.3 billion media impressions and becoming LinkedIn's most talked-about campaign. The campaign's bold messaging and various media assets encourage everyday consumers to reflect on the significance and inequality of an issue they may have otherwise overlooked. The response was overwhelmingly positive, with 98 percent favorable media sentiment and an 81 percent net sentiment on social media. More importantly, the campaign led to tangible change. As part of the initiative, e.l.f. Beauty sponsored a group of diverse candidates through the National Association of Corporate Directors, and companies have already placed 10 percent of these candidates on corporate boards.[15]

e.l.f. Beauty seems to know what people want. In a fresh collaboration (the only ones that pop are surprising ones), e.l.f. Beauty created an eyeshadow palette featuring twelve matte, shimmer, and metallic shades inspired by iconic Chipotle ingredients. Movers+Shakers, the agency behind this, stated that it was the collab "you never knew you needed. A tidal wave of press (from *Good Morning America* to [*The Late Show with*] *Stephen Colbert*) drove the full collection to sell out in three days, with most products selling out in just forty-four minutes! We brought two of Gen Z's favorite brands together for an epic collaboration, complete with an avocado makeup sponge and the limited-edition 'Eyes. Chips. Face.' vegan bowl. e.l.f.'s website nearly crashed!"[16]

Worldbuilding and Reinterpretation

Brands that "create worlds" go beyond selling; they build narrative-rich (often immersive) environments that capture consumers' imaginations and offer meaningful ways to engage. These brands craft a unique identity, aesthetic, or ecosystem that stimulates curiosity, inspires creativity, and helps consumers make sense of their own lives and the culture they inhabit. This approach attracts attention and earned media (publicity gained through organic efforts, such as word-of-mouth, social media mentions, earned media, or influencer endorsements, rather than paid media). It builds lasting emotional connections, earning recognition and financial success.

"As a marketer, so often we think in terms of campaigns and channels when we should be thinking in terms of outcomes and relationships," said Jonathan Emmins, founder and CEO of creative agency Amplify, in an interview with *The Drum*. Emmins explained that a world-building marketer takes a broader view, considering how a campaign fits into the larger narrative of the world they are creating. This involves asking, "How do you ensure the intellectual property becomes a chapter in the brand's overarching story?" It also requires recognizing that brands are "co-authored" with their audiences and being willing to embrace the loss of control that comes with that collaboration.[17]

LEGO brand play materials are iconic and adaptable to new interpretations, from collaborating with major franchises such as *Star Wars* to the FIRST Lego League, a guided, global robotics program using LEGO® technology. Now LEGO can add a documentary titled *Piece by Piece* to its vast repertoire. Conceived as such by musician and entrepreneur Pharrell Williams, *Piece by Piece* feels authentic rather than gimmicky. Although the documentary follows a relatively conventional biopic narrative, is it predictable?

"No, 'Piece by Piece' pops because everyone—including Williams and the film's director, Morgan Neville—is played by animated Legos," Alissa Wilkinson writes in the *New York Times* review of the film.[18]

The LEGO bricks become as tangible as Williams' life, embodying his playful and boundless creative essence. Whether producing chart-topping hits like "Happy," collaborating on streetwear, fragrances, and sneakers, or envisioning new possibilities in eyewear and skincare, Williams treats the world as a sandbox of opportunities for reinvention. LEGO bricks couldn't be a more fitting vehicle for his storytelling, each piece part of a larger, evolving narrative.[19]

This concept—that each revelation contributes to a larger, evolving narrative—aligns seamlessly with Nick Law's insight in chapter 2 about the power of storytelling: "A good story should make the audience feel like they've gained a deeper understanding of themselves or the world. Without these revelatory moments, a story falls flat. While anyone can tell a story, great storytellers excel in creating these impactful, dramatic moments." Williams' life and work exemplify this principle, showing how stories—whether built from LEGO bricks or crafted through music and design—can spark discovery and inspire.

Solving Tensions in Culture

"If I can't imagine what it's going to be when it lands in culture, then it's probably not going to be a great idea," said Rob Reilly, WPP's global chief creative officer.[20]

Reilly describes what he refers to as the Press Release Process, which he developed when at CPB (Crispin Porter Bogusky) and employs wherever he works. The essential "ask" is always the same:

> It's going to solve some tension that's out there in culture. And when this idea lands in culture, what's the thing that the press writes about? What's that thing people love to share and spread? . . . If you can't figure that out in a sentence or two, there's no way you're going to be able to make an entire campaign that's going to pop in culture.[21]

Brands that solve cultural tensions in creative, bold ways—such as *Barbie* or e.l.f.'s "So Many Dicks"—achieve relevance and spark meaningful conversations.

Reilly believes the key is figuring out how to "pop in culture"—getting people to notice, talk about, and spread your brand. With so many platforms, technologies, and AI, the need for a relevant, big idea is greater than ever. Brands that don't have one likely aren't making the cultural impact they need to pop.[22]

"Young people, especially, really want to see a brand that's got big ideas, but also stands for something. Young people will cancel you if you're not really doing the right thing, so I think it's a combination of doing it by a big idea but also doing the right thing by society. That's the combination," Reilly said.[23]

When Reilly says that effective advertising "solves some tension that's out there in culture," he likely refers to how successful campaigns often address existing societal issues, contradictions, a collective mood, or unmet needs. These cultural, emotional, economic, or social tensions often center on themes such as identity, freedom, leisure, belonging, or justice, and on how advertising or branding can help address these tensions or spark conversations that resonate with audiences.

Branding often mirrors cultural shifts, such as the growing concerns people have about the impact of artificial intelligence (AI) on their jobs, lives, and futures. When a brand positions itself as part of the solution, it fosters an emotional connection with consumers. Layne Braunstein, creative principal, ESI | NBBJ & founder of Fake Love, a NYT Company (see chapter 6), described "True Experiential Design" as "designed to stir feelings in the audience that leave a lasting emotional impact long after the experience ends." By presenting a product or service as a solution, brands can promote their offerings and connect emotionally with audiences by addressing issues they care about or feel conflicted over.

A "tension" often arises from discomfort, frustration, or unmet desires within the cultural landscape. Microsoft sought to address one such tension.

"If you design for people who have the greatest need, that same technology can make its way into the mainstream and help everyone," said Saqib Shaikh, founder and leader of Microsoft Seeing AI. For individuals who are blind or have low vision, AI can narrate daily experiences. Accessible through a smartphone camera, Microsoft's Seeing AI can read text, scan barcodes, describe scenes, recognize faces, and much more. The app delves into the details of the surrounding world, creating a vivid narrative that immerses users in the moment. It continues to evolve, driven by community feedback and advancements in AI research.[24]

Seeing AI is part of Microsoft's AI for Good program, which supports nonprofits, startups, and researchers using AI to address global challenges, such as improving accessibility and protecting biodiversity. One commitment of Microsoft's AI for Good program is to ensure that everyone can thrive in a digital, AI-enabled economy, and it extends to empowering other organizations to address society's biggest challenges.

Celebrated for his inquisitiveness, Trevor Noah, South African comedian, writer, producer, political commentator, and television host, is Microsoft's chief questions officer. Featured in each episode of a Microsoft series titled *The Prompt*, Noah and a guest engage with a timely prompt, exploring how AI is being used to tackle pressing global challenges and its impact on public safety, health, education, and more. In this effort, which is part of Microsoft's AI for Good, Noah examines the forefront of technology, breaking barriers, and gaining insights from technologists, engineers, scientists, and communities worldwide.

Unlike Microsoft's Seeing AI, Coca-Cola's AI-generated remake of its iconic Christmas ad, *Holidays Are Coming*, serves as a cautionary tale of misreading public sentiment regarding AI. Instead of resonating with audiences, the updated commercial amplified concerns about technology replacing human creativity. Public backlash ensued, with critics labeling it a marketing gimmick, and others expressing more profound anxieties about AI's role in eroding creative industries.[25]

One TikToker highlighted these fears, stating, "AI is going to steal so many jobs, and a company like Coca-Cola actually using it and endorsing it is very bad for the rest of the world. Why hire animators or directors when you can just type into AI and get an entire commercial?"[26] Similarly, Alex Hirsch, animator and creator of *Gravity Falls*, took to social media, describing Coca-Cola's iconic red as "the blood of out-of-work artists."[27]

This reaction underscores the importance of thoughtful decision-making in creative endeavors, particularly when integrating emerging technologies. Revamping a beloved classic using technology that sparks public anxiety carries significant risk—both to a brand's reputation and its connection with audiences.

In chapter 14, Lesley-Ann Noel, PhD, dean of the Faculty of Design at OCAD University, emphasized a proactive approach to managing such challenges. She advised: "Intentionally look for unintended consequences before, during, and after the design process. This awareness can help us better understand the impact of our work." Coca-Cola's misstep serves as a powerful reminder of the need to evaluate not only the creative potential of new technologies but also their broader implications on societal perception and cultural values. By integrating this mindfulness into the design process, brands can navigate innovation while maintaining trust and relevance.

In contrast, a highly effective "solve" employing technology is the "Shah Rukh Khan-My-Ad" by creative agencies Ogilvy and Wavemaker for Cadbury. Because the COVID-19 pandemic took a heavy toll on small businesses in India, the campaign leveraged machine learning to create ads promoting Cadbury and thousands of local businesses. With the enthusiastic support of Cadbury's brand ambassador, Bollywood superstar Shah Rukh Khan, Ogilvy crafted personalized ads featuring the actor encouraging people to shop locally for Diwali. The AI-driven ads highlighted over 2,000 stores across categories such as groceries, electronics, home décor, and clothing. Wavemaker developed a strategic media plan, optimizing ad reach with Google and YouTube.[28]

To enhance accessibility, a microsite enabled small business owners to generate customized ads, featuring Shah Rukh Khan "endorsing" their stores. Geotargeted ads ensured consumers saw promotions for nearby businesses. The campaign created 130,000 ads, garnered 94 million views on YouTube and Facebook, and empowered countless small businesses nationwide.[29]

This ability to identify and address tensions is not new—it has historical roots that laid the foundation for contemporary branding.

The Cracker Barrel

When I share with my Gen-Z university students that, in the 1880s in the United States, general stores sold crackers in bulk, stored in baskets or barrels, they often cringe at the thought. To them, the practice seems antediluvian, unsanitary, and messy, far removed from the modern advertising touts of convenience, hygiene, and safety. Yet, this evolution allowed brands like Nabisco to redefine consumer expectations, elevate perceptions of product quality, and establish trust in national brands.

Uneeda Biscuit: A Revolution in Packaging

In 1898, Adolphus Green helped organize over 40 Midwestern bakeries in the United States, to form the National Biscuit Company, which would later become Nabisco. The company's first product, Uneeda Biscuit, revolutionized the cracker industry by introducing packaging designed to preserve freshness and ensure hygiene, essential at a time when sanitation was a cultural tension in the United States.

Uneeda Biscuits were sold in moisture-proof, dust-proof cartons, which became a symbol of trust. No longer were crackers sold in open containers subject to contamination. This innovation established a new standard for packaged goods, earning consumer trust for the brand's commitment to quality and cleanliness. As the company's first million-dollar national advertising campaign boomed (created by N.W. Ayer & Son in Philadelphia), with the memorable slogan "Lest you forget, we say it yet, Uneeda Biscuit," the brand became synonymous with not only freshness but also transformation. By 1900, Americans were purchasing ten million packages of Uneeda Biscuits each month, and the brand's mascot—a little boy in a yellow raincoat—became a pop-culture icon.[30]

Brand Promises: The Foundation of Trust and Transformation

The success of Uneeda Biscuit laid the groundwork for a broader cultural shift. As packaged goods grew in popularity, so did consumers' trust in name-brand promises. Uneeda Biscuit delivered on its promise of sanitary, fresh crackers, while Nabisco continued to grow and began to introduce other now-iconic products: Ritz crackers (1934), which promised "a bite of the good life" during the Depression; and Oreos (1912), still much-loved and often aligned with pop cultural events, such as Pride Month.[31]

The appeal of brands such as Ritz went beyond their product functionality. They tapped into consumers' desires for transformation—offering not just a snack, but a glimpse into a better life. For many during the mid-to-late 1930s, buying Ritz crackers wasn't just about satisfying hunger, but about connecting to an aspirational ideal. Over time, this symbolic value became as important as the product itself.

We can see the same desire for transformation in brands such as Barbie, which, like Uneeda Biscuits, delivers more than a product—promising a connection to a larger cultural narrative of self-improvement and aspiration.

The Appeal of Transformation

In the late nineteenth century in the United States, "patent medicines" surged in popularity. Advertisements promised cures for ailments ranging from chronic pain and headaches to "female complaints" and kidney trouble. Over time, these dubious remedies became known as "snake oil."[32]

The origins of the term snake oil trace back to the 1860s when Chinese laborers working on the Transcontinental Railroad used a traditional Chinese ointment derived from the fat of the Erabu sea snake to soothe their sore muscles, which they brought with them from China to North America.[33] Enter Clark Stanley, a cowboy and showman known as "The Rattlesnake King." Claiming to have learned his Snake Oil Liniment formula not from Chinese émigrés but from Indigenous medicine, Stanley became famous for his dramatic live demonstrations. Dressed in colorful Western garb, he would battle rattlesnakes before mesmerized crowds, such as those at the 1893 World's Columbian Exposition in Chicago.[34]

As tales of snake oil's miraculous properties spread, opportunistic patent medicine vendors sought to capitalize on the craze, crafting their own "snake oil" remedies. Many, however, took shortcuts, often omitting any genuine snake-derived ingredients. As consumers grew wary of the extravagant claims, distrust of these "snake oil salesmen" grew. In an attempt to regain trust, some vendors began prominently displaying their names and faces on bottles, offering a personal guarantee of authenticity. Despite these efforts, "snake oil" became a byword for empty promises and fraudulent cures, a legacy that endures in conversations about advertising and trust.

A key element in the success of patent medicines was the traveling medicine show, popular across the southern and western regions of the United States from the 1870s to the 1930s. These events blended entertainment with salesmanship, drawing crowds with dramatic demonstrations of the medicines' supposed powers. Strongmen performing extraordinary feats, such as pulling horses with their bare hands, became symbols of the elixirs' transformative effects.[35] Figures such as Harry Houdini and P. T. Barnum even began their careers in this spectacle-driven trade, leveraging themes of transformation to captivate audiences.[36]

Marketers didn't just hawk patent medicines as cures; they framed them as pathways to the "good life," blending tangible promises with aspirational ideals.[37] However, their advertising often exploited marginalized groups, including Indigenous and Black communities, using harmful stereotypes to broaden appeal.[38]

Initially, these products appealed to consumers not just for physical healing but also for promising elevated social standing alongside improved health.[39] This strategy, which linked prosperity, morality, and personal success, mirrors contemporary marketing tactics. For example, Coca-Cola evokes human connection and happiness, while Jeep's "Go Anywhere. Do Anything" slogan embodies the spirit of freedom and adventure, positioning the brand not merely as a product but as a lifestyle.[40]

The Shape and Speed of Culture

To be clear, there is history, and there are histories.

There is culture, and there are cultures.

Broadening the definition of culture—by breaking down traditional boundaries—enables people to engage with and appreciate a wider range of cultural expressions, intellectual work, nonoperational thought, and social realities. This shift enriches a society's aesthetic sensibilities, fostering openness to diverse tastes, ideas, and experiences that were once marginalized or dismissed. It's not about redefining "what is good," but dismantling outdated hierarchies that constrain what could be valued and celebrated. As creative director Nijel Taylor states in chapter 15, "Design shapes culture." Similarly, as Sadie Red Wing highlights in chapter 13, "Graphic design is a powerful practice—it visually communicates the identity of something, making it real and recognizable." These insights underscore the role of design in making cultural expressions visible.

Subcultures naturally arise within larger cultures, characterized by groups of individuals who embrace distinct norms, values, beliefs, consumption habits, and lifestyles that often differ significantly from the dominant main-stream culture. Language plays a pivotal role in forming and maintaining these subcultures, acting as a marker of their unique identity.[41] For example, slang gradually infiltrates mainstream culture, often emerging from the vibrant lex-icon of diverse subcultures. For brands, subcultures offer a valuable source of borrowed cachet and a pathway to authentic street credibility. Drawing from phenomenological theory, Douglas B. Holt might describe this approach as life-world emplacement, a strategy that fosters the perception that brands pro-vide consumers with "original cultural resources untainted by the instrumental motivations of sponsoring companies."[42]

An example is New Balance's seven-minute film, *Grey Days*, shot in black-and-white 16mm, showcasing the brand's influence on various subcultures through minimalist vignettes. When a brand aligns itself with a subculture, it borrows that authenticity and credibility, making its narrative more compel-ling to both members of the subculture and those outside it who admire its values or aesthetic.[43] New Balance states, "The color grey embodies everything that makes New Balance stand out as a brand. Grey reflects an independent approach, dedicated to quality and style."[44]

Grey Days is a seven-minute film celebrating grey as the signature color of New Balance. Directed by Elliott Power and created by the Brooklyn agency American Haiku, the film traces New Balance's history, from its roots in run-ning to its cultural impact in 1980s DMV (D.C., Maryland, and Virginia) sub-cultures and the rise of the iconic 990 sneaker. Featuring appearances by UK rapper Dave, NFL star Chase Young, and skateboarding legend Andrew Reyn-olds, the film highlights the subcultures New Balance has influenced, with grey as a unifying symbol of authenticity and timelessness.

"This film celebrates what grey represents—not only for us as a brand but also for our consumers," said Chris Davis, chief marketing officer and senior vice president of merchandising at New Balance. "Grey transcends boundaries, appealing to everyone from supermodels in London to dads in Ohio to sneaker enthusiasts in Tokyo. It's a color for all—versatile, authentic, and enduring—carrying our heritage into the future."[45]

The marketing appeal of sneaker and sneakerhead (sub)culture, as exem-plified in *Grey Days*, is massive and influential. Sneakerheads are enthusiasts or collectors who are deeply passionate about sneakers, often treating them as cultural artifacts rather than just footwear, typically knowledgeable about sneaker history, limited-edition releases, collaborations, and the brands and designers that shape sneaker culture.[46] On Reddit, these groups boast over ten million members, representing just a fraction of the countless blogs, websites, Instagram accounts, and real-world gatherings that are too vast to quantify. Their economic impact is equally impressive, with the global sneaker industry valued at up to $90 billion and a resale market exceeding $10 billion.[47]

A recent YouGov report highlighted sneakerheads as a marketer's dream: predominantly younger individuals with significant disposable income, culturally attuned, highly active on social media, easily reachable online, and receptive to advertising.[48] Sneakerheads' passions often go beyond footwear, encompassing fashion, music, sports, and street culture—elements deeply intertwined with the sneaker world. In recent years, they have become influential cultural tastemakers, shaping trends and driving a brand landscape increasingly intent on embedding itself in culture. Recognizing their impact, brands across industries now view these communities as pivotal, investing heavily to earn their favor. Young people in particular have played a transformative role in elevating sneakers from functional sports gear to powerful tools of cultural expression, fueling the sector's growth into a multibillion-dollar industry.[49]

There is mainstream culture and the countless countercultures that challenge or deviate from it. Mainstream culture reflects the dominant ideas, practices, and values widely accepted and propagated within a particular society or group—often shaped by media, institutions, majority religion, political climate, or shared traditions. Countercultures emerge as responses to or rejections of the mainstream, creating spaces for alternative values, beliefs, and lifestyles; for example, the 1960s counterculture was a widespread social movement in the United States, Canada, and Western Europe that challenged conventional norms and traditional authority. Its members championed ideals such as peace, love, social justice, and revolution.[50]

Beyond subcultures, fringe subcultures thrive on the periphery, often influencing or being co-opted by the mainstream over time. As individuals and brands strive more than ever to stand out from one another, aspects of subcultures are becoming increasingly sought after due to their ties to the fringes and impassioned niche communities. This dynamic interplay—where elements of subcultures or countercultures are adopted, diluted, or reshaped by the mainstream—shows how culture emerges and is ever-evolving, blending the unorthodox or reactionary with tradition, for instance, sneakerhead culture as previously noted. Or consider steampunk, "a subculture that is the aesthetic expression of a time-traveling fantasy world, one that embraces music, film, design and now fashion, all inspired by the extravagantly inventive age of dirigibles and steam locomotives, brass diving bells and jar-shaped protosubmarines," which later became a stylish protest against the digital age.[51]

Yet culture or subculture is not an objective thing. In an interview, art historian George Kubler said, "Culture has been reified a great deal, been turned into a 'thing.' But it isn't a thing."[52]

Culture isn't a fixed entity that exists independently of the people and practices that shape it. It is dynamic, fluid, and constantly evolving through human exchange, values, beliefs—both accurate and misguided—and shared practices. Rather than being something that can be neatly categorized or boxed in, we can better understand culture as an ongoing process, constructed and experienced through social interactions, art, language, music, fashion, and even branding.

Viewing culture as a thing diminishes its complexity and adaptability. Instead, we should see it as a living, ever-evolving force that mirrors the fluidity of human experience. While some cultural shifts happen gradually, others occur rapidly during pivotal moments in history. The shift from the Medieval period to the Renaissance highlights how culture transitions between different modes of expression and inquiry, reflecting humanity's capacity for continuity and transformation.

By the "speed of culture," I refer to the pace at which cultural trends, ideas, and movements emerge, spread, and gain influence within a society. It reflects how quickly shifts in societal values, behaviors, technologies, and artistic expressions take root and evolve, locally or globally. In branding and media, this concept highlights the rapid journey of ideas or products from niche appeal to mainstream acceptance—and, just as quickly, their potential decline into irrelevance. (Think flash mobs of the early 2010s, or the pop-punk music genre of the early 2000s that faded from prominence, versus more recent phenomena like TikTok dances or Wordle that achieved massive cultural penetration in a matter of months). AI represents both a watershed moment and a cultural revolution. It marks a historic turning point, radically transforming how we communicate and reshaping who holds the power to create, distribute, and define culture in real time.

With the rise of digital platforms and social media, the speed of culture has accelerated dramatically. Trends encompass the general direction of development or change, often reflecting shifts in consumer behavior, preferences, and styles across various industries and contexts. Rooted in shared experiences, technological advancements, and community interactions, they shape diverse aspects of life, including art, entertainment, social norms, lifestyles, and consumer habits. At a broader level, macrotrends represent significant, overarching shifts with widespread implications, transcending industries, geographies, and demographics, while also acting as catalysts for the emergence of microtrends—short-term phenomena driven by specific influencers, creators, or groups within niche subcultures. At an even more focused level, nanotrends highlight ultra-specific cultural phenomena tied to hyper-localized events or niche subcultures, resonating with small, targeted audiences.[53] Platforms such as TikTok amplify this dynamic, creating "TikTok aesthetics"—distinct visual, cultural, and stylistic trends shaped by user-generated content, influencers, and algorithm-driven discovery, which can emerge, peak, and evolve within days or even hours. This fast-paced environment demands agility from brands and creators, requiring them to monitor cultural shifts closely and respond swiftly to remain relevant and resonant.

Subcultures have become more fluid and fragmented, often manifesting as short-lived micro-trends. The aspects of rebellion and resistance that once defined them are now embraced, even commodified, by commercial industries. This shift indicates that the line between subcultures and mainstream culture is increasingly blurred. What was once considered rebellious or underground is now frequently adopted by major brands and integrated into mass media, making it harder to distinguish the "alternative" in today's interconnected, globalized world.[54] Subcultures often innovate and develop new practices to preserve their distinct identity, particularly when mainstream media or culture co-opts their traditions. For instance, when skateboarding tricks or aesthetic elements gain mainstream adoption through commercialized video games and fashion brands, they can lose their original countercultural spirit and community significance. In response, core skateboarding communities may gravitate toward more technical disciplines or underground venues to preserve their subcultural distinctiveness and cultural authenticity. This ongoing cycle underscores the dynamic nature of cultural expression as both a marker of identity and a form of resistance to cultural homogenization.

There was a time in the United States when most people watched the same TV commercials across a few broadcast stations, creating a shared pop-cultural experience. However, with the rise of accessible media such as streaming services, social media, and video-sharing platforms, marketers now must focus on niche cultures and communities. Unlike the top-down cultural influence once driven by TV commercials, social media has enabled a more democratized, decentralized, and bottom-up process for culture to emerge and evolve. The speed, reach, and amplification power of social platforms are reshaping cultural dynamics, by empowering subcultures, microtrends, and individual creators—shifting the power of influence toward consumers, content creators, influencers, and niche communities.[55]

For a brand to "pop in culture," to make an impact, or even shape it, it must align with the zeitgeist, hitting the cultural moment at precisely the right time for the target audience. In chapter 12, Yousuke Ozawa, creative director at Ultra-SuperNew K.K. in Tokyo, shares three key elements for creating impactful work that drives business forward: a strong relationship, a clear vision, and a creative solution. He explains, "You have to take all that into account and crystallize it into something people find entertaining and exciting. It's a battle between logic and art, emotion and information, common and uncommon. Yet, when you find the right idea, it will penetrate the market like a giant arrow. Sneaking into people's subconscious, giving them a strong feeling about that brand."

• • •

During graduate school, one book that profoundly shaped my understanding of art and history was *The Shape of Time: Remarks on the History of Things* by George Kubler. Kubler challenges the traditional art historical approach that organizes artistic development primarily around stylistic categories and periods. Drawing from anthropology and linguistics, he shifts the focus to historical sequence and continuous change, emphasizing how time shapes and transforms cultural expressions. Kubler writes: "Let us suppose that the idea of art can be expanded to embrace the whole range of man-made things, including all tools and writing in addition to the useless, beautiful, and poetic things of the world. By this view the universe of man-made things simply coincides with the history of art. It then becomes an urgent requirement to devise better ways of considering everything man has made."[56]

Kubler's perspective challenges the linear narratives often associated with art history, proposing instead that objects and ideas exist in an ongoing sequences, shaped by both their predecessors and contemporaries. This framework reveals that cultural artifacts are not isolated but part of a larger, ever-evolving dialogue spanning generations.

Culture, much like Kubler's view of art, functions as a reflection of various collective identities—whether those identities are subcultures, national, religious, generational, or otherwise. It encapsulates shared values, beliefs, and experiences that evolve. For brands, these cultural expressions offer powerful tools for engagement. By aligning with and reflecting these cultural narratives, brands resonate with their audiences in the present as well as shape the collective understanding of the era they inhabit. Gradually, a brand's identity becomes part of a larger cultural story, influencing how it is perceived and remembered, ultimately shaping its legacy and place in history. We can see this dynamic at work in two landmark advertising campaigns. For example, Coca-Cola's iconic 1971 spot, "Hilltop," featuring the "I'd Like to Buy the World a Coke" jingle, emphasized a small yet powerful commonality shared by a diverse group of people, with the simple act of sharing a Coke serving as a symbol of global unity. Or take Budweiser's iconic "Wassup" commercial, which aired during Super Bowl XXXIV in 2000 and quickly became a cultural phenomenon. The spot, featuring friends casually exclaiming, "watchin' the game, havin' a Bud," became one of the most memorable and widely recognized campaigns in advertising history. Inspired by the short film *True*, written and directed by Charles Stone III and starring Stone and his friends, the spot connected with audiences across diverse communities. It captured the essence of friendship and laid-back moments, transforming into a global pop culture phenomenon that continues to resonate.

Branding as a Cultural Force

A reasonable observer from another planet might wonder, "Why would someone choose a branded product or service when a simple commodity could suffice? What motivates consumers to engage with a brand on social media, watch branded entertainment, or be influenced by a creator hired by a company to promote its wares?" This question points to the deeper emotional and cultural drivers behind consumer behavior—forces beyond mere functionality or price.

Emotional connections, personal values, and cultural significance, all amplified by social media, often drive people to choose a branded product over a generic alternative. Brands don't just sell products or services—they sell identities, stories, allegiances, and experiences that speak to people's sense of self. In chapter 6, when discussing how design makes data accessible and relatable, Giorgia Lupi, partner at Pentagram, emphasizes, "We have to see ourselves in the stories." Lupi's view speaks to how brands weave narratives in which consumers can see themselves, creating bonds that transcend the basic transactions and data to tap into something more meaningful.

Brands often provide a sense of identity, status, and connection. For instance, according to a report by YouGov, 77 percent of adidas wearers like products that reflect their lifestyles.[57] Consumers engage with brands to fulfill practical needs and project an aspirational vision of their desired lifestyle.[58] Through social media interactions, they can express themselves, feel a sense of belonging, converse, share content, and connect with a community that aligns with their values, activities, and interests. It's not just about the product—it's about what the brand represents and how it resonates with personal values, aspirations, or broader cultural moments.

As Emma Robbins, chief creative officer at M&C Saatchi Melbourne, shared in her interview in chapter 12, "The best brand storytelling happens when a brand is telling the story of their customer. Their customer's need, their customer's life, their customer's success—not their own. Brands can appear arrogant and unapproachable when they tell a 'we' story. We're the biggest. We're the most awarded. We're the most popular. People don't care about that. They care about how being the biggest will help them feel, or how being the most awarded will make them feel safer. Telling a brand's story is only relevant if it's about how customers will benefit from it."

● ● ●

It's late December; I'm deciding whether to rejoin a gym.

A study by *U.S. News* found that approximately 80 percent of individuals who join a gym in January stop attending by February.[59] Drawing on this data and insight, Babies Uganda launched Soul Gym, a campaign developed by Accenture Song, which encourages people to channel their unused gym memberships into support for vulnerable communities in Uganda. Babies Uganda is an international development NGO that operates two orphanages, a primary school serving over 650 children, a high school with more than 250 students, a primary care clinic for the local community, and a specialized school for over sixty children who are visually impaired.

Juan Silva, chief creative officer at Accenture Song, explained, "There's a powerful parallel between the discipline required in a gym to see tangible results and the discipline needed in showing solidarity to make a meaningful impact in the community you're supporting. Soul Gym serves as a metaphor for the value of sponsorship, leveraging a familiar concept and insight to maximize visibility and recognition."[60]

In my interview with Pancho González in chapter 8, the co-founder and chief creative Officer of INBRAX in Santiago, he emphasized one crucial criterion for assessing creative work: "What I value most is purpose. Originality and execution are important, but without positive impact, the work has no foundation—it won't progress." Creating purpose-driven campaigns is no easy feat, particularly in an environment where consumers and advocacy groups quickly call out anything that feels performative or inauthentic. Yet despite this heightened scrutiny, brands and nonprofits continue to develop impactful and genuine initiatives. Whether responding to fleeting nano-cultural moments or tackling enduring social issues, brands shape culture, just as their audiences, creators, and critics shape them.

To stay culturally relevant, successful brands must define their role in the cultural landscape and deploy strategies that make a significant impact. As Juliana Constantino, group creative director at Dentsu, notes in chapter 7, "Some brands jump on social issues for short-term campaigns without a genuine commitment to the cause. These efforts can come across as insincere or opportunistic, especially when their actions don't align with their promises. In today's hyper-aware consumer landscape, these discrepancies are often quickly noticed and can erode trust. The authenticity and ongoing commitment of purpose-driven branding set it apart from short-lived, opportunistic campaigns. It's not just about joining a conversation; it's about living your brand's values every day."

Understanding popular culture means recognizing the ever-evolving dynamics of human connections, interests, and (micro)trends—and finding innovative ways to engage with them. A standout example is the collaboration between German luxury brand Montblanc and filmmaker Wes Anderson, centered around the Meisterstück, a writing instrument. To celebrate "100 Years of Meisterstück," Montblanc launched a short film featuring Anderson himself along with Jason Schwartzman, Rupert Friend, and frequent collaborators, including Adrien Brody and Waris Ahluwalia. The film debuted alongside a Montblanc pop-up store on Rodeo Drive in Los Angeles, where they painted the exterior in Anderson's chosen shade of green, and the interior mirrored the set he created at Studio Babelsberg in Berlin. By embracing Anderson's distinctive visual storytelling—a style celebrated for its whimsy, attention to detail, and creativity—Montblanc infused its brand with the unique voice of a renowned auteur while resonating with audiences who value artistic vision and craftsmanship.

Vincent Montalescot, chief marketing and merchandising officer at Montblanc, explained that the brand chose to make the Meisterstück the centerpiece of its century-long legacy, telling a fresh story brought to life through a collaboration with Wes Anderson. By inviting a renowned storyteller to lend his unique perspective, Montblanc ensured that the iconic writing instrument would remain engaging and relevant in today's cultural landscape.[61]

Industry experts like Teresa Barreira, global chief marketing communications officer at Publicis Sapient, echo this emphasis on cultural relevance and the need for brands to continuously prove their worth. In an interview for *Financial Express*, Barreira remarked that "the biggest threat to brands today is irrelevance," stressing that brands must consistently demonstrate their value in consumers' lives to maintain their significance.[62] (For other insights, see the interview with Barreira in chapter 9.)

Each Sweethearts candy heart traditionally carries a short, sweet message, such as "Bestie," "Cutie Pie," "Love Bug," or "Be Mine." Recently, Sweethearts cleverly transformed a misprinted batch of conversation hearts into a fresh line perfectly in sync with a current top dating trend—"Situationships." Just in time for Valentine's Day, the brand released a limited-edition "Situationship Boxes" that playfully nod to romantic or sexual entanglements where the relationship is undefined, and commitment is often absent. This highly contemporary twist on the 120-year-old brand resonates particularly with Gen Z, demonstrating its ongoing cultural relevance. Indy Selvarajah, chief creative officer at Ketchum and a judge for D&AD, commented on the campaign, "They took a wasted product and turned it into a new line—culturally relevant, attracting a new audience that was in decline. It also became a sought-after product that played into exclusive 'drop culture,' all done on a shoestring budget."[63] ("Dropping" is a marketing and consumer technique centered around the launch of limited-edition or exclusive products in restricted quantities, typically announced with minimal notice.)

Sweethearts' clever integration of a trending cultural concept like Situationships shows how even heritage brands can remain relevant by listening to cultural shifts and engaging with humor, creativity, and authenticity.

Montblanc and Sweethearts illustrate how brands can do more than react to culture; they can actively engage with and shape it. Whether through collaborations with creative visionaries like Wes Anderson or addressing evolving relationship dynamics such as Situationships, successful brands position themselves at the intersection of core values, cultural tensions, and emerging microtrends. By doing so, they spark cultural influence rather than simply chase it.

Tim Walsh, head of strategy at Momentum, emphasizes this evolving approach, noting a shift from sponsorship to partnership, rooted in "cultural intersectionality." Speaking to *The Drum*, he underscored the importance of tapping into diverse subcultures and the influence of digital natives: "The key trend this year has been the focus on cultural intersectionality. While traditional strategies still exist, real innovation emerges when brands connect with smaller, highly engaged communities that share specific interests. These niche groups are gaining momentum, and brands are increasingly investing in them to achieve deeper relevance."[64]

Revisiting Barbie: Harnessing Tensions to Spark Cultural Change

As a child, I adored my Barbie doll and dreamed of growing up to be as glamorous as she was. But a close friend of mine loathed Barbie for her "stereotypically perfect body" and even destroyed her doll in protest. While my friend's actions weren't the direct inspiration for "Weird Barbie," it turns out she wasn't alone in her critique.

Spoiler alert for the *Barbie* film: Weird Barbie, portrayed by Kate McKinnon, is an eccentric character shaped by her owner's modifications—cut hair, marker-drawn face, and flexible limbs—which led to her isolation in Barbie Land. Initially feared and avoided, Weird Barbie eventually becomes essential in guiding Stereotypical Barbie (played by Margot Robbie) with the knowledge needed to access the real world. Beyond the film, Weird Barbie has become a cultural sensation, with the hashtag #WeirdBarbie amassing 53.9 million views on TikTok. Her relatable charm has made her a standout character, even prompting the release of a purchasable Weird Barbie doll. As Olivia-Anne Cleary wrote in *Glamour UK*, "Margot Robbie's Stereotypical Barbie is great, but Weird Barbie is the MVP."[65]

Another standout character in the film is Allan, played by Michael Cera. Through Allan, director Gerwig sends an important message: not every man fits the mold of a Ken doll. Some men navigate a male-dominated world without resorting to exaggerated bravado, as seen in the various portrayals of Ken throughout the film. With its mix of awkward charm and subtle exasperation about being an Allan in a Ken world, Cera's portrayal perfectly captures this sentiment in his limited yet memorable scenes, resonating deeply with many viewers.[66]

Tapping into Culture

Leveraging cultural moments to build emotional connections with audiences is key to creating content that truly resonates. A social media trends report by creative agency Ogilvy aptly asks, "Wasn't 2023's Barbie mania a live-action masterclass in the power of content with culture at its heart?"[67] This phenomenon reached beyond the screen, exemplified by the *Barbie: A Cultural Icon* exhibit at the Museum of Arts and Design in New York City, which attracted long lines for months. Celebrating Barbie's 65th anniversary, the exhibit chronicles her sixty-five-year history, highlighting her profound influence on fashion and global popular culture while tracing her evolution from 1959 to the present.[68] Barbie mania demonstrates how brands can transcend their original purpose to shape conversations about identity, gender, and social expectations across generations.

Brands hold the power to shape culture and influence societal values in substantial ways. In today's rapidly shifting landscape, where cultural dynamics evolve constantly, brands must be bold and proactive in driving progress. They can transcend profit-focused goals by remaining committed to creating positive change, even amid political divides and backlash. The most impactful brands are those that actively contribute to advancing communities by addressing real social needs and creating tangible impact, as demonstrated by initiatives like Babies Uganda's Soul Gym campaign that channel consumer behavior into community support.

In parts of Africa and Asia, persistent taboos surrounding menstruation often result in millions of girls missing school. To address this, feminine hygiene brand Whisper launched an educational lobbying campaign in India to challenge these societal taboos and help girls stay in school. Procter & Gamble India's #Whisper initiative, *#KeepGirlsInSchool*, seeks to normalize menstruation as a natural and healthy process, while empowering parents and educators to approach the topic in a supportive and informative manner.[69]

The true power of branding lies not just in messaging, but in meaningful action—investing in communities, supporting causes, and addressing the issues that resonate with audiences. Brands have the potential to inspire, challenge, and ignite cultural shifts that leave lasting legacies. In chapter 10, Ari Halper, global executive creative director and head of creative excellence at R/GA, recalled a lecture by Oliviero Toscani, the Italian photographer and mastermind behind Benetton's purpose-driven and provocative campaigns. Halper shared Toscani's reflections on his controversial campaigns in the 1980s and '90s, which featured stark images, including scenes of genocide and a person living with AIDS. Though unconventional for selling clothes, the campaigns forced consumers to confront social issues they might otherwise ignore, transforming a fashion brand into a platform for global awareness. As Toscani told the *New York Times*, "We are a little bit in advance of everyone, not by what we say, but by using advertising as communication" to address social, political, and environmental issues. He added, "I have found out that advertising is the richest and most powerful medium existing today, so I feel responsible to do more than to say, 'Our sweater is pretty.' "[70]

Brands have the power to shape cultures. In a rapidly evolving world, they must actively drive progress and stand firm in the face of uncertainty. Profit alone is no longer enough; the most effective brands recognize their responsibility to contribute positively. As Karen R. Baker, CEO of Seven Concepts, emphasized in chapter 13, "When it comes to corporate social responsibility, we need major brands to step up. They're the ones with the visibility, the history, and often, the financial resources to make a significant impact. If we have more socially responsible businesses taking a leading role, it will drive conversations about the need for diverse creative directors to deliver socially responsible campaigns."

Branding's true power lies in authentic actions that drive lasting, positive change. It can inspire and foster meaningful connections that extend beyond the marketplace. As consumers, we expect businesses to actively contribute to communities, protect the environment, and be inclusive of diverse cultures. For branding to be impactful, companies must accept this responsibility. With their powerful societal position, businesses can lead change through tangible actions, reshaping how they are perceived globally. In my interview with Christina Carey Dunleavy, vice president of Entertainment Brand Solutions, Disney CreativeWorks, and Multicultural & Inclusive Solutions, Disney Advertising, she explains that their approach is to "drive relevance for brands through creativity, connection, and collaboration." This perspective underscores the role of cultural stewardship: relevance depends on a brand's ability to connect authentically, collaborate meaningfully, and continually earn cultural resonance.

In chapter 4, during my interview with Ben Miles, chief design officer for APAC, R/GA, I asked how advertising and branding could drive positive change. His response perfectly captured the essence of this book's theme—a call to harness creativity and influence as powerful forces for meaningful impact: "The key is differentiating between a nice idea and actual impact. Brands and advertisers driving long-term change really contribute to moving the dial positively. Design is a tool that bridges gaps, that creates inclusivity, that creates space for people. That has to be intentional."

ACKNOWLEDGMENTS

R enowned practitioners and thought leaders shared their expertise with remarkable generosity and wisdom. Their insights sharpened the ideas presented here and grounded them in real-world applications. I am profoundly grateful to each of them for enriching this work with their remarkable perspectives: Christiano Abrahao, Karen R. Baker, Teresa Barreira, Layne Braunstein, César Chinchilla, Brian Collins, Juliana Constantino, Jonathan Daniel, Melissa Grady Dias, Christina Carey Dunleavy, Nancy Crimi-Lamanna, Luke Flynn, Pancho González, Kelcey Gray, Ari Halper, Joseph Han, Stuart Haury, Alexander Isley, Nick Law, Giorgia Lupi, Kristie Malivindi, Ben Miles, Leslie-Ann Noel, Eddie Opara, Yousuke Ozawa, Gaëtan du Peloux, Alison Place, Sadie Red Wing, Emma Robbins, Kristen Schiele, Nijel Taylor, Jessica Walsh, and Yoshihiro Yagi.

I am deeply grateful to Leland Maschmeyer, Co-Founder and CEO of COLLINS, for generously contributing the foreword to this book. His visionary perspective and insights into creativity and branding set the perfect tone for what follows. Thank you, Leland, for lending your expertise and voice to this project—it's an honor to have your thoughtful words open this work.

For their support and contributions, my humble thanks to Diane Anton, Alan Bethke, Greg Braun, Steven Brower, Phillip Cox, Tim Crino, Dolly Dunn, Abby Evans, Madeleine Garner, Diane Gibbs, Maggie Giles, Caitlin Gilles-Grabinsky, Catalina Gomez, Jane Ha, Emily Hofstetter, Adam Leiter, Laura Lyman, Frank Macera, Sumita Masahiko, Julian McBride, Paul Mehnert, Rosie Milton-Schönemann, Mike Schnaidt, Yuka Nakamura, Kate Neill, Casey

Powers, Nick Sonderup, Emma Swanson, Penny Taylor, Jessica Thompson, Paula Tobo, Lauren Walsh, Tim Welsh, and Doug White. Also, my thanks to the experts who reviewed the manuscript.

At Columbia University Press, I am truly grateful to the editorial team for believing in this subject and in me. A special thank you to my exceptional editor, Brian C. Smith, whose keen insights, thoughtful guidance, and unwavering support shaped this book in countless ways.

I'm also grateful to former publisher, Myles C. Thompson, and to the faculty and editorial boards of Columbia University Press. My thanks to Ben Kolstad, Kathryn Jorge, and the production team at KGL.

At Kean University, for their invaluable support I am deeply indebted to Dr. Lamont Repollet, president; Dr. David Birdsell, provost; Dr. Susannah Porterfield, vice president for research; Laura Baecher, associate provost for faculty development; David Mohney, dean of Michael Graves College; Rose Gonnella, associate dean; Linda O'Shea, chairperson of the Robert Busch School of Design, and my brilliant colleagues and fellow citizen-designers near and far: Deborah Ceballos (Kean), Meaghan Dee (Virginia Tech), Meena Khalili (University of South Carolina), and Camile Sherod (Kean). I'm grateful to Meaghan Dee for not only being part of this illustrious group but for stepping in to design when I needed an alternate cover—you're a rare gem.

Heartfelt thanks to Amaya Grullon Hernandez for her creative vision in designing the cover, and to the incomparable Deborah Ceballos for refining it with such generosity and aplomb. Together, they brought this cover to life.

For putting up with me and endless takeout, I thank my loving husband, Harry, and our darling daughter, Hayley.

TOOL: SCRUTINIZING ARCHETYPES

When employing archetypal models such as the Hero, Rebel, or Caregiver in branding, storytelling, or character development, it's crucial to ensure these representations align with principles of social justice and genuinely reflect the values of the target audience. To effectively evaluate and refine these archetypes, assess them through the lens of the following three categories:

1. Biased Archetypes

Biased archetypes reinforce stereotypes, perpetuate harmful narratives, and misrepresent or marginalize certain groups. These portrayals often lack inclusivity and overlook the broader social and cultural implications of their traits and actions. Favoring specific groups due to existing disparities reinforces the status quo, sustaining or exacerbating systemic inequities. Bias manifests in two primary forms: explicit and implicit. *Explicit bias* involves conscious, intentional beliefs and attitudes that individuals are aware of and can control. *Implicit bias* operates unconsciously, shaping perceptions and actions through automatic associations linked to characteristics such as race, ethnicity, gender, age, disability, neurodiversity, religion, sexual orientation, educational level, or economic status.[1]

Characteristics of Biased Archetypes:

- *Stereotypical traits*: Relies on clichéd, reductive attributes that reinforce harmful or limiting perceptions
- *Exclusionary narratives*: Diminishes or overlooks the lived experiences and perspectives of historically marginalized groups
- *Lack of complexity*: Portrays characters or narratives in a one-dimensional, overly simplistic manner
- *Cultural appropriation*: Uses cultural symbols, language, or practices without understanding, respect, credit, or proper context
- *Representation bias*: Centers dominant or majority groups while minimizing or omitting others
- *Gender bias*: Prioritizes one gender's experience or perspective, often reinforcing historically biased or unjust norms or roles
- *Exclusion of people living with disabilities and neurodivergence*: Marginalizes people with disabilities or neurodivergent individuals, restricting visibility and agency
- *Limited family depictions*: Focuses exclusively on nuclear, heterosexual family structures
- *Core values and authenticity*: Bias often signals a lack of awareness, ethical principles, or cultural competence. When a company fails to integrate equity and social justice principles into its identity, any alignment with social or environmental causes may appear performative, damaging credibility, and weakening relationships with the public and stakeholders.

Assessment Questions:

- Does the archetype meaningfully challenge stereotypes?
- Are a broad range of experiences and identities thoughtfully represented?
- Is there a demonstrated effort to adapt and evolve the archetype based on feedback?

2. Conscious Archetypes

We carefully craft conscious archetypes with an awareness of social and cultural dynamics. They aim to be inclusive and respectful, stereotype-defying, promoting representation and meaningful cultural resonance. Even well-intentioned portrayals can fall short of fully embodying social justice principles.

Characteristics of Conscious Archetypes:

- *Inclusive representation*: Reflects a wide range of experiences, identities, and backgrounds.
- *Challenging misconceptions*: Actively subverts stereotypes and reframes dominant narratives.
- *Cultural sensitivity:* Demonstrates respect and understanding for different cultures and identities.
- *Evolving narratives*: Shows openness to growth and adaptation based on feedback and shifting social contexts.
- *Core values and authenticity*: A company embeds social justice in the brand's identity. Marketing efforts often fall short when this is not a core value.
- *Tokenism*: Representation appears superficial, such as performative gestures during cultural observances, without sustained, structural commitment.
- *Gender inequalities*: Acknowledges gender disparities but fails to offer meaningful inclusion or leadership opportunities (e.g., including a lone woman on a team framed as representative).
- *Disability representation*: Often limited to portrayals of individuals with visible disabilities and reliant on stereotypical or inspirational tropes.
- *Diverse family models*: Recognizes nontraditional family structures, such as single-parent households or same-sex couples, but rarely integrates them in substantive ways.

Assessment Questions:

- Does this archetype meaningfully challenge stereotypes or conventions?
- Are a wide range of experiences and identities thoughtfully represented?
- Is there a consistent effort to evolve the archetype based on feedback and cultural shifts?

3. Upstanding Archetypes

We intentionally craft *upstanding* archetypes to fully embody and advance social justice principles. Design them to be empowering, inclusive, and transformative, serving as positive models that inspire and uplift a wide range of audiences. These portrayals actively confront existing disparities, advocate for equity, and empower historically marginalized populations. Brands that use upstanding archetypes represent diverse identities and also respond with scalable solutions tailored to the needs of different family structures, individuals living with disabilities, various cultural backgrounds, and all gender identities and expressions.

Characteristics of Upstanding Archetypes:

- *Empowerment*: Inspires individuals and communities to effect positive change
- *Authenticity*: Portrays identities and lived experiences with depth, accuracy, and respect
- *Equity and inclusion*: Actively promotes fairness and embraces a wide range of identities across all dimensions
- *Social impact*: Brings attention to pressing social issues, encourages dialogue, and drives collective action
- *Responsiveness*: Listens to feedback and evolves to address systemic inequities and challenges
- *Core values and authenticity*: Embeds social justice principles into the brand's voice, portrayals, actions, and mission
- *Gender identity and gender expression*: Affirms and supports all gender identities and expressions, striving for equity and empowerment
- *Representation*: Portrays individuals from a range of racial, ethnic, socioeconomic, and cultural backgrounds, challenging dominant or one-dimensional narratives
- *Disability representation*: Includes individuals with visible and nonvisible disabilities as active, multidimensional participants in society, reflecting the full spectrum of disability experiences
- *Diverse family models*: Positively depicts various family structures, such as extended, blended, LGBTQ+, multigenerational, and economically diverse households, as valid and valued

Assessment Questions:

- Does this archetype actively promote and advance social justice causes?
- Are historically marginalized voices centered, empowered, and authentically represented?
- Does the archetype inspire positive change and foster meaningful connections across a wide range of communities?

Action Steps:

- *Lead by example:* Use the archetype to model high standards for inclusivity, equity, and social responsibility.

- *Amplify marginalized voices*: Center and elevate perspectives from historically marginalized communities.
- *Foster engagement*: Create meaningful ways for audiences to engage with and contribute to the brand's mission.
- *Engage with communities*: Collaborate with diverse groups to ensure portrayals are authentic, respectful, and co-created.
- *Continuous improvement*: Regularly review and evolve the archetype based on feedback and shifting cultural insights.
- *Build depth and nuance*: Craft layered, multidimensional characters that reflect the complexity of lived human experiences.
- *Measure impact*: Track how the archetype influences perception, representation, and measurable social change.

Using the Three Categories to Assess and Develop Archetypes

Utilize the Biased, Conscious, and Upstanding categories as a guiding framework to evaluate and develop archetypal models that resonate with your audience while upholding social justice principles. This approach ensures that the brand contributes positively to society, fosters meaningful connections, and demonstrates a commitment to equity and inclusion.

1. **Evaluation Process:**

   o *Identify the current state*: Analyze the archetype's traits, narratives, and cultural impact to determine where it currently falls within the three-category framework.
   o *Gather feedback*: Collect insights from diverse audiences, communities, and subject experts to uncover blind spots and opportunities for growth.
   o *Set goals*: Establish clear objectives to move the archetype toward the "Upstanding" category.

2. **Development Strategies:**

   o *Educate the teams*: Provide training on equity, representation, and inclusive storytelling practices.
   o *Focus on collaborative creation*: Involve a diverse group of creators, cultural consultants, and lived-experience experts in the development process.
   o *Use iterative design*: Incorporate continuous feedback loops to refine and enhance the archetype's alignment with social justice values.

3. **Implementation:**

 o *Integrate thoughtfully*: Apply the archetype consistently across branding, marketing, communications, and "storiestelling" to reinforce its upstanding attributes.
 o *Monitor and adapt*: Regularly assess how people receive and make any necessary adjustments to maintain relevance, authenticity, and impact.

4. **Communication:**

 o *Offer transparent messaging*: Clearly articulate the intent, values, and purpose behind the archetype to internal and external audiences.
 o *Engage in dialogue*: Encourage open conversation around the archetype's role in promoting social good.

The Difference Between Archetypes and Stereotypes

An archetype is a universal symbol or motif that recurs across literature, art, mythology, and culture, reflecting fundamental human experiences and truths. By contrast, a stereotype is a reductive and biased generalization about specific groups. While archetypes offer shared, meaningful narratives that resonate broadly, stereotypes amplify prejudice, oversimplify identity, and foster misunderstanding.

As Sadie Red Wing, designer and assistant professor at OCAD University's Faculty of Design in Toronto, emphasizes in her interview in chapter 13: "Stereotypes are exaggerated identities that are neither appropriate nor accurate for representing nationalities." She further notes: "Currently, the dominant imagery showcasing Indigenous nations is rooted in stereotypes." Red Wing's insights highlight how stereotypes, particularly those targeting Indigenous communities and nations, perpetuate harm and erase nuance. These portrayals distort cultural realities and contribute to systemic inequality.

By embracing archetypes—symbols rooted in shared human experiences— brands can forge more respectful connections with people. Archetypes can transcend boundaries and inspire understanding, whereas stereotypes reinforce harmful biases and exclusion.

Stereotypes perpetuate negative perceptions and biases, fueling societal inequality and discrimination. For brands, relying on stereotypes risks alienating audiences, eroding trust, and even inviting legal consequences, such as lawsuits for defamation or discrimination.

Ethically and strategically, brands have a responsibility to portray people accurately and inclusively. Beyond ethical obligation, a commitment to diversity and authenticity enhances brand reputation, strengthens identity, and broadens audience appeal. Fostering accurate and inclusive representation isn't just good citizenship—it's good business.

When Archetypes Imbue Meaning

China is the world's largest beer-drinking market.[2]

For Corona, the challenge of securing high-quality limes grew as nearly a quarter of the country's farmers live in poverty. Rather than resorting to lime imports, Corona partnered with local governments and industry leaders to support farmers. Through the Corona Extra Lime initiative, the brand provided farmers with the knowledge and tools to grow high-quality limes and boost their yields. This approach resolved Corona's lime supply issue and also created a sustainable business model that offered essential economic support to struggling farmers in China.[3]

After 1,000 days of research, development, and farming, the company finally introduced Corona Extra Lime to shelves across China. This initiative not only elevated the quality standard of limes in the market and enhanced the Corona drinking experience but also profoundly impacted the lives of thousands of farmers. By directing all profits from the initiative back to the farmers, Corona enabled them to expand their farms and improve their living conditions.[4]

In this campaign context, Corona embodies the "Angel" archetype by taking bold action to address a pressing issue while uplifting a community in need. This initiative is part of a broader commitment to sustainability: Corona is the first brand to achieve a net-zero plastic footprint, meaning it recovers and recycles as much or more plastic than it uses globally, thus "preventing it from ever polluting paradise."[5]

Corona, a subsidiary of Constellation Brands, adheres to an Environmental, Social, and Governance (ESG) strategy. This commitment includes protecting the environment, supporting underserved communities, and promoting responsible alcohol consumption to ensure consumer safety and well-being. Constellation Brands' vision—to "elevate human connections and communities, creating a future that is truly Worth Reaching For"—reflects their broader goals. Through these initiatives, Corona exemplifies the Activist archetype.

Brands frequently utilize multiple archetypes in their campaigns, provided they align with the core narrative. For example, Corona embodies both the Angel and Activist archetypes, while Nike combines the Hero and Rebel archetypes.

Some creative professionals and marketers have mixed views on archetypes. While some find them valuable tools for building emotional connections, others consider them overly simplistic or struggle to apply them to a brand's unique identity. In my experience, even chief marketing officers sometimes struggle to articulate their brand's essence. Still, exploring a brand's archetype can yield valuable insights into how it fits into people's lives and why it matters.

When studying branding, students often appreciate archetypes for their literary roots and universal appeal. Much like film archetypes such as the Hero or Rebel, brand archetypes can facilitate emotional connections with consumers. However, true emotional resonance and differentiation come from crafting nuanced narratives that move beyond broad archetypal outlines. While archetypes offer useful structure, compelling brand campaigns require more than these generalizations.

Conceptualizing a Brand as a Character

Our brains process brands much like they do close relationships, sometimes with influence that surpasses our conscious awareness.[6] A brain imaging study found that the medial prefrontal cortex, the region that evaluates intentions, responds similarly to "socially oriented brands" and to people, suggesting our brains process both in comparable ways.[7] This underscores the powerful influence brands have on consumer behavior, revealing that a "caring" brand can affect us as profoundly as a conversation with a friend.[8]

FOCUS: "CARS TO WORK" / RENAULT AND PUBLICIS CONSEIL, PARIS

According to a government report, around 20 percent of France's working-age population experiences mobility challenges due to limited transportation options.[9] As a result, up to 28 percent of individuals entering the workforce may forgo employment or training opportunities.[10]

The Renault and creative agency Publicis Conseil, Paris, "Cars to Work" campaign exemplifies the friend and caregiver archetypes, characterized by a commitment to support and nurture others. This initiative provides practical assistance to new job starters by offering a vehicle lease option with payments deferred until after their probation period, addressing a key barrier to employment. "The campaign was truly dedicated to those in need. From the outset, it was about addressing a real problem for real people. The offer is genuinely tailored for them," Marie Donnedieu, Publicis' senior artistic director, said in an interview with Contagious, an advertising consultancy.[11]

"It's an idea that benefits both people and business," said Gustavo Lauria, Cannes Lions Sustainable Development Goals Jury President and cofounder, president, and chief creative officer of We Believers. "Sustainable initiatives often focus primarily on people and the planet, potentially overlooking business impact. In this case, the solution achieves both: it supports people and simultaneously drives car sales."[12]

In brand-building, emphasis often lies on the brand's attributes. Utilizing archetypal characters from literature, such as the Hero or the Sage, can help define the brand's persona, clarify its strategic relationship with the audience, and position it effectively against competitors. For example, TOMS exemplifies the "Caregiver" archetype through its one-for-one model, which focuses on social good, while Virgin Atlantic embodies the "Innovator" archetype with its groundbreaking use of 100 percent sustainable aviation fuel and commitment to sustainable energy solutions.[13]

The Floating Boat installation exemplifies the Magician archetype, characterized by transformation, unveiling the unseen, and fostering change. Created by contemporary artist Oscar Oiwa for E.On Italy, this artwork features a boat suspended 75 cm above the water level of Lake Garda, highlighting the invisible impact of climate change—specifically the reduction in water levels. The installation's striking presentation captured widespread attention and remains visible on Google Maps.

Created by Dentsu Creative Amsterdam for Dutch telecommunications firm KPN, the "A Piece of Me" campaign reflects the Sage archetype, representing wisdom and guidance. This initiative addresses the critical issue of intimate photo sharing among teens and the associated online shaming. By promoting the message "think twice before you forward," the campaign acts as a moral guide, aiming to educate and foster responsible digital behavior.

Featuring a film and original music by popular Dutch singer-songwriter Meau, the campaign effectively engages Gen Z, evoking emotional resonance and sparking conversations. Dentsu Creative stressed the urgency of the issue, stating, "In the past six months alone, 33,000 young people in the Netherlands have fallen victim to the unwanted forwarding of intimate photos. Victims are often blamed and unfairly portrayed as perpetrators—a serious problem with severe consequences that must change."[14]

Since its release, the campaign has achieved 10 million streams, reached the top three on music charts, and has been used in hundreds of schools to educate students about the consequences of online shaming. "Understanding the challenge of reaching Gen Z, we crafted a piece of musical entertainment designed to resonate with them and encourage sharing," said Gijs Sluijters and Joris Tol, the campaign's creative directors. "This approach has transformed the stories of online shaming into meaningful conversations, both in schools and at home."[15]

Telecommunications companies such as KPN, recognized for their essential services and reliable information, embody the Sage archetype by positioning themselves as trusted advisors. KPN strengthens its role as a leader in promoting responsible digital behavior with initiatives like the "A Piece of Me" campaign. This effort marks the beginning of KPN's #BetterInternet brand platform, aimed at creating a safer, more socially responsible, and environmentally conscious internet.

Integrating Archetypes into Brand Strategy and Stories

Jung's theory of archetypes continues to provoke discussion; however, in branding, archetypes offer a powerful tool for crafting an emotionally resonant identity. By aligning with a specific archetype, brands can clearly articulate their values, foster a shared sense of purpose, and build deeper connections with their audiences. This strategic approach can help distinguish brands from competitors and ensures a cohesive identity, where every element—from visuals to messaging—reinforces the intended brand image.

Archetypes are central to shaping a brand's personality and influencing consumer perception. Whether a brand embodies the Caregiver (like Renault), the Magician (such as E.On Italy), or the Sage (exemplified by KPN), the chosen archetype defines its tone, values, and the way it engages with its audience. For example, a brand aligned with the Angel archetype (like Corona) emphasizes guardianship, which becomes integral to its identity and market positioning. By aligning with a clear archetype, a brand can intentionally and consistently shape its core values and personality.

When a brand's strategy, essence, archetype, construct, and personality align, they form a cohesive narrative that brings its identity to life. This unity ensures every story resonates with audiences, reflects core values, and fosters emotional connections. A holistic approach amplifies cultural and societal impact, providing context for past actions, clarity for current initiatives, and a compelling vision for the future. (See chapter 12 for more on the power of stories.)

The Role of Brand Archetypes in Shaping Brand Identity

Archetypes play a central role in defining a brand's identity by embodying its core characteristics and values. For instance, a Hero archetype conveys courage, resilience, and transformation. Yet, a disconnect can exist between how a brand sees itself and how consumers perceive it. When used effectively, archetypes help bridge this gap by shaping narratives and experiences that resonate authentically with the audience.

Marketers use archetypes to boost relatability and forge emotional connections, helping ensure brand messaging and experiences remain consistent. To be effective, these archetypes must align with the target audience's values and aspirations as well as the brand's identity.

Brands often embody one or more archetypes, and their positioning can evolve. For example, Nike originally aligned itself with the Idealist and Hero archetypes, but has since broadened its identity to reflect more inclusive values, primarily through initiatives supporting disability rights and adaptive sports.

Below are examples of core archetypes and brands that exemplify them effectively.

Activist: Advocates for significant social or political causes
Marketing niche: Champions issues such as human rights, sustainability, and systemic injustice with bold, action-oriented messaging
Examples: Ben & Jerry's is known for outspoken campaigns on racial equality, climate justice, and LGBTQ+ rights. Corona supports ocean conservation and environmental protection. Patagonia leads climate advocacy and environmental activism. Nike's "Dream Crazy" and related campaigns elevate social justice themes through sports.

Advocate (related to Activist): Champions marginalized and overlooked communities by raising awareness and driving social change
Marketing niche: Focuses on community well-being through advocacy for gender equity, women's rights, and LGBTQ+ inclusion
Examples: Again, Ben & Jerry's leverages brand influence to advance social justice. The company leverages its platform to advocate for these causes, raise awareness, and drive meaningful change. Similarly, The Body Shop has long championed animal rights, most notably through its Forever Against Animal Testing campaign in partnership with Cruelty Free International, which advocates for a global ban on cosmetic animal testing.[16]

Angel: Embodies benefactor and guardian qualities, symbolizing purity, goodness, and benevolence
Marketing niche: Champions ethical practices, social responsibility, and philanthropy through ongoing, mission-driven actions
Examples: Corona engages in beach clean-up efforts and environmental protection, reflecting its commitment to sustainability and positive social impact. Newman's Own, founded by actor Paul Newman, donates 100 percent of profits to charity, supporting education, health, and environmental causes. TOMS is known for its "One for One" model, providing a pair of shoes for every pair sold, and has since expanded to support access to clean water, safe childbirth, and vision care globally.

Best Friend: Known for being trusted, dependable, and emotionally supportive, with a strong focus on loyalty and service
Marketing niche: Builds lasting relationships through personalized service, reliability, and emotional warmth
Examples: Customers celebrate Nordstrom for its legendary customer service and commitment to customer satisfaction. Starbucks creates a welcoming "third space" between work and home, fostering comfort and community.

Caregiver: Characterized by nurturing, protective, and service-oriented qualities

Marketing niche: Prioritizes care, safety, and emotional support through products or services that promote well-being and stability

Examples: Volvo emphasizes safety, dependability, and family-first design, reinforcing its role as a protector on the road. Campbell's evokes warmth and comfort, offering nourishment that taps into memories of home and family care.

Citizen: Embraces the shared humanity of all people, closely aligned with the Advocate archetype

Marketing niche: Champions community well-being, equity, and social responsibility through inclusive, humanitarian initiatives

Examples: IBM is committed to driving positive impact across the environment, communities, and ethical business practices, earning recognition on the Kantar Gen Z Sustainability Index. For over two decades, Unilever has led a robust sustainability agenda, consistently advancing social and environmental responsibility.

Creator: An artist and visionary who sparks innovation and drives cultural conversations

Marketing niche: Champions creativity, originality, and self-expression, emphasizing innovation, craftsmanship, and boundary-pushing ideas

Examples: Apple is renowned for its groundbreaking technology and design, continually reshaping how we interact with devices. LEGO fuels imagination across generations, inviting users to build, invent, and explore. Google pioneers new frontiers in information and services, aiming to organize the world's knowledge and make it universally accessible and useful.

Everyday person: Connects with the average consumer through relatability, authenticity, and practicality

Marketing Niche: Resonates by addressing familiar needs, shared values, and everyday experiences

Examples: State Farm is trusted "like a good neighbor," helping customers navigate life's uncertainties. Dunkin' captures the spirit of the daily grind, providing coffee and food for people on the move.

Explorer: Seeks new experiences and embraces adventures

Marketing niche: Appeals to curiosity, independence, and a desire for discovery, ideal for those eager to explore the world and push boundaries

Examples: Jeep embodies the spirit of adventure with rugged vehicles designed for off-road exploration. The North Face equips adventurers with durable outdoor apparel and gear, encouraging enthusiasts to face the elements and challenge themselves.

Free Spirit: Embodies independence, creativity, and a sense of adventure
Marketing niche: Values personal freedom, self-expression, and the courage to defy convention
Examples: Virgin Group, founded by Richard Branson, disrupts norms across industries, from airlines to space exploration, by championing innovation. Oatly, the oat milk company, embraces authenticity and transparency, using its voice and packaging to challenge norms, spark dialogue, and advocate for planetary and human well-being.[17]

Guardian: Embodies responsibility, protection, and safety
Marketing niche: Delivers security, reliability, and a steadfast commitment to customer well-being
Examples: ADT offers dependable security services that protect homes and families. AARP advocates for the needs and rights of older adults, acting as a trusted advocate for their interests.

Hero: Empowers individuals to overcome obstacles, achieve greatness, and make a positive impact on their lives and communities
Marketing niche: Inspires courage, resilience, and a pursuit of excellence, tapping into the universal desire to be bold and purpose-driven
Examples: Doctors Without Borders / *Médecins Sans Frontières* (MSF) exemplifies the Hero archetype through its courageous commitment to delivering emergency medical care in the world's most dangerous crises, demonstrating bravery and compassion. Procter & Gamble (P&G) channels heroic spirit in their "Thank You, Mom" campaign, celebrating the strength and sacrifice of mothers who help athletes rise and persevere against the odds.

Idealist: Driven by unwavering ideals, prioritizing social responsibility, sustainability, and ethical integrity while embedding these principles into every facet of business
Marketing niche: Establishes emotional connections by aligning with their audience's values, sharing purpose-driven stories, and demonstrating a genuine commitment to making a difference
Examples: The *New York Times* champions journalistic integrity, positioning itself as a trusted defender of truth and democracy. Seventh Generation

leads with a sustainability-first approach with products that protect people and the planet, reinforcing its ethical and environmental mission.

Innovator: Visionary and pioneering, in constant pursuit of what's next, setting new standards

Marketing niche: Leads industry transformation by introducing groundbreaking products, technologies, or ideas that shift paradigms and redefine consumer expectations

Examples: Netflix redefined the entertainment landscape by pioneering streaming, creating binge-worthy original content, and leveraging personalized algorithms, transforming how the world consumes media. Beyond Meat popularized plant-based meat in the US, gaining mainstream retail and fast-food traction.

Jester or *Joker*: Uses humor and irreverence to entertain and engage

Marketing niche: Stands out by creating joyful, memorable experiences, using clever narratives, satire, and playfulness to spark emotional connections and make messages stick

Examples: Geico grabs attention with absurd, unexpected scenarios that turn mundane insurance messaging into whimsical moments. Skittles leans into quirky, surreal humor to reflect its whimsical personality.

Lover: Romantic, sensual, and emotionally expressive

Marketing niche: Builds emotional bonds by focusing on intimacy, passion, and indulgence, often appealing to the senses and heart

Examples: Hallmark evokes heartfelt moments and emotional expression, using cards and gifts to help people articulate love and affection. Chocolatier Godiva seduces the senses with chocolate, positioning indulgence as an act of pleasure and intimacy.

Magician: An alchemist who harnesses imagination to turn dreams into reality and inspire transformation

Marketing niche: Focuses on transformation and possibility, offering products or experiences that feel almost magical in how they empower people

Examples: L'Oréal promises transformation through beauty science, positioning its products as catalysts to unlock personal potential and confidence. Google and Anthropic embody the Magician archetype by using AI systems to deliver information and augment human capabilities.

Maverick (or Rebel): Challenge the status quo and champion those who defy convention

Marketing niche: Empower consumers to break the rules, stand out, and forge their own path, often appealing to those who value freedom, authenticity, and disruption

Examples: Red Bull fuels a rebellious spirit by sponsoring extreme sports and daring individuals who push physical and mental boundaries. Harley-Davidson embodies rugged independence, attracting those who reject conformity and ride to their own rhythm.

Provocateur: Bold, defiant, and unapologetically disruptive

Marketing niche: Captivate by confronting convention, stirring debate, and pushing cultural buttons to ignite conversation

Examples: Benetton sparks global dialogue with controversial advertising campaigns that address race, politics, and human rights, using fashion as a platform for activism. Burger King disrupts fast food marketing through provocative stunts and direct jabs at competitors, standing out for its audacity. Dollar Shave Club broke into a stagnant market with irreverent humor and a subscription model, challenging legacy brands.

Ruler: Authoritative, refined, and in control

Marketing niche: Attracts consumers who value power, success, and elevated status, offering products and experiences that signal achievement and command respect

Examples: Rolex stands as a symbol of luxury and status, with its timepieces marking success. Mercedes-Benz delivers on the promise of automotive excellence, appealing to those who prioritize status and performance.

Sage (or Expert): Wise, analytical, and trusted

Marketing niche: Offers trusted guidance and expertise, positioning the brand as a reliable source of information and authority

Examples: *National Geographic* illuminates science, history, and culture through captivating storytelling and research, inspiring discovery. The Mayo Clinic delivers expert medical care through evidence-based practice and accessible health information.

NOTES

Introduction

1. "2024 Gen Z and Millennial Survey," Deloitte, accessed July 12, 2024, https://www.deloitte.com/global/en/issues/work/content/genz-millennialsurvey.html.
2. Harris Reed et al., "Edelman's Gen Z Lab: Building Trust with the Future Generation of Consumers," Edelman, accessed July 13, 2024, https://www.edelman.com/future-consumer.
3. Gaëtan du Peloux in an interview with Robin Landa, June 5, 2024.

1. Moving at the Speed of Culture

1. Gaëtan du Peloux, interview with Robin Landa, June 5, 2024.
2. "Towards Victory for Gender Equality," Unesco.org, March 13, 2024, accessed July 9, 2024, https://www.unesco.org/en/articles/towards-victory-gender-equality.
3. Jennifer Corn, "Viral Women's Soccer Ad Uses Doctored Footage to Prove a Point," CNN.com, July 20, 2023, accessed July 9, 2024, https://www.cnn.com/2023/07/20/tech/french-soccer-ad-gender-swap/index.html.
4. Jennifer Corn, "Viral Women's Soccer Ad."
5. Purple, M&M'S Spokescandy—Topic, "I'm Just Gonna Be Me" YouTube video, 2:18, 2023, accessed August 202, 204, https://www.youtube.com/watch?v=L6oSZq_zFM4.
6. "News: M&Ms® Welcomes First New Character in a Decade," Mars.com, September 28, 2022, accessed May 28, 2024, https://www.mars.com/news-and-stories/press-releases-statements/mms-welcomes-new-character-purple.
7. "First New Character in a Decade," Mars.com.

8. "We Help People Feel Included by Championing Fun as a Way to Share our True-Self and Connect With Others," Mars.com, https://www.mms.com/en-us/explore?, accessed May 28, 2024.

9. Milos Bujisic et al., "2022 Corporate Social Value Index," NYU School of Professional Studies, New York University, October 25, 2022, Accessed May 18, 2024, https://www.sps .nyu.edu/content/dam/sps/academics/departments/division-of-programs-and-business /integrated-marketing/research-leadership/NYU_IMC_2022_Corporate_Social_Value _Index.pdf.

10. Robin Landa and Greg Braun, *Shareworthy: Advertising That Creates Powerful Connections Through Storytelling* (Columbia University Press, 2024), 5.

11. Bujisic et al., "2022 Corporate Social Value Index."

12. "Global Gender Gap Report 2021," World Economic Forum, accessed May 15, 2025, https://www3.weforum.org/docs/WEF_GGGR_2021.pdf.

13. Ommara Raza Ali and Hannah Hilali, "Empowering Girls Through Education in Pakistan," EduFinance.org, April 15, 2021, accessed June 2, 2024, https://edufinance.org /latest/blog/2021/empowering-girls-through-education-in-pakistan.

14. "Awards: Schoolgirl Newscasters," DandAD.org, 2023, accessed June 2, 2024, https:// www.dandad.org/awards/professional/2023/237585/schoolgirl-newscasters/.

15. Kim Shaw, "BBDO and EBM Win First Glass Lion for Pakistan at the 2023 Cannes Lions Festival," *Campaign Brief Asia*, June 26, 2023, accessed June 2, 2024, https:// campaignbriefasia.com/2023/06/26/bbdo-and-ebm-win-first-glass-lion-for-pakistan -at-the-2023-cannes-lions-festival/.

16. "REI Co-op Studios Celebrates the Release of New Co-produced Films for Fall," REI Co-op Newsroom, REI.com, September 13, 2023, accessed June 2, 2024, https://www .rei.com/newsroom/article/rei-co-op-studios-celebrates-the-release-of-new-co -produced-films-for-fall.

17. "REI Co-op Studios Celebrates Release."

18. Evan Horowitz, "The Six Best Ways to Connect Brands to Culture," AdvertisingWeek. com, accessed June 23, 2024, https://advertisingweek.com/the-six-best-ways-to-connect -brands-to-culture/.

19. David Salazar and Rebecca Barker, "Here Are Sixteen Brands Making a Cultural Splash Everywhere, from Summer Blockbusters to TikTok," Fast Company, October 3, 2023, accessed July 9, 2024, https://www.fastcompany.com/90953679/cultural-brands -johnnie-walker-hoorae-starz.

20. Evan Horowitz, "The Six Best Ways."

21. Luke Flynn, email message to Robin Landa, June 18, 2024.

2. Differentiation

1. "2024 ONE SHOW—Music & Sound Craft: The Lost Voice, OneClub, accessed July 16, 2024, https://www.oneclub.org/awards/theoneshow/-award/53306/the-lost-voice.

2. Leland Maschmeyer, LinkedIn, post, June 2024, accessed July 13, 2024, https://www .linkedin.com/feed/update/urn:li:activity:7201318025130639363/.

3. Koen Pauwels and Oliver Koll, "Why Brands Grow: The Power of Differentiation and Penetration," *Management and Business Review* 2, no. 3 (Summer 2022): 28–35, https:// doi.org/10.1177/2694105820220203004.

4. Mary Kyriakidi, "What Role Does Brand Play In the Consumer Decision Journey?," Kantar, April 20, 2022, accessed August 1, 2024, https://www.kantar.com/north-america

/inspiration/brands/modern-marketing-dilemmas-what-role-does-brand-play-in-the
-consumer-decision-journey.

5. "Analysis of 6.5 Billion Consumer Datapoints Reveals the Three Rules of Brand Growth,"
Kantar, May 14 2024, accessed August 22, 2024, https://www.kantar.com/company-news
/analysis-of-6-5-billion-consumer-datapoints-reveals-the-three-rules-of-brand-growth.

6. David Mayer, "The Myth of Brand Differentiation: Why Being Meaningful Matters
More," Lippincott, January 5, 2024, accessed July 13, 2024, https://www.lippincott.com
/ideas/myth-of-brand-differentiation/.

7. Jane Ostler, "The Blueprint for Brand Growth: How Marketers Can Influence Revenue and Profit," Kantar, May 14, 2024, accessed July 24, 2024, https://www.kantar.com
/north-america/inspiration/brands/the-blueprint-for-brand-growth-how-marketers
-can-influence-revenue-and-profit.

8. "Kantar, WARC, Ehrenberg-Bass Institute: Three New Rules of Brand Growth,"
WARC, May 14, 2024, accessed July 12, 2024, https://www.warc.com/content/feed/three
-new-rules-of-brand-growth/en-GB/9484.

9. Gabija Velykytė, "Creativity in Distinctive Brand Asset," *Creativity Studies* 16, no. 2
(2023): 384–96, https://doi.org/10.3846/cs.2023.19035.

10. Arash Ahmadi and Afsoon Ataei, "Emotional Attachment: A Bridge Between Brand
Reputation and Brand Advocacy," *Asia-Pacific Journal of Business Administration* 16,
no. 1 (2022): 1–20, https://doi.org/10.1108/APJBA-11-2021-0579.

3. North Star Brand Construct

1. Dove, (@Dove) "No filter should tell you how to look," 2023, Instagram, March 12,
2023, accessed May 18, 2025, https://www.instagram.com/dove/p/CpgUoofvJdh/?hl
=en&img_index=1.

2. Tate-Ryan Mosley, "Artificial Intelligence: Beauty Filters Are Changing the Way Young Girls
See Themselves," *MIT Technology Review*, April 2, 2021, https://www.technologyreview
.com/2021/04/02/1021635/beauty-filters-young-girls-augmented-reality-social-media/.

3. "No filter should tell you how to look," Dove.

4. "DAVID, Ogilvy and Mindshare: Dove's #TurnYour Back," WPP, accessed June 28, 2024,
https://www.wpp.com/en/featured/work/2023/05/david-and-ogilvy-doves-turnyourback.

5. "The Dove Real Beauty Pledge," Dove, March 21, 2024, accessed June 28, 2024, https://
www.dove.com/us/en/stories/campaigns/real-beauty-pledge.html.

6. Jack Neff and Tim Nudd, "How Twenty Years of Dove's Campaign for Real Beauty
Have Changed Marketing," *Ad Age*, April 10, 2024, https://adage.com/article/marketing
-news-strategy/doves-campaign-real-beauty-how-its-20-years-changed-marketing
/2552441

7. "Twenty Years of Dove's Campaign," *Ad Age*.

8. "Twenty Years On: Dove and the Future of Real Beauty," Unilever, April 23, 2024,
accessed June 28, 2024, https://www.unilever.com/news/news-search/2024/20-years-on
-dove-and-the-future-of-real-beauty.

9. "Wolff Olins: About," Wolff Olins, accessed July 15, 2024, https://www.wolffolins.com
/about.

10. *2024 Edelman Trust Barometer Special Report: Brands and Politic*, Edelman Trust Institute, https://www.edelman.com/sites/g/files/aatuss191/files/2024-06/2024%20Edelman
%20Trust%20Barometer%20Special%20Report%20Brands%20and%20Politics%20
Final.pdf.

11. "Conscious Brands 100: Thinking: The Race to Make a Better Brand: Conscious Brand Launch," Wolff Olins, accessed July 4, 2024, https://wolffolins.com/news/the-race-to-make-a-better-brand-conscious-brand-launch.

12. "Inployable: Canadian Down Syndrome Society," FCB Toronto, accessed August 2, 2024, https://fcbtoronto.com/our-work/inployable/.

13. "Connecting Jobseekers to Employers in Canada," Canadian Down Syndrome Society, accessed August 2, 2024, https://cdss.ca/inployable/.

14. Luz Corona, host, with Jameson Fleming, "Promoting Women's Sports Through Storytelling with Kristyn Cook of State Farm," *Yeah, That's Probably An Ad*, podcast, season 3, episode 51, June 17, 2024, https://shows.acast.com/yeah-thats-probably-an-ad/episodes/promoting-womens-sports-through-storytelling-with-kristyn-co.

15. David Goldman, "Tim Cook: How Steve Jobs Changed the World," *CNN Business*, May 17, 2015. https://money.cnn.com/2015/05/17/technology/tim-cook-gwu-graduation/.

16. *2024 Edelman Trust Barometer Special Report*, Edelman Trust Institute, 25.

17. *Bentley–Gallup Business in Society Report*, May 2023, 7, https://www.bentley.edu/files/gallup/Bentley_Gallup_Business_in_Society_Report.pdf.

18. *2024 Edelman Trust Barometer Special Report*, Edelman Trust Institute, 13.

19. Nick Law, interview with the author, May 22, 2024.

20. Leland Maschmeyer, "What Is a Brand?," LinkedIn, June 2024, https://www.linkedin.com/posts/activity-7201318025130639363-rFr3?utm_source=share&utm_medium=member_desktop&rcm=ACoAAAC3VE0BL2YDieuo9TLZdaEj4ZqHBjpYTfo

21. Simon Sinek, *Start with Why: How Great Leaders Inspire Everyone to Take Action* (Portfolio, 2011).

4. Brand-Building Ideas

1. "Mastercard's Where to Settle Platform to Offer New Features, Job Listings and Apartment rentals," Mastercard, February 20, 2023, accessed July 15, 2024, https://www.mastercard.com/news/europe/en/newsroom/press-releases/en/2023/mastercard-s-where-to-settle-platform-to-offer-new-features-job-listings-and-apartment-rentals/.

2. Adriana Sas, "Number of Ukrainian Refugees in Poland 2022–2024, by Date of Report," Statista, February 18, 2025, https://www.statista.com/statistics/1293564/ukrainian-refugees-in-poland/.

3. "Mastercard: Room for Everyone," McCann Worldgroup, accessed June 24, 2024, https://mwcannes.com/work/room-for-everyone/.

4. "Mastercard: Inclusive by Design," McCann Worldgroup, accessed May 25, 2025, https://mwcannes.com/work/inclusive-by-design/.

5. "About Mastercard: Always Moving Forward," Mastercard, accessed July 15, 2024, https://www.mastercard.us/en-us/vision/who-we-are.html.

6. "Mastercard's Purpose Manifesto, Connecting Everyone to Priceless Possibilities," Mastercard.com, accessed May 25, 2025, https://www.mastercard.us/content/dam/public/mastercardcom/na/global-site/documents/mastercard-sustainability-report-2020.pdf

7. Martin Guerrieria, "Revealed: The World's Most Valuable Brands of 2024," Kantar, June 12, 2024, accessed July 15, 2024, https://www.kantar.com/north-america/inspiration/brands/revealed-the-worlds-most-valuable-brands-of-2024.

8. Amanda Edelman, "Winning with Gen Z: Embracing Intention and Values for Brand Success," Edelman, June 13, 2024, accessed July 4, 2024, https://www.edelman.com/trust/2024/trust-barometer/special-report-brand/gen-z-embracing-intention-values-brand-success.

9. *The 2024 Edelman Trust Barometer Special Report: Brands and Politics*, Edelman Trust Institute, fieldwork conducted April 13–24, 2024, accessed July 4, 2024, https://www.edelman.com/trust/2024/trust-barometer/special-report-brand/gen-z-embracing-intention-values-brand-success.

10. Robin Landa, *The New Art of Ideas: Unlock Your Creative Potential* (Berrett-Koehler, 2022).

5. Designing Brand Identity

1. Lisa Smith, "Pack Talks: Be Distinctive Everywhere: How Do You Reshape a Brand to Reflect Its 'True Self' and Show up Authentically Across the Entire Consumer Experience?," Food and Beverage Innovation Forum, June 16, 2023, Shenzhen, China.

2. "The Courage to Let Culture Lead," Contagious, July 8, 2024, accessed August 5, 2024, https://www.contagious.com/news-and-views/the-courage-to-let-culture-lead.

6. Designing Brand Experiences

1. Kat Eschner, "Four Things Happen When Language Dies and One Thing You Can Do to Help," *Smithsonian Magazine*, February 21 2017, https://www.smithsonianmag.com/smart-news/four-things-happen-when-language-dies-and-one-thing-you-can-do-help-180962188/.

2. AdLam, "Can an Alphabet Save a Culture?," Microsoft, accessed May 25, 2025, https://unlocked.microsoft.com/adlam-can-an-alphabet-save-a-culture/.

3. Eschner, "When Language Dies."

4. AdLam, "Can an Alphabet Save a Culture?"

5. Christiano Abrahao, email to Robin Landa, June 26, 2024.

6. Luke Flynn, email to Robin Landa, June 18, 2024.

7. Anton Chekhov, letter to Nikolay Chekhov, March 1886, in *Letters of Anton Chekhov to His Family and Friends*, trans. Constance Garnett (Macmillan, 1920), accessed September 15, 2024, https://www.gutenberg.org/cache/epub/6408/pg6408-images.html.

8. "Climate Realism," World Wild Fund for Nature, accessed September 15, 2024, https://www.wwf.de/climaterealism.

9. Yoshihiro Yagi, email to Robin Landa, August 2, 2024.

10. Yagi, email to Robin Landa.

11. "FCB Chicago and Current Global Launch 'Banned Book Club,'" Interpublic Group, July 2, 2023, accessed August 13, 2024, https://www.interpublic.com/case-study/fcb-chicago-current-global-launch-banned-book-club/.

12. "2024 One Show Experiential & Immersive: The DiversiTree Project," The One Club for Creativity, accessed August 13, 2024, https://www.oneclub.org/awards/theoneshow/-award/53606/the-diversitree-project. Claritan: The DiversiTree Project. Creative agency: Energy BBDO Chicago; chief creative officers: Josh Gross, Pedro Perez; executive creative directors: Susan Treacy, Allison Hayes, Andrea Siqueira; global group creative director: Doug Malcom; creative directors: Ricardo Salgado, Murilo Santos, Jenna Nussbaun; associate creative directors: Josh Parmenter, Abigail Chieppa; art director: Abigail Chieppa, Murilo Santos; senior copywriter: Lucy Butka; copywriter: Jenna Nussbaum; senior designer: Tess Barnes; PR/marketing agency: Coyne PR, twelvenote

13. Sean Thomas, executive creative director at Jones Knowles Ritchie, LinkedIn, June 21, 2024, accessed May 25, 2025, https://www.linkedin.com/posts/sean-thomas-6a46691b _cannes-is-usually-a-party-that-the-branding-activity-7209978749864292353-kUKY?utm _source=share&utm_medium=member_desktop&rcm=ACoAAAC3VEoBL2YDieuo9 TLZdaEj4ZqHBjpYTfo.

14. Matt Alagiah, "Giorgia Lupi Becomes First Pentagram Partner in New York for Seven Years," *It's Nice That*, May 20, 2019, accessed August 4, 2024, https://www.itsnicethat.com /news/giorgia-lupi-pentagram-partner-new-york-announcement-200519.

7. A Brand Is a Promise Kept

1. "Michelob ULTRA Presents: For the First Time Ever. A Blind Person Commentated a Basketball Game. Live. On TV.," Michelob ULTRA, accessed July 11, 2024, https://www .michelobultra.com/dreamcaster.

2. "Michelob ULTRA Dreamcaster," FCB New York, accessed July 10, 2024, https://www .fcb.com/work/dreamcaster.

3. "Michelob ULTRA DreamCaster," FCB New York.

4. "Responsible Drinking," Anheuser-Busch, accessed July 11, 2024, https://www.anheuser -busch.com/community/responsible-drinking.

5. "About Us," L'Oréal Paris USA, accessed June 20, 2024, https://www.lorealparisusa.com /about-us.

6. "About Us," L'Oréal Paris USA.

7. State Farm, "Our Promise," State Farm Good Neighbor Center, accessed June 20, 2024, https://goodneighborcenter.statefarm.com/our-promise/index.html.

8. Brian Collins, "Ideas: 101 Design Rules," COLLINS, accessed July 11, 2024, https://www .wearecollins.com/ideas/101-design-rules/.

9. Harris Reed et al., "Edelman's Gen Z Lab: Building Trust with the Future Generation of Consumers," Edelman, accessed July 13, 2024, https://www.edelman.com/future-consumer.

10. François Faelli et al., "Selling Sustainability Means Decoding Consumers," Bain & Company, November 13, 2023, accessed September 5, 2024, https://www.bain.com/insights /selling-sustainability-means-decoding-consumers-ceo-sustainability-guide-2023/.

11. *2023 Edelman Trust Barometer Special Report: Trust and Climate Change*, Edelman Trust Institute, accessed July 12, 2024, https://www.edelman.com/trust/2023/trust-barometer /special-report-trust-climate.

12. Annabelle Timsit and Sarah Kaplan, "At Least 85 Percent of the World's Population Has Been Affected by Human-Induced Climate Change, New Study Shows," *Washington Post*, October 11, 2021, https://www.washingtonpost.com/climate-environment /2021/10/11/85-percent-population-climate-impacts/.

13. "Reasons for Consumers in the United States to Gain Trust in Companies as of January 2023," Statista, accessed July 13, 2024, https://www.statista.com/statistics/1381237 /trust-companies-us-consumers-influence-factors/.

14. Jane Ostler and J. Walker Smith, "Marketing Trends 2024," Kantar, accessed July 12, 2024, https://www.kantar.com/campaigns/marketing-trends-2024.

15. "Buying Time: How the Young Spend Their Money," *The Economist*, January 16, 2023, https://www.economist.com/business/2023/01/16/how-the-young-spend-their-money.

16. *2024 Gen Z and Millennial Survey: Living and Working with Purpose in a Transforming World*, Deloitte, accessed July 12, 2024, https://www.deloitte.com/global/en/issues /work/content/genz-millennialsurvey.html.

17. Brian Collins, "The Future of Brand," Cannes Lions session, June 2023.
18. Dole, "Our Promises," DoleSunshine.com, accessed July 25, 2024, https://dolesunshine
    .com/us/en/sustainability/.
19. "Fitchix: Changing the Egg Industry One Step at a Time," Honest Eggs Co., accessed
    August 4, 2024, https://honesteggsco.com.au/fitchix/.
20. "Campaign of the Week: Produce Brand Prints Chickens' Step Counts on Eggs as
    Proof of Welfare," Contagious, March 28, 2023, accessed August 4, 2024, https://www
    .contagious.com/news-and-views/campaign-of-the-week-produce-brand-prints
    -chickens-step-counts-on-eggs-as-proof-of-welfare.

8. Planet-First Brand Building

1. Reef-World, "What Would Happen If There Were No Coral Reefs?," The Reef-World
   Foundation, March 1, 2021, accessed July 6, 2024, https://reef-world.org/blog/no-coral
   -reefs.
2. "The Sheba Hope Grows™ Program Expands to Hawaii in Partnership with Kuleana
   Coral Reefs," Sheba, accessed July 5, 2024, https://www.sheba.com/sustainability.
3. Jordan Bar Am et al., "Consumers Care About Sustainability—and Back It Up With
   Their Wallets," McKinsey & Company, accessed June 21, 2024, https://www.mckinsey
   .com/industries/consumer-packaged-goods/our-insights/consumers-care-about
   -sustainability-and-back-it-up-with-their-wallets.
4. "Our Company: We Believe in a Seventh Generation," Seventh Generation, accessed
   August 6, 2024, https://www.seventhgeneration.com/company.
5. "The 17 Goals," United Nations Department of Social and Economic Affairs, Sustainable Development, accessed May 26, 2024, https://sdgs.un.org/goals.
6. "The 17 Goals," United Nations Department of Social and Economic Affairs.
7. "History," United Nations Department of Social and Economic Affairs, Sustainable
   Development, accessed May 12, 2025, https://sdgs.un.org/goals#history.
8. "Climate Group RE100: We Are Accelerating Change Towards Zero Carbon Grids,"
   RE100, accessed August 6, 2024, https://www.there100.org/.
9. *Project Contrails*, Google, accessed July 17, 2024, https://sites.research.google/contrails/.
10. "Project Contrails," Google.
11. Carl Elkin and Dinesh Sanekommu, "Sustainability: How AI Is Helping Airlines Mit-
    igate the Climate Impact of Contrails," Google Blog, August 8, 2023, accessed June 21,
    2024, https://blog.google/technology/ai/ai-airlines-contrails-climate-change/.
12. "Project Contrails," Google.
13. "Grey: Sol Cement's Sightwalks: Helping the Visually Impaired to Navigate City
    Streets," WPP, accessed June 24, 2024, https://www.wpp.com/featured/work/2024/06
    /grey-cemento-sols-sightwalks.
14. "14: Life Below Water," The Global Goals, accessed June 21, 2024, https://www.global
    goals.org/goals/14-life-below-water/.
15. TBWA Finland, "Fortum + Fishheart," accessed June 21, 2024, https://www.tbwa.fi
    /work/case-study-fortum-fishheart/.
16. Damien Guiol, LinkedIn, post, June 17, 2024, accessed May 16, 2025, https://www.linkedin
    .com/posts/damienguiol_cannes-contenders-how-fcb-is-using-creativity-activity
    -7203354428748259328-X7ZH/?originalSubdomain=fr.
17. "15: Life on Land," The Global Goals, accessed June 21, 2024, https://www.globalgoals
    .org/goals/15-life-on-land/.

18. "VML: Makro's Life Extending Stickers: Data Visualization Inspired by Nature," WPP, accessed June 2, 2025, https://www.wpp.com/featured/work/2024/01/grey-makros-life-extending-stickers.

19. "Our Work: Seeding Songs," VML, accessed July 5, 2024, https://www.vml.com/work/seeding-songs.

20. Céline Fenech et al., "The Sustainable Consumer 2023: What Consumers Need in Order to Adopt a More Sustainable Lifestyle," Deloitte UK, October 20, 2023, accessed July 5, 2024, https://www.deloitte.com/uk/en/Industries/consumer/research/sustainable-consumer-what-consumers-need.html.

21. Fenech et al., "The Sustainable Consumer."

9. Audience-Focused Brand Building

1. McCann Worldgroup, "Creative: 'Translators' Tells the Story of Young Interpreters Helping Their Families Navigate and Survive Life in the US," *Little Black Book*, May 6, 2023, accessed June 10, 2024, https://lbbonline.com/news/translators-tells-the-story-of-young-interpreters-helping-their-families-navigate-and-survive-life-in-the-us.

2. McCann Worldgroup, "Story of Young Interpreters."

3. "Searches for 'Quick-Fix Weight Loss Exercises' Surge by Over 500 Percent as Research Shows Focus on Exercise Purely for Weight Loss Impacts Our Mental Health," News-emea.Asics.com, June 11, 2024, accessed August 7, 2024, https://news-emea.asics.com/latest-news/searches-for--quick-fix-weight-loss-exercises--surge-by over 500--as-research-shows-focus-on-exercis/s/7f7d5723-8b0d-47e9-b5f4-8b1e976fa7fc#C.

4. "Introducing the Asics State of Mind Study," Asics, accessed August 7, 2024, https://www.asics.com/gb/en-gb/mk/smsb-state-of-mind-index.

5. "Global State of Mind Study 2024," Asics, accessed August 7, 2024, https://www.asics.com/gb/en-gb/mk/stateofmindstudy2024?asics-orig-path=%2fmk%2fstateofmindstudy2024.

6. "Specsavers: The Misheard Version—The World's First Mass Hearing Test," Golin, accessed July 7, 2024, https://golin.com/work/specsavers-the-misheard-version/.

7. "Lions: Insights and Trends," Canneslions.com, accessed May 27, 2025, https://www.lovethework.com/inspiration/the-official-cannes-lions-wrap-up-2024-insights-and-trends-vfRzr24bpGAWluzZ6ZIGO

8. Yaling Jiang, "China Is Munching Toward a Fast Food Revolution," *Time*, February 17, 2024, accessed July 10, 2024, https://time.com/6695341/china-fast-food-revolution-tastien/.

9. Li Yingxue, "Talent: Cultural Elements See Surge in Demand," *China Daily*, May 2, 2024, accessed July 10, 2024, https://www.chinadailyasia.com/upload/main/pdf/2024/05/02/730e3199edb5aacc84292a90a43cc4a6.pdf.

10. "Our Work: Recycle Me—Coca-Cola," Ogilvy, accessed July 29, 2024, https://www.ogilvy.com/work/recycle-me.

11. Sunil Bajaj, "When You Have 138 Years Under Your Wing, Your Brand Can Go Two Ways," Contagious, July 23, 2024, accessed July 29, 2024, https://www.contagious.com/news-and-views/coca-cola-recycle-me-interview-contagious.

12. Dentsu Creative Canada, "Creative: SkipTheDishes Launches AI-Powered Grocery Shopping Tool to Help Canadians Take Inflation Out of Their Cart," *Little Black Book*, December 4, 2023, accessed June 10, 2024, https://www.lbbonline.com/news/skipthedishes-launches-ai-powered-grocery-shopping-tool-to-help-canadians-take-inflation-out-of-their-cart.

13. Kenan Thompson, "Cannes Lions 2024: Ready to Laugh Again: The Return of Comedy," Cannes Lions and VML, June 18, 2024, YouTube video, 0:29, https://www.youtube.com/watch?v=TeUyL-ZvlbQ.

14. Kashmira Joshi, "Insights Unveiled: Four Key Themes from Winning Ad Campaigns," Kantar, May 2, 2024, accessed June 11, 2024. https://www.kantar.com/north-america/inspiration/advertising-media/insights-unveiled-four-key-themes-from-winning-ad-campaigns.

15. "A Pink, Plastic Paradigm Shift: Branded Entertainment in a Post-Barbie World," *Little Black Book*, March 7, 2024, accessed June 11, 2024. https://lbbonline.com/news/a-pink-plastic-paradigm-shift-branded-entertainment-in-a-post-barbie-world.

16. Oracle and Gretchen Rubin, "The Happiness Report: Oracle Advertising and CX: Emotions and Experiences," Oracle, accessed July 7, 2024, https://www.oracle.com/uk/a/ocom/docs/humor-happiness-cx.pdf.

17. Tim Minchin, "Play It Safe: Sydney Opera House 50th Anniversary," Sydney Opera House, premiered October 17, 2023, YouTube video, 4:21, https://www.youtube.com/watch?v=QshKJQQyCAE.

18. "Dumb Ways to Die—the PSA," DumbWaystoDie.com, accessed June 19, 2024, https://www.dumbwaystodie.com/psa.

19. "E.L.F. Cosmetics—TikTok," Movers+Shakers, accessed July 8, 2024, https://moversshakers.co/elf-tiktok-challenge.

20. Kim Shaw, "'Charge Full of Love' This Tet Season with Re-Charge—A Free Power Supply Service for Small Businesses from the Dat Bikers Community," *Campaign Brief Asia*, February 7, 2024, accessed June 12, 2024, https://campaignbriefasia.com/2024/02/07/charge-full-of-love-this-tet-season-with-recharge-a-free-power-supply-service-for-small-businesses-from-the-dat-bikers-community/.

21. David Mogensen, "Uber VP of Marketing David Mogensen on Marketing Strategy and Great Creative," interview by Joshua Spanier, Modern Marketers Podcast, YouTube video, 25:25, https://www.youtube.com/watch?v=Wlc2A9076HA.

22. "What We Know About Category Disruption," WARC, accessed May 28, 2025, https://www.warc.com/content/paywall/article/bestprac/what-we-know-about-category-disruption/en-gb/111765?

23. "Creative Impact Unpacked: Eleven Effectiveness Trends from Cannes Lions 2024," WARC, accessed July 8, 2024, https://page.warc.com/11-effectiveness-trends-from-cannes-lions-2024.html.

24. "Cannes Lions 2024: Creative Business Transformation," Contagious, June 20, 2024, accessed July 10, 2024, https://www.contagious.com/news-and-views/cannes-lions-2024-creative-business-transformation.

25. Ian Kahn et al., "How to Gain a Competitive Advantage on Customer Insights," *Harvard Business Review*, October 20, 2022, accessed June 12, 2024, https://hbr.org/2022/10/how-to-gain-a-competitive-advantage-on-customer-insights.

26. "New and Events/Press Releases: It's the Event of the Season: E.L.F. Cosmetics x Chipotle Launch a Limited-Edition Makeup Collection," Elfbeauty, March 4, 2021, accessed June 11, 2024. https://investor.elfbeauty.com/news-and-events/press-releases/landing-news/2021/03-04-2021-073715282.

27. Lillian Stone, "The Unhinged Product Mash-Ups That Sell Out in Hours," BBC, March 13, 2024, accessed June 11, 2024, https://www.bbc.com/worklife/article/20240312-the-unhinged-product-mash-ups-that-sell-out-in-hours.

28. "The Courage to Let Culture Lead," Contagious, July 8, 2024, accessed July 10, 2024, https://www.contagious.com/news-and-views/the-courage-to-let-culture-lead.

29. Thomas H. Davenport et al., "Use GenAI to Uncover New Insights Into Your Competitors," *Harvard Business Review*, November 17, 2023, accessed June 12, 2024, https://hbr.org/2023/11/use-genai-to-uncover-new-insights-into-your-competitors.

10. Brand Building: Forging Emotional Connections

1. "Subaru: Love Campaign," Carmichael Lynch, accessed June 16, 2025, https://carmichaellynch.com/project/subaru-love/.

2. Eileen Falkenberg-Hull and Jake Lingeman, "Subaru's Former CEO Left a Lasting Impact of Important Change," *Newsweek*, March 26, 2024, https://www.newsweek.com/2024/04/12/subarus-former-ceo-left-lasting-impact-important-change-1882747.html.

3. "News: Why Are Memories Attached to Emotions So Strong?," Columbia University Irving Medical Center, July 13, 2020, accessed June 14, 2024, https://www.cuimc.columbia.edu/news/why-are-memories-attached-emotions-so-strong.

4. "How Advertising Really Works," Wieden + Kennedy, April 28, 2014, accessed August 20, 2024, https://wklondon.com/2014/04/how-advertising-really-works/.

5. Leonardo Aureliano-Silva et al., "The Relationship between Brand Attachment and Consumers' Emotional Well-Being," *Journal of Relationship Marketing* 17, no. 1 (2018): 1–16, https://doi.org/10.1080/15332667.2017.1391058.

6. Gailynn Nicks, "Emotion, Attention and Memory in Advertising," Ipsos, November 10, 2016, accessed September 16, 2024, https://www.ipsos.com/en/emotion-attention-and-memory-advertising.

7. Salman E. Qasim et al., "Neuronal Activity in the Human Amygdala and Hippocampus Enhances Emotional Memory Encoding" *Nature Human Behavior* 7, no. 5 (2023): 754–64, https://doi.org/10.1038/s41562-022-01502-8.

8. Holly Evarts, "News: Why Do We Remember Emotional Events Better?," Columbia Engineering, Columbia University, January 19, 2023, accessed June 14, 2024, https://www.engineering.columbia.edu/news/why-do-we-remember-emotional-events-better.

9. Daren Poole, "The Five Habits of Highly Effective Advertisers," Kantar, June 16, 2021, accessed June 19, 2024, https://www.kantar.com/inspiration/advertising-media/the-5-habits-of-highly-effective-advertisers.

10. Gerald Zaltman, *How Customers Think: Essential Insights Into the Mind of the Markets* (Harvard Business School Press, 2003), 8.

11. "Warc X Lions Creative Impact Unpacked: Eleven Effectiveness Trends from Cannes Lions 2024," WARC, accessed July 8, 2024, https://www.warc.com/content/feed/creative-impact-unpacked-warcs-insights-from-cannes-lions-2024/9639.

12. Ian Forrester, "Creative Impact Track: Top Ads Have Distinct Emotional Traits," WARC, Creative Impact track at the Cannes Lions International Festival of Creativity, Cannes Lions, June 21, 2024, https://www.warc.com/content/feed/top-ads-have-distinct-emotional-traits/9621.

13. Patrick McHenry, "Super Bowl 2019: What the Hell Happened at the Skittles Musical?," *Vulture*, February 4, 2019, https://www.vulture.com/2019/02/skittles-the-musical-commercial-michael-c-hall-broadway.html#/.

14. "We Are Ayenda," WhatsApp, D&AD, accessed August 20, 2024, https://www.dandad.org/awards/professional/2024/238504/we-are-ayenda/.

15. Adrianne Pasquarelli. "'We Are Ayenda' Short Film for WhatsApp Wins Grand Prix for Entertainment," *Ad Age*, June 18, 2024, accessed August 20, 2024, https://adage.com/article

/special-report-cannes-lions/creative-x-and-modern-arts-we-are-ayenda-whatsapp-wins
-grand-prix-entertainment/2565976.

16. "Cannes Lions 2024 Grand Prix Winners in Entertainment, Gaming, Music, Sport, Design, Digital Craft, Film Craft and Industry Craft," *Little Black Book*, accessed June 19, 2024, https://www.lbbonline.com/news/cannes-lions-2024-grand-prix-winners-in -entertainment-gaming-music-sport-design-digital-craft-film-craft-and-industry -craft/?mc_cid=02f9440e0d&mc_eid=09367cd08d.

17. "Sheer Driving Pleasure: The History of the BMW Slogan," BMW, August 27, 2020, accessed June 19, 2024, https://www.bmw.com/en/automotive-life/the-history-of-the -bmw-slogan.html.

18. "Sheer Driving Pleasure," BMW.

19. "Nielsen Study Reveals Majority of Consumers Actively Avoid Ads Across Podcasts, Streaming, and Live TV Platforms," Nielsen, November 2023, accessed August 20, 2024, https://www.nielsen.com/news-center/2023/nielsen-study-reveals-majority-of-consumers -actively-avoid-ads-across-podcasts-streaming-and-live-tv-platforms/.

20. "Digital Ads Which Evoke Strong Emotions Are Four Times More Likely to Drive Brand Equity," Kantar, March 1, 2023, accessed June 16, 2024, https://www.kantar.com /company-news/digital-ads-which-evoke-strong-emotions-are-four-times-more-likely -to-drive--brand-equity.

21. Alan Zorfas and Daniel Leemon, "Marketing: An Emotional Connection Matters More Than Customer Satisfaction," *Harvard Business Review*, August 29, 2016, accessed June 15, 2024, https://hbr.org/2016/08/an-emotional-connection-matters-more-than -customer-satisfaction.

11. Brand Building: Manifestos

1. "Murder Your Thirst," Liquid Death, accessed May 28, 2025, https://liquiddeath.com /pages/manifesto.

2. Katie Roof, "Liquid Death Is Valued at $1.4 Billion in New Financing Round," *Bloomberg*, March 11, 2024, https://www.bloomberg.com/news/articles/2024-03-11 /liquid-death-is-valued-at-1-4-billion-in-new-financing-round?sref=BGQFqz7X

3. "Plastic Recycling Is a Myth. And Most Plastic Is Sent to Landfills," Liquid Death, accessed June 15, 2024, https://liquiddeath.com/pages/death-to-plastic.

4. Jacob Stern, "Of Course America Fell for Liquid Death: How Is a Company That Sells Canned Water Worth $1.4 Billion?," *The Atlantic*, March 14, 2024, https://www.theatlantic .com/technology/archive/2024/03/liquid-death-canned-water-marketing/677752/.

5. Karen Heller, "Liquid Death Is a Mind-Set. And Also Just Canned Water," *Washington Post*, June 17, 2023, https://www.washingtonpost.com/lifestyle/2023/06/17/liquid -death-water-brand/.

6. "Our Credo, 1943," Johnson & Johnson, accessed June 13, 2024, https://ourstory.jnj.com /our-credo.

7. "Our Credo," Johnson & Johnson.

8. "Our Credo," Johnson & Johnson.

9. Robin Landa and Greg Braun, *Shareworthy* (Columbia University Press, 2024), 44–45.

10. Landa and Braun, *Shareworthy*, 43–44.

11. Nick Sonderup, email message to Robin Landa, May 2, 2023.

12. Kristen Schiele, email message to Robin Landa, March 4, 2024.

13. "Manifesto Page," Lululemon Australia, accessed May 28, 2025, https://www.lululemon.com.au/en-au/content/lululemon-manifesto-page.html.

14. @lululemon, Twitter post, August 21, 2018, 8:43 a.m., https://twitter.com/lululemon/status/1031884600992256002?lang=en.

12. Brand Building: The Power of Stories

1. Xiaozhi Zhang et al., "Descriptive Analysis of Depression Among Adolescents in Huangshi, China," *BMC Psychiatry* 23 (2023); 176, doi: 10.1186/s12888-023-04682-3

2. Mandy Zuo, "Mental Health: Social Phobia with Chinese Characteristics, Growing Number of Young People Speaking About Battle with Condition," *South China Morning Post*, April 5, 2022, https://www.scmp.com/news/people-culture/social-welfare/article/3173075/mental-health-social-phobia-chinese.

3. "Shot on iPhone: Little Garlic: Chinese New Year," 2024 One Show, The One Club, accessed June 28, 2024, https://www.oneclub.org/awards/theoneshow/-award/51779/shot-on-iphone-little-garlic-chinese-new-year.

4. Jonathan J. B. Mijs et al., "Confronting Racism of Omission," *Du Bois Review: Social Science Research on Race* 21, no. 1 (2023):1–23, https://doi.org/10.1017/S1742058X23000140.

5. Kimeko McCoy, "Marketing Briefing: Diversity Execs Sound Off on the Current State of DE&I in Advertising—A Work in Progress," *Digiday*, August 22, 2023, https://digiday.com/marketing/marketing-briefing-diversity-execs-sound-off-on-the-current-state-of-dei-in-advertising-a-work-in-progress/.

6. "Agencies Owned or Run by White Execs Jump to 90 percent, 4A's Diversity Report Finds," *Ad Age*, July 20, 2023, https://adage.com/article/agency-news/agencies-owned-or-run-white-execs-jump-90-4as-diversity-report-finds/2504951.

7. *The State of DEI 2023: What Marketers Need to Do to Close Inclusion Gaps*, Kantar, July 6, 2023, https://www.kantar.com/north-america/inspiration/advertising-media/the-state-of-dei-2023.

8. "Disability," World Health Organization, March 7, 2023, accessed June 29, 2024, https://www.who.int/news-room/fact-sheets/detail/disability-and-health.

9. *The State of DEI 2023*, Kantar.

10. Michael Prieler, "Representations of Older People in Advertising: A Review," *Advertising & Society Quarterly* 25, no. 1 (2024), https://doi.org/10.1353/asr.2024.a924348.

11. "Fuzzy Feelings," D&AD, accessed June 28, 2024, https://www.dandad.org/awards/professional/2024/237811/fuzzy-feelings/.

12. "The #Share the Load Journey," Ariel, accessed July 19, 2024, https://www.ariel.in/en-in/about-ariel/share-the-load/the-share-the-load-journey.

13. Amit Bapna, "Ariel's Award-Winning 'Share The Load' Campaign Returns for Sixth Edition," *The Drum*, April 19, 2023, accessed July 19, 2024, https://www.thedrum.com/news/2023/04/19/ariel-s-award-winning-sharetheload-campaign-returns-sixth-edition.

14. *Shauna* Lewis, "KVI Brave Fund Wins Innovation Grand Prix at Cannes Lions 2024," *Campaign Live*, June 21, 2024, https://www.campaignlive.com/article/kvi-brave-fund-wins-innovation-grand-prix-cannes-lions-2024/1878104.

15. Harry A. Taute and Jeremy. J. Sierra, "Brand Tribalism: An Anthropological Perspective," in *Marketing Dynamism & Sustainability: Things Change, Things Stay the Same . . .*, ed. Leroy Robinson (Springer, 2015), https://doi.org/10.1007/978-3-319-10912-1_67.

16. Kells McPhillips, "New Documentary Chronicles One Runner's Race to Qualify for the Refugee Olympic Team," *Runner's World*, June 20, 2023, accessed July 19, 2024, https://www.runnersworld.com/news/a44271791/the-right-to-race-film/.

17. Hungry Man UK, "Sportswear Brand On Premieres Epic Short Film 'The Right to Race' at Cannes Lions," *Little Black Book*, June 21, 2023, accessed July 19, 2024, https://lbbonline.com/news/sportswear-brand-on-premieres-epic-short-film-the-right-to-race-at-cannes-lions.

18. Jonathan Bond and Richard Kirschenbaum, *Under the Radar: Talking to Today's Cynical Consumer* (Wiley, 1997), 3.

19. "Consumers Expect Personalized Experiences, Social Engagement and Diverse Content: Can Media Deliver?," Deloitte, March 20, 2024, accessed August 31, 2024, https://www2.deloitte.com/us/en/pages/about-deloitte/articles/press-releases/consumers-expect-personalized-experiences-social-engagement-and-diverse-content.html.

13. Social Impact

1. "Unilever: Ben & Jerry's: Leading with Progressive Values Across Our Business," Unilever, accessed June 21, 2024, https://www.unileverusa.com/brands/ice-cream/ben-jerrys.

2. "Ben & Jerry's: Leading with Progressive Values."

3. "2024 Edelman Trust Barometer: Innovation in Peril," Edelman, https://www.edelman.com/trust/2024/trust-barometer.

4. "2023 Edelman Trust Barometer: Navigating a Polarized World," Edelman, https://www.edelman.com/trust/2023/trust-barometer

5. Jura Liaukonyte et al., "Lessons from the Bud Light Boycott, One Year Later," *Harvard Business Review*, March 20, 2024, accessed June 22, 2024, https://hbr.org/2024/03/lessons-from-the-bud-light-boycott-one-year-later.

6. Liaukonyte et al., "Bud Light Boycott."

7. Heather Newman, "Meet America's Best Brands For Social Impact 2024," *Forbes*, Apr 16, 2024, accessed May 28, 2025, https://www.forbes.com/sites/hnewman/2024/04/16/meet-americas-best-brands-for-social-impact-2024/.

8. PRNewswire, "New Guide for Business Helps Companies to Effectively Address Critical Social Justice Issues," *PR Newswire*, Feb 28, 2024, accessed May 28, 2025, https://www.prnewswire.com/news-releases/new-guide-for-business-helps-companies-to-effectively-address-critical-social-justice-issues-302073385.html.

9. PRNewswire, "New Guide for Business Helps Companies."

10. Ari Halper, interview with Robin Landa, January 17, 2024.

14. Advancing Equity

1. "See My Skin," Vaseline, in collaboration with Hued and VisualDx, searchable database, accessed July 15, 2024, https://vaseline.huedco.com.

2. "See My Skin: Vaseline," Edelman, accessed July 15, 2024, https://www.edelman.com/work/vaseline-see-my-skin.

3. "Campaign of the Week: Vaseline Restores Faded Murals to Promote Skin Healthcare for People with Darker Skin Tones," Contagious, March 12, 2024, accessed July 15, 2024, https://

www.contagious.com/news-and-views/skincare-brand-restores-faded-community
-street-art-to-promote-skin-health-resources-for-people-with-darker-skin-tones.

4. "Vaseline Restores Faded Murals."
5. "Pride Research," Monks, accessed July 16, 2024, https://www.monks.com/case-studies
   /pride-research.
6. Nathalie Spielmann et al., "Brands and Social Justice Movements: The Effects of True
   Versus Performative Allyship on Brand Evaluation," *Journal of the Association for Consumer Research* 8, no. 1 (2023): 83–94, https://doi.org/10.1086/722697.
7. "The Lego Group Unveils 'Fly Away Isles,' a New Playful Installation by Artist Hebru
   Brantley That Celebrates the Imaginations of Children," Lego, August 10, 2022, accessed
   August 5, 2024, https://www.lego.com/en-gb/aboutus/news/2022/august/build-the-change
   -new-york-city-installation?locale=en-gb.
8. Tim Nudd, "The Top Five Creative Campaigns You Need to Know About Right Now,"
   Ad Age, August 5, 2024, accessed August 5, 2024, https://adage.com/article/special-report
   -creativity-top-5/top-5-creative-ads-fanatics-vitaminwater-jd-jelly-quilted-northern
   -bodyform/2573506.
9. Geeta Menon and Tina Kiesler, "When a Brand Stands Up for Racial Justice, Do People Buy It?," HBR, July 31, 2020, accessed June 22, 2024, https://hbr.org/2020/07/when
   -a-brand-stands-up-for-racial-justice-do-people-buy-it?
10. Sabrina Sanchez, "Mental Health Awareness Month 2024—How McDonald's, MTV
    and More Are Promoting the Cause," *Ad Age*, May 15, 2024, accessed June 25, 2024,
    https://adage.com/article/marketing-news-strategy/mental-health-awareness-month
    -2024-ads-mtv-mcdonalds-calm-and-more/2560366.
11. David Gelles, "Billionaire No More: Patagonia Founder Gives Away the Company," *New
    York Times*, September 14, 2022, https://www.nytimes.com/2022/09/14/climate/patagonia
    -climate-philanthropy-chouinard.html.
12. "Let's Make Some Motherchunkin' Change!," Ben & Jerry's, accessed August 5, 2024,
    https://www.benjerry.com/whats-new/2024/06/mother-chunkin-change.
13. Gillian Friedman, "Uncle Ben's Rice Products will be rebranded as Ben's Originals," *New
    York Times*, September 23, 2020, https://www.nytimes.com/2020/09/23/business/uncle
    -ben-name-change.html
14. Brian Collins, "101 Design Rules," COLLINS, accessed June 28, 2024, https://www
    .wearecollins.com/ideas/101-design-rules/.
15. "Design Justice Network Principles," Design Justice, Summer 2018, accessed August 5,
    2024, https://designjustice.org/read-the-principles.
16. Deepa Iyer, "Mapping Our Social Change Roles in Times of Crisis," *Medium*, March 27,
    2020, accessed August 5, 2024, https://dviyer.medium.com/mapping-our-social-change
    -roles-in-times-of-crisis-8bbe71a8ab01.

15. Brand Building: Archetypes

1. FCB Toronto, "Behind the Work: Who Is Runner 321? The Campaign Increasing Visibility for Neurodivergent Athletes," *Little Black Book*, May 4, 2022, accessed
   July 7, 2024, https://lbbonline.com/news/who-is-runner-321-the-campaign-increasing
   -visibility-for-neurodivergent-athletes.
2. World Changing Ideas: "How Runner 321 is Celebrating Neurodivergent Athletes,"
   Fast Company, May 14, 2024, accessed May 28, 2025, https://www.fastcompany.com
   /91073477/fcb-canada-adidas-world-changing-ideas-2024

3. Rebecca Fulleylove, "ABAAD's Film Reveals the Culture of Shame Facing Sexual Abuse Victims," *Creative Review*, January 30, 2023, https://www.creativereview.co.uk /abaad-leo-burnett-bierut-advertising-film/.

4. The Clios, "Dirty Laundry," content page in *Ads of the World*, accessed May 28, 2025, https://www.adsoftheworld.com/campaigns/dirty-laundry-897fd787-317c-49ae-9d96 -beb263bf561e.

5. "From the Fifteenth Annual Shorty Awards: #NoShameNoBlame: A Campaign Demanding a Serious Sentence for a Serious Crime," The Shorty Awards, accessed July 8, 2024, https://shortyawards.com/15th/noshamenoblame-a-campaign-demanding-a-serious -sentence-for-a-serious-crime.

6. "#KeeptheGray Dove Canada," Edelman, accessed July 8, 2024, https://www.edelman .com/work/dove-keepthegrey.

7. Adrianne Pasquarelli and E. J. Schultz, "Nike is *Ad Age*'s Marketer of the Year for 2018," *Ad Age*, December 03, 2018, accessed July 8, 2024, https://adage.com/article/cmo -strategy/nike-ad-age-s-marketer-year-2018/315795.

8. Carl Gustav Jung, *The Archetypes and the Collective Unconscious* (Routledge, 2014).

9. Toms Kreicbergs et al., "Brand and Masculinity Archetypes as an Innovative Research Approach for Analyzing Consumer Preferences on Masculinity in Advertising," *Journal of Open Innovation: Technology, Market, and Complexity* 10, no. 1 (2024): 100184, https://doi.org/10.1016/j.joitmc.2023.100184.

16. Connecting to Culture(s)

1. Chuck Arnold, "Meet the Woman Behind Black Barbie's Groundbreaking, 'Dynamite' Style," *New York Post*, July 17, 2023, accessed December 22, 2024, https://nypost .com/2023/07/17/how-the-first-black-barbie-got-her-dynamite-style/.

2. Laura Carollo, "Global Box Office Revenue of 'Barbie' as of April 5, 2024, by Region," Statista, May 16, 2024, accessed December 22, 2024, https://www.statista.com/statistics /1401601/global-box-office-revenue-barbie-by-region-worldwide/.

3. Adrianne Pasquarelli, "How Duolingo Is Moving Beyond Social Media to Connect with Customers," *Ad Age*, April 25, 2024, accessed January 3, 2025, https://adage .com/article/special-report-agency-list-creativity-awards/creativity-awards-2024-brand -year-duolingo/2551071.

4. Gillian Follett, "How Duolingo's Marketing Shaped Pop Culture While Driving Huge User Growth," *Ad Age*, November 18, 2024, accessed December 25, 2024, https:// adage.com/article/special-report-marketers-year/duolingo-marketers-year-2024 /2590931.

5. Douglas B. Holt, "Why Do Brands Cause Trouble? A Dialectical Theory of Consumer Culture and Branding," *Journal of Consumer Research* 29, no. 1 (2002): 70–90, DOI:10.1086/339922.

6. "Duolingo and Netflix Partner Launch 'Learn Korean or Else' Campaign Ahead of Squid Game Season 2," Duolingo, December 10, 2024, accessed December 25, 2024, https:// investors.duolingo.com/news-releases/news-release-details/duolingo-and-netflix -partner-launch-learn-korean-or-else.

7. Follett, "How Duolingo's Marketing Shaped Pop Culture."

8. Duolingo Team, "How We Turned Duo's Butt into a Viral Super Bowl Commercial," Duolingo, February 12, 2024, accessed December 25, 2024, https://blog.duolingo.com /super-bowl-commercial-2024/.

9. Olivia Morley, "Duo's BBL Takes Center Stage in Duolingo's Super Bowl Spot," *Adweek*, February 11, 2024, accessed January 2, 2025, https://www.adweek.com/brand-marketing /duos-new-bbl-explodes-in-duolingos-5-second-regional-super-bowl-ad.

10. "Duolingo and Netflix Partner Launch."

11. Izzy Pugh and Charlie Chidley, "Why Playing a Greater Role in Culture is Key to Growth," Kantar, accessed December 27, 2024, https://www.kantar.com/inspiration/brands/why -playing-a-greater-role-in-culture-is-key-to-growth.

12. J. G. Navarro, "Advertising Consumption and Perception in the United States—Statistics and Facts," Statista, June 20, 2024, accessed January 2, 2025, https://www.statista.com /topics/4457/advertising-consumption-and-perception/.

13. "So Many Dicks, So Few of Everyone Else," Elfbeauty.com, accessed December 25, 2024, https://www.elfbeauty.com/changing-the-board-game/so-many-dicks.

14. "So Many Dicks."

15. "E.L.F. So Many Dicks: E.L.F. X Oberland Take Over Wall Street," ThisIsOberland.com, https://www.thisisoberland.com/casestudies/e-l-f-x-oberland.

16. "E.L.F. X Chipotle—Brand Partnership," MoversShakers.com, accessed January 2, 2025, https://moversshakers.co/elf-chipotle-brand-partnership.

17. Sam Anderson, "According to Amplify, Brand Building Is Evolving—into 'Worldbuilding,'" *The Drum*, April 21, 2023, https://www.thedrum.com/news/2023/04/21/according -amplify-brand-building-evolving-worldbuilding.

18. Alissa Wilkinson, "'Piece by Piece' Review: Pharrell Williams's Life, in Legos," *New York Times*, October 10, 2024, accessed December 27, 2024, https://www.nytimes.com /2024/10/10/movies/piece-by-piece-review-pharrell-williams.html.

19. Alissa Wilkinson, "'Piece by Piece' Review."

20. Bob Pittman, "Rob Reilly: 'Be a Fountain of Ideas,'" *Math and Magic*, iHeartPodcasts, March 27, 2024, podcast, 36:00, https://www.iheart.com/podcast/1119-math-magic-stories -from-t-31150153/episode/rob-reilly-be-a-fountain-of-162715259/.

21. Bob Pittman, "Rob Reilly: 'Be a Fountain of Ideas.'"

22. Rob Reilly, "The Need for a Big Idea Is Bigger Than Ever," interview by Addison Capper, *Little Black Book*, June 26, 2024, accessed December 24, 2024, https://lbbonline.com /news/rob-reilly-the-need-for-a-big-idea-is-bigger-than-ever.

23. Reilly, "Need for a Big Idea."

24. "The Prompt: Independence in an App," Microsoft Unlocked, accessed December 21, 2024, https://unlocked.microsoft.com/the-prompt/.

25. Brittaney Kiefer, "How Coca-Cola's AI Holiday Ad Went from Praise to Rage," *Adweek*, November 20, 2024, accessed December 25, 2024, https://www.adweek.com/creativity /how-coca-colas-ai-holiday-ad-went-from-praise-to-rage/.

26. Joseph Lamour, "Coca-Cola's AI-Generated Holiday Ad Fizzles with Consumers," *Today*, November 18, 2024, accessed December 24, 2024, https://www.today.com/food /trends/coca-cola-ai-generated-holiday-ad-backlash-rcna180647.

27. Alex Hirsch (@_AlexHirsch), X (formerly Twitter), Nov 16, 2024, accessed December 24, 2024, https://x.com/_AlexHirsch/status/1857847598054518921.

28. "Ogilvy and Wavemaker: Not Just a Cadbury Ad and Shah Rukh Khan-My-Ad," WPP.com, https://www.wpp.com/en/featured/work/2022/03/ogilvy-and-wavemaker -notjustacadburyad.

29. "Not Just a Cadbury Ad."

30. Bee Wilson, "How Crackers Went from Survival Food to Gourmet Treat," April 26, 2024, *WSJ*, accessed January 4, 2025, https://www.wsj.com/arts-culture/food-cooking /how-crackers-went-from-survival-food-to-gourmet-treat-cdf78e2f.

31. Wilson, "Survival Food to Gourmet Treat."
32. Lakshmi Gandhi, "A History Of 'Snake Oil Salesmen,'" NPR, August 26, 2013, accessed December 24, 2024, https://www.npr.org/sections/codeswitch/2013/08/26/215761377/a-history-of-snake-oil-salesmen.
33. Peter Gwin, "How Ancient Remedies Are Changing Modern Medicine," *National Geographic*, December 12, 2018, accessed January 2, 2025, https://www.nationalgeographic.com/magazine/article/ancient-chines-remedies-changing-modern-medicine.
34. Gandhi, "A History Of 'Snake Oil Salesmen.'"
35. "Here Today . . . Here Tomorrow, Varieties of Medical Ephemera: Medical Show," The National Institute of Medicine, accessed December 2024, https://www.nlm.nih.gov/exhibition/ephemera/medshow.html.
36. Ann Anderson, *Snake Oil, Hustlers and Hambones: The American Medicine Show* (McFarland, 2004), 15.
37. Michael Ortiz-Castro, "Patent Medicines, Medicine Shows, and The Secret Life of Blackface," *Yale Medical Library*, October 13, 2023, accessed December 24, 2024, https://library.medicine.yale.edu/news/patent-medicines-medicine-shows-and-secret-life-blackface.
38. Ortiz-Castro, "Patent Medicines."
39. Ursula Klein and E. C. Spary, "Introduction: Why Materials?," in *Materials and Expertise in Early Modern Europe: Between Market and Laboratory*, ed. Ursula Klein and E. C. Spary (University of Chicago Press, 2010), 22.
40. "Jeep Brand History: An American Legend," Jeep, accessed December 27, 2024, https://www.jeep.com/history.html.
41. Cecelia Cutler, "Subcultures and Countercultures," in *Encyclopedia of Language & Linguistics*, 2nd ed., ed. Keith Brown (Elsevier, 2006), 236–39.
42. Holt, "Why Do Brands Cause Trouble?"
43. Holt, "Why Do Brands Cause Trouble?"
44. New Balance, "Grey Days: New Balance History," director: Elliott Power, cinematographer: Norm Li, animation: Stray London, still photography: Samuel Bradley, 16 mm film, 7 min. 12 sec., posted May 10, 2024, accessed December 25, 2024, https://www.youtube.com/watch?v=QjUiywy1aNQ.
45. Tim Nudd, "New Balance's Artful Seven-Minute Film Tells Seven Stories of Its Reach in Subcultures," *Ad Age*, May 10, 2024, accessed December 27, 2024, https://adage.com/creativity/work/new-balances-artful-seven-minute-film-tells-seven-stories-its-reach-subcultures/2559381.
46. Starlight Williams, "How Sneaker Culture Took Over the World," *National Geographic*, April 27, 2023, https://www.nationalgeographic.com/culture/article/sneaker-culture-sneakerheads-air-jordans-history-expression.
47. Sam Andersen, "Inside the Rise (and Coming Fall?) of Marketing's Infatuation with Sneakerheads," *The Drum*, October 4, 2024, https://www.thedrum.com/news/2024/10/04/inside-the-rise-and-coming-fall-marketing-s-infatuation-with-sneakerheads.
48. "The Sole Obsession: Inside the World of Sneakerheads," YouGov, 2023, https://commercial.yougov.com/rs/464-VHH-988/images/2023-03-YouGov-US-Sneakerheads-Report.pdf.
49. Elizabeth Paton, "The Art of the Sneaker," *New York Times*, May 19, 2021, https://www.nytimes.com/2021/05/19/style/sneakers-collectibles-design-museum.html.
50. Fred Frommer, "1960s Counterculture," *Britannica*, accessed January 3, 2025, https://www.britannica.com/topic/1960s-counterculture.
51. Alex Williams, "Steampunk Moves Between Two Worlds," *New York Times*, May 8, 2008, reprinted May 14, 2018, https://www.nytimes.com/2018/05/14/style/steampunk-style.html.

52. Robert Joseph Horvitz, "A Talk with George Kubler," *Artforum*, June 29, 1973, https://www.artforum.com/features/a-talk-with-george-kubler-214132/.

53. Mike Silver, "Culture on Macro, Micro and Nano Level," January 5, 2024, Creative-brief, accessed January 6, 2025, https://www.creativebrief.com/bite/trend/guest-trend/culture-on-macro-micro-and-nano-level.

54. Mireille Silcoff, "Teen Subcultures Are Fading. Pity the Poor Kids," *New York Times*, February 21, 2024, https://www.nytimes.com/2024/02/21/magazine/aesthetics-tiktok-teens.html.

55. "Social Media Trends 2024," Ogilvy, accessed December 24, 2024, https://www.ogilvy.com/ideas/social-media-trends-2024-culture-first-reset-brands-social.

56. George Kubler, *The Shape of Time: Remarks on the History of Things* (Yale University Press, 1962), 1.

57. "The Sole Obsession."

58. Claudiu-Cătălin Munteanu and Pagalea Andreea, "Brands as a Mean of Consumer Self-Expression and Desired Personal Lifestyle," *Procedia—Social and Behavioral Sciences* 109 (2014): 103–107, 10.1016/j.sbspro.2013.12.427.

59. Elaine K. Howley, "Why Most New Year's Resolutions Fail," *U.S. News & World Report*, December 22, 2023, https://health.usnews.com/wellness/articles/why-new-years-resolutions-fail.

60. Accenture Song Spain, "Babies Uganda Launches Gym Campaign to Support Vulnerable Communities in Uganda," *Little Black Book*, February 19, 2024, accessed December 27, 2024, https://lbbonline.com/news/babies-uganda-launches-gym-campaign-to-support-vulnerable-communities-in-uganda.

61. Charlotte Rawlings, "Wes Anderson Brings Unmistakable Style to Montblanc Campaign," *Campaign Live*, May 2, 2024, accessed December 30, 2024, https://www.campaignlive.com/article/wes-anderson-brings-unmistakable-style-montblanc-campaign/1871155.

62. Teresa Barreira, "Why Brands Seeking Relevance Must Become an Integral Part of People's' Lives," *Financial Express*, October 4, 2020, https://www.financialexpress.com/business/brandwagon-why-brands-seeking-relevance-must-become-an-integral-part-of-peoples-lives-2097715/.

63. "Sweethearts Situationships," D&AD, accessed January 3, 2025, https://www.dandad.org/awards/professional/2024/238413/sweethearts-situationships/.

64. Oscar Quine, "As We Enter the Era of Microtrends, How Are Marketers Keeping Up?," *The Drum*, December 23, 2024, https://www.thedrum.com/news/2024/12/23/we-enter-the-era-microtrends-how-are-marketers-keeping-up.

65. Olivia-Anne Cleary, "An Ode to Weird Barbie and Everything She Represents," *Glamour Magazine UK*, August 3, 2023, https://www.glamourmagazine.co.uk/article/ode-to-weird-barbie-kate-mckinnon.

66. Evan Romano, "Why *Barbie* Needed Michael Cera's Allan," *Men's Health*, August 4, 2023, https://www.menshealth.com/entertainment/a44735449/barbie-allan-michael-cera/.

67. Ogilvy, "Social Media Trends 2024."

68. "Barbie®: A Cultural Icon," MAD Museum of Arts and Design, accessed January 5, 2025, https://madmuseum.org/exhibition/barbie-cultural-icon.

69. WhisperIndia, "Whisper Presents 'Keep Girls in School,'" advertising short, 3 min. 22 sec., director: Gary S, executive producer: Khalil Bachooali, cinematographer: Shanker Raman, posted May 15, 2024, YouTube, 3:22, https://www.youtube.com/watch?v=gFZTpxk5DaU.

70. Stuart Elliott, "Benetton Stirs More Controversy," *New York Times*, July 23, 1991, https://www.nytimes.com/1991/07/23/business/the-media-business-advertising-benetton-stirs-more-controversy.html.

Tool: Scrutinizing Archetypes

1. Research shows that there are "measurable negative effects of ethnic brand imagery on implicit stereotypes and supports the view that the use of such imagery can carry detrimental societal consequences." Justin Angle et al., "Activating Stereotypes with Brand Imagery: The Role of Viewer Political Identity," *Journal of Consumer Psychology* 27, no. 1 (2017): 28–41, 10.1016/j.jcps.2016.03.004.
2. Lim Hui Jie, "China's Beer Market, the World's Largest, Set for Bounce as Drinkers Go High-end," *CNBC*, July 14, 2024, https://www.cnbc.com/2024/07/15/china-beer -consumption-expected-to-recover-in-the-second-half-.html.
3. "Corona Extra Lime Corona—Our Work," Ogilvy.com, accessed July 1, 2024, https:// www.ogilvy.com/work/corona-extra-lime.
4. "Corona Extra Lime," DandAD.org, accessed July 1, 2024, https://www.dandad.org /awards/professional/2024/237900/corona-extra-lime/.
5. "Corona Extra: Our Commitment," Corona, accessed July 1, 2024, https://www.corona .com/en/our-commitment.
6. Michael Schaefer and Michael Rotte, "Combining a Semantic Differential with fMRI to Investigate Brands as Cultural Symbols," *Social Cognitive and Affective Neuroscience* 5, nos. 2–3 (2010): 274–81, https://doi.org/10.1093/scan/nsp055.
7. Schaefer and Rotte, "Combining a Semantic Differential."
8. Eszter Boczan, "Inspiration: What Role Do Brand Cues Have in Brand Equity," Kantar, June 16, 2021, accessed July 1, 2024, https://www.kantar.com/north-america/inspiration /brands/what-role-do-brand-cues-have-in-brand-equity.
9. "Renforcement des solutions de mobilité pour améliorer l'accès à l'emploi," *Ministère du Travail*, May 28, 2021, https://travail-emploi.gouv.fr/actualites/l-actualite-du-ministere /article/renforcement-des-solutions-de-mobilite-pour-ameliorer-l-acces-a-l-emploi.]
10. "Renault Targets Isolated Communities with Rentals for Job Hunters," Contagious, April 23, 2024, accessed July 15, 2024, https://www.contagious.com/news-and-views /campaign-of-the-week-renault-targets-isolated-communities-with-rental-scheme-for -job-hunters.
11. "Cannes Lions 2024: Creative Commerce Lions: Renault Speeds Ahead to Grab the Grand Prix at the Cannes Lions Festival," Contagious, June 20, 2024, https://www .contagious.com/news-and-views/cannes-lions-2024-creative-commerce.
12. Jack Neff, "Renault's 'Cars to Work' From Publicis Conseil Wins Sustainable Development Goals Grand Prix," *Ad Age*, June 21, 2024, https://adage.com/article/special -report-cannes-lions/renaults-cars-work-wins-sustainable-development-goals-grand -prix/2566451.
13. "Virgin Atlantic Flies World's First 100% Sustainable Aviation Fuel Flight from London Heathrow to New York JFK," Virgin Atlantic, November 28, 2023, https://corporate .virginatlantic.com/gb/en/media/press-releases/worlds-first-sustainable-aviation-fuel -flight.html.
14. Dentsu Creative, LinkedIn, March 2024, https://www.linkedin.com/posts/dentsucreative _betterinternet-activity-7169366766651961344-yRPk/.
15. Dentsu Creative Amsterdam, "Creative: Dentsu Creative Amsterdam's Hit Single 'Piece of Me' Launches Internationally," *LBB*, April 23, 2024, https://lbbonline.com/news /dentsu-creative-amsterdams-hit-single-piece-of-me-launches-internationally.
16. "Forever Against Animal Testing," The Body Shop, accessed June 12, 2024, https://www .thebodyshop.com/en-gb/about-us/activism/faat/a/a00018.
17. "Oatley Who?," Oatly, accessed July 1, 2024, https://www.oatly.com/oatly-who.

INDEX